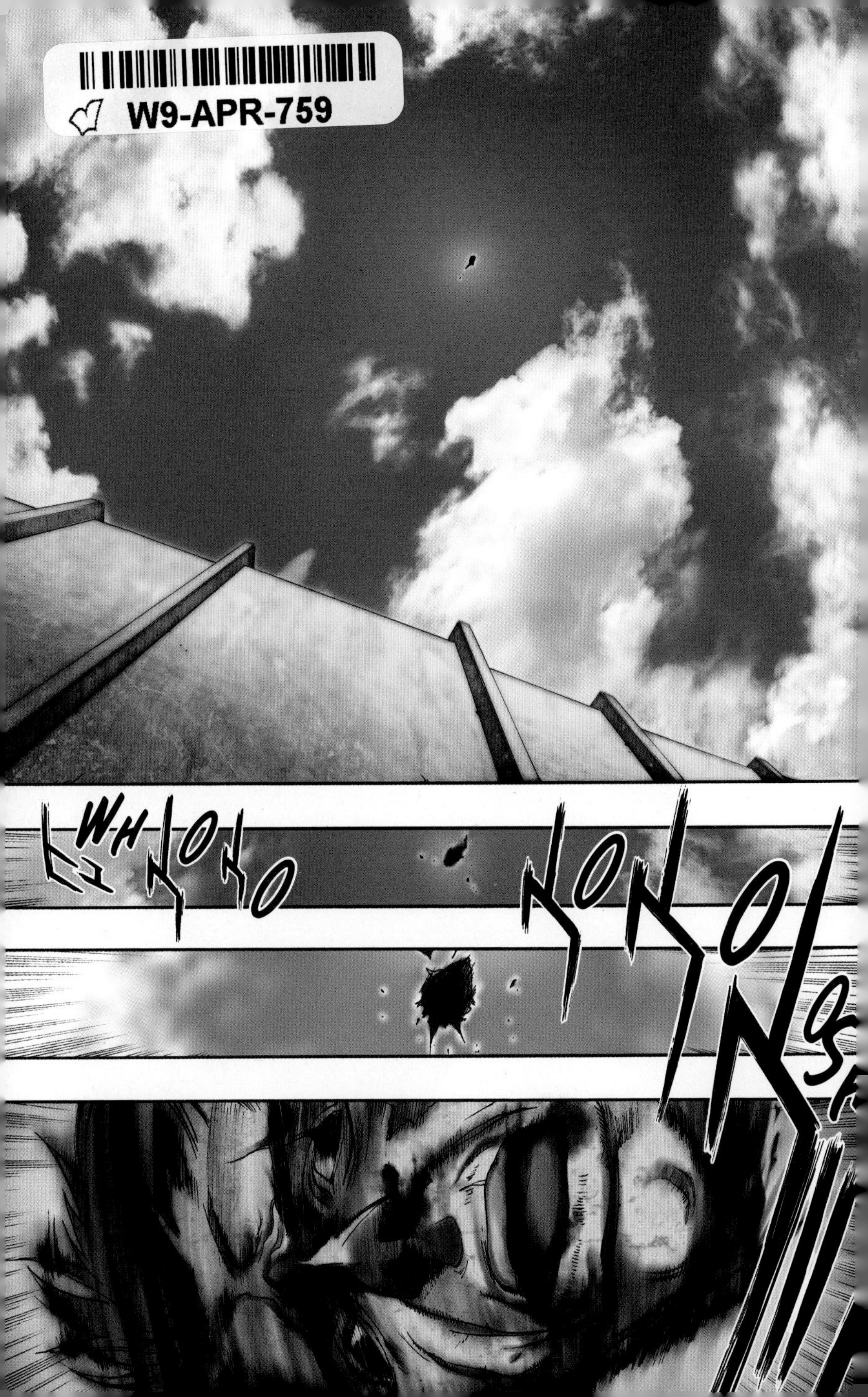
WHOOOO
OOOOSH

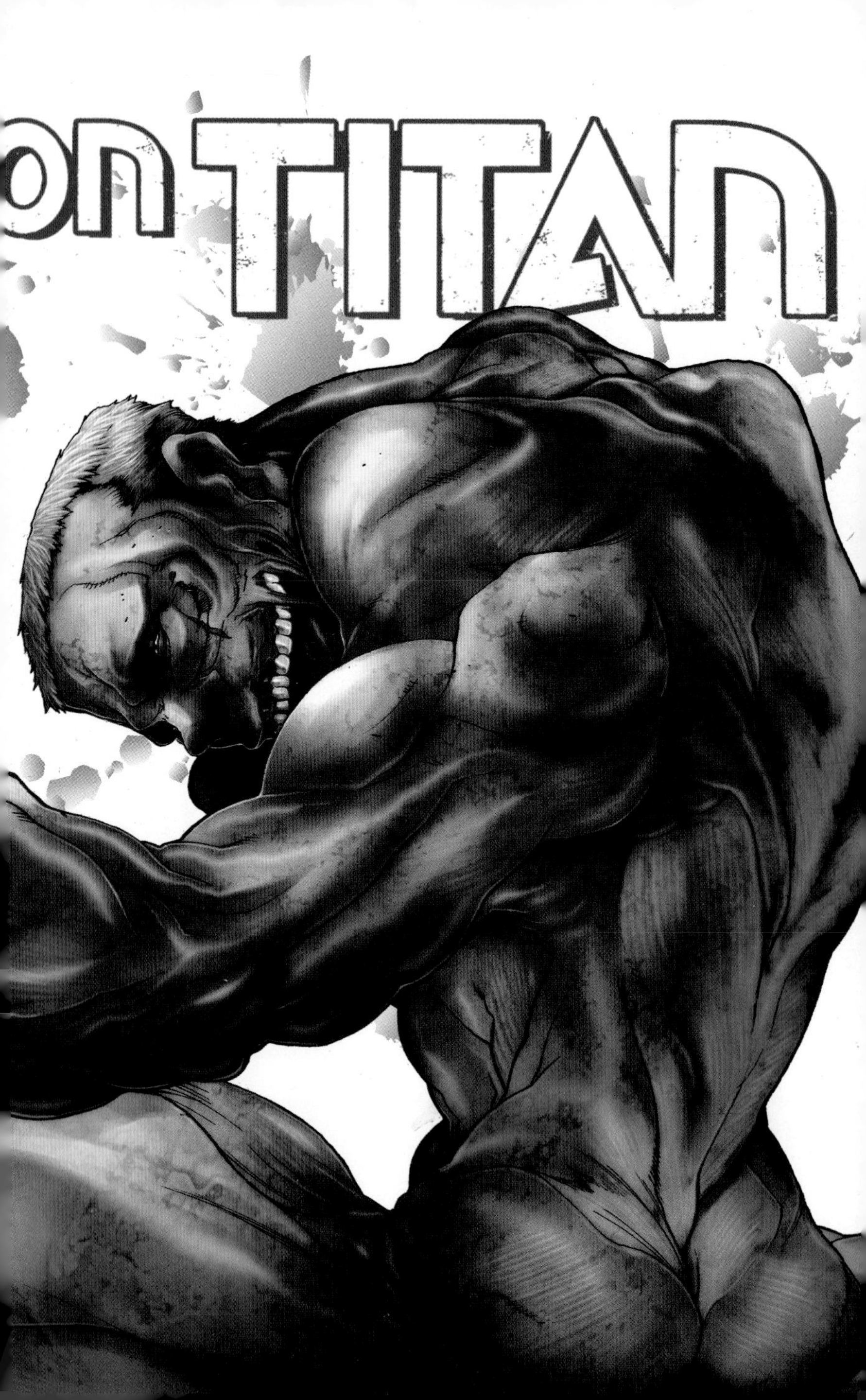
on TITAN

ATTACK BEFORE THE FALL

Chapter 1: The Titan's Son

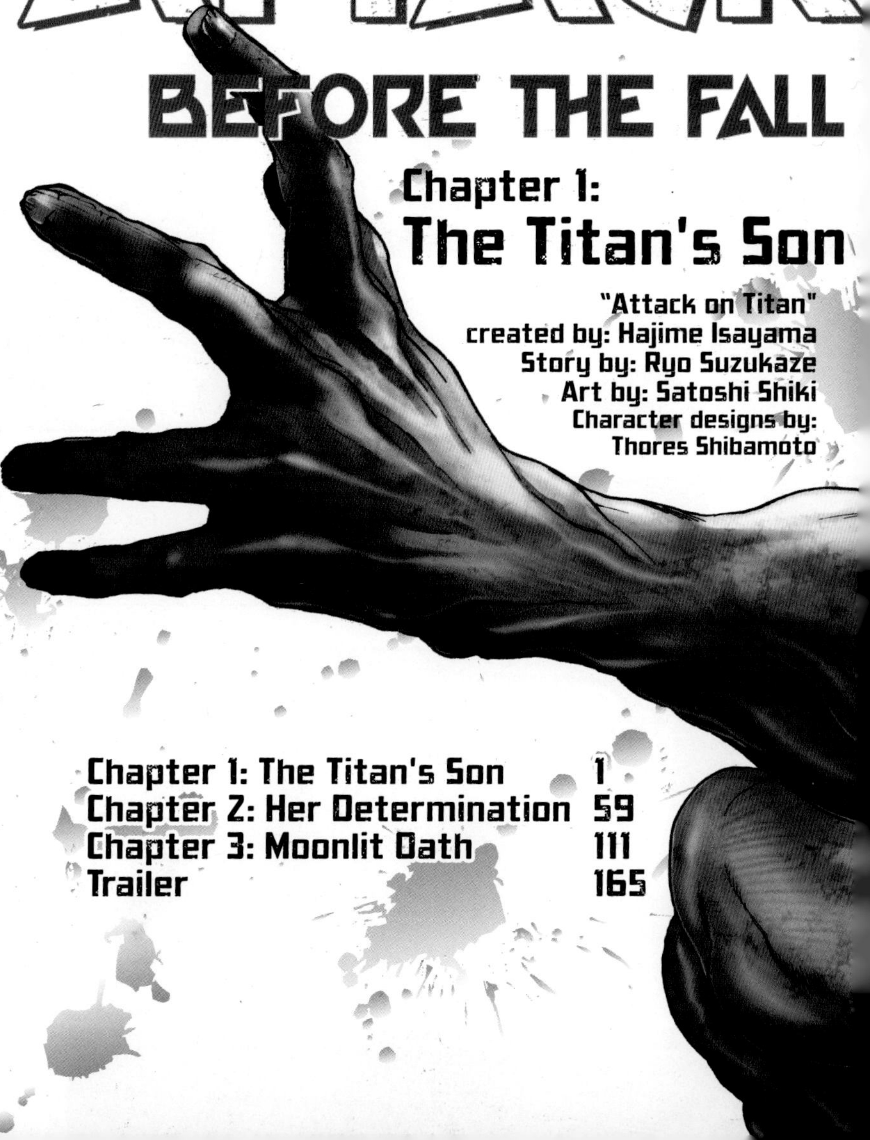

"Attack on Titan"
created by: Hajime Isayama
Story by: Ryo Suzukaze
Art by: Satoshi Shiki
Character designs by:
Thores Shibamoto

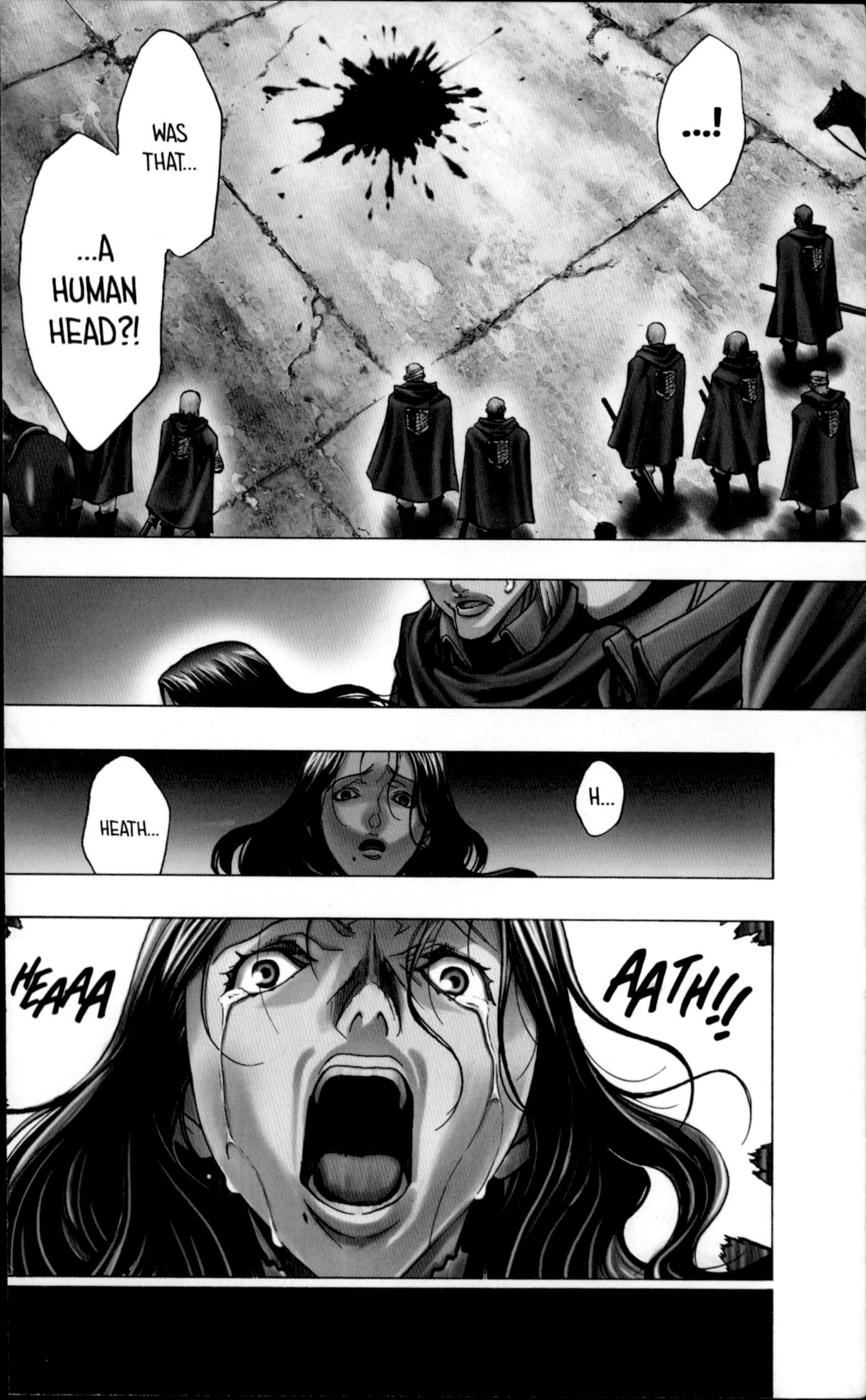
...!
WAS THAT...
...A HUMAN HEAD?!
H...
HEATH...
HEAAA AATH!!

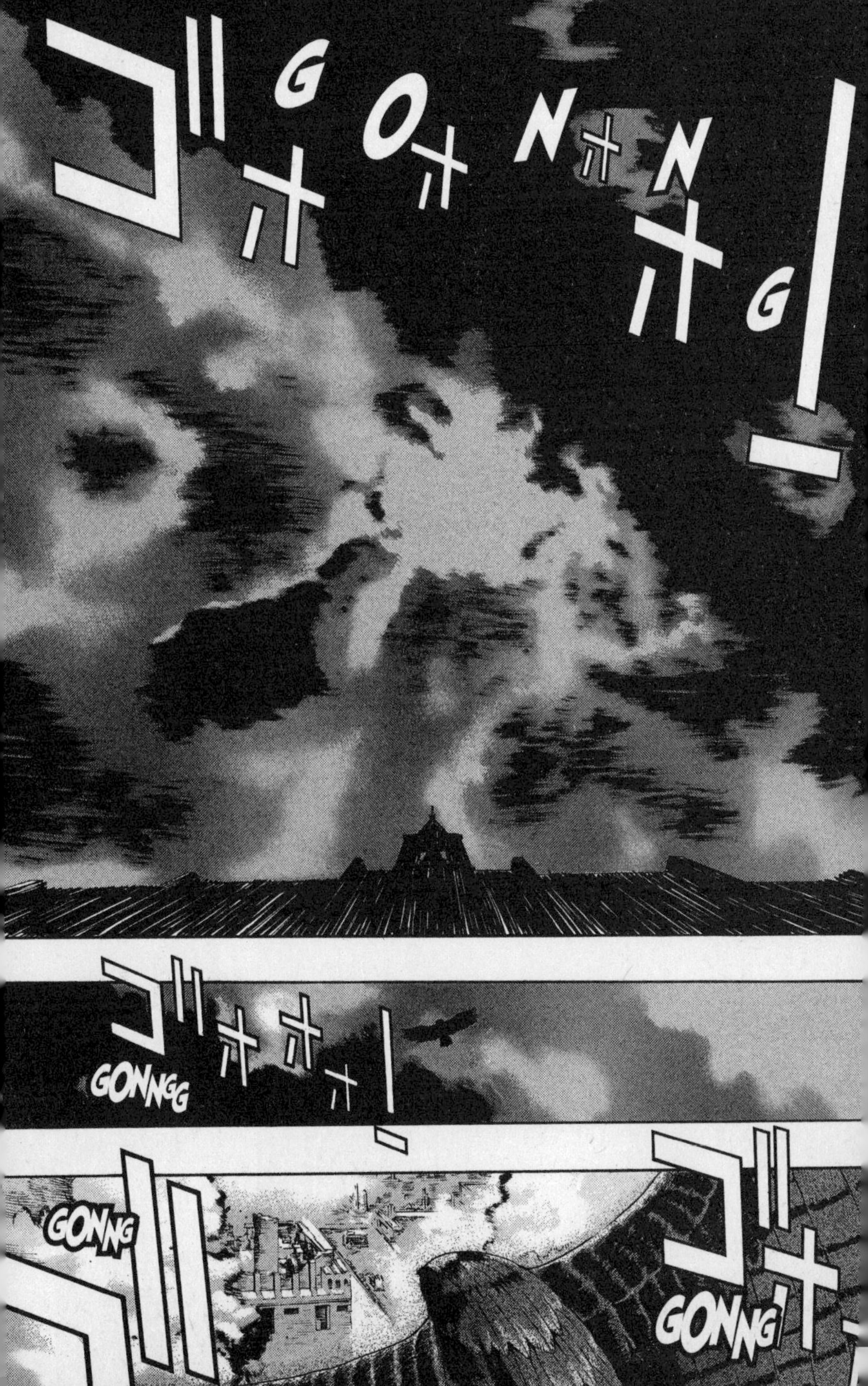
GONNG
GONNGG
GONNG
GONNG

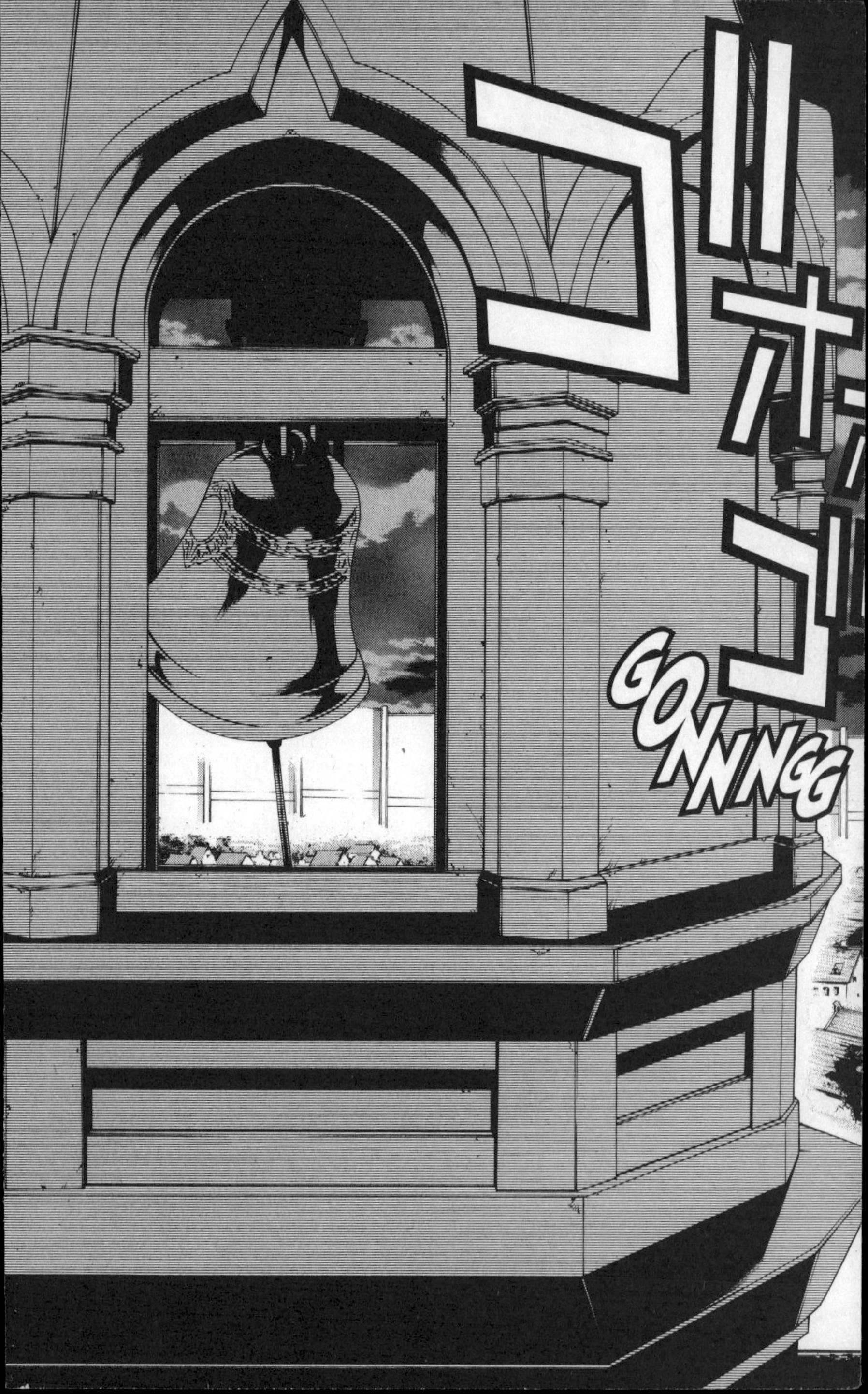
GONNNGG

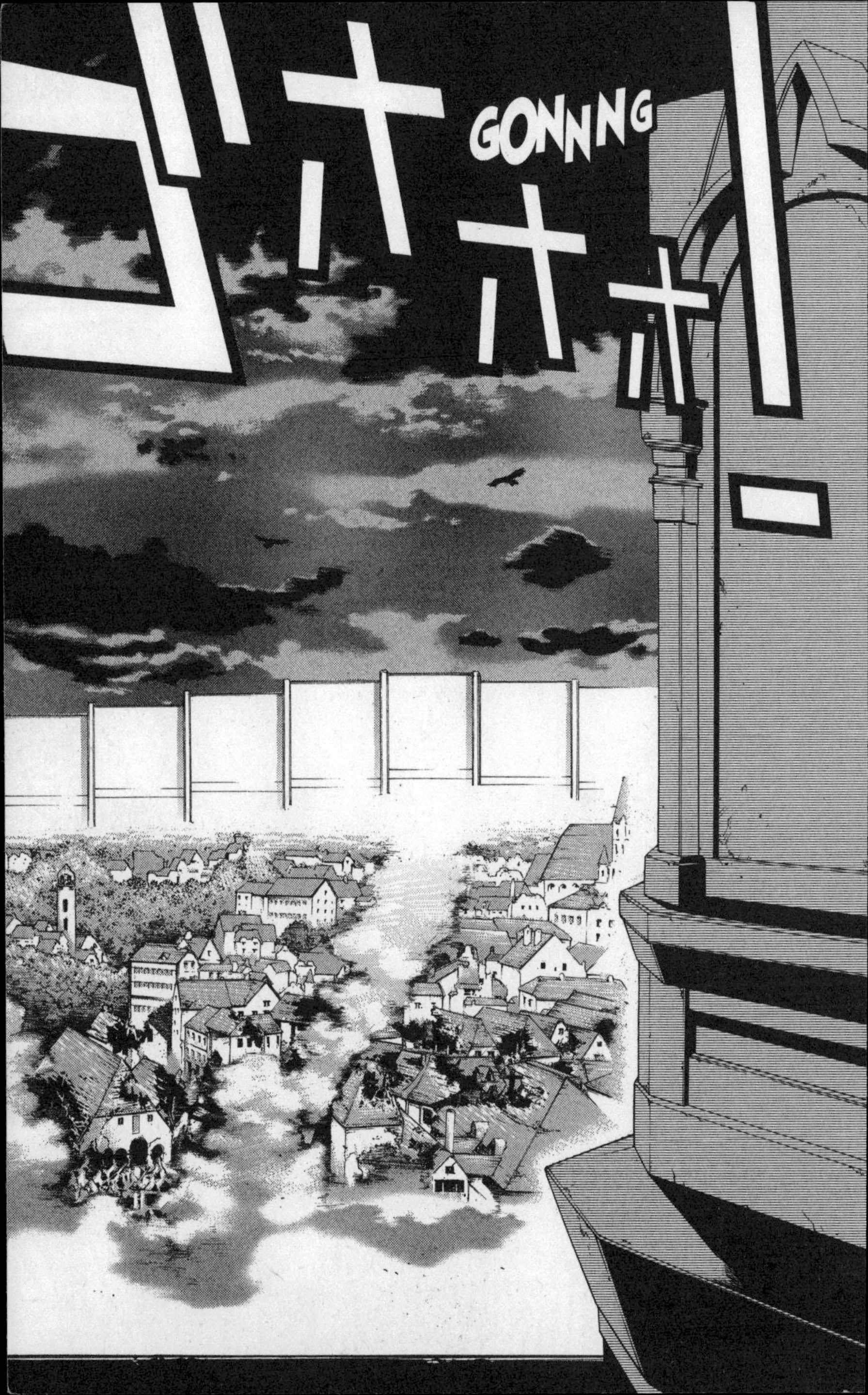
ゴオォォォン
GONNNG

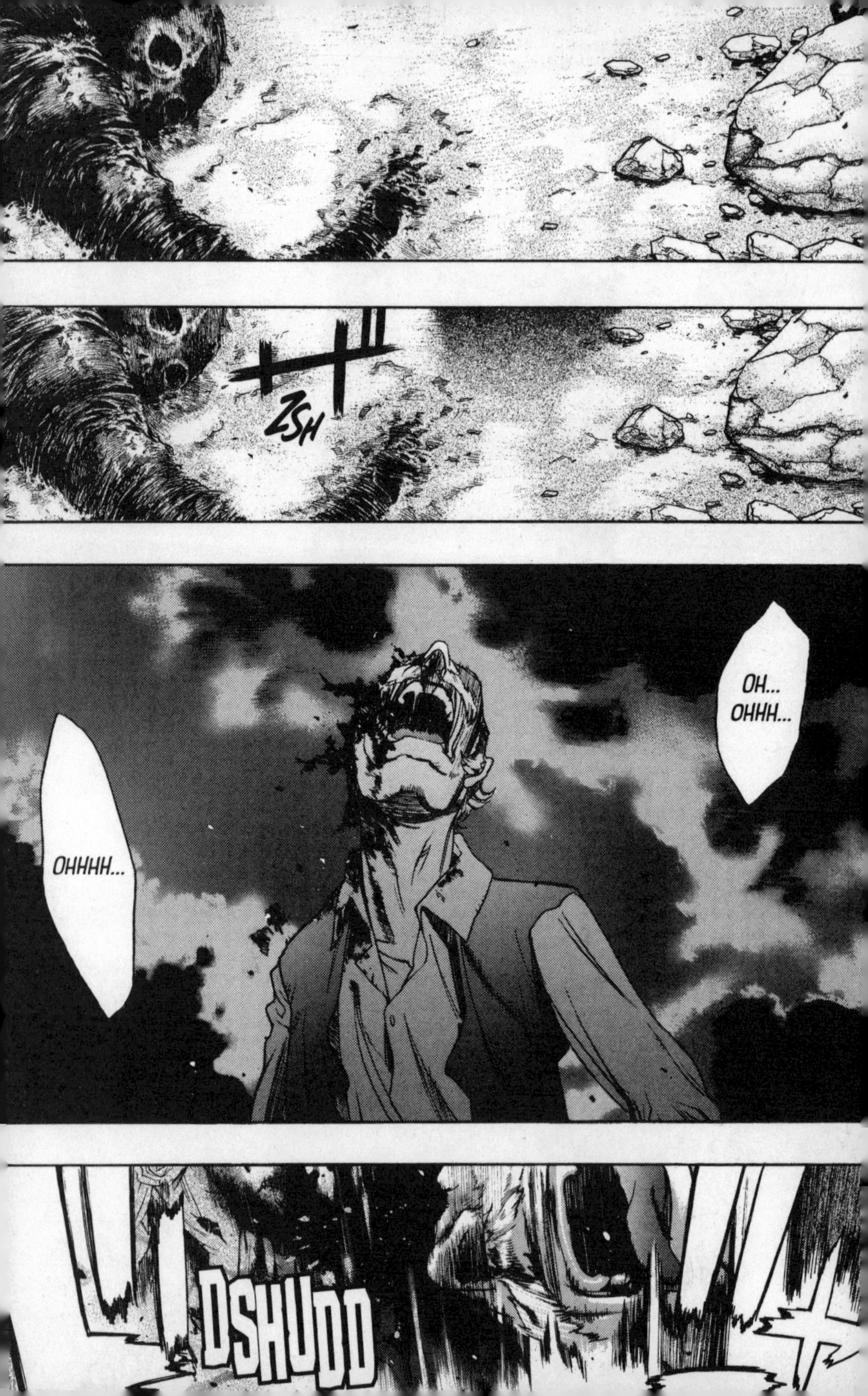
ZSH
OH... OHHH...
OHHHH...
DSHUDD

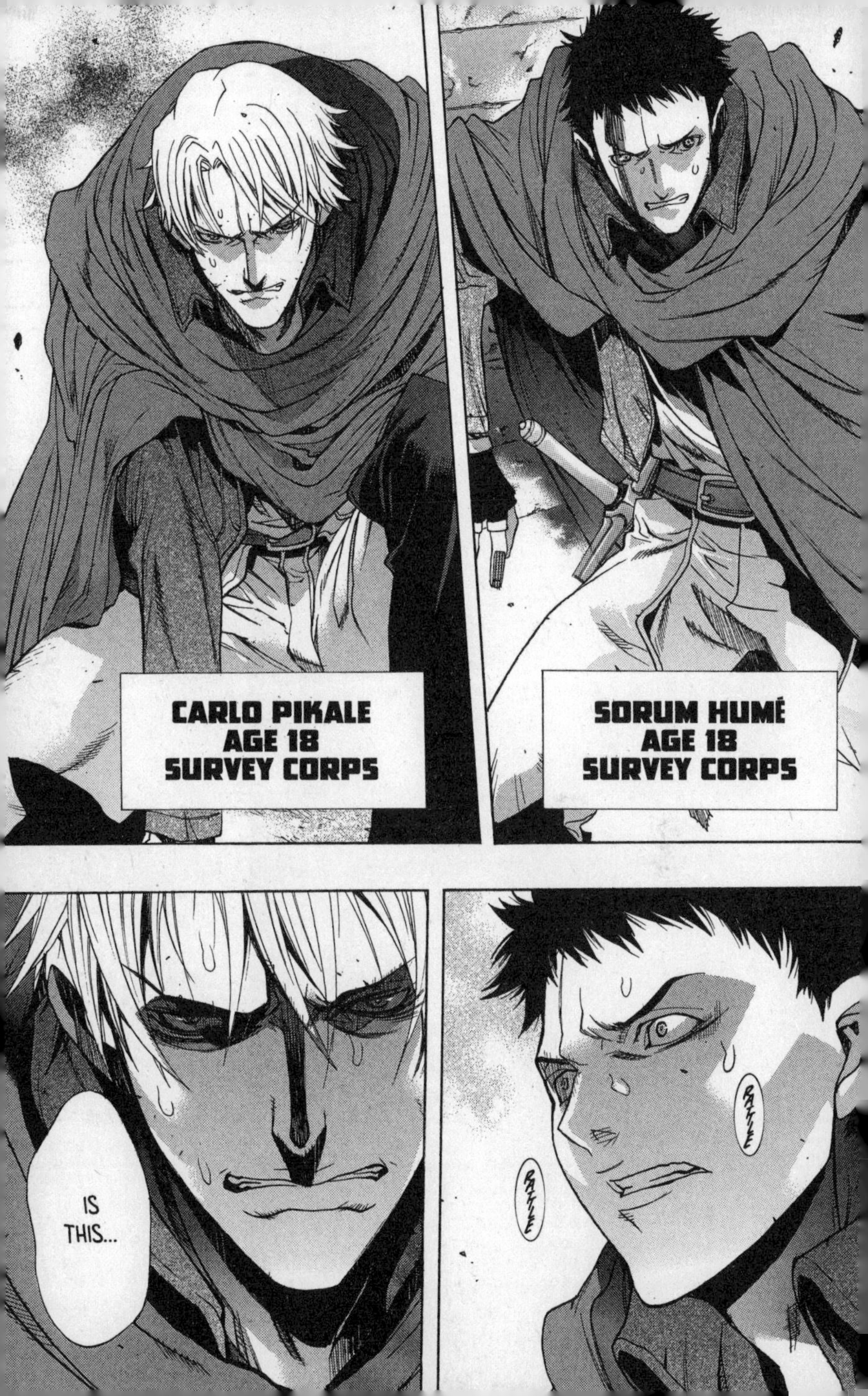
SORUM HUMÉ
AGE 18
SURVEY CORPS
CARLO PIKALE
AGE 18
SURVEY CORPS
RATTLE
RATTLE
IS THIS...

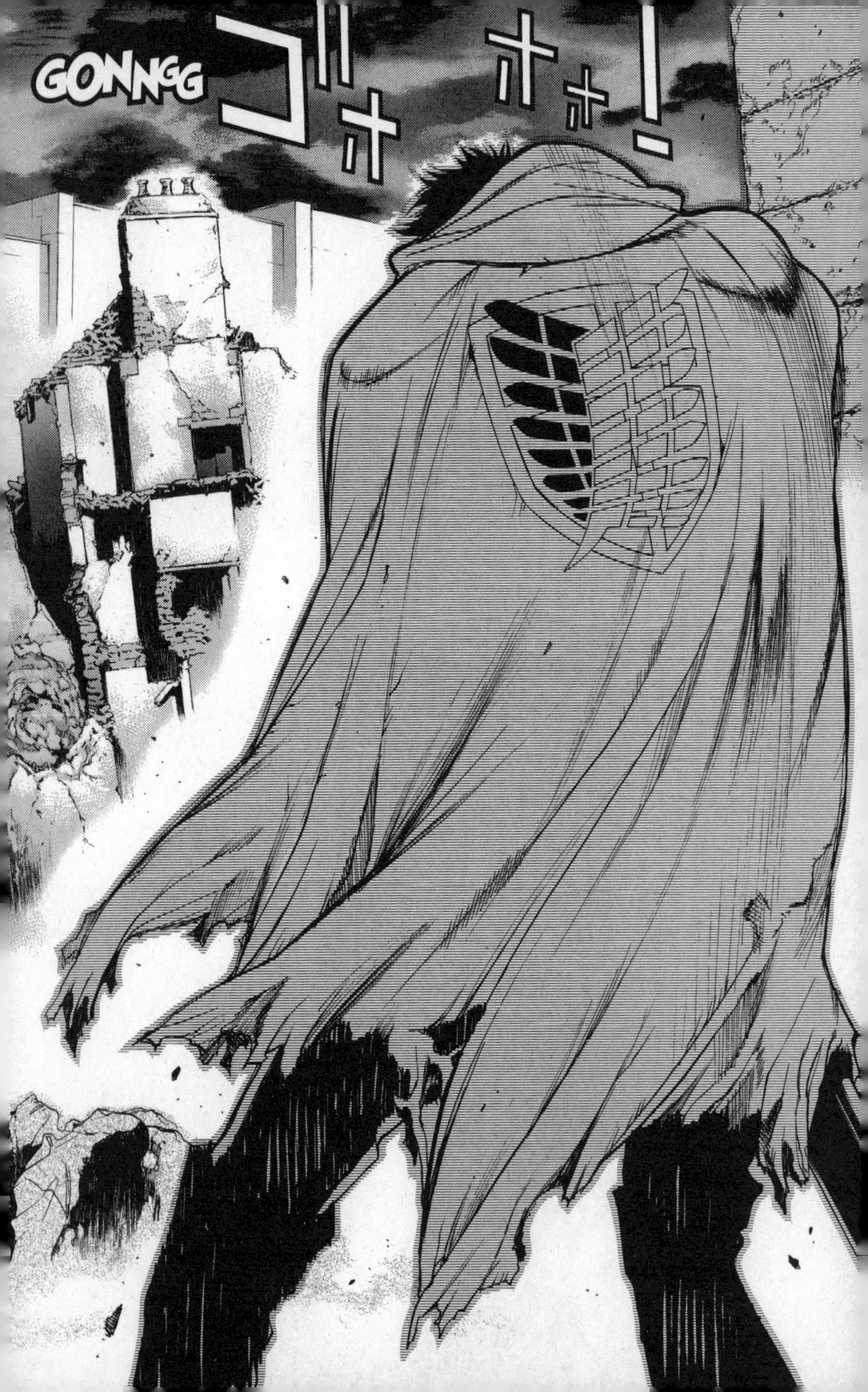
GONNGG
ゴォォォ…

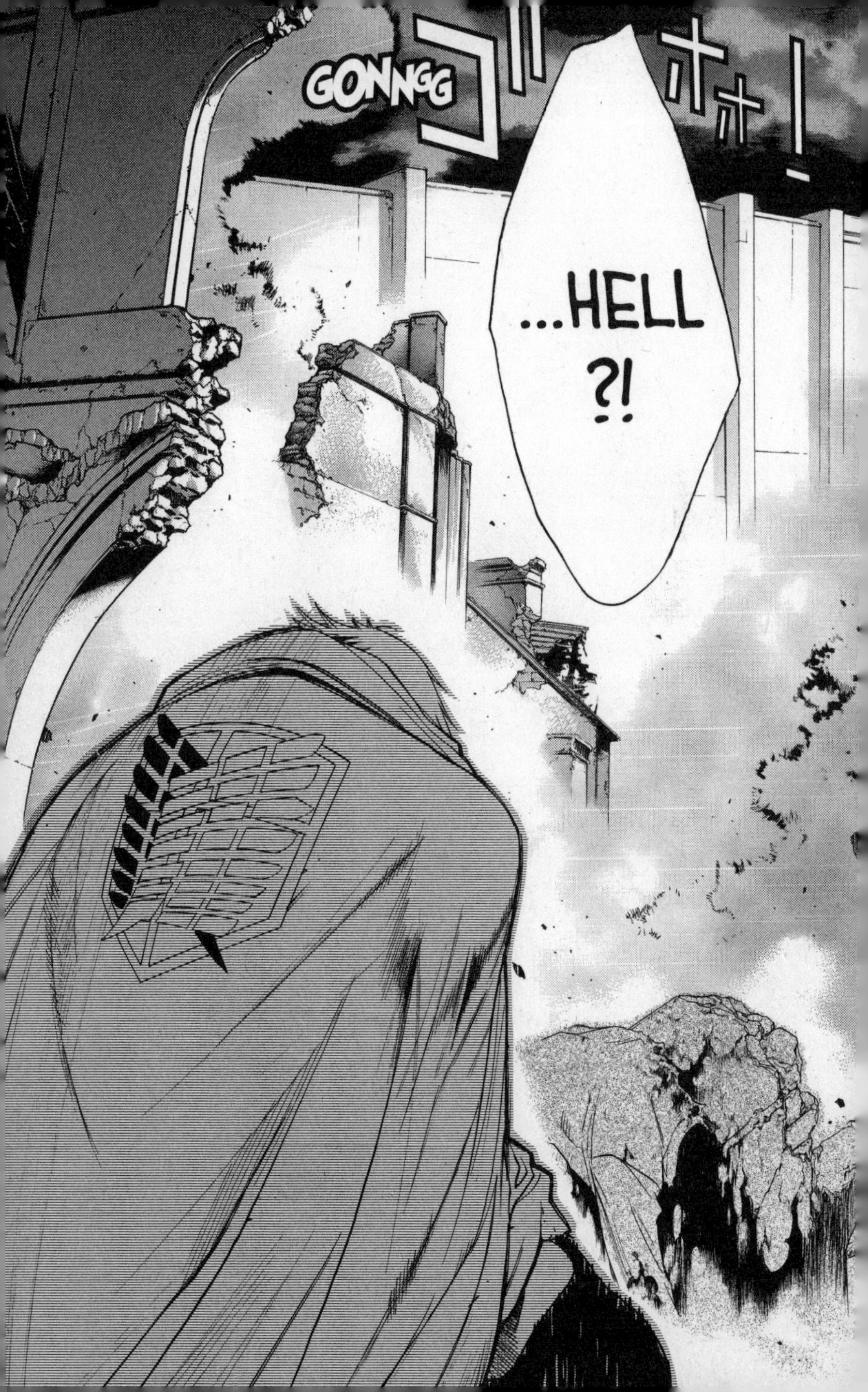
GONNGG
ゴォォー
...HELL ?!

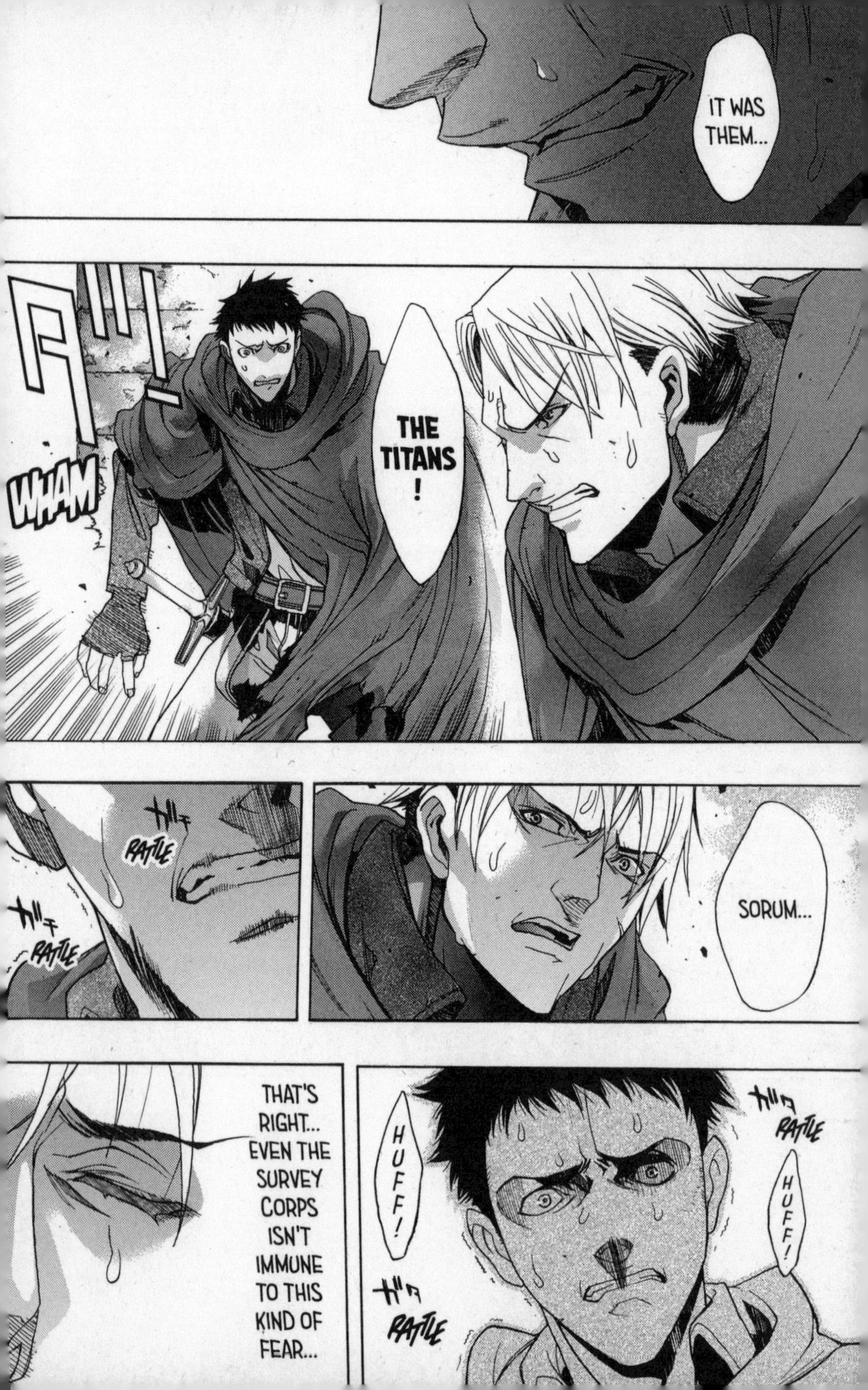
IT WAS THEM...
THE TITANS!
WHAM
SORUM...
RATTLE
RATTLE
HUFF!
HUFF!
RATTLE
RATTLE
THAT'S RIGHT... EVEN THE SURVEY CORPS ISN'T IMMUNE TO THIS KIND OF FEAR...

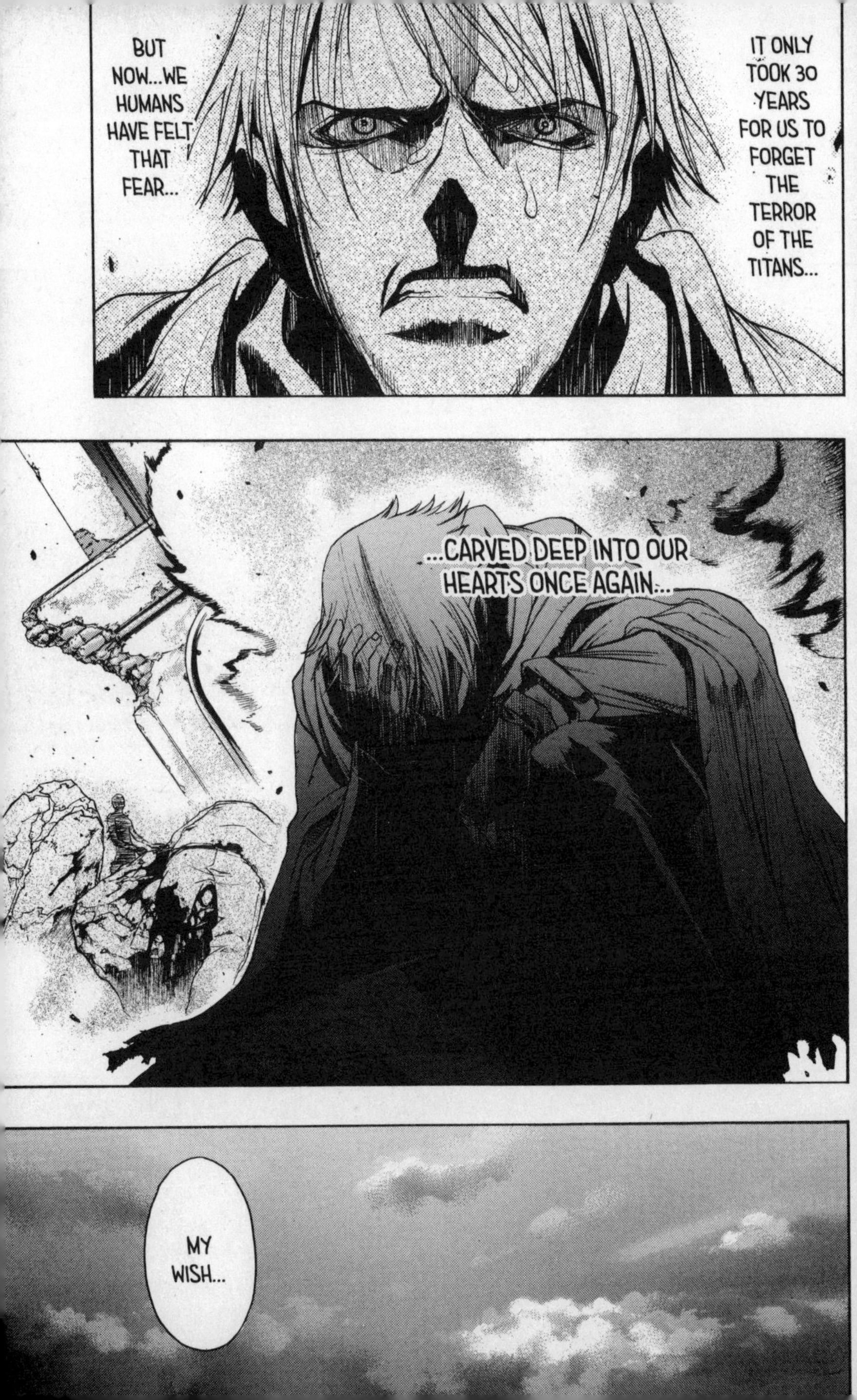
IT ONLY TOOK 30 YEARS FOR US TO FORGET THE TERROR OF THE TITANS...
BUT NOW...WE HUMANS HAVE FELT THAT FEAR...
...CARVED DEEP INTO OUR HEARTS ONCE AGAIN...
MY WISH...

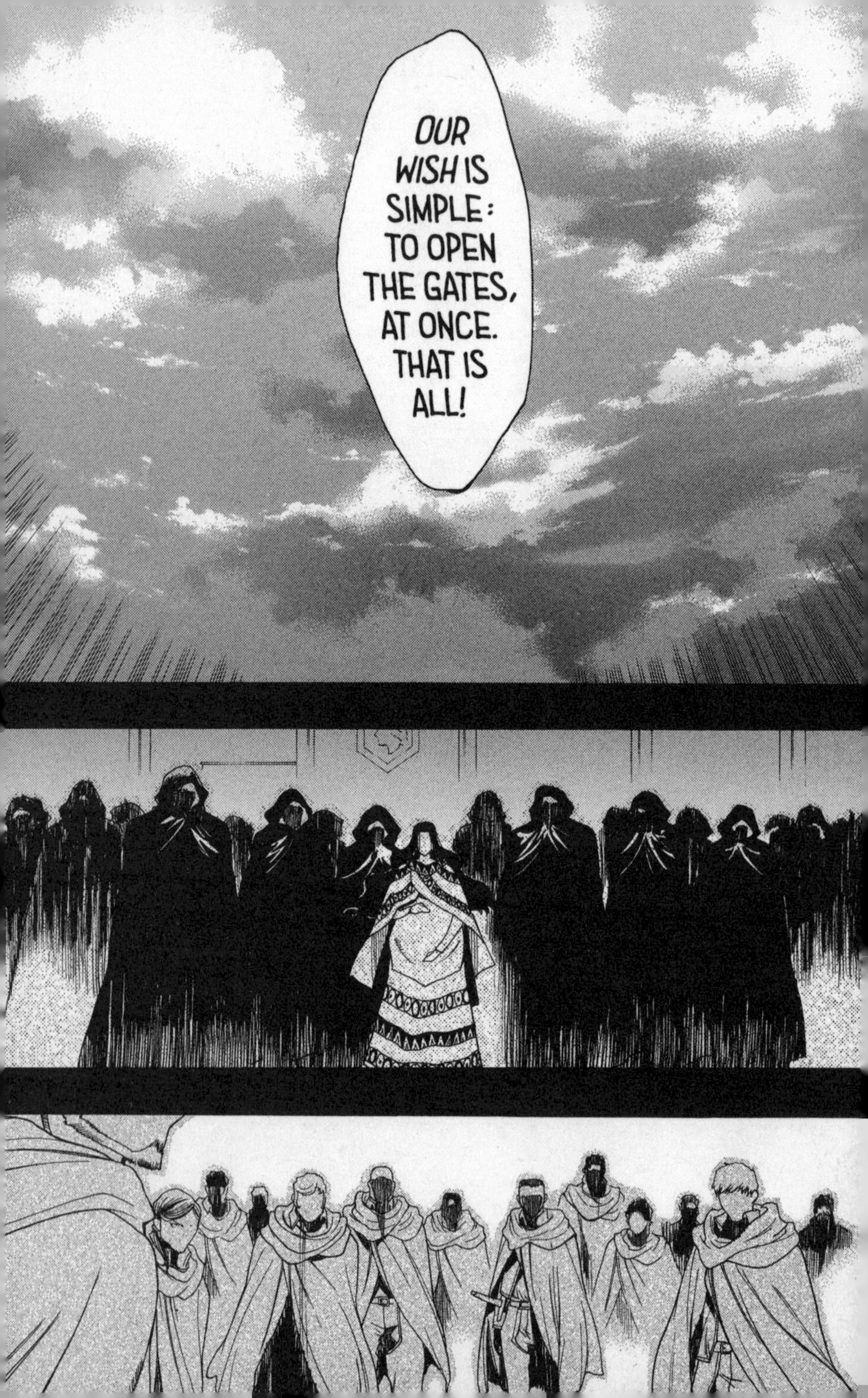
OUR WISH IS SIMPLE: TO OPEN THE GATES, AT ONCE. THAT IS ALL!

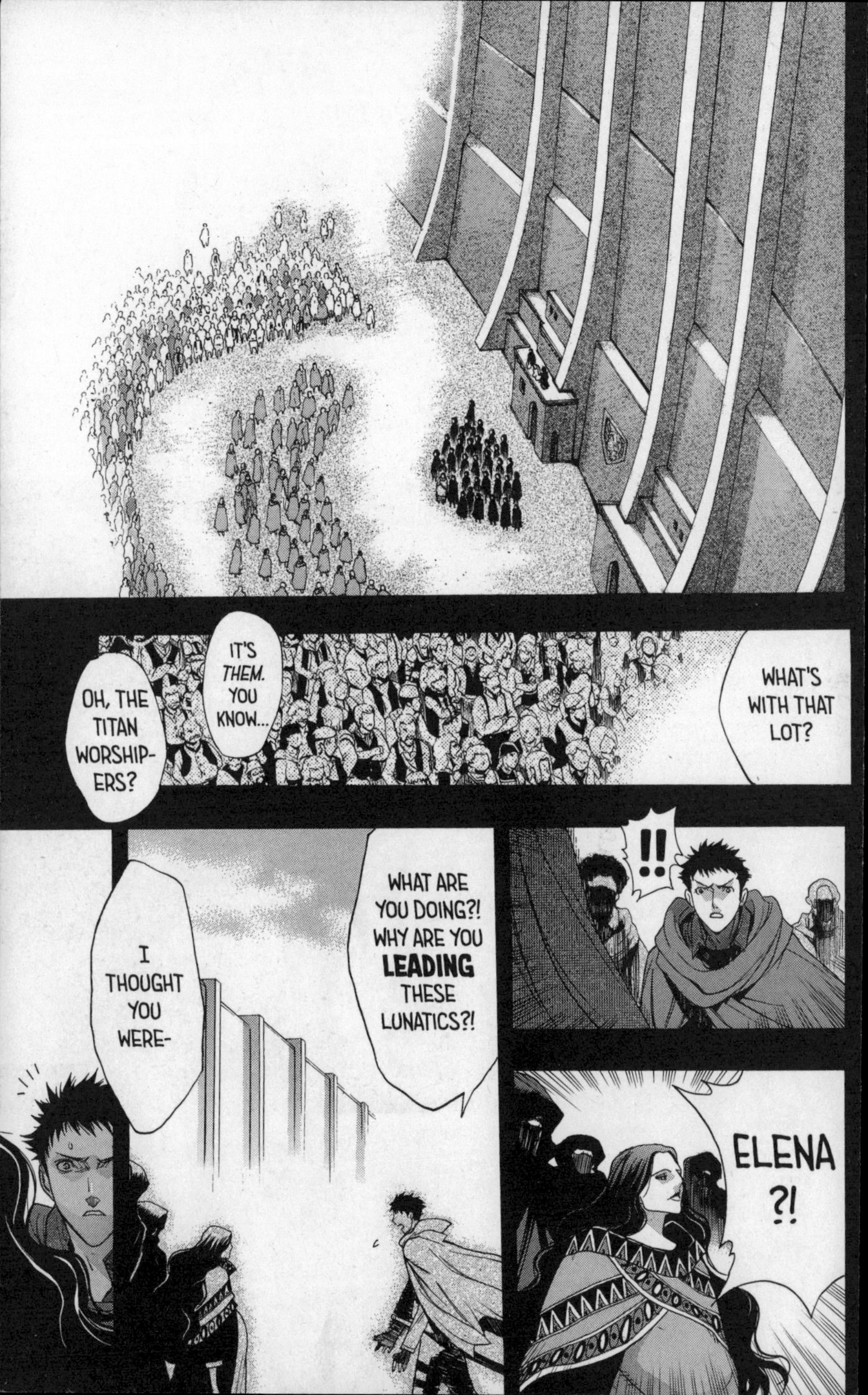
WHAT'S WITH THAT LOT?
IT'S *THEM.* YOU KNOW...
OH, THE TITAN WORSHIP-ERS?
!!
ELENA ?!
WHAT ARE YOU DOING?! WHY ARE YOU **LEADING** THESE LUNATICS?!
I THOUGHT YOU WERE-

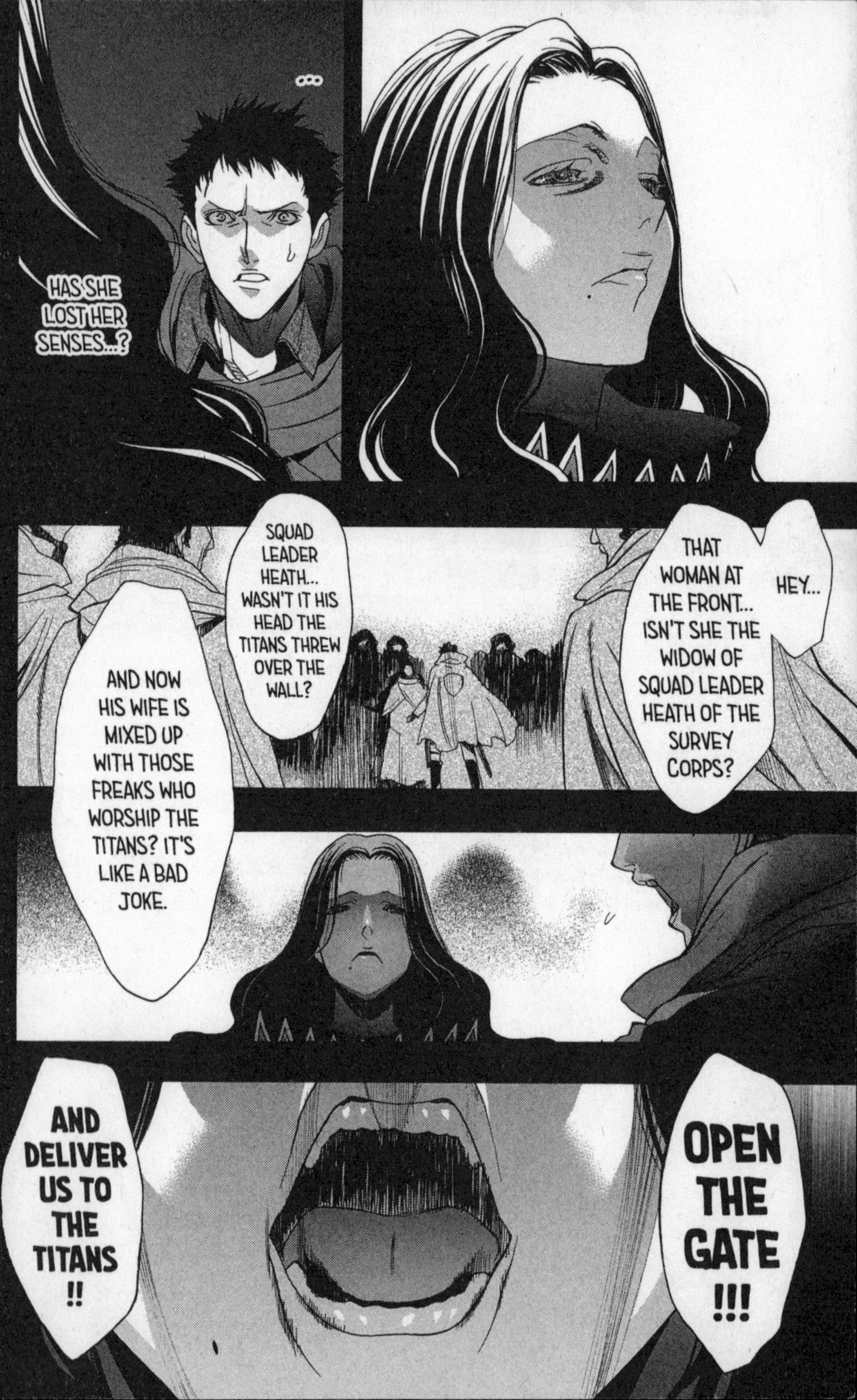
...
HAS SHE LOST HER SENSES...?
HEY...
THAT WOMAN AT THE FRONT... ISN'T SHE THE WIDOW OF SQUAD LEADER HEATH OF THE SURVEY CORPS?
SQUAD LEADER HEATH... WASN'T IT HIS HEAD THE TITANS THREW OVER THE WALL?
AND NOW HIS WIFE IS MIXED UP WITH THOSE FREAKS WHO WORSHIP THE TITANS? IT'S LIKE A BAD JOKE.
OPEN THE GATE!!!
AND DELIVER US TO THE TITANS!!

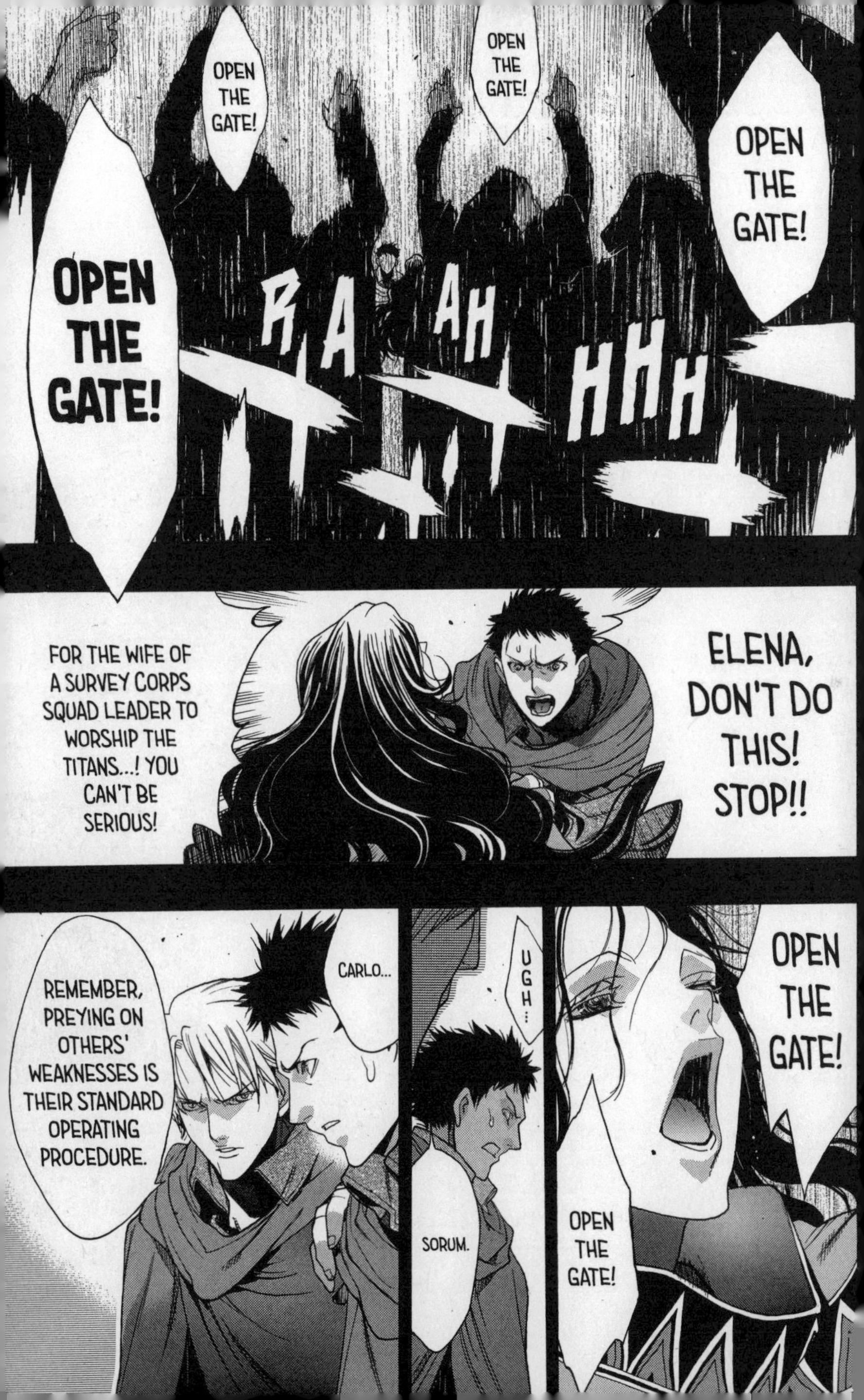
OPEN THE GATE!
OPEN THE GATE!
OPEN THE GATE!
RAAHHHH
OPEN THE GATE!
ELENA, DON'T DO THIS! STOP!!
FOR THE WIFE OF A SURVEY CORPS SQUAD LEADER TO WORSHIP THE TITANS...! YOU CAN'T BE SERIOUS!
OPEN THE GATE!
OPEN THE GATE!
UGH...
SORUM.
CARLO...
REMEMBER, PREYING ON OTHERS' WEAKNESSES IS THEIR STANDARD OPERATING PROCEDURE.

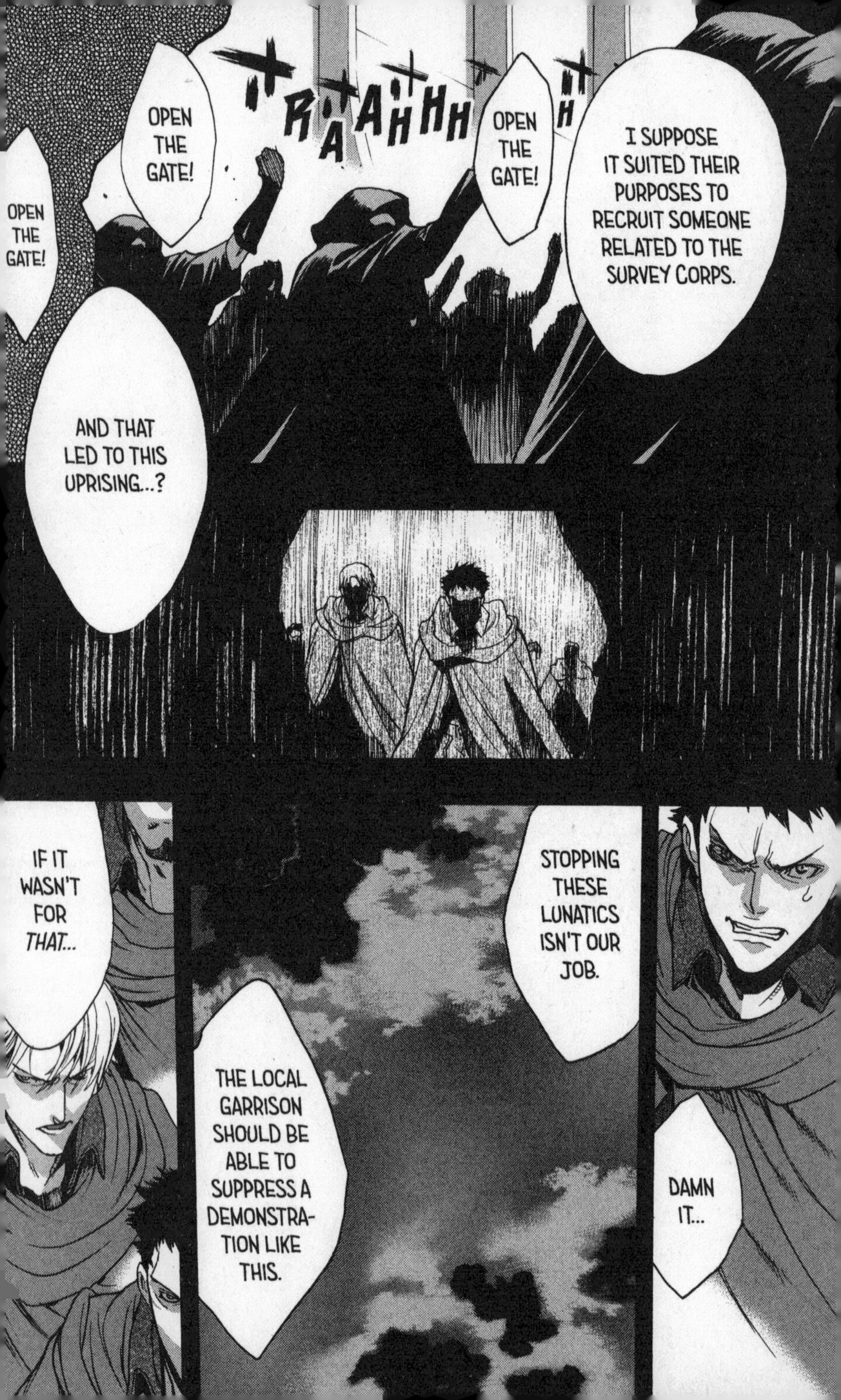
I SUPPOSE IT SUITED THEIR PURPOSES TO RECRUIT SOMEONE RELATED TO THE SURVEY CORPS.
OPEN THE GATE!
RAAHHHHH
OPEN THE GATE!
OPEN THE GATE!
AND THAT LED TO THIS UPRISING...?
DAMN IT...
STOPPING THESE LUNATICS ISN'T OUR JOB.
THE LOCAL GARRISON SHOULD BE ABLE TO SUPPRESS A DEMONSTRATION LIKE THIS.
IF IT WASN'T FOR *THAT*...

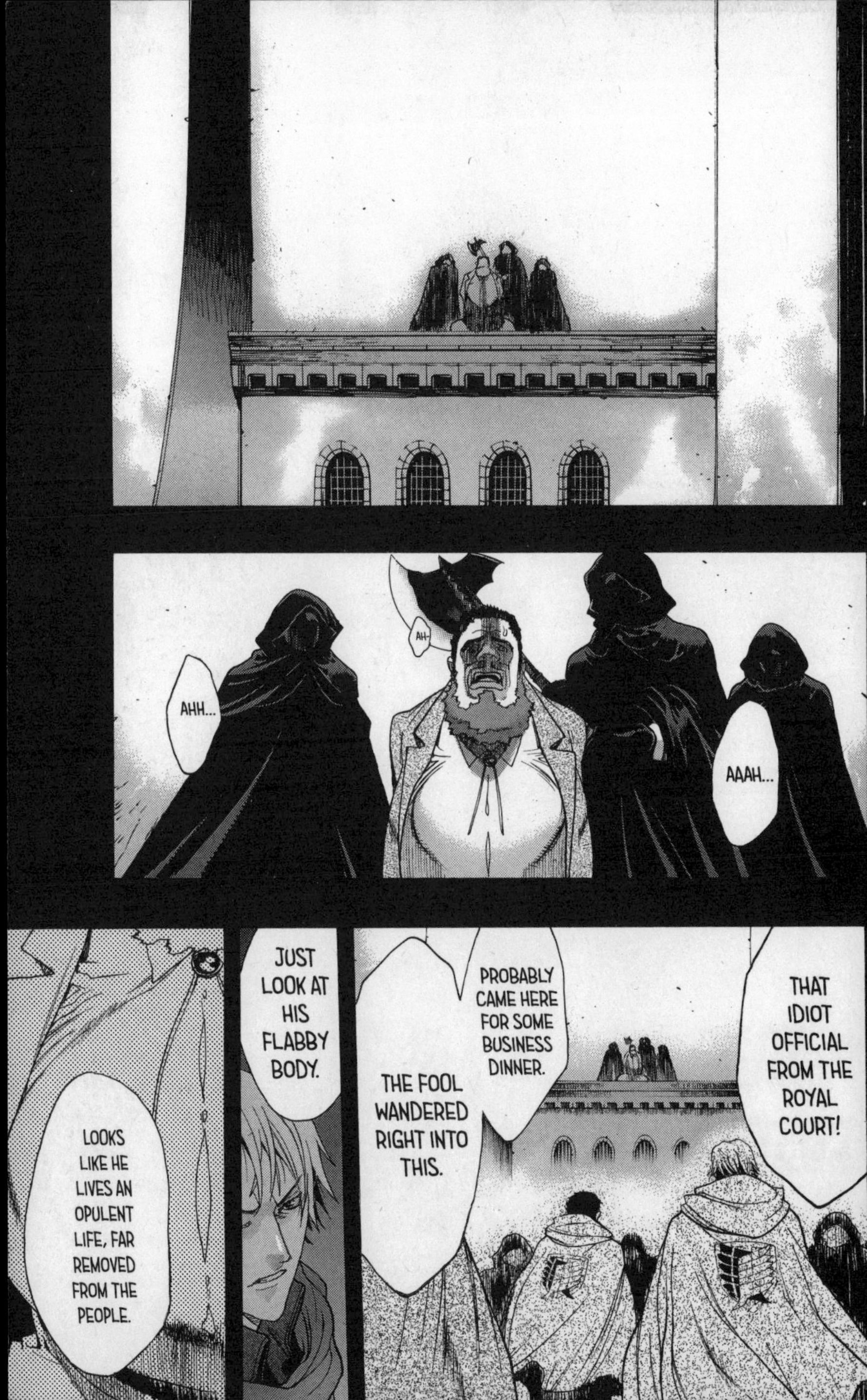
AAAH...
AH-
AHH...
THAT IDIOT OFFICIAL FROM THE ROYAL COURT!
PROBABLY CAME HERE FOR SOME BUSINESS DINNER.
THE FOOL WANDERED RIGHT INTO THIS.
JUST LOOK AT HIS FLABBY BODY.
LOOKS LIKE HE LIVES AN OPULENT LIFE, FAR REMOVED FROM THE PEOPLE.

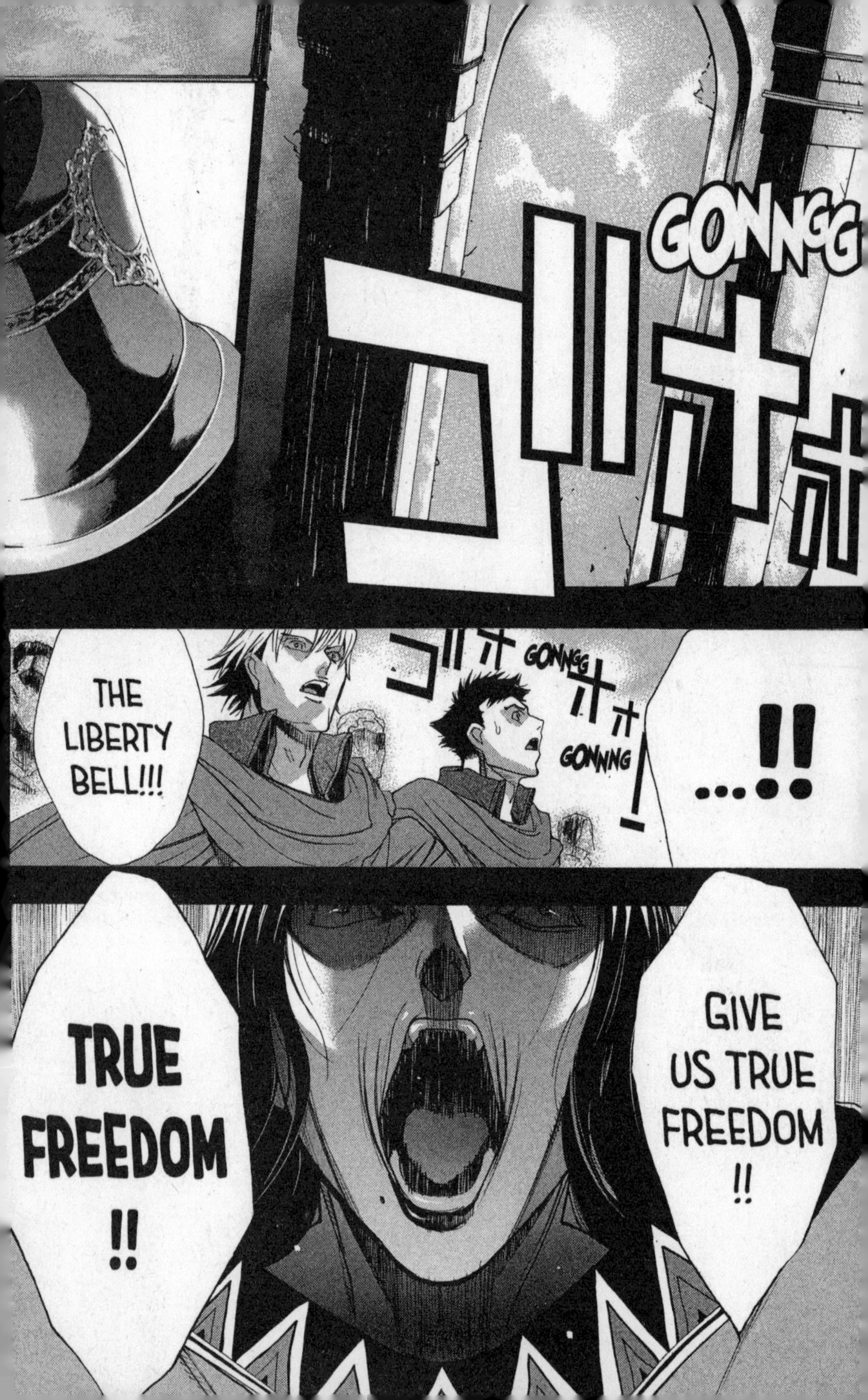
ゴォォ
GONNGG
...!!
ゴォォ GONNGG
ォォ GONNNG
THE LIBERTY BELL!!!
GIVE US TRUE FREEDOM !!
TRUE FREEDOM !!

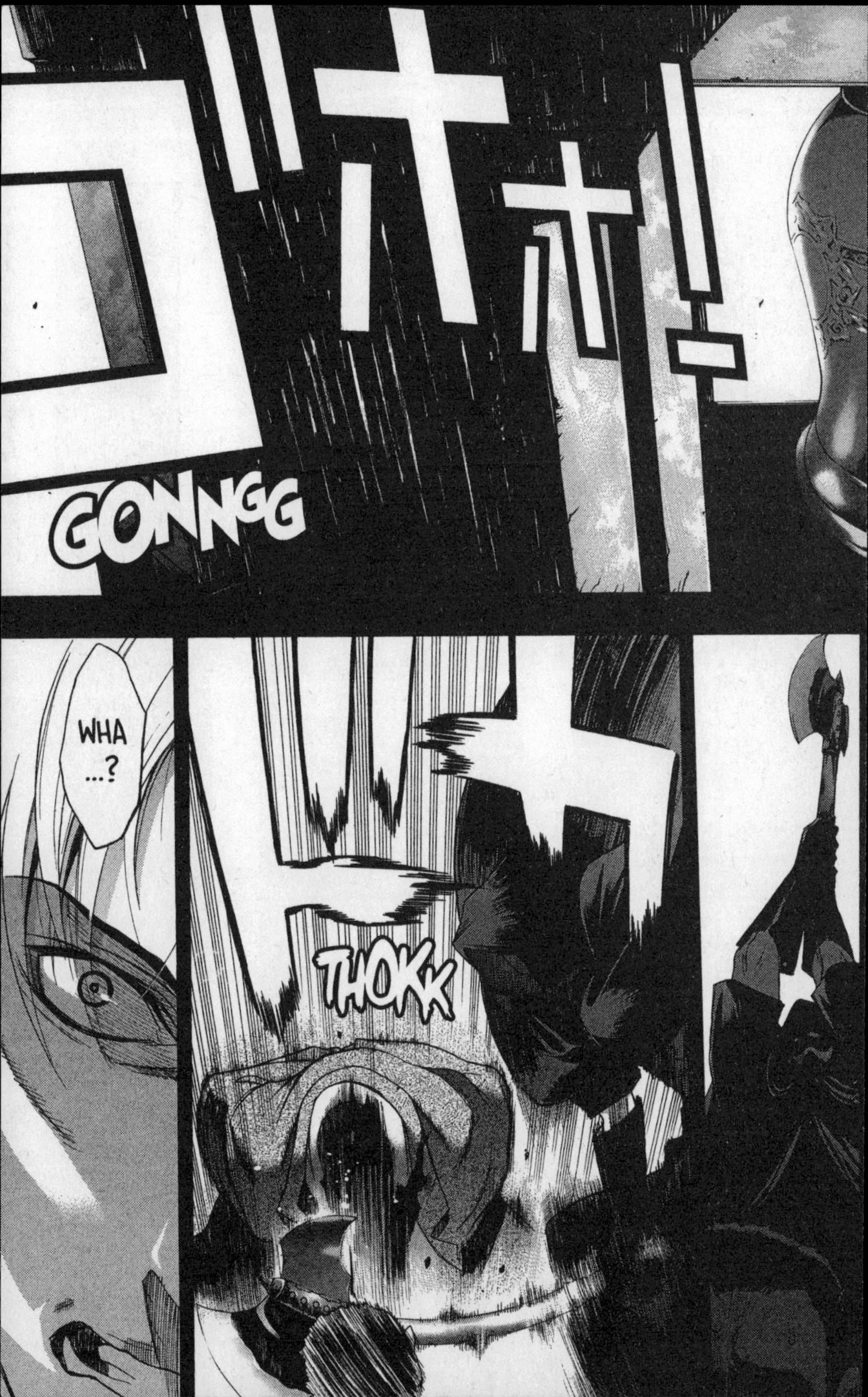
GONNGG
THOKK
WHA ...?

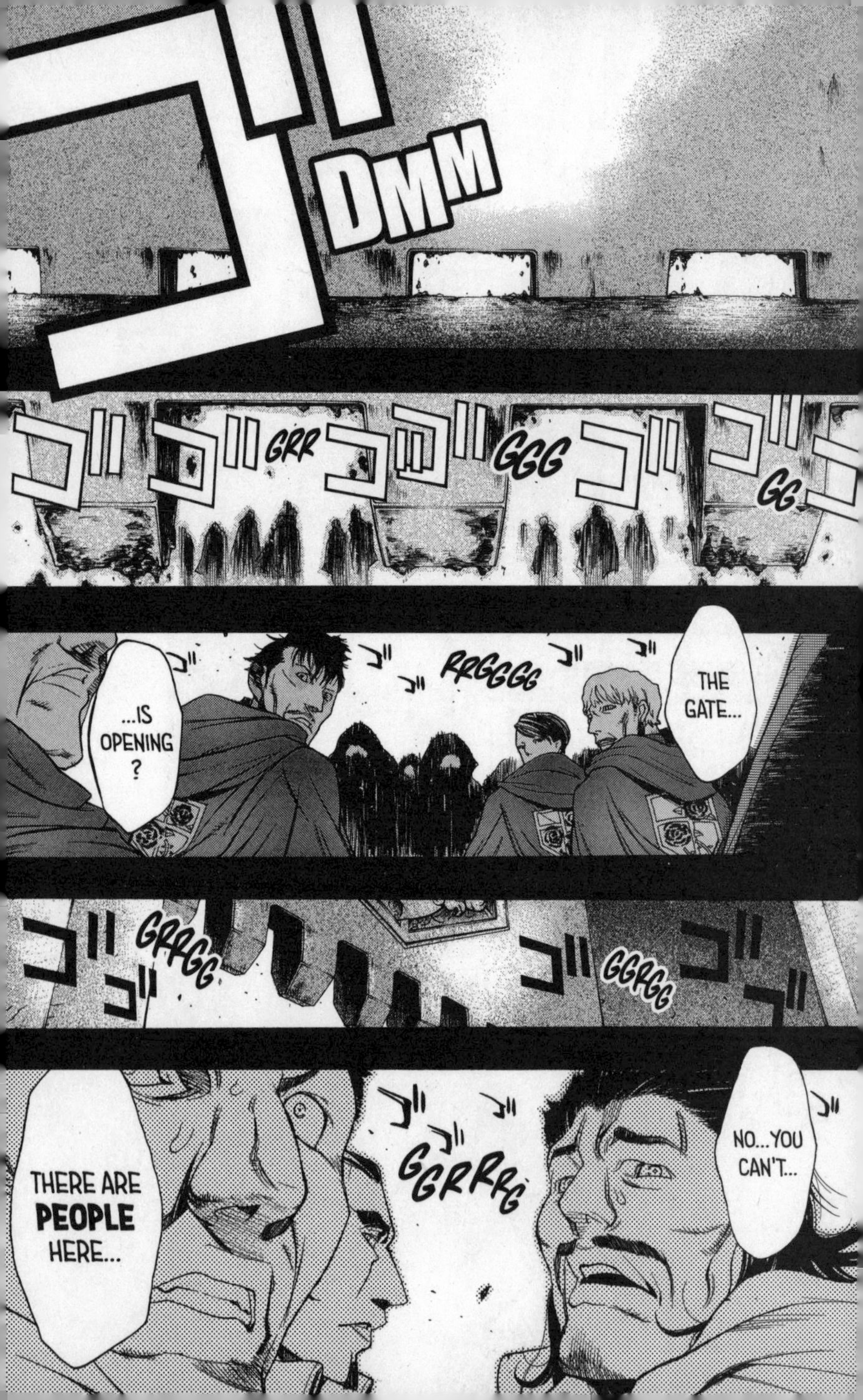
DMM
GG
GGG
GRR
THE GATE...
RRGGGG
...IS OPENING ?
GGRGG
GRRGG
NO...YOU CAN'T...
GGRRRG
THERE ARE **PEOPLE** HERE...

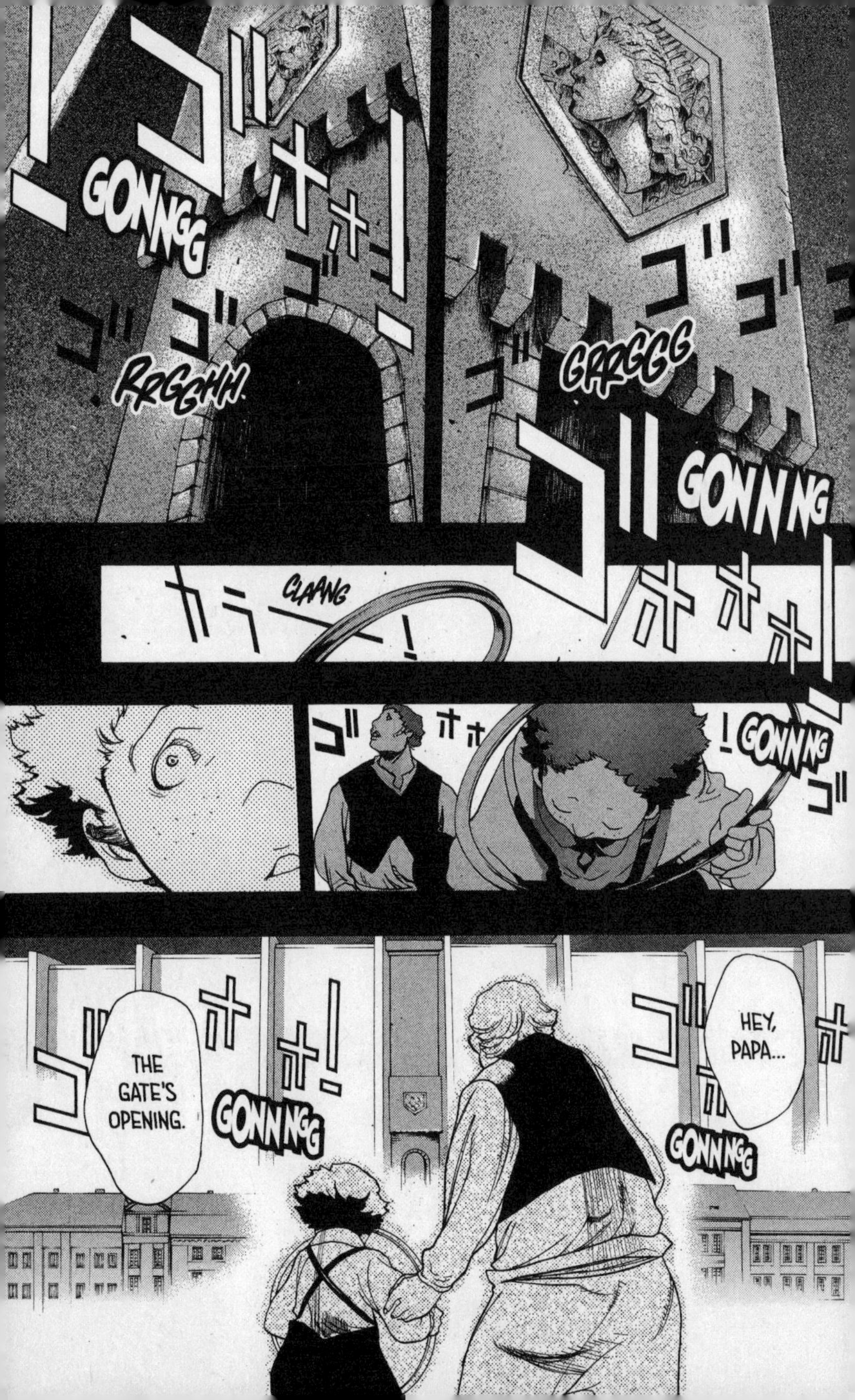
GARGGG
GONNNG
GONNGG
RRGGHH
CLAANG
GONNNG
HEY, PAPA...
GONNGG
THE GATE'S OPENING.
GONNGG

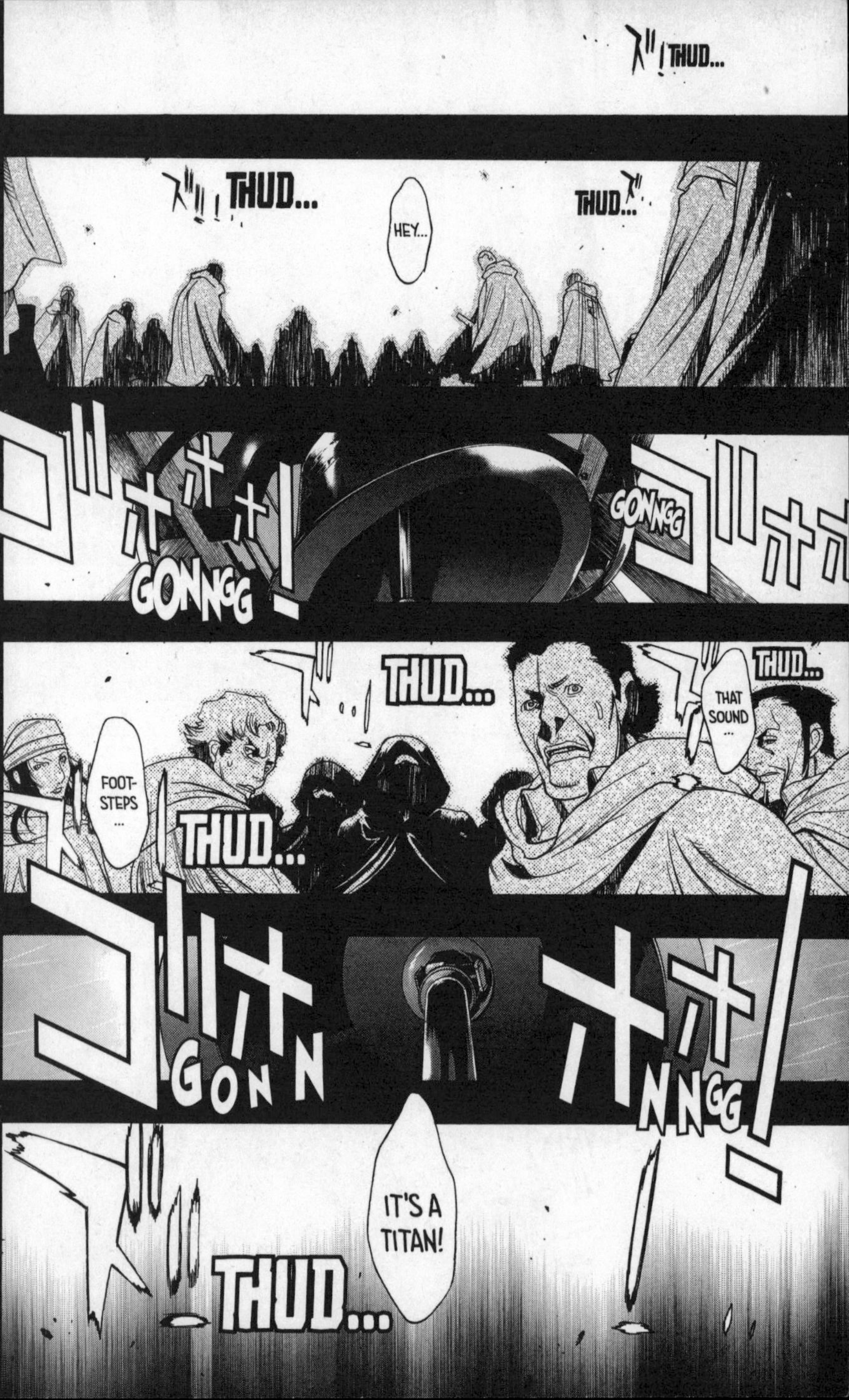
THUD...
THUD...
HEY...
THUD...
GONNGG
GONNGG!
THUD...
THAT SOUND...
THUD...
FOOT-STEPS...
THUD...
GONN NNGG!
IT'S A TITAN!
THUD...

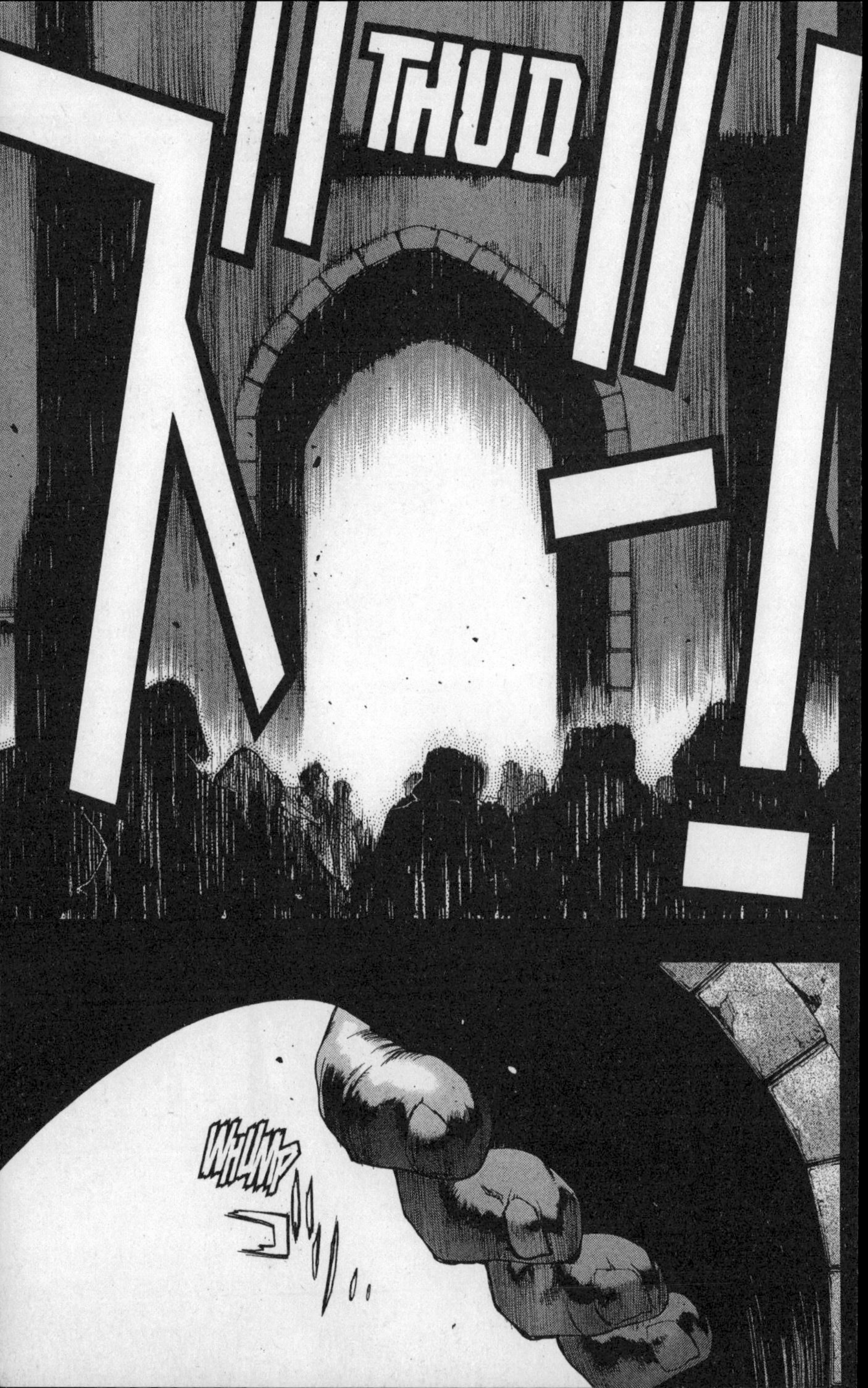
THUD
WHUMP

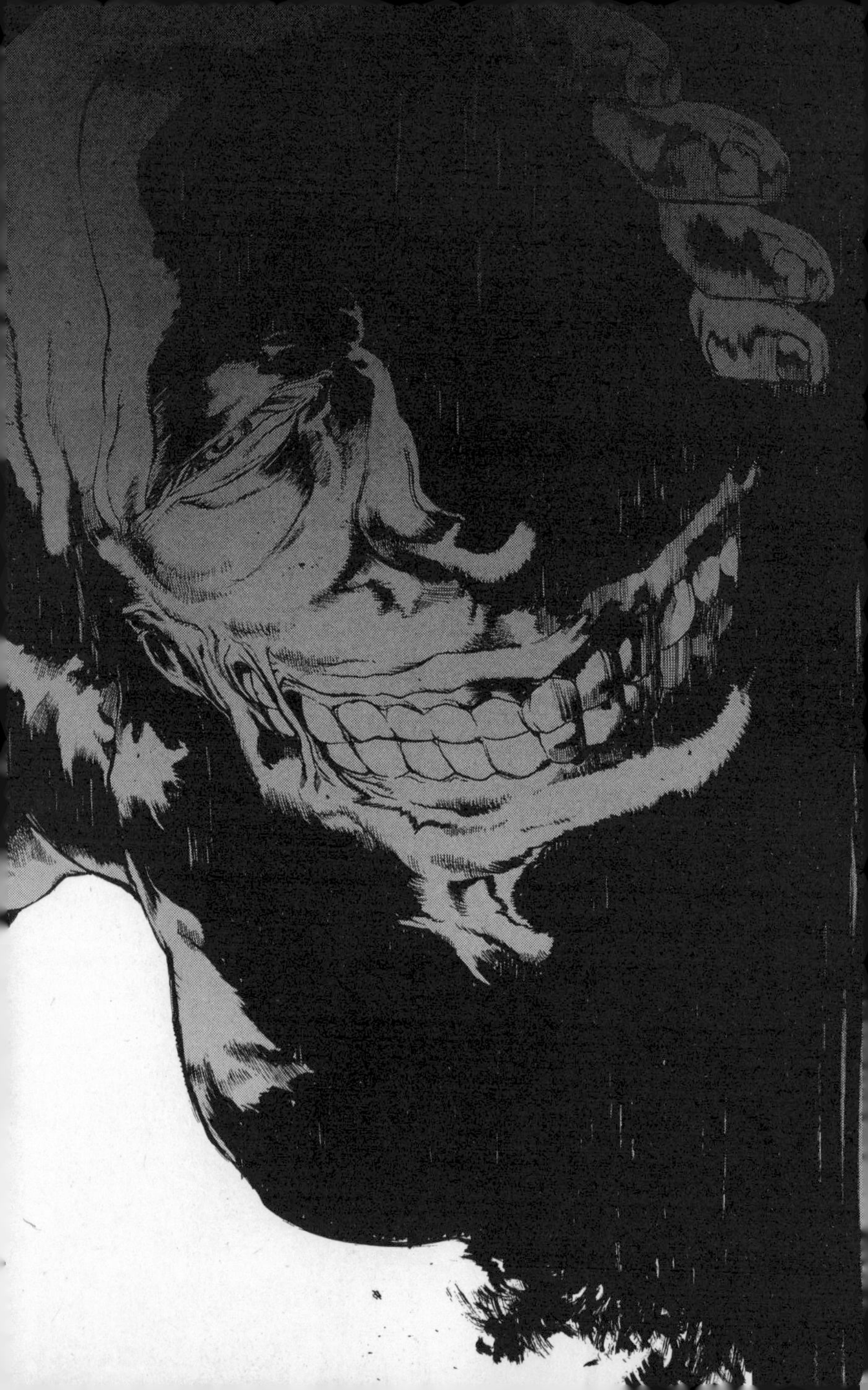

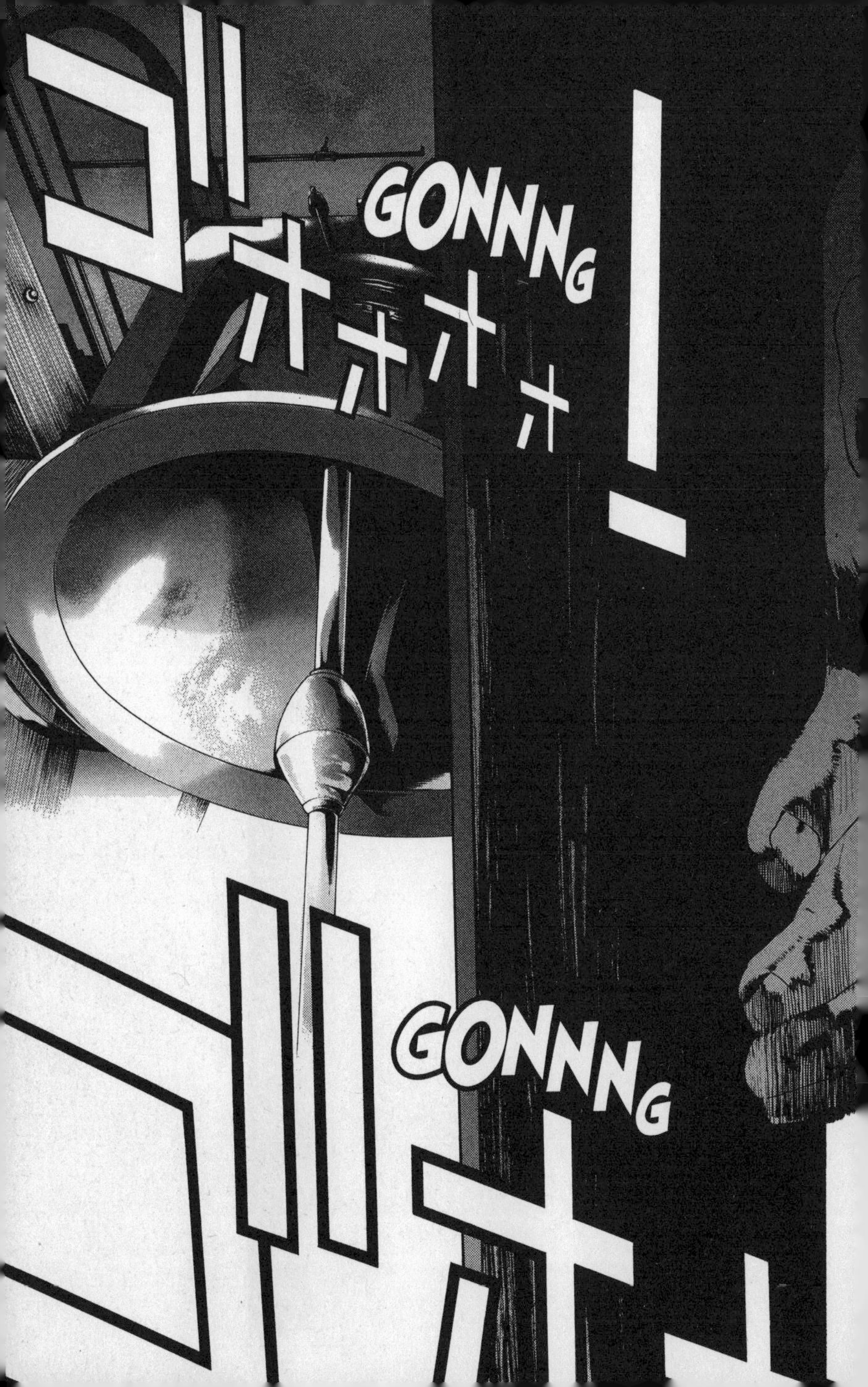
ゴォォォォォー!
GONNNG
ゴォー
GONNNG

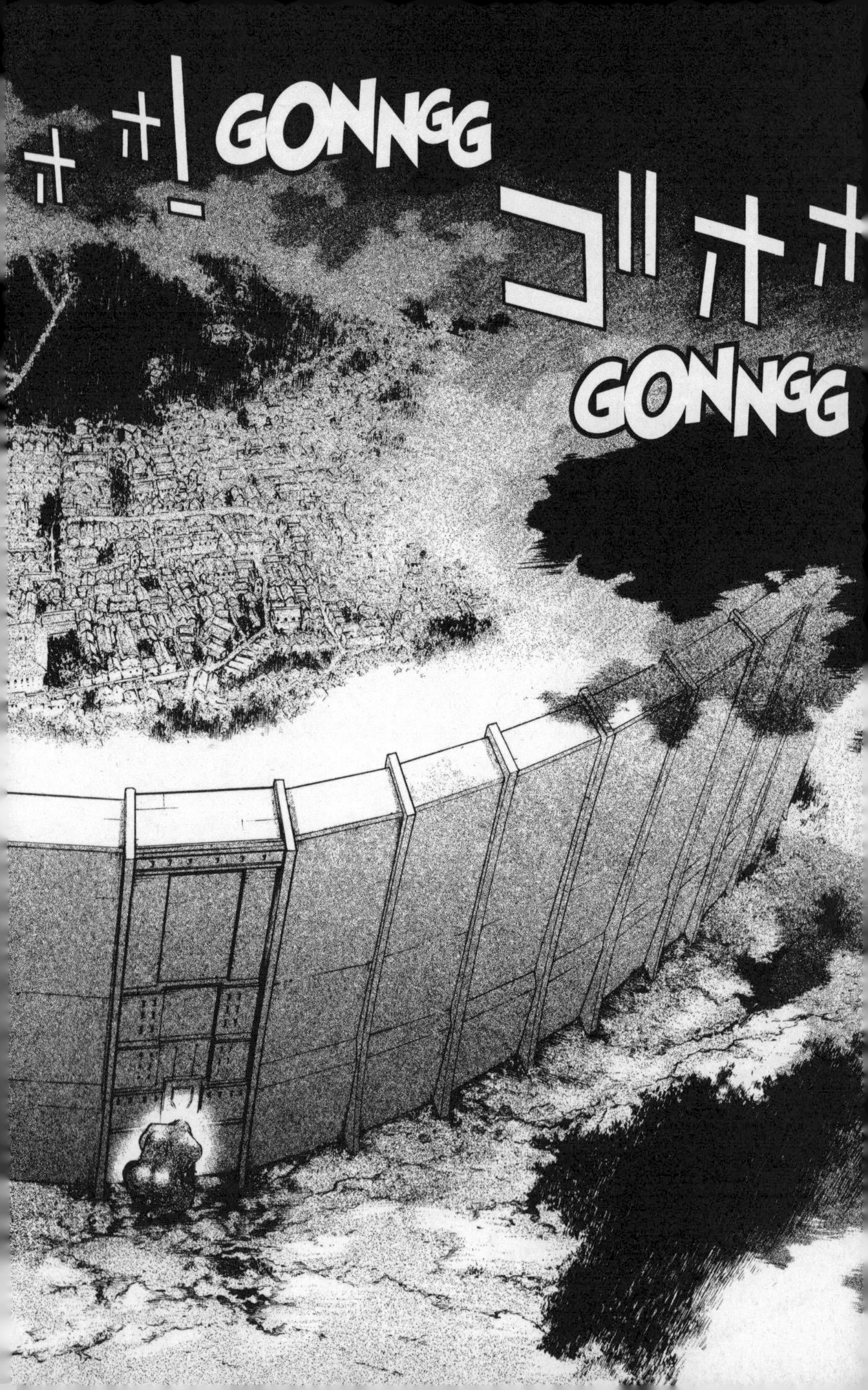
ゴォォ
GONNGG
GONNGG

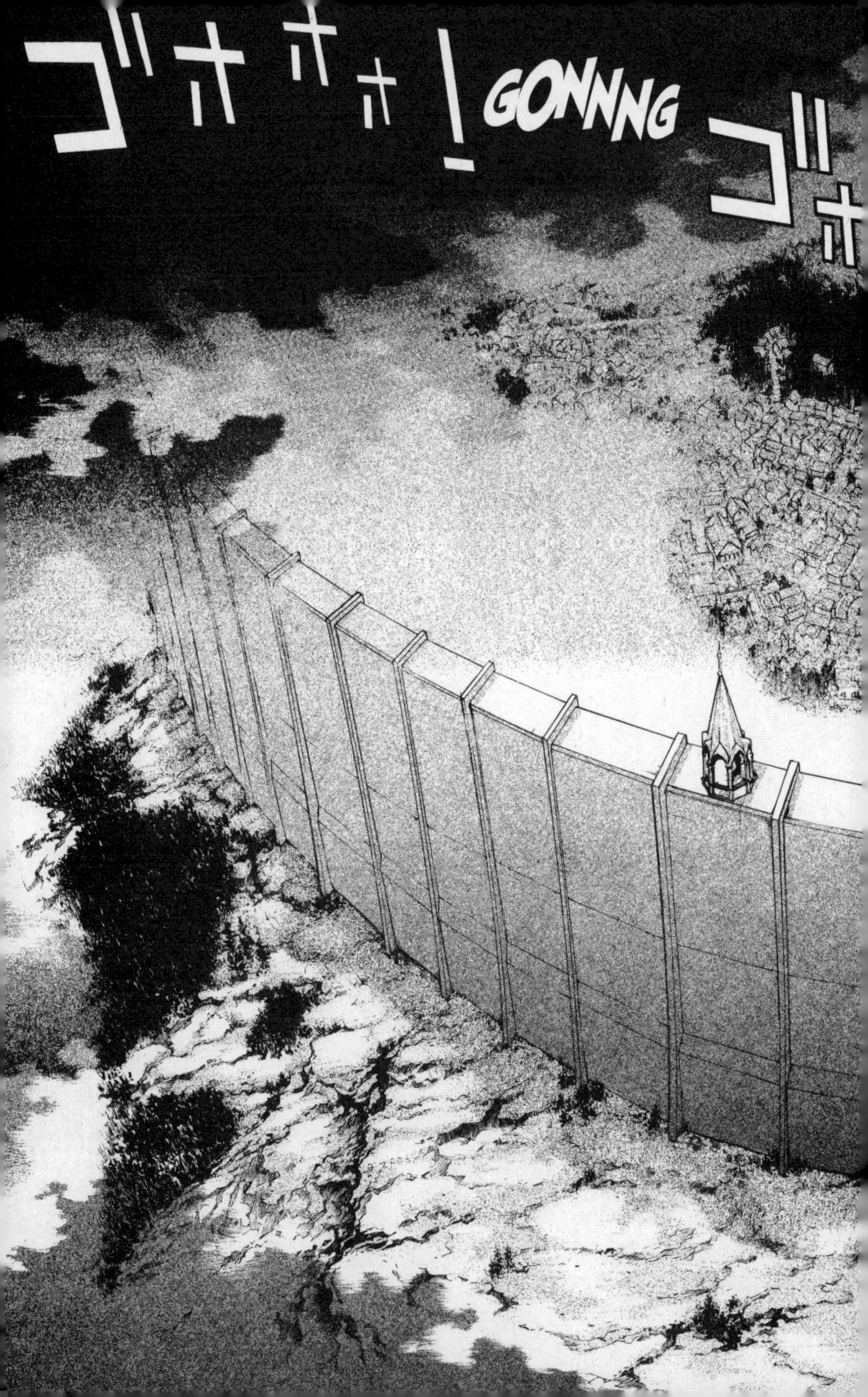
ゴォォォ！
GONNNG
ゴォ

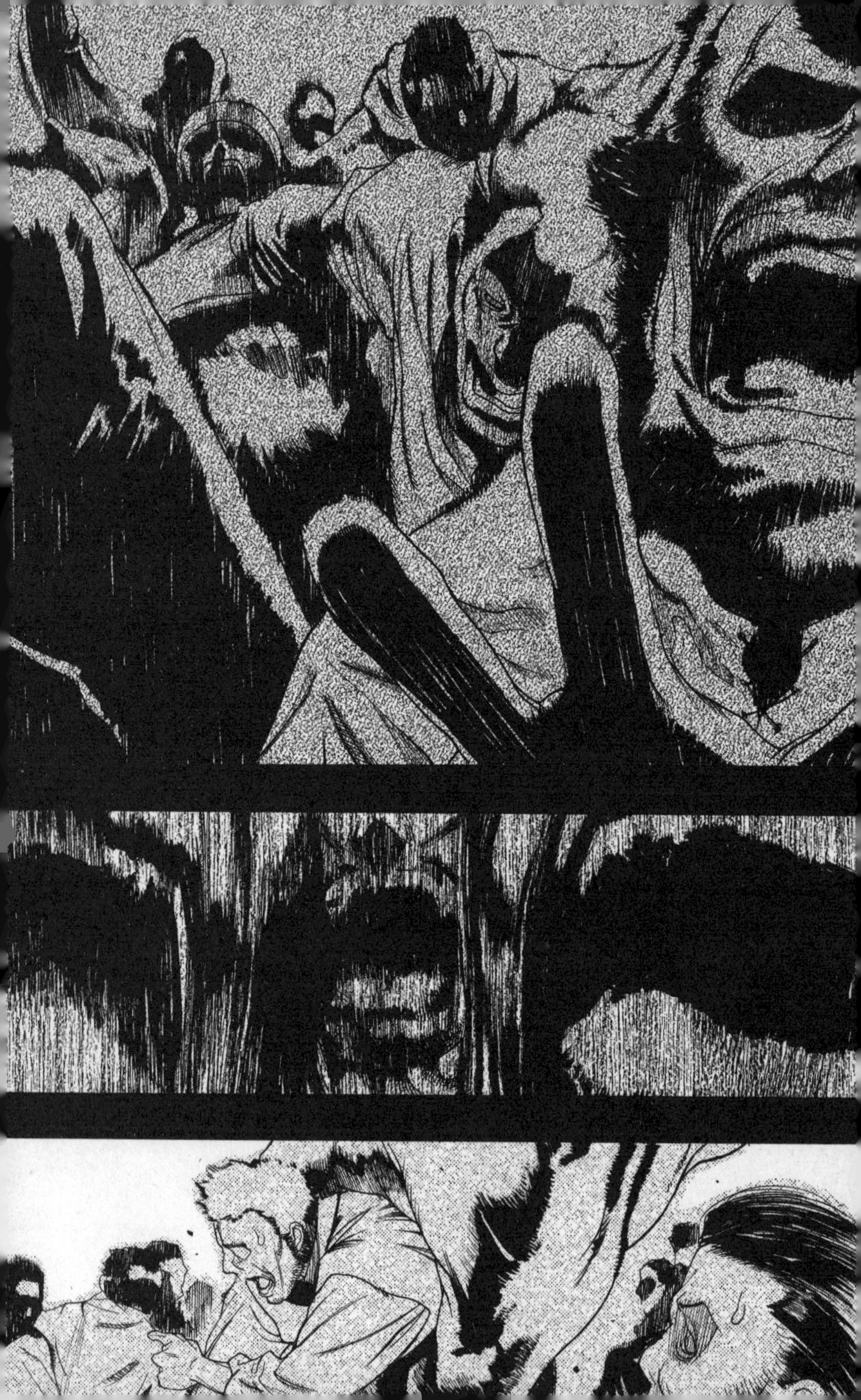

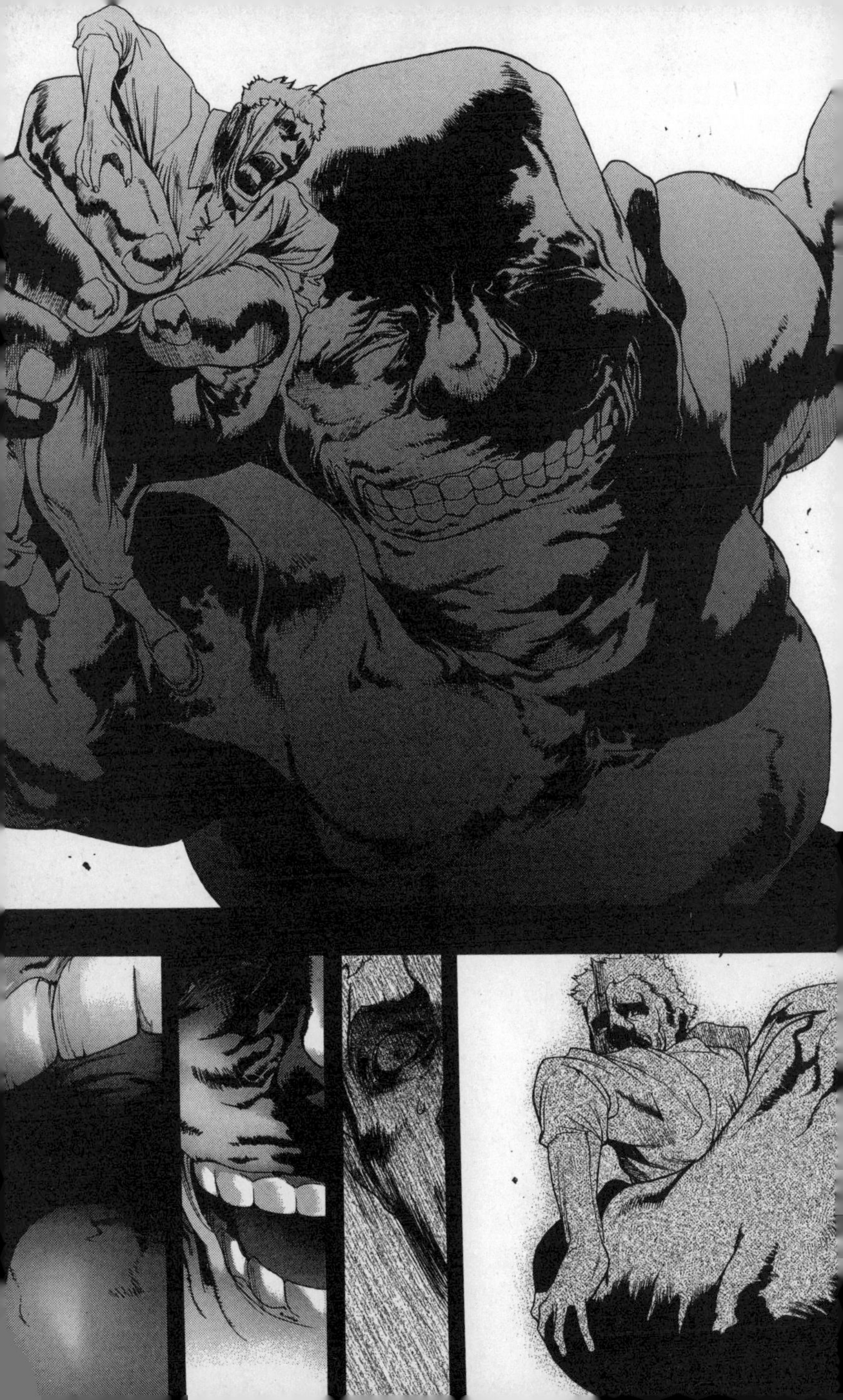

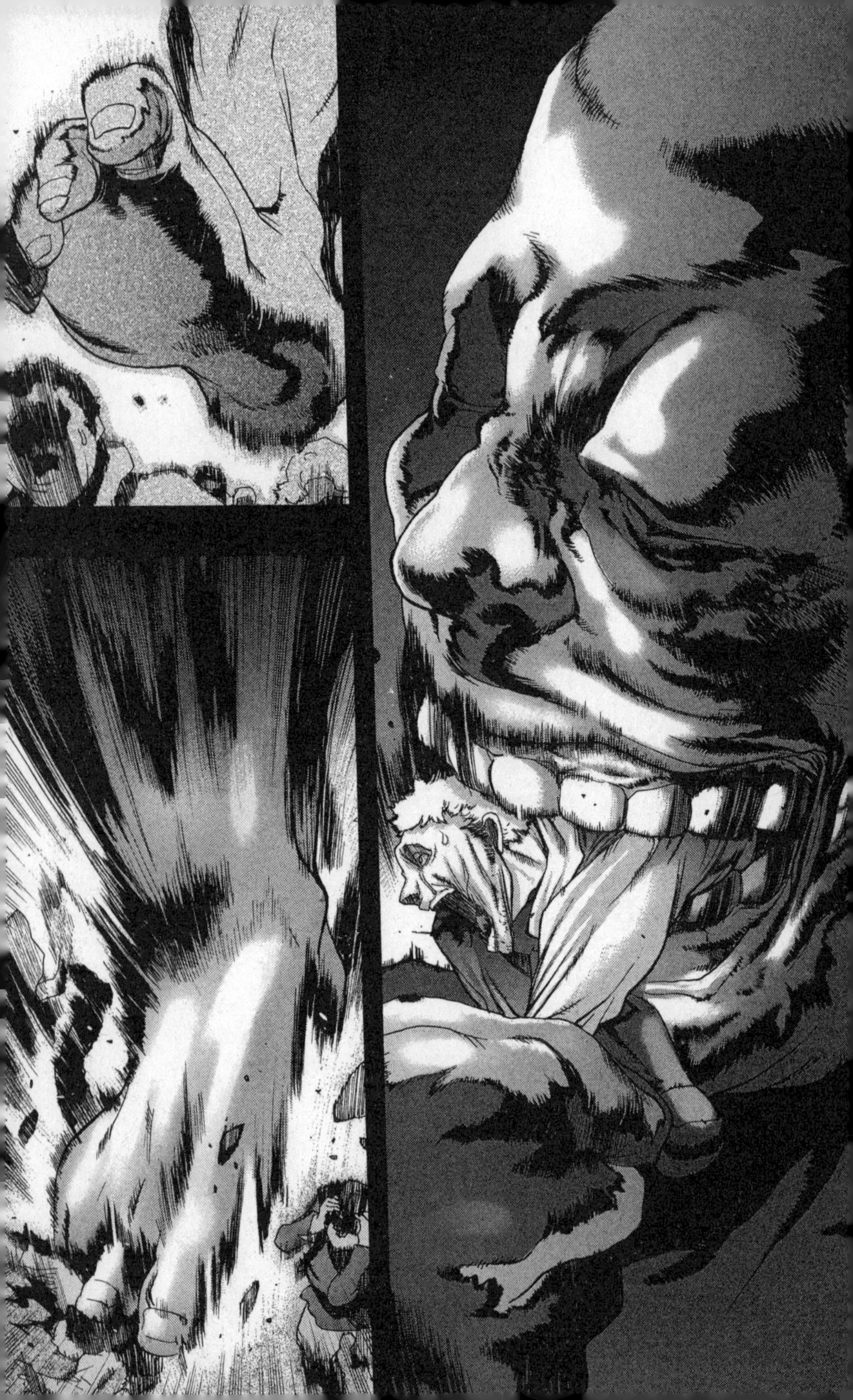

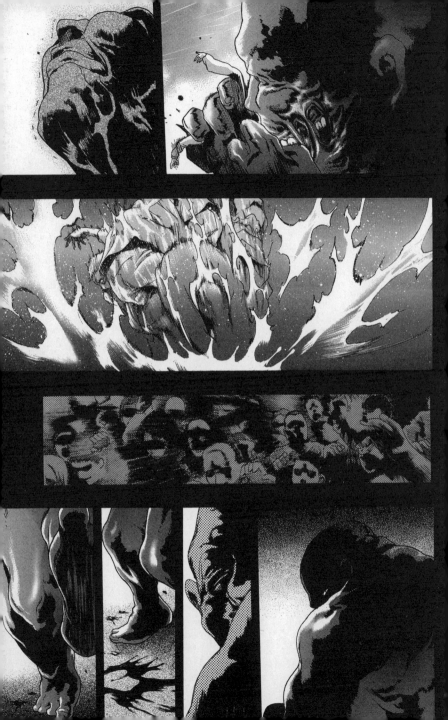

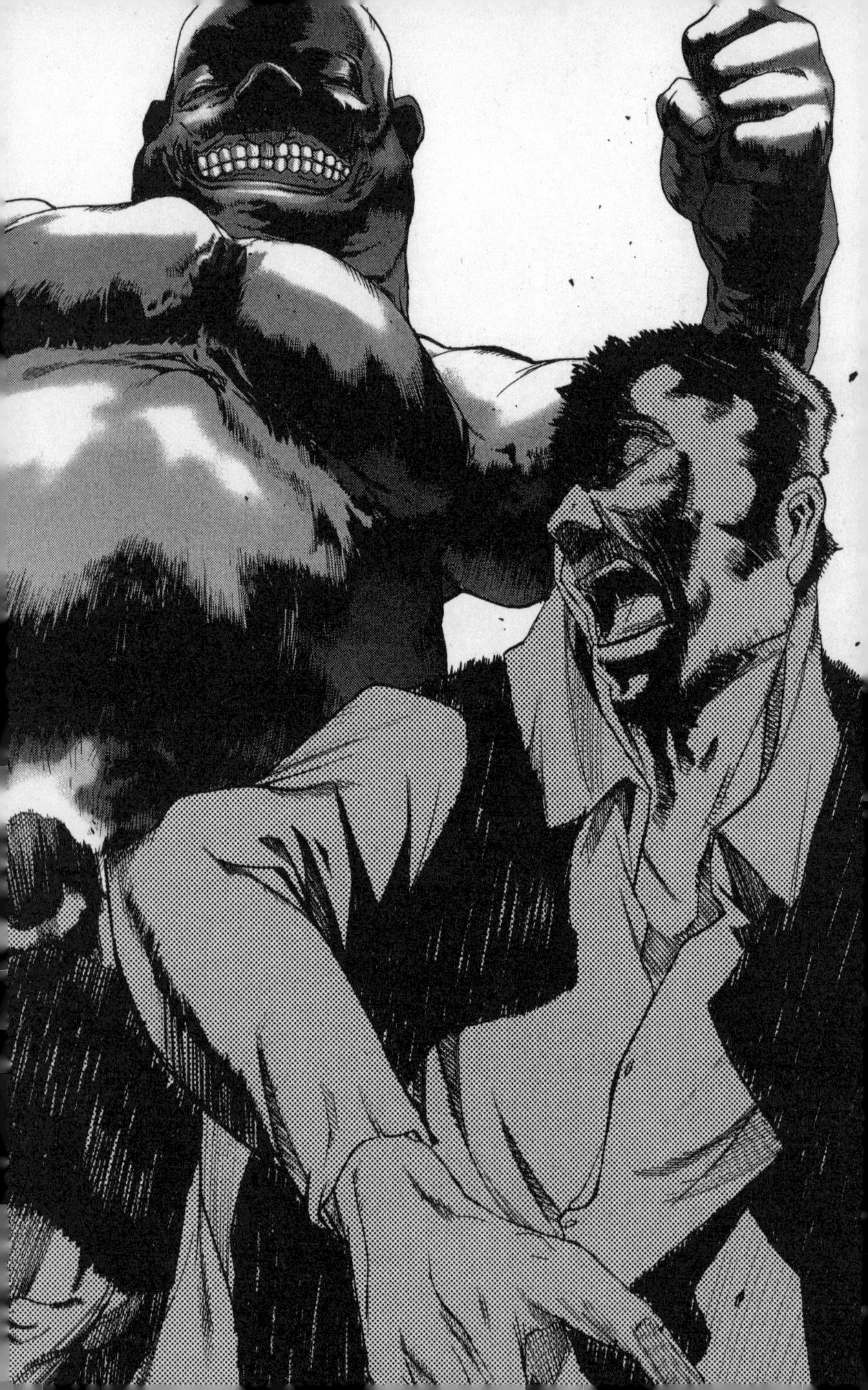

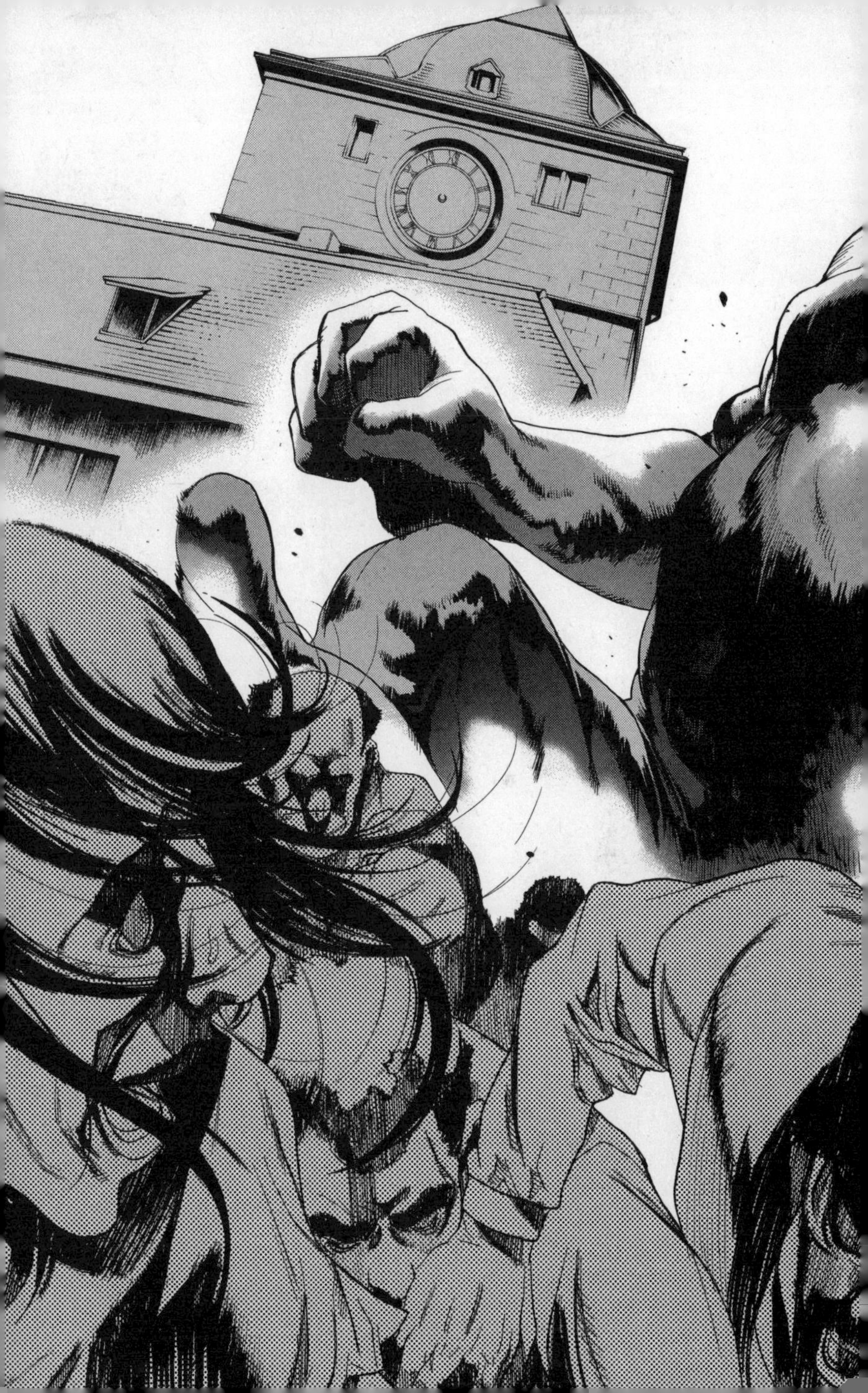

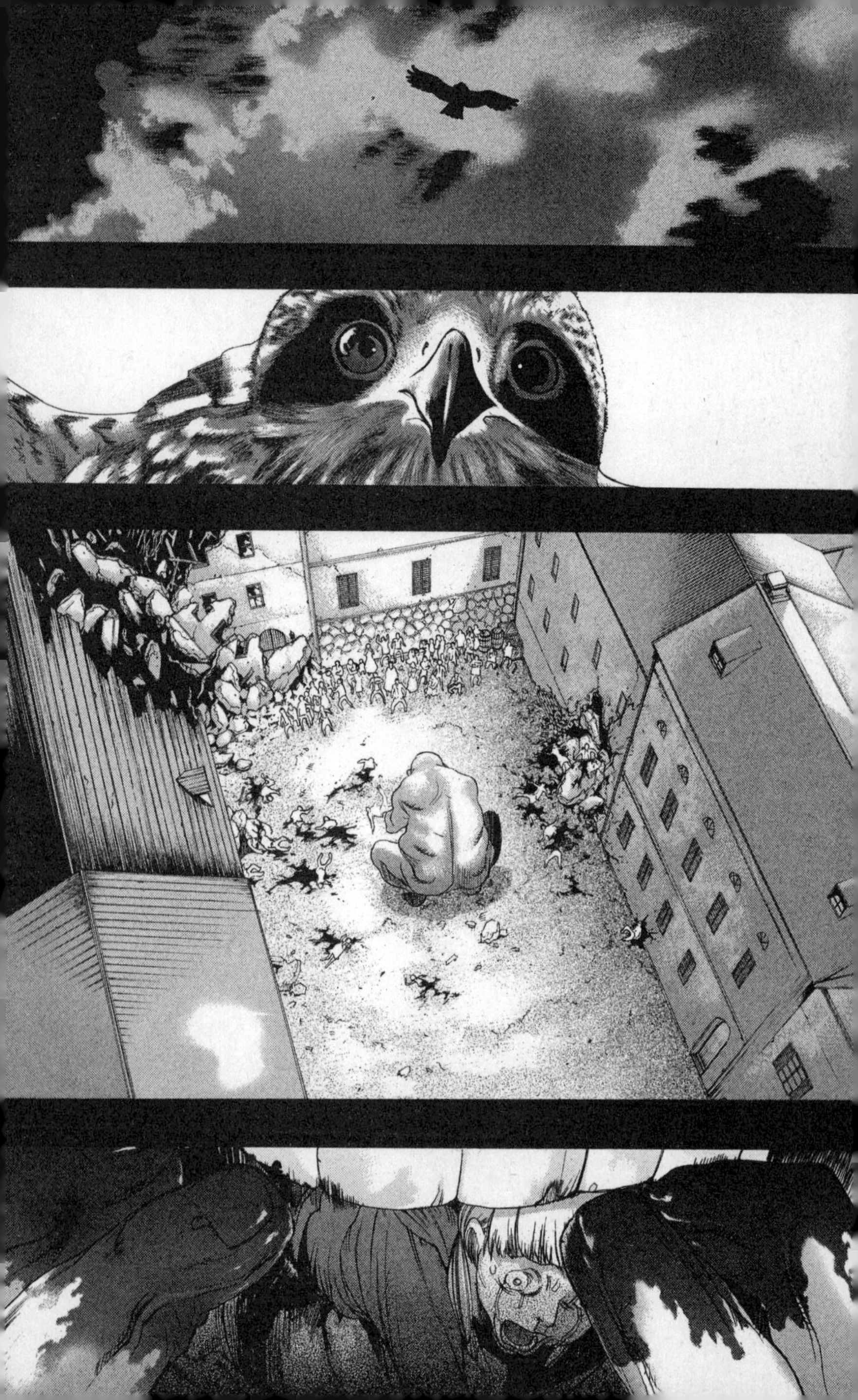

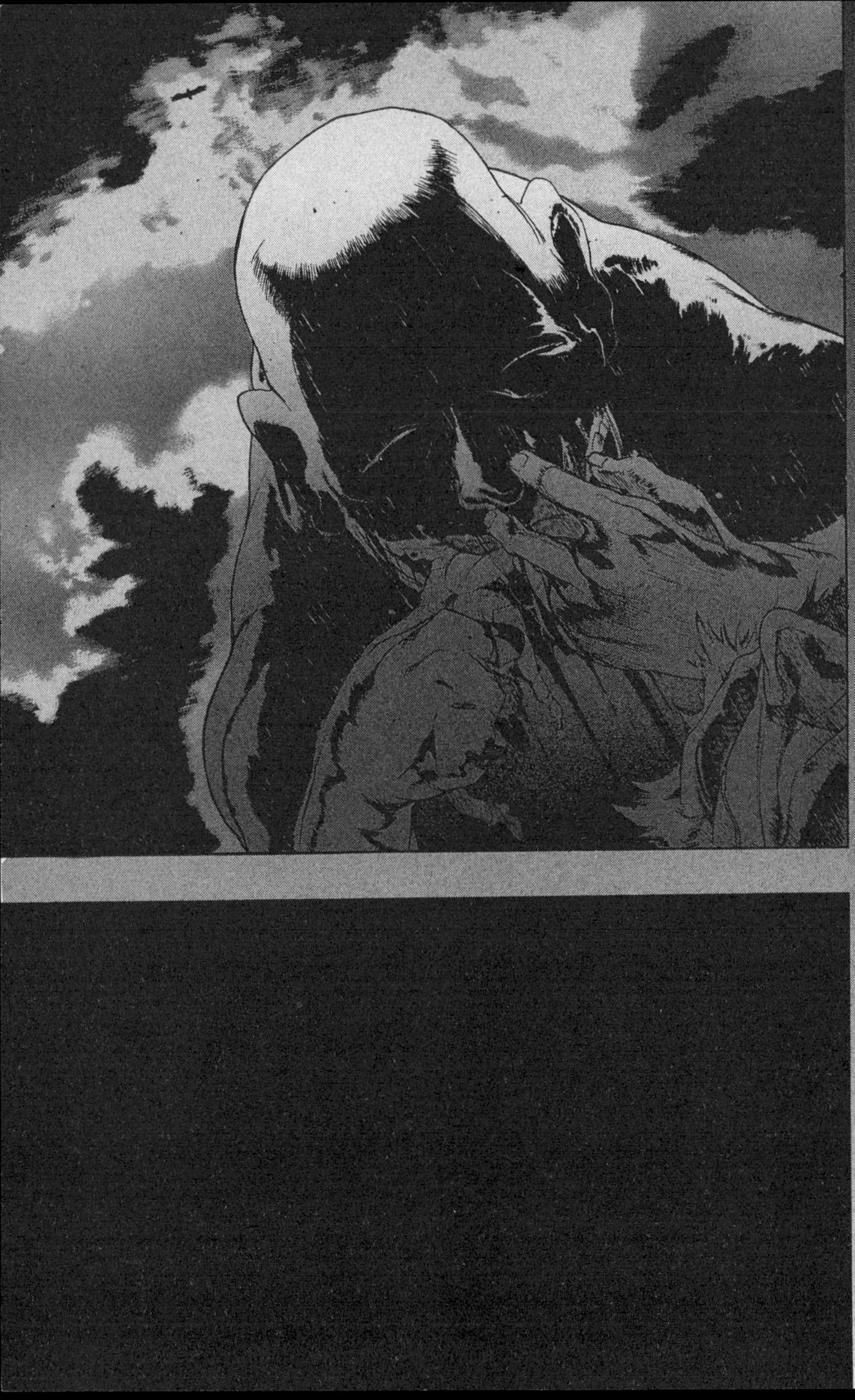

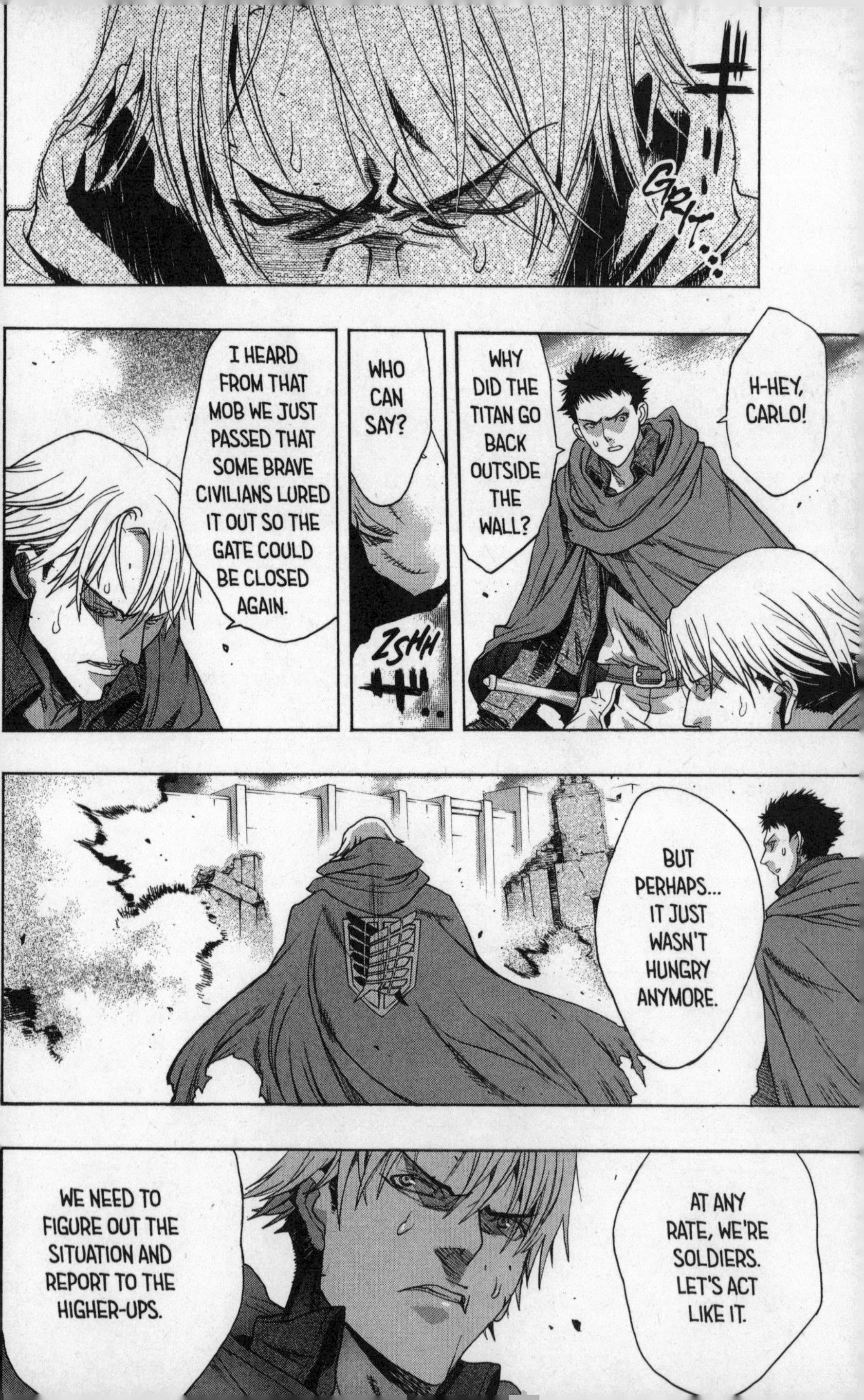
GRIT...
H-HEY, CARLO!
WHY DID THE TITAN GO BACK OUTSIDE THE WALL?
WHO CAN SAY?
ZSHH
I HEARD FROM THAT MOB WE JUST PASSED THAT SOME BRAVE CIVILIANS LURED IT OUT SO THE GATE COULD BE CLOSED AGAIN.
BUT PERHAPS... IT JUST WASN'T HUNGRY ANYMORE.
AT ANY RATE, WE'RE SOLDIERS. LET'S ACT LIKE IT.
WE NEED TO FIGURE OUT THE SITUATION AND REPORT TO THE HIGHER-UPS.

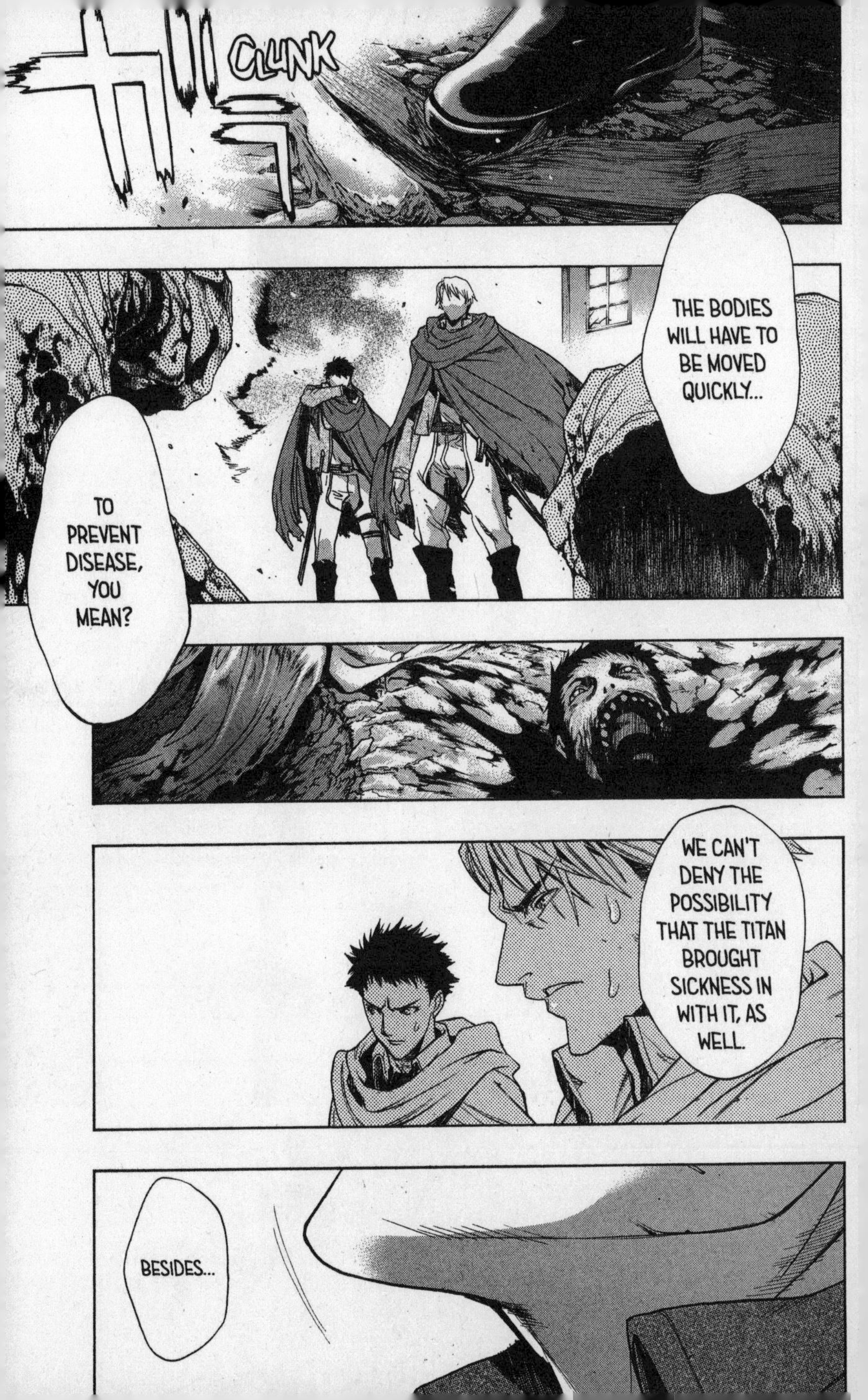
CLUNK
THE BODIES WILL HAVE TO BE MOVED QUICKLY...
TO PREVENT DISEASE, YOU MEAN?
WE CAN'T DENY THE POSSIBILITY THAT THE TITAN BROUGHT SICKNESS IN WITH IT, AS WELL.
BESIDES...

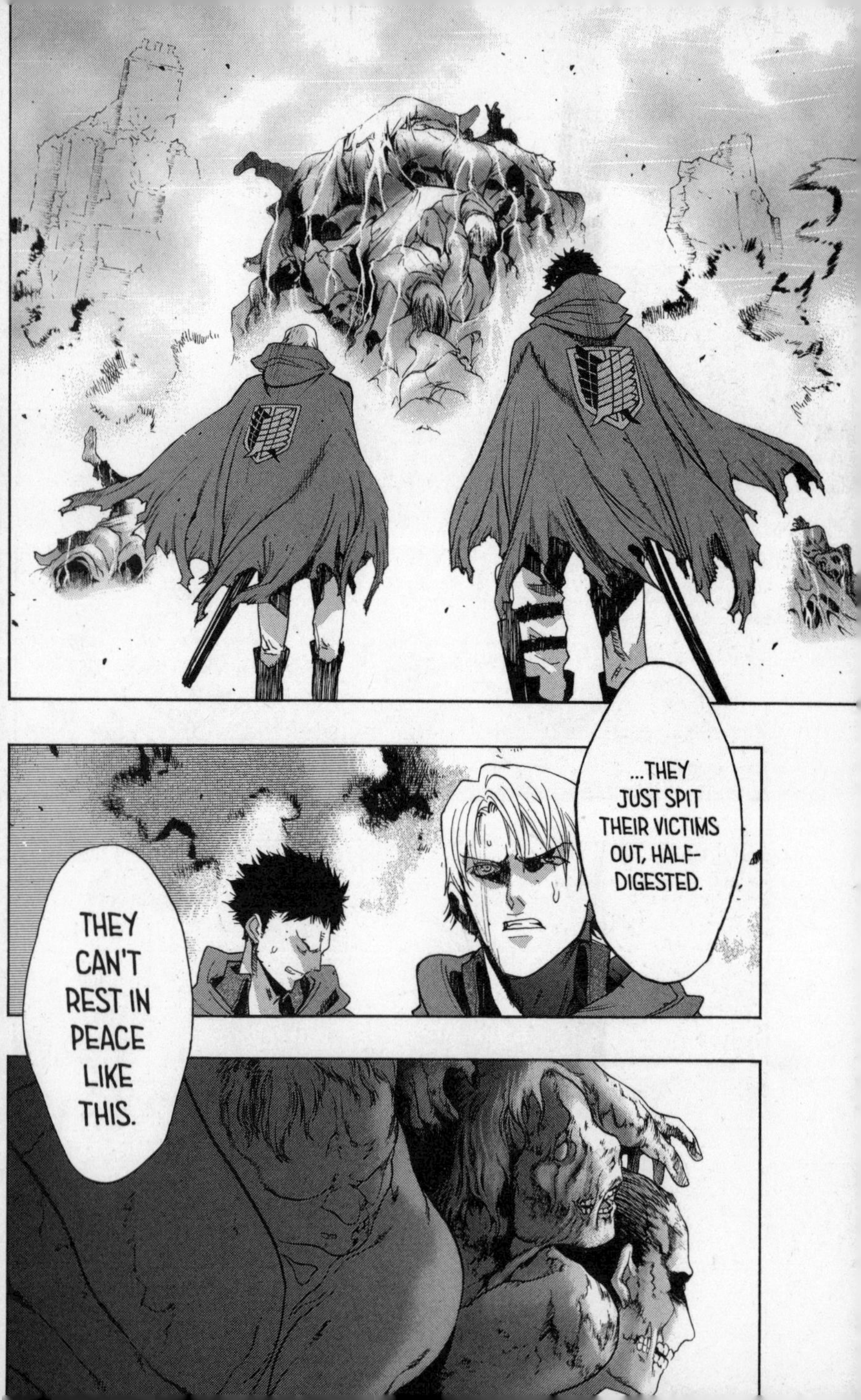
...THEY JUST SPIT THEIR VICTIMS OUT, HALF-DIGESTED.
THEY CAN'T REST IN PEACE LIKE THIS.

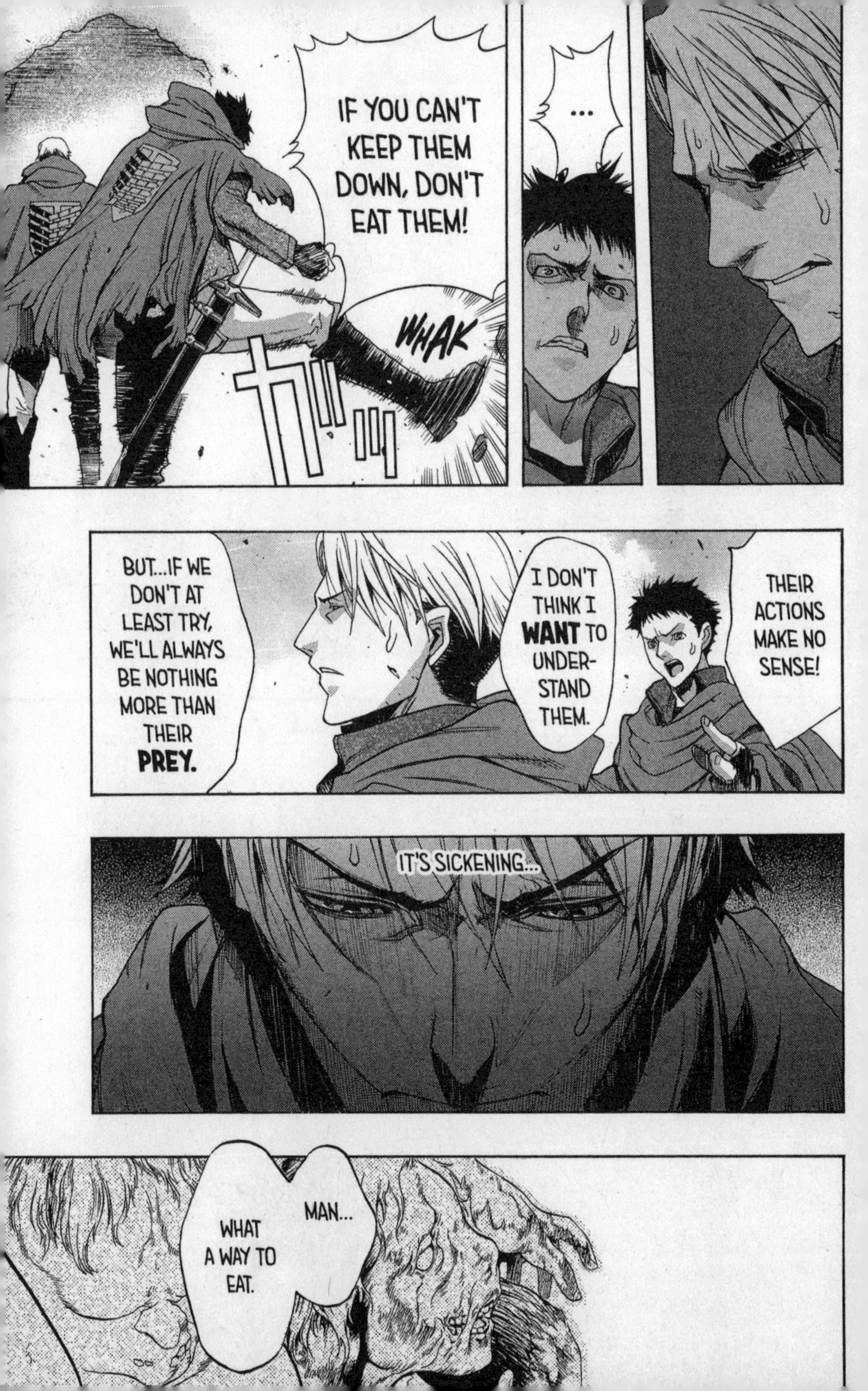
...
IF YOU CAN'T KEEP THEM DOWN, DON'T EAT THEM!
WHAK
ガッ
THEIR ACTIONS MAKE NO SENSE!
I DON'T THINK I **WANT** TO UNDER-STAND THEM.
BUT...IF WE DON'T AT LEAST TRY, WE'LL ALWAYS BE NOTHING MORE THAN THEIR **PREY.**
IT'S SICKENING...
MAN...
WHAT A WAY TO EAT.

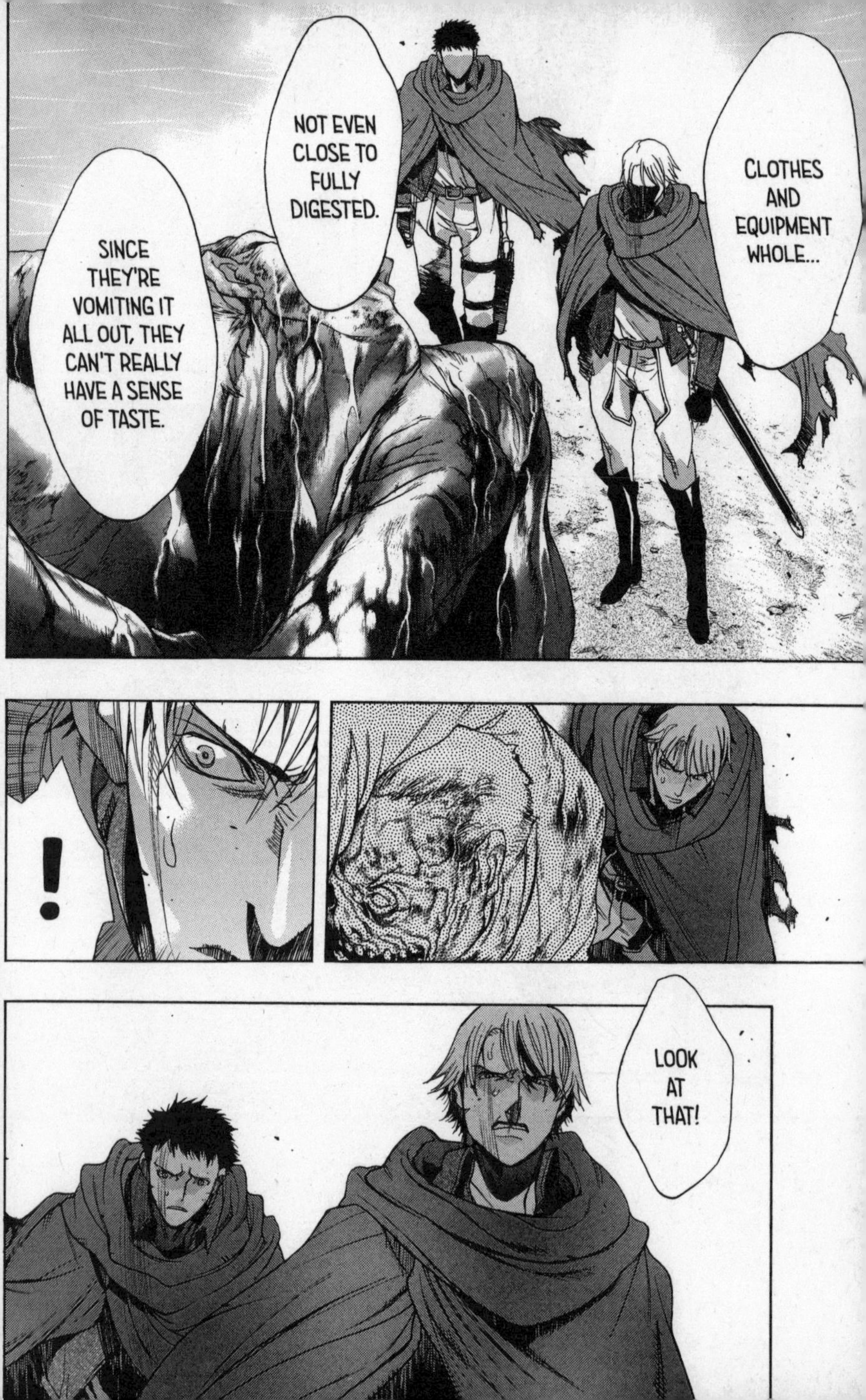
CLOTHES AND EQUIPMENT WHOLE...
NOT EVEN CLOSE TO FULLY DIGESTED.
SINCE THEY'RE VOMITING IT ALL OUT, THEY CAN'T REALLY HAVE A SENSE OF TASTE.
!
LOOK AT THAT!

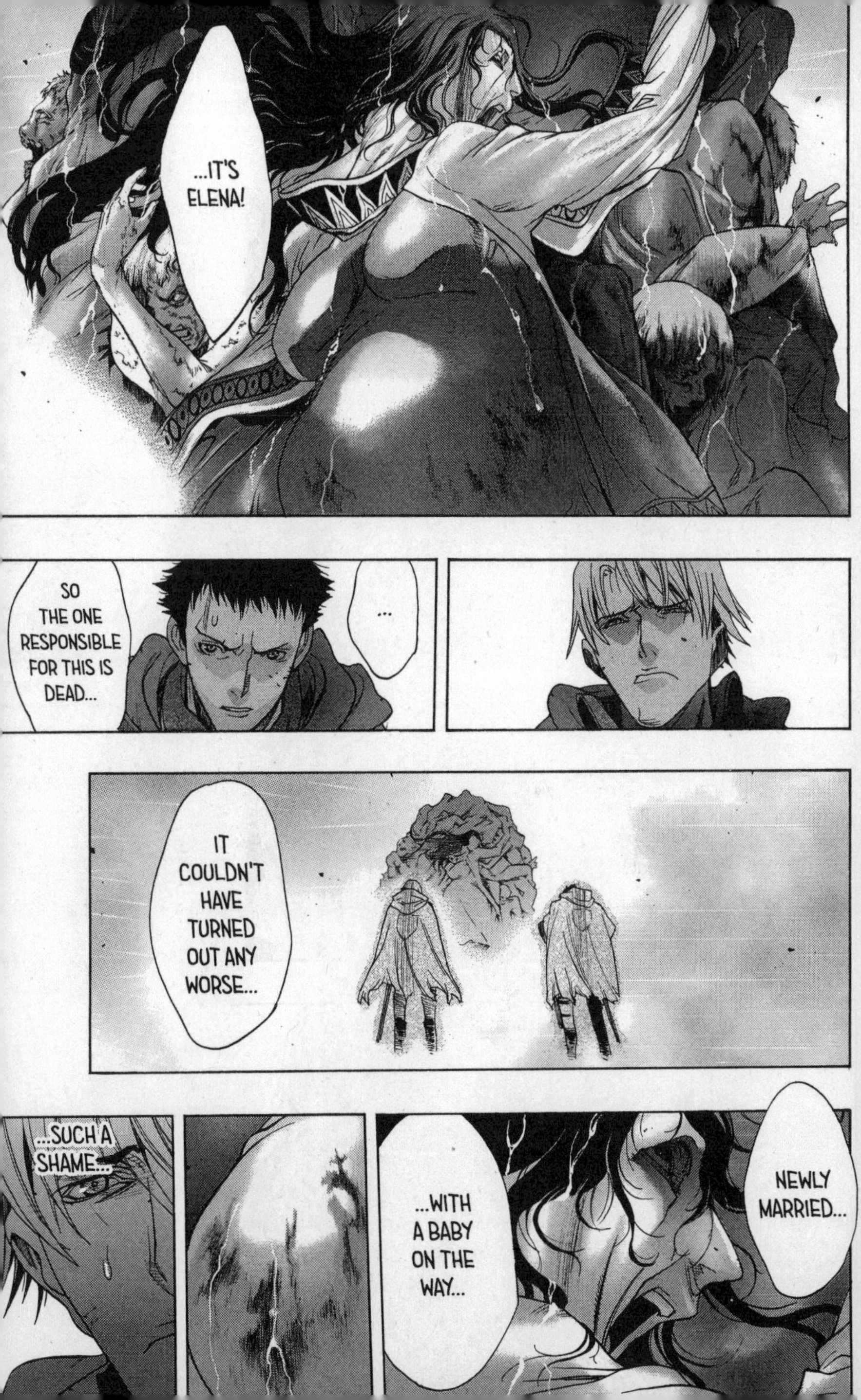
...IT'S ELENA!
...
SO THE ONE RESPONSIBLE FOR THIS IS DEAD...
IT COULDN'T HAVE TURNED OUT ANY WORSE...
NEWLY MARRIED...
...WITH A BABY ON THE WAY...
...SUCH A SHAME...

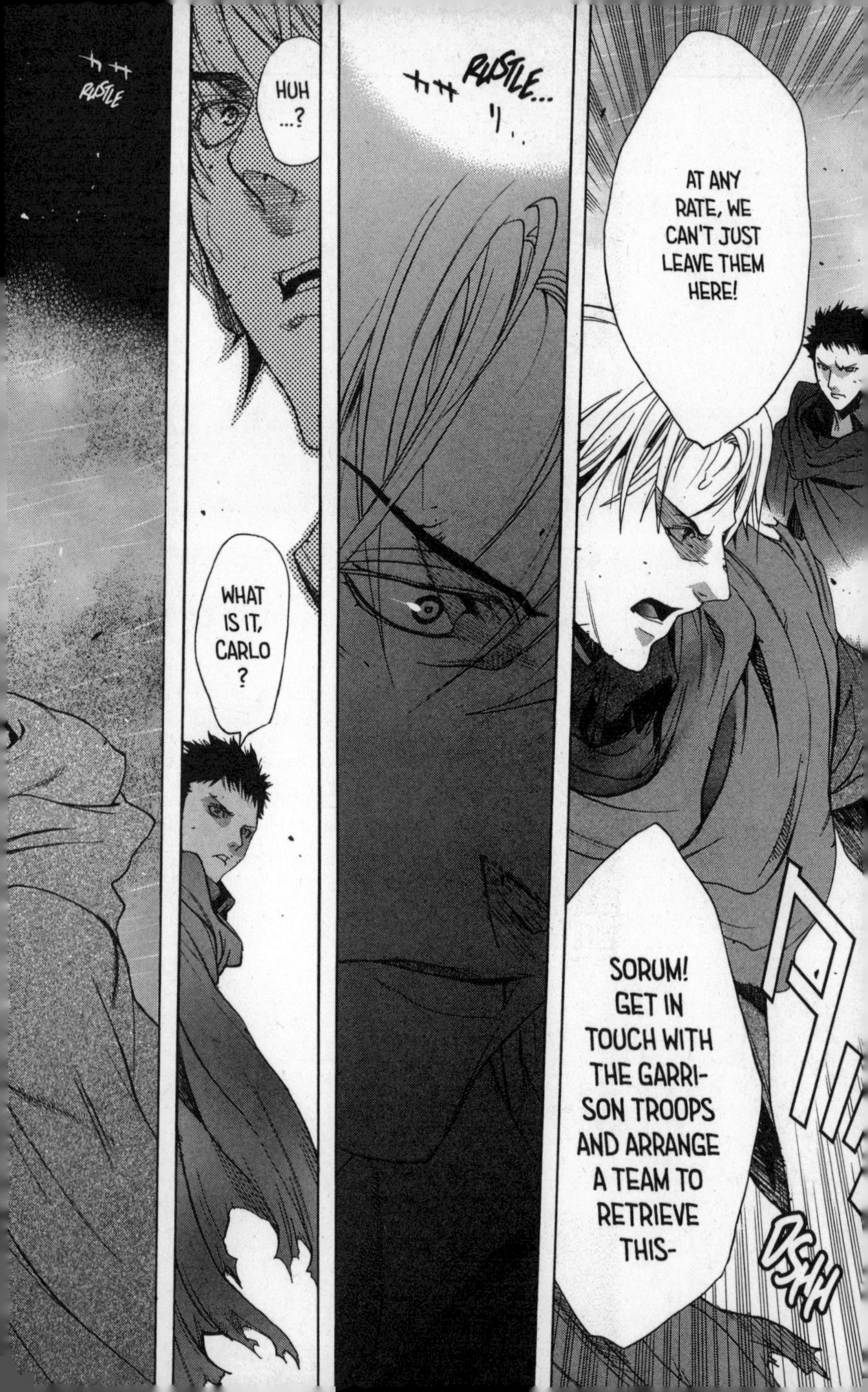
AT ANY RATE, WE CAN'T JUST LEAVE THEM HERE!
SORUM! GET IN TOUCH WITH THE GARRI-SON TROOPS AND ARRANGE A TEAM TO RETRIEVE THIS-
DSHH
RUSTLE...
HUH ...?
WHAT IS IT, CARLO ?
RUSTLE

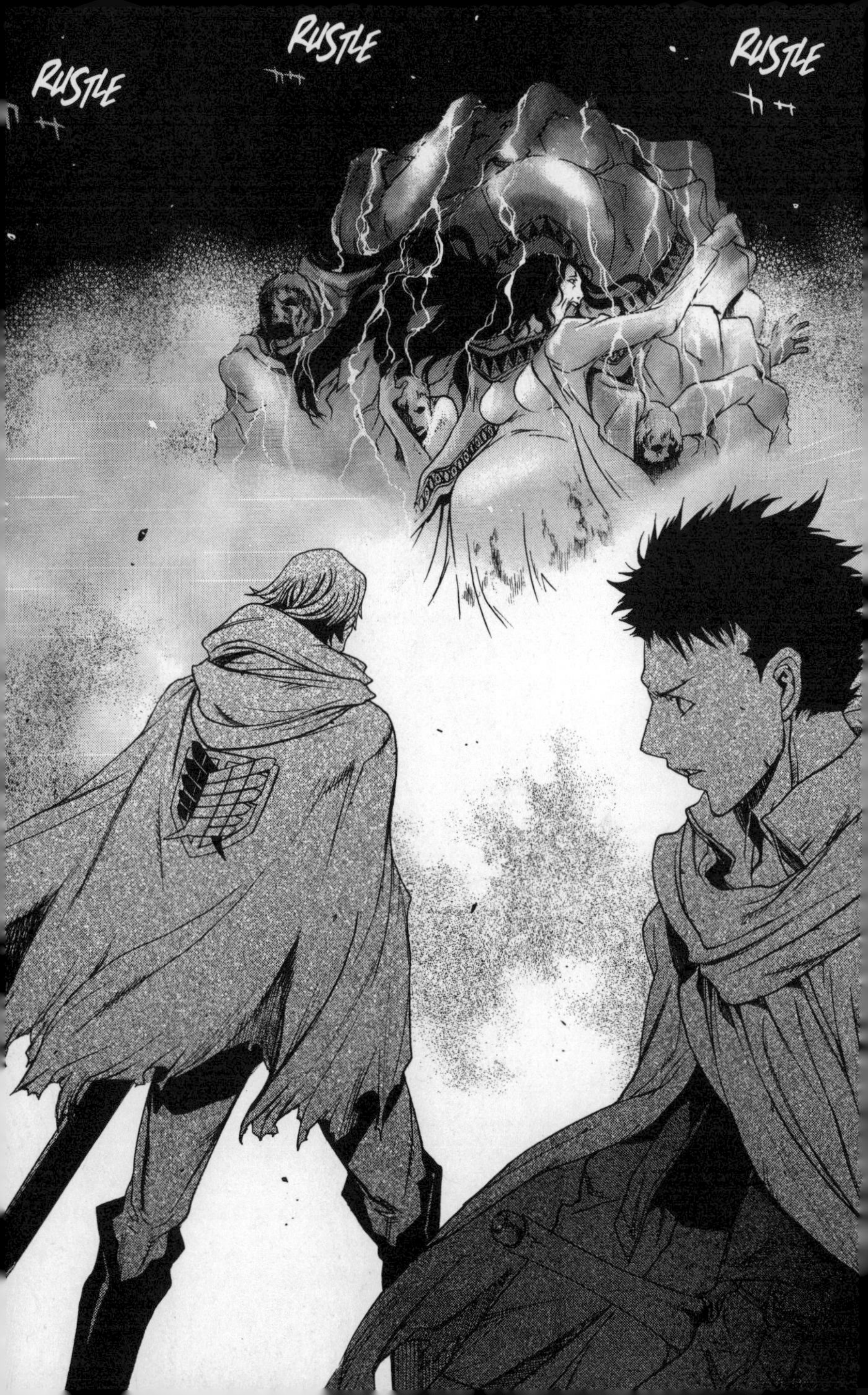
RUSTLE
RUSTLE
RUSTLE

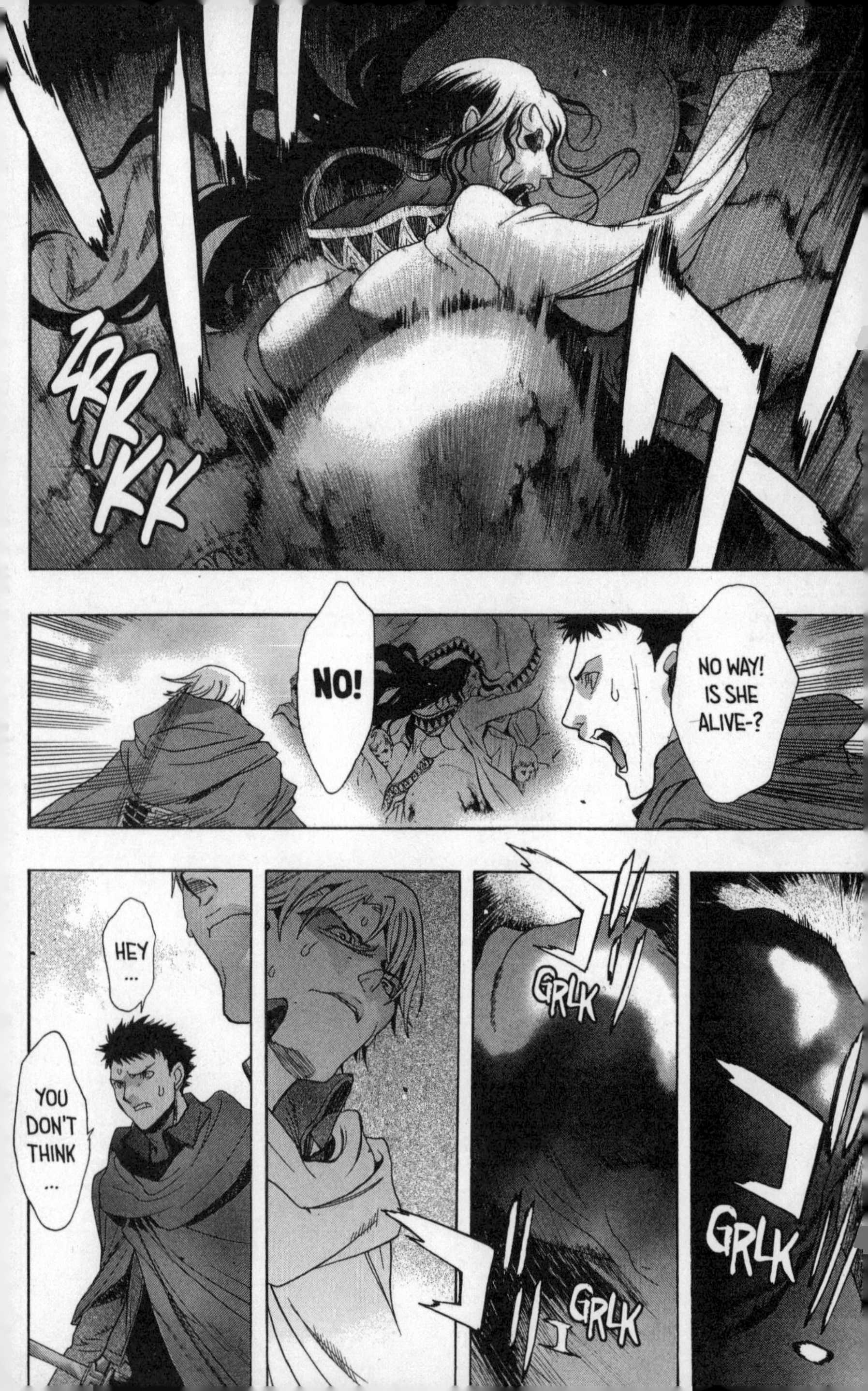
ZRRKK
NO WAY! IS SHE ALIVE-?
NO!
GRLK
GRLK
GRLK
HEY ...
YOU DON'T THINK ...

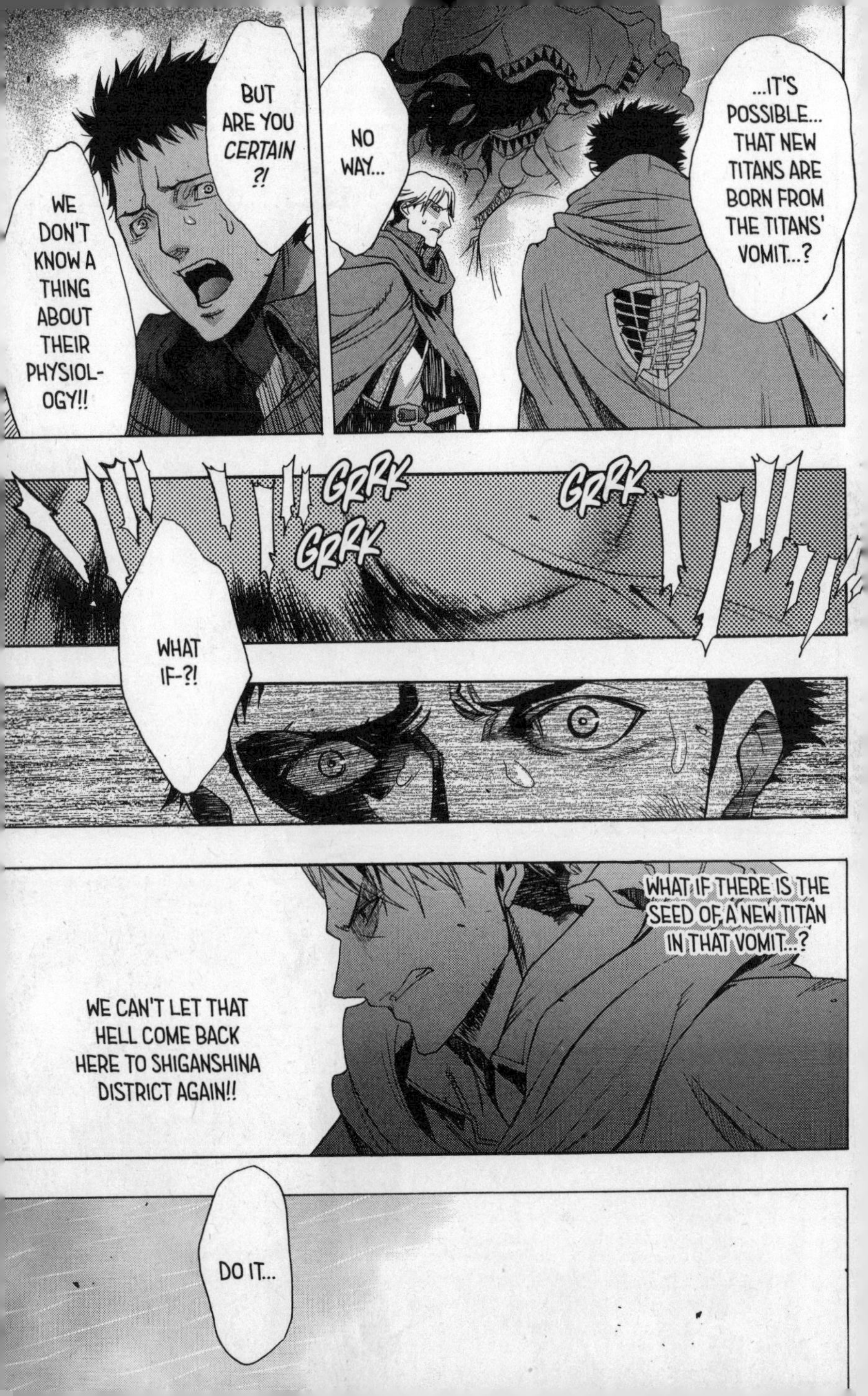
...IT'S POSSIBLE... THAT NEW TITANS ARE BORN FROM THE TITANS' VOMIT...?
NO WAY...
BUT ARE YOU *CERTAIN* ?!
WE DON'T KNOW A THING ABOUT THEIR PHYSIOL-OGY!!
GRRK
GRRK
GRRK
WHAT IF-?!
WHAT IF THERE IS THE SEED OF A NEW TITAN IN THAT VOMIT...?
WE CAN'T LET THAT HELL COME BACK HERE TO SHIGANSHINA DISTRICT AGAIN!!
DO IT...

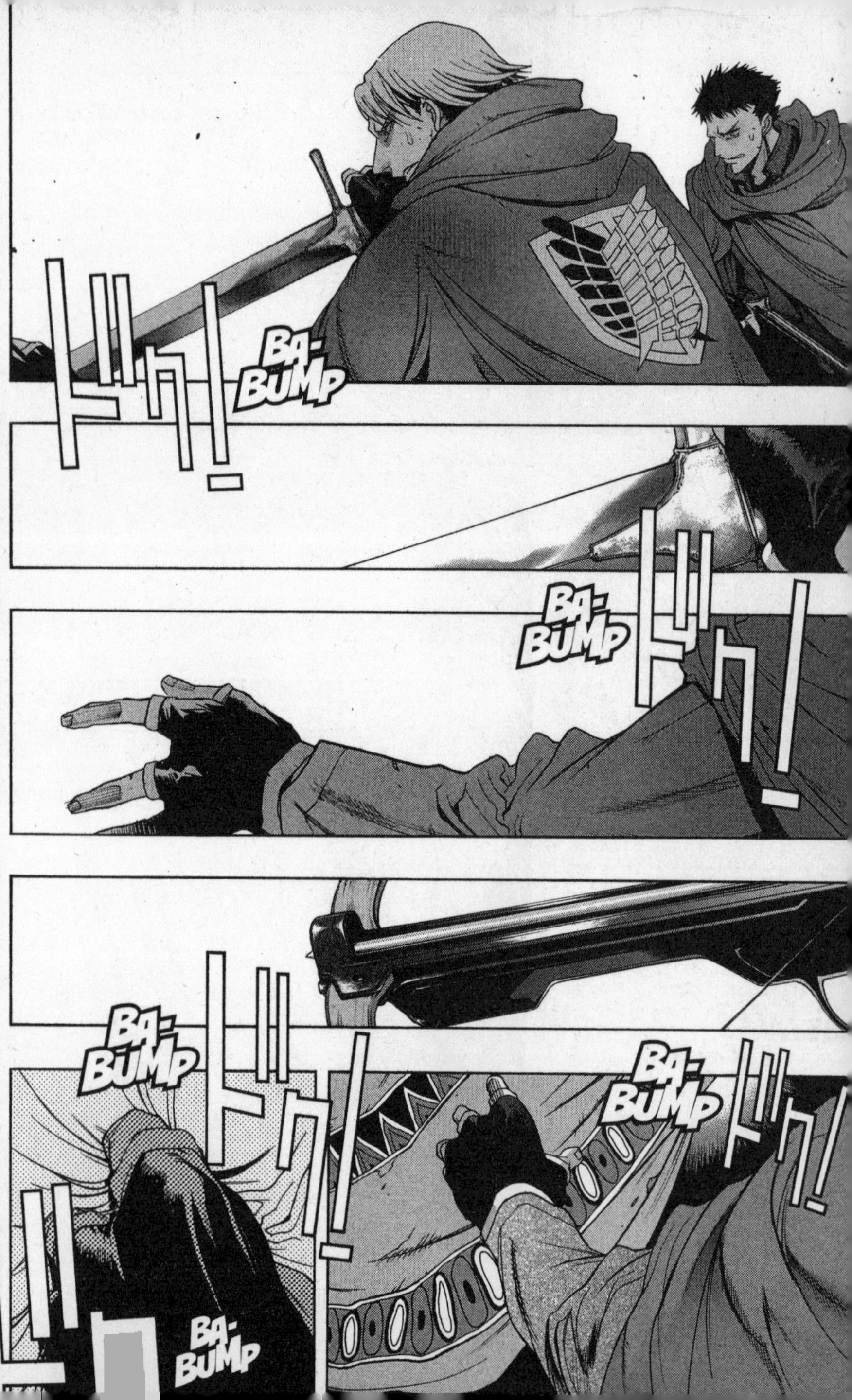
BA-BUMP
ドク!
BA-BUMP
ドク!
BA-BUMP
ドク!
BA-BUMP
ドク!
BA-BUMP
ドク

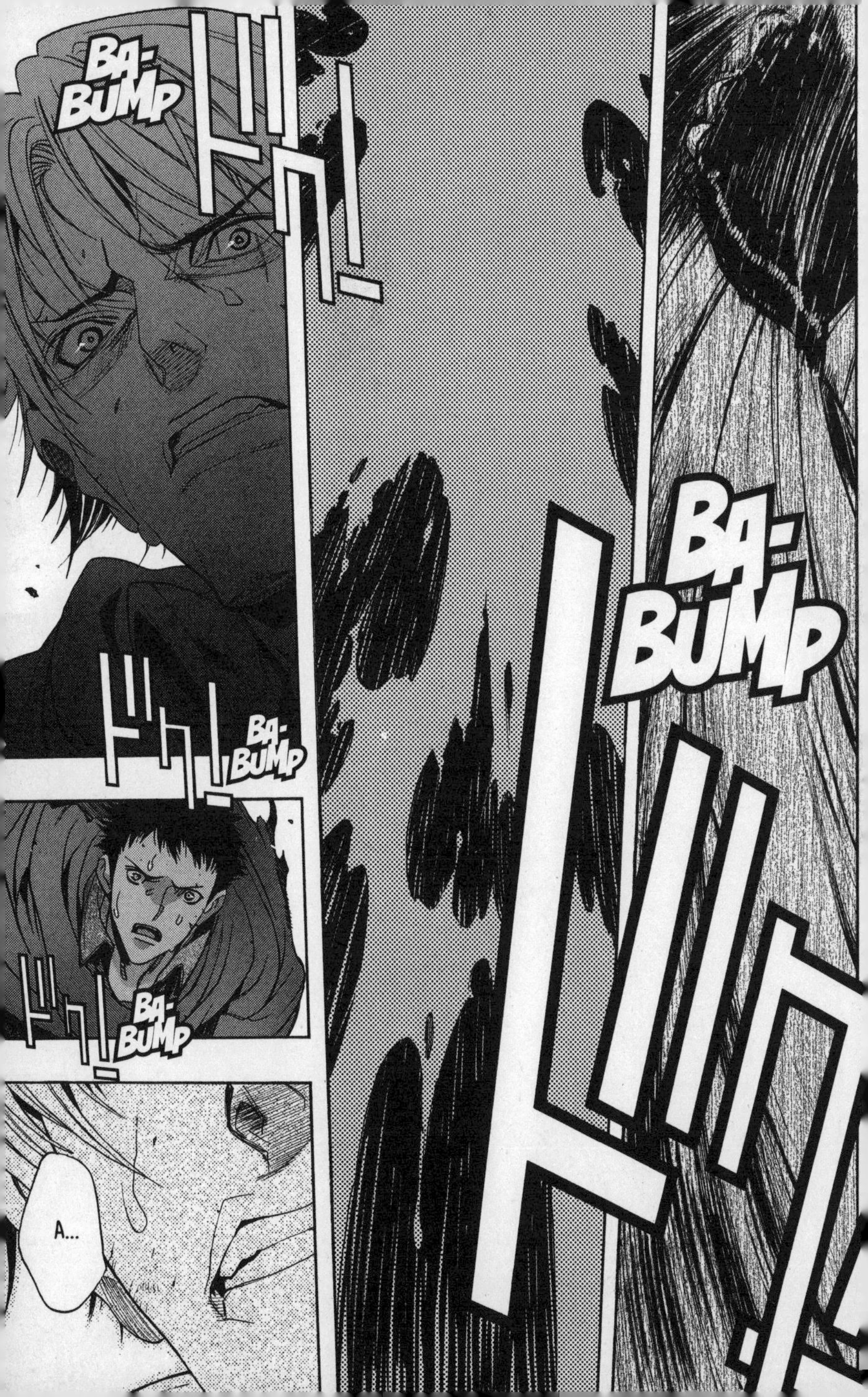
BA-BUMP
BA-BUMP
BA-BUMP
BA-BUMP
A...

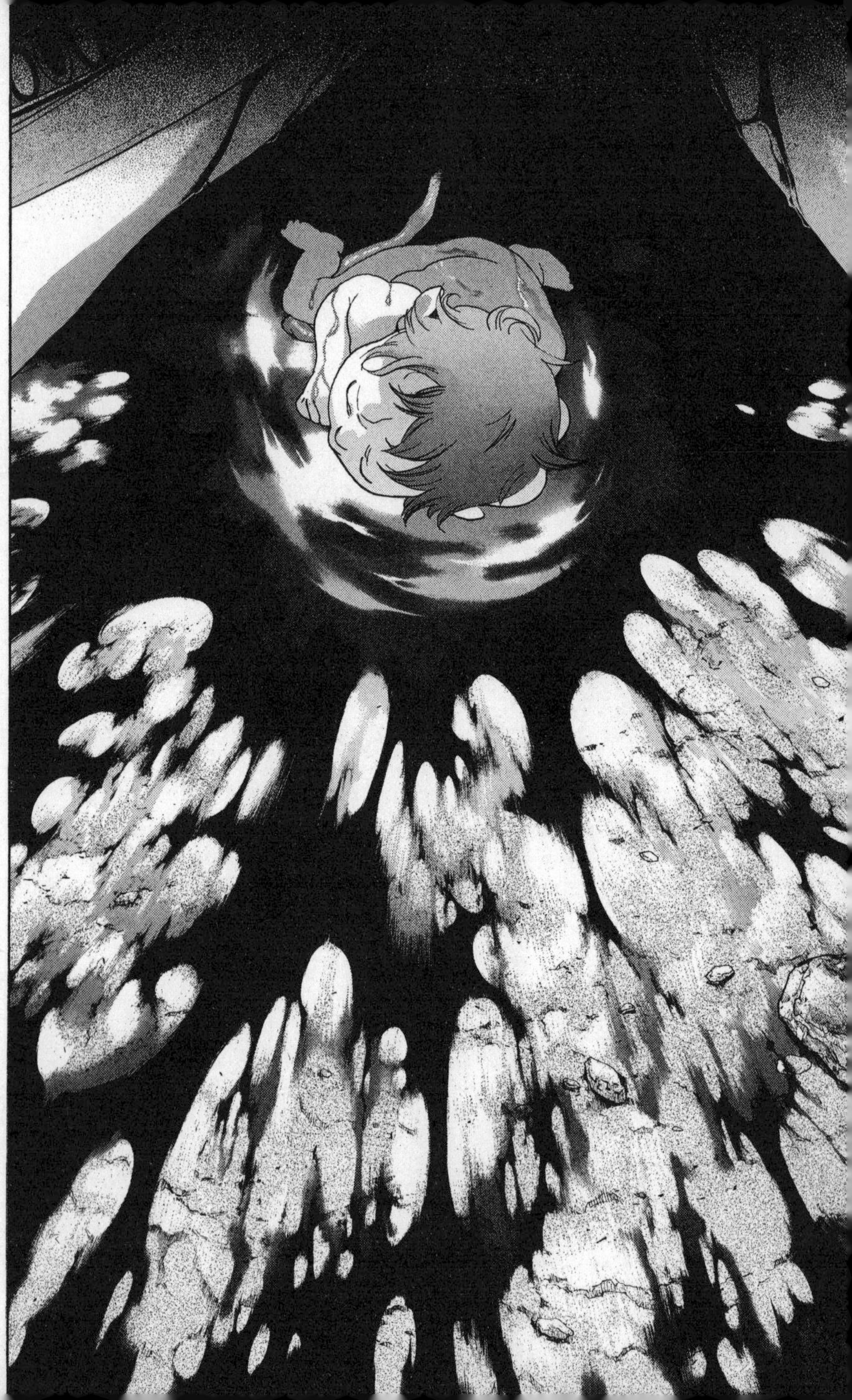

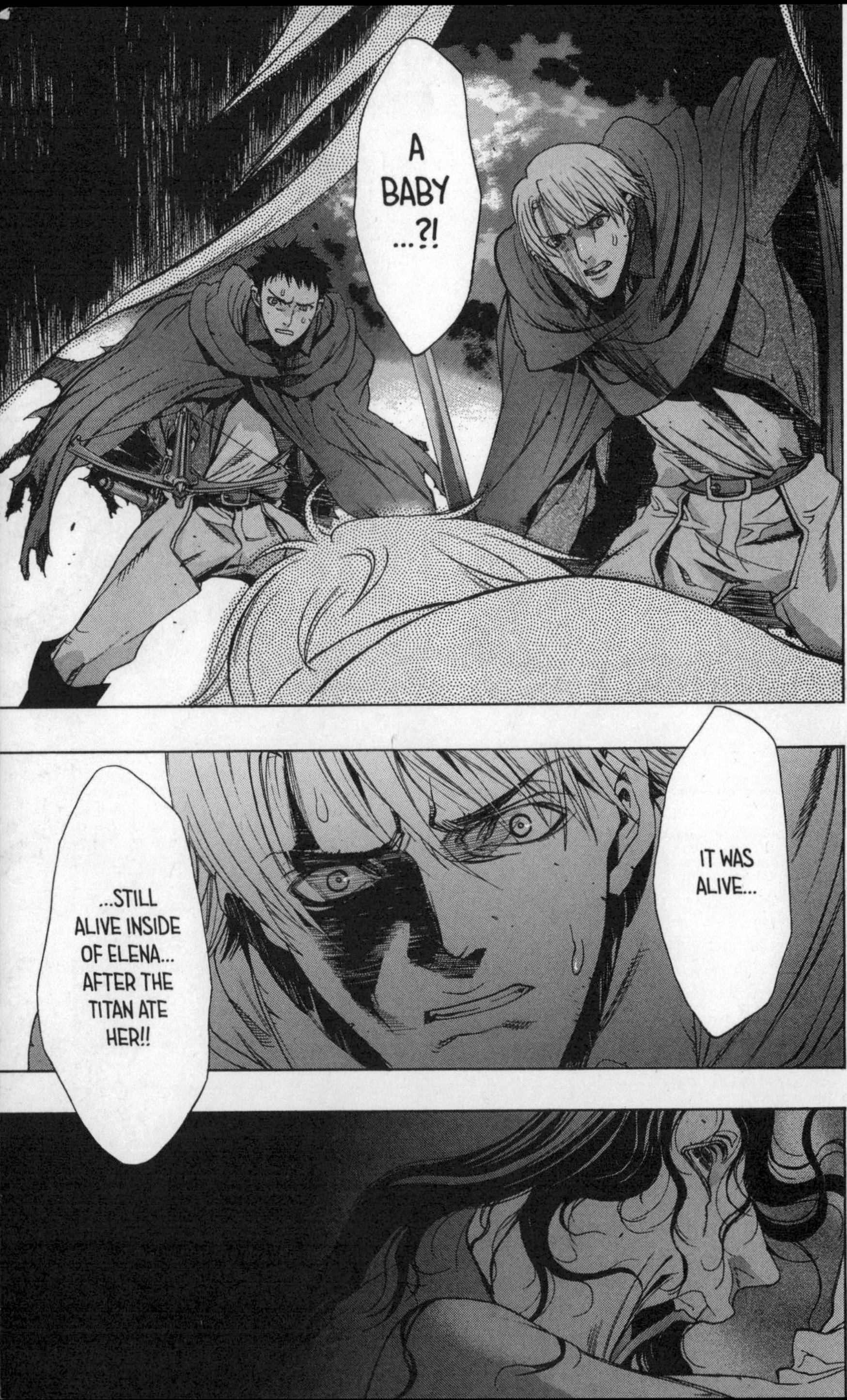
A BABY ...?!
IT WAS ALIVE...
...STILL ALIVE INSIDE OF ELENA... AFTER THE TITAN ATE HER!!

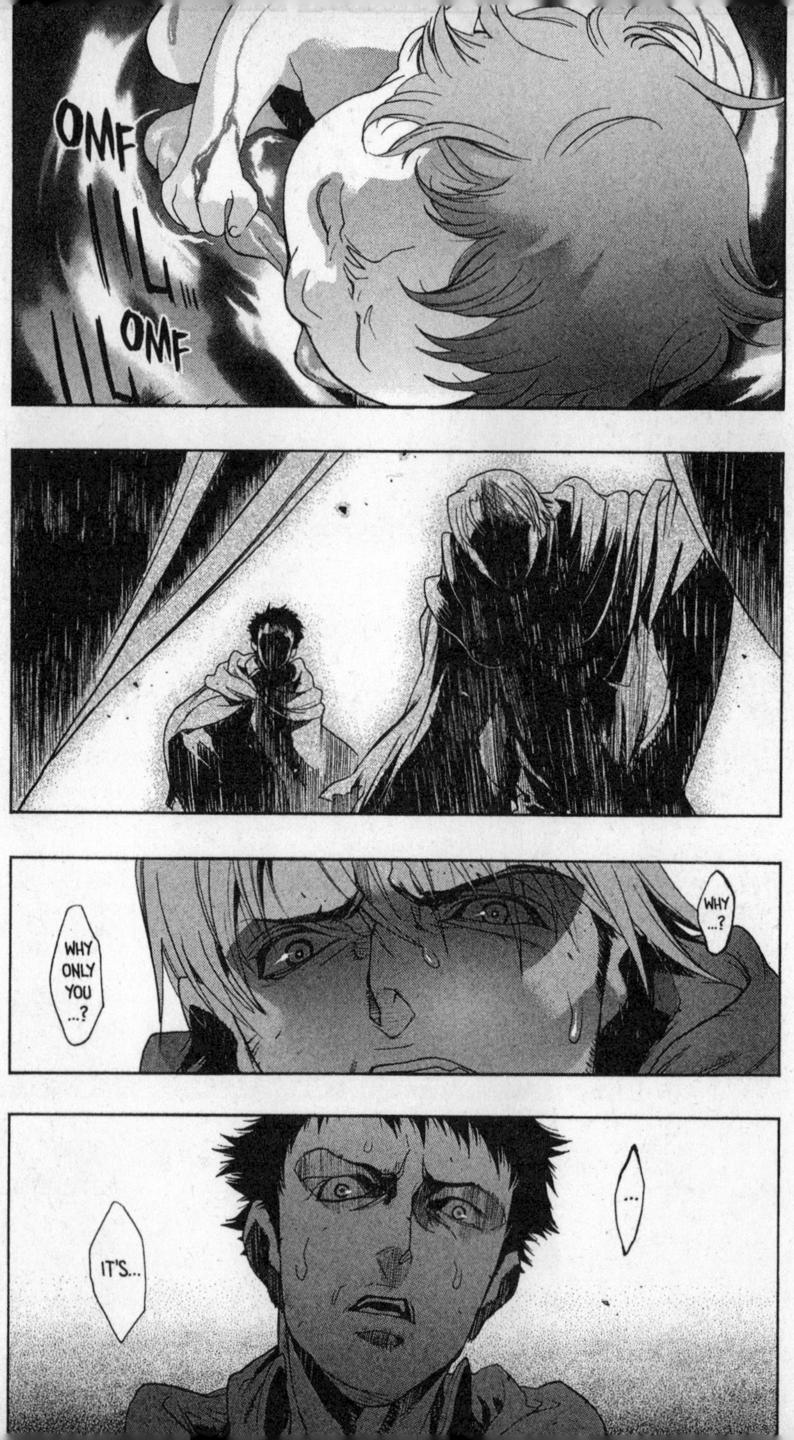
OMF
OMF
WHY ...?
WHY ONLY YOU ...?
...
IT'S...

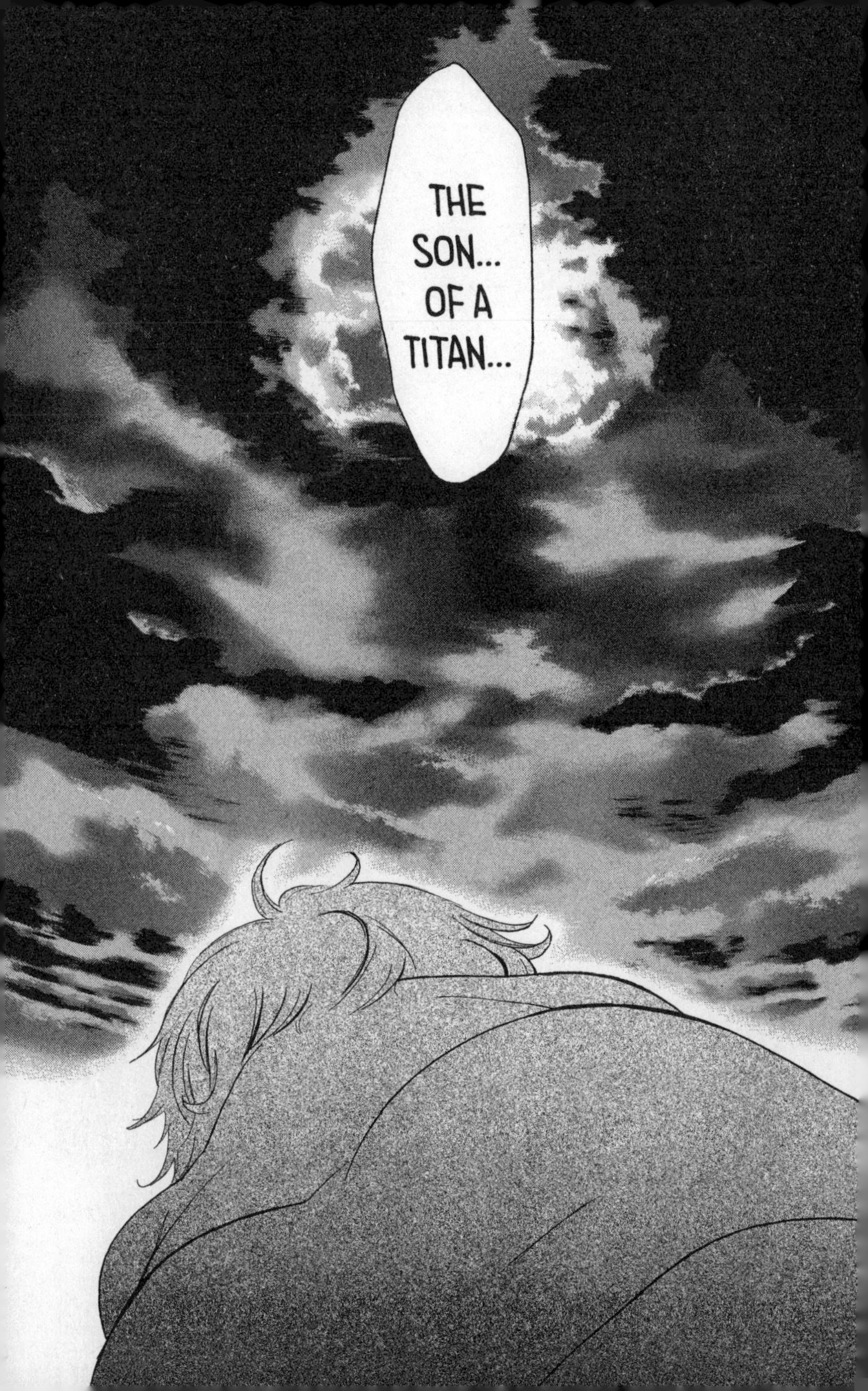
THE SON... OF A TITAN...

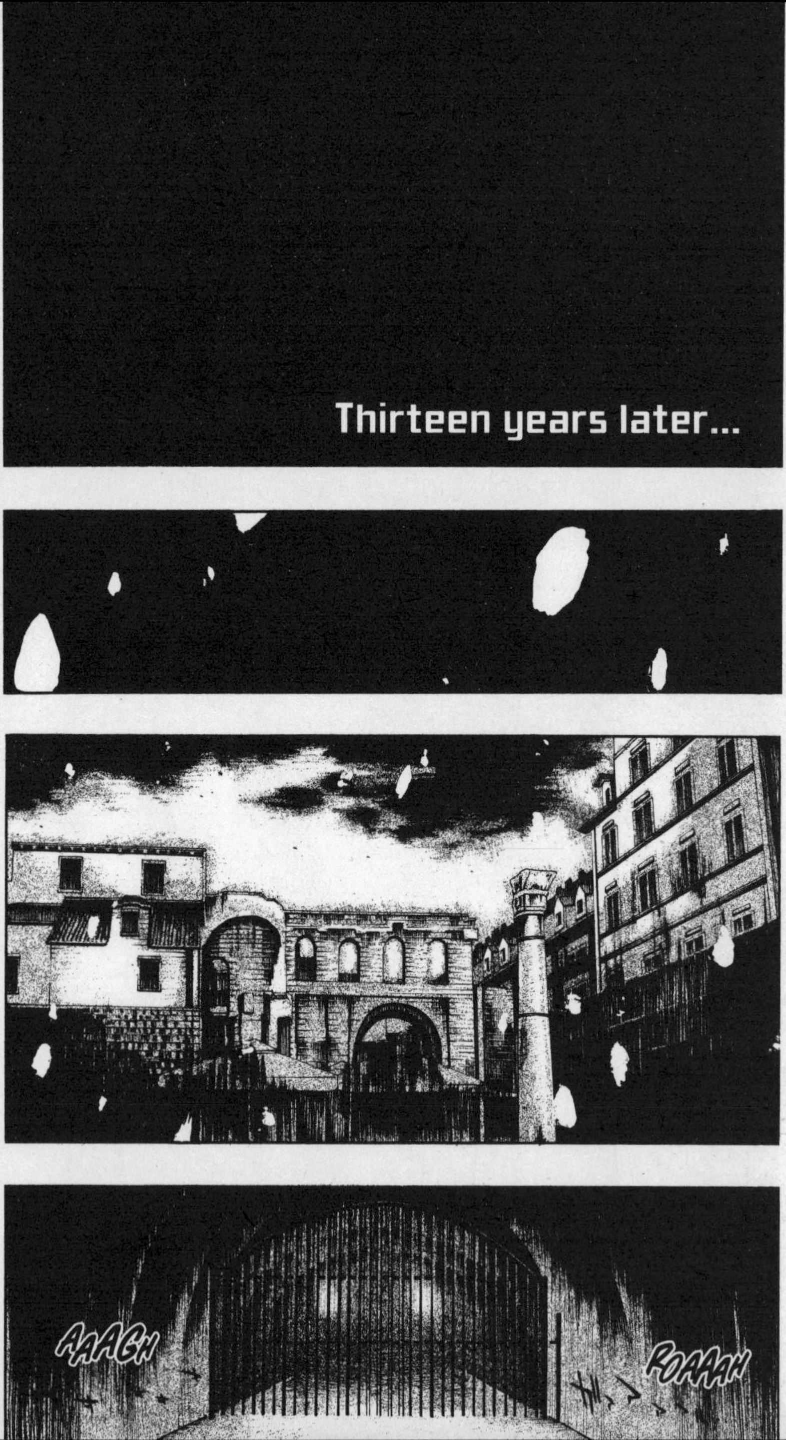
Thirteen years later...
ROAAAH
AAAGH

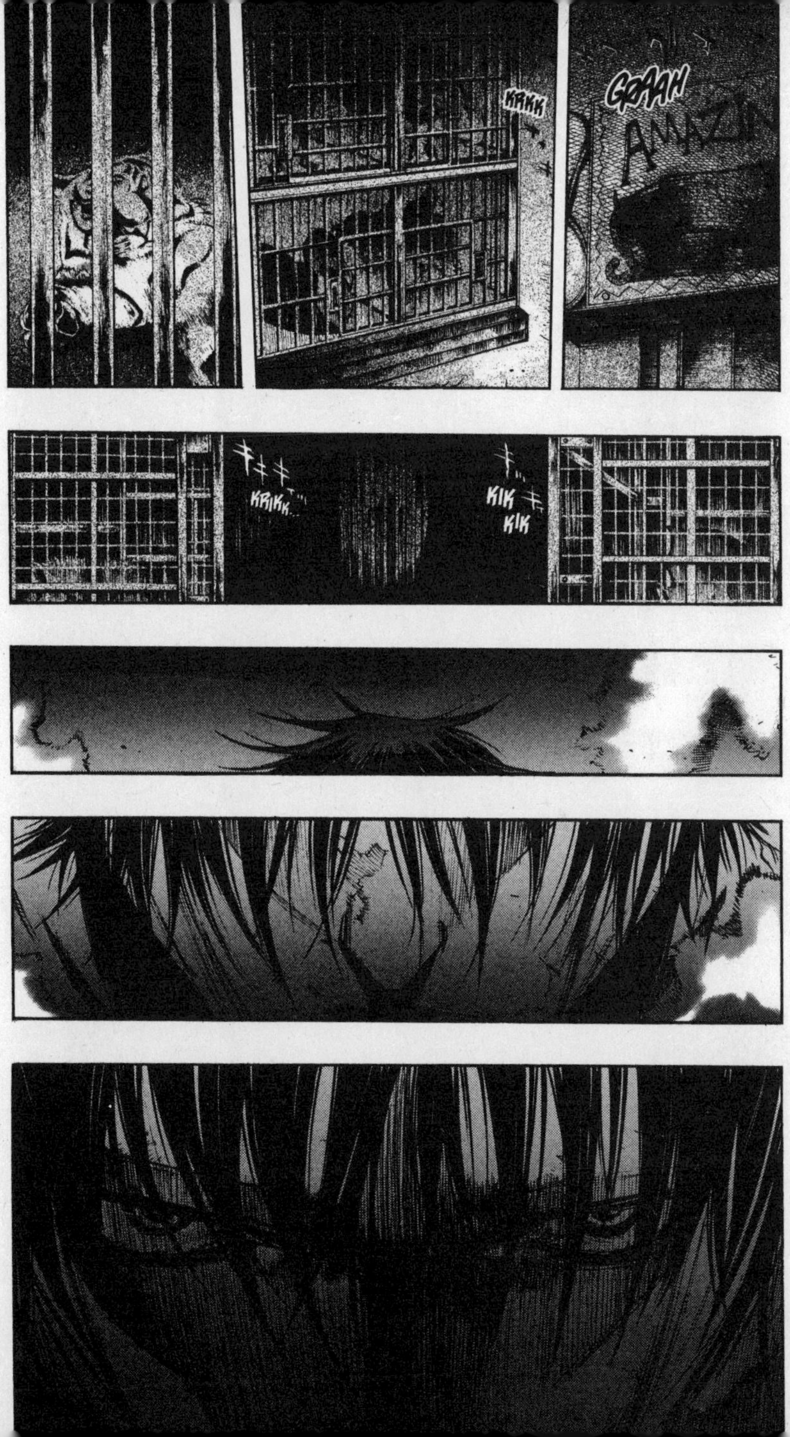
GRAAH
KRKK
KIK KIK
KRIKK...

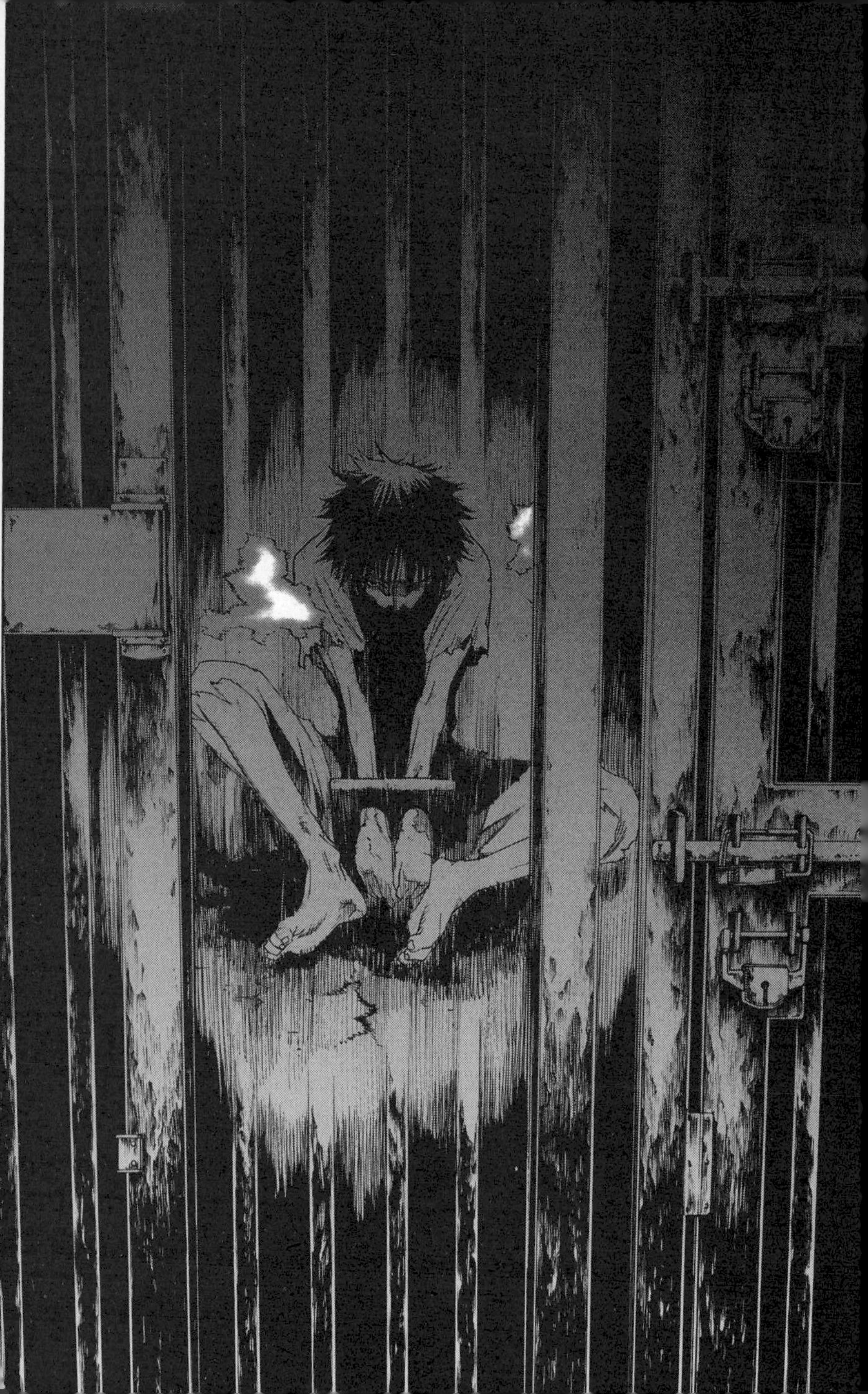

Chapter 1: The Titan's Son END

ATTACK on TITAN

BEFORE THE FALL

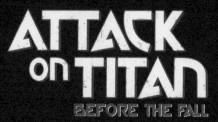

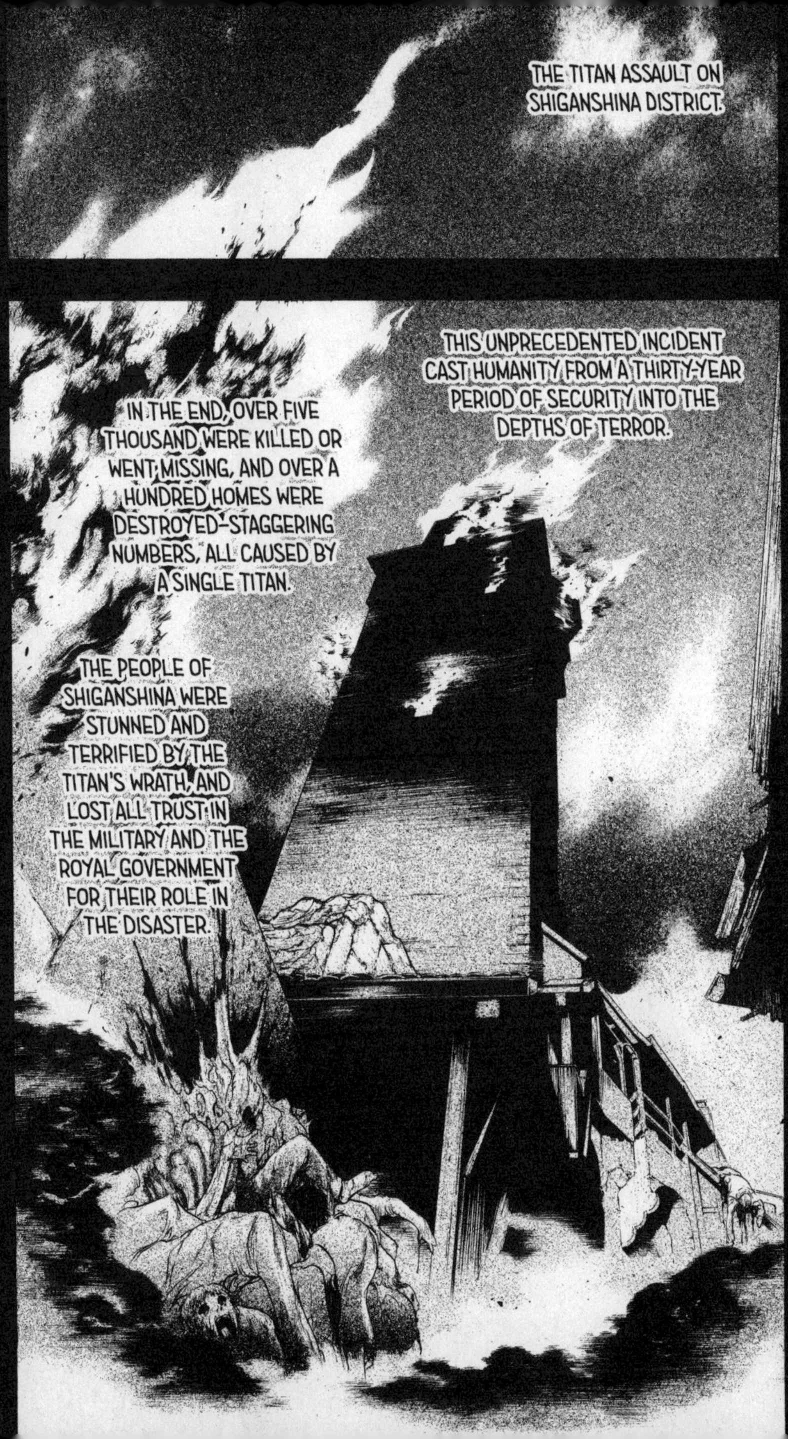
THE TITAN ASSAULT ON SHIGANSHINA DISTRICT.
THIS UNPRECEDENTED INCIDENT CAST HUMANITY FROM A THIRTY-YEAR PERIOD OF SECURITY INTO THE DEPTHS OF TERROR.
IN THE END, OVER FIVE THOUSAND WERE KILLED OR WENT MISSING, AND OVER A HUNDRED HOMES WERE DESTROYED–STAGGERING NUMBERS, ALL CAUSED BY A SINGLE TITAN.
THE PEOPLE OF SHIGANSHINA WERE STUNNED AND TERRIFIED BY THE TITAN'S WRATH, AND LOST ALL TRUST IN THE MILITARY AND THE ROYAL GOVERNMENT FOR THEIR ROLE IN THE DISASTER.

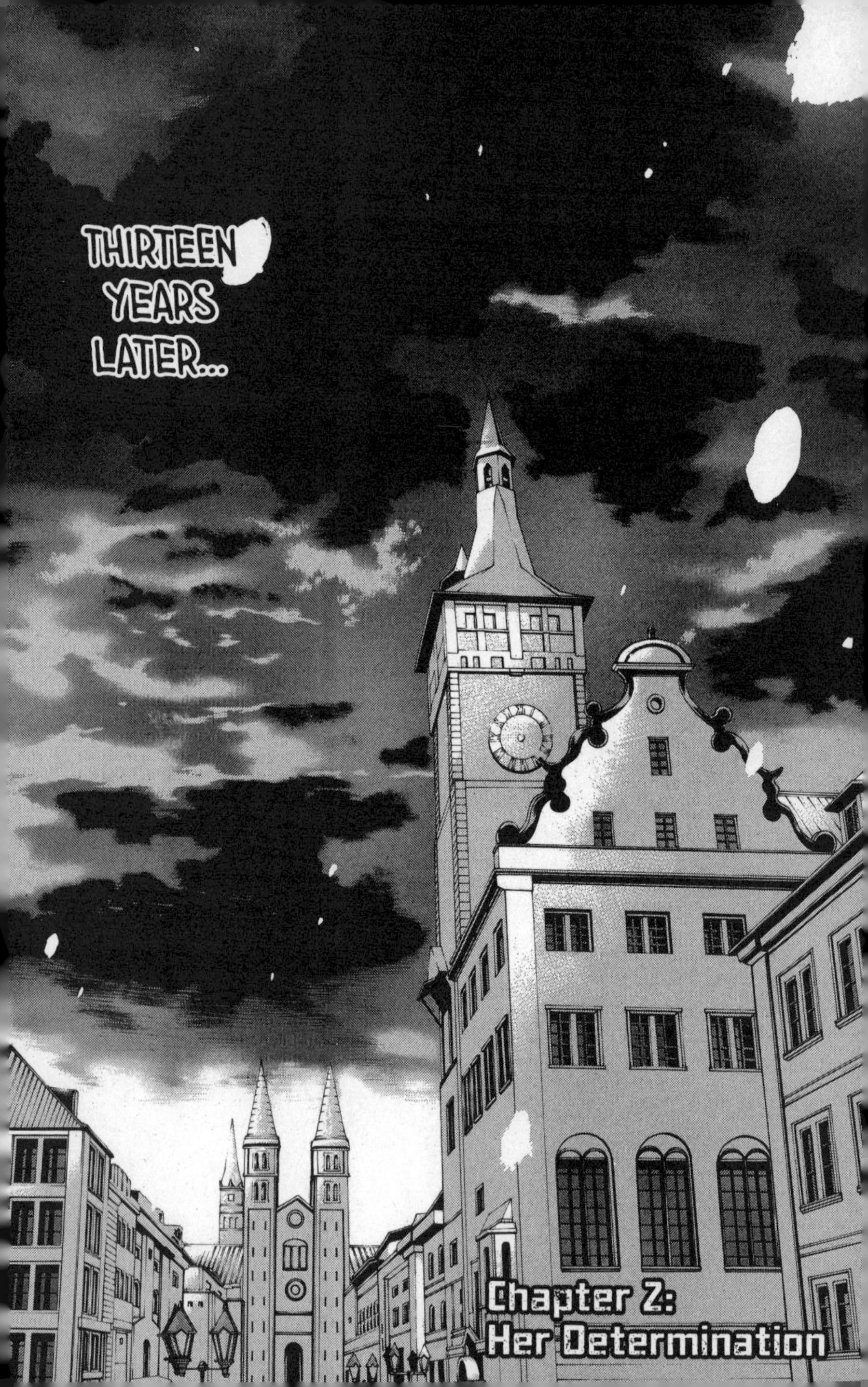
THIRTEEN YEARS LATER...
Chapter 2:
Her Determination

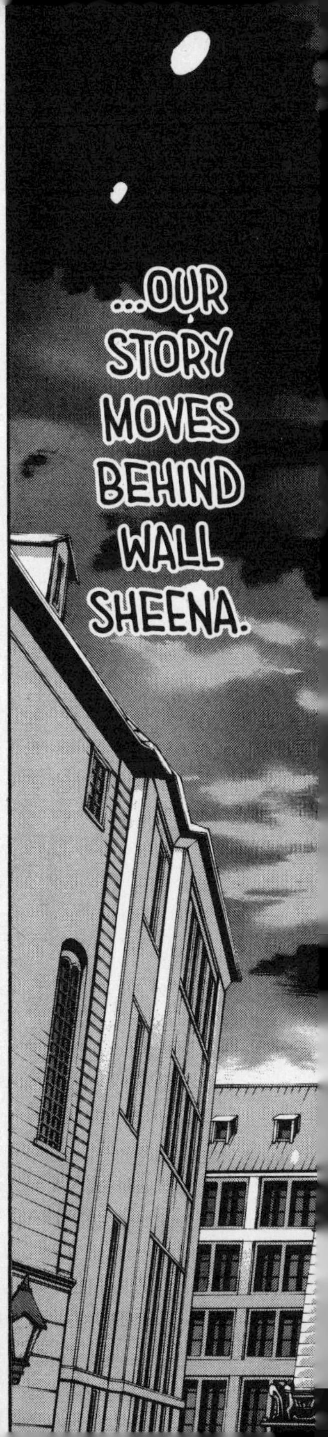
...OUR STORY MOVES BEHIND WALL SHEENA.
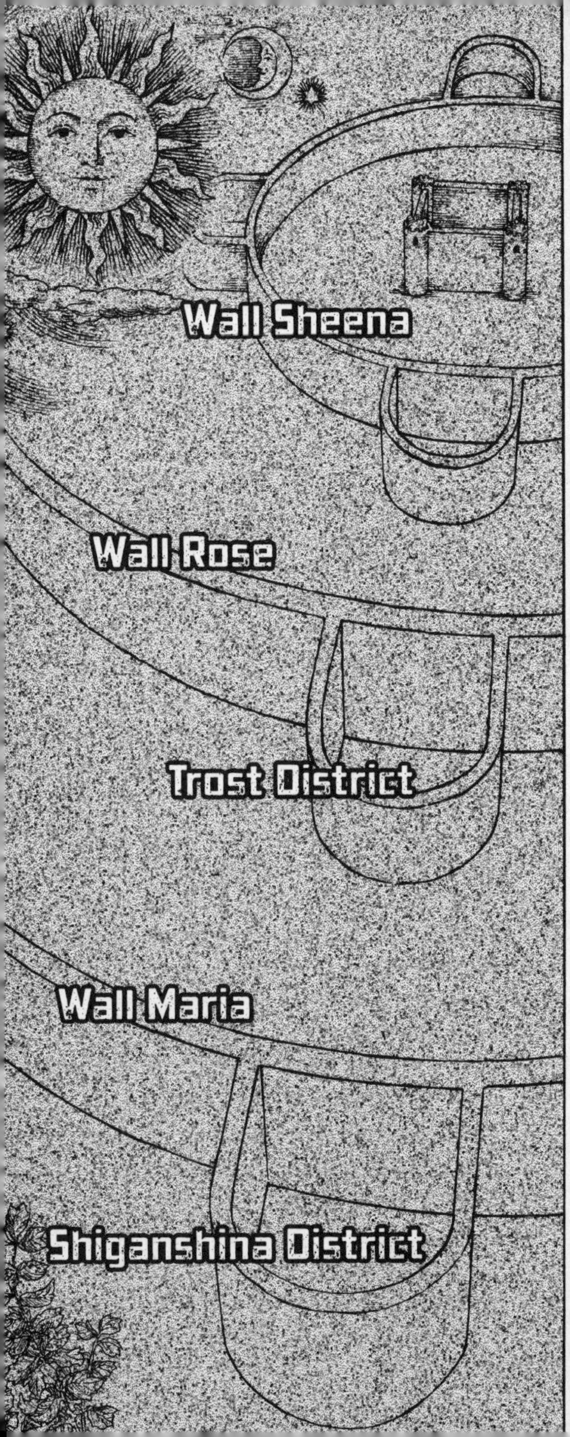
Wall Sheena
Wall Rose
Trost District
Wall Maria
Shiganshina District

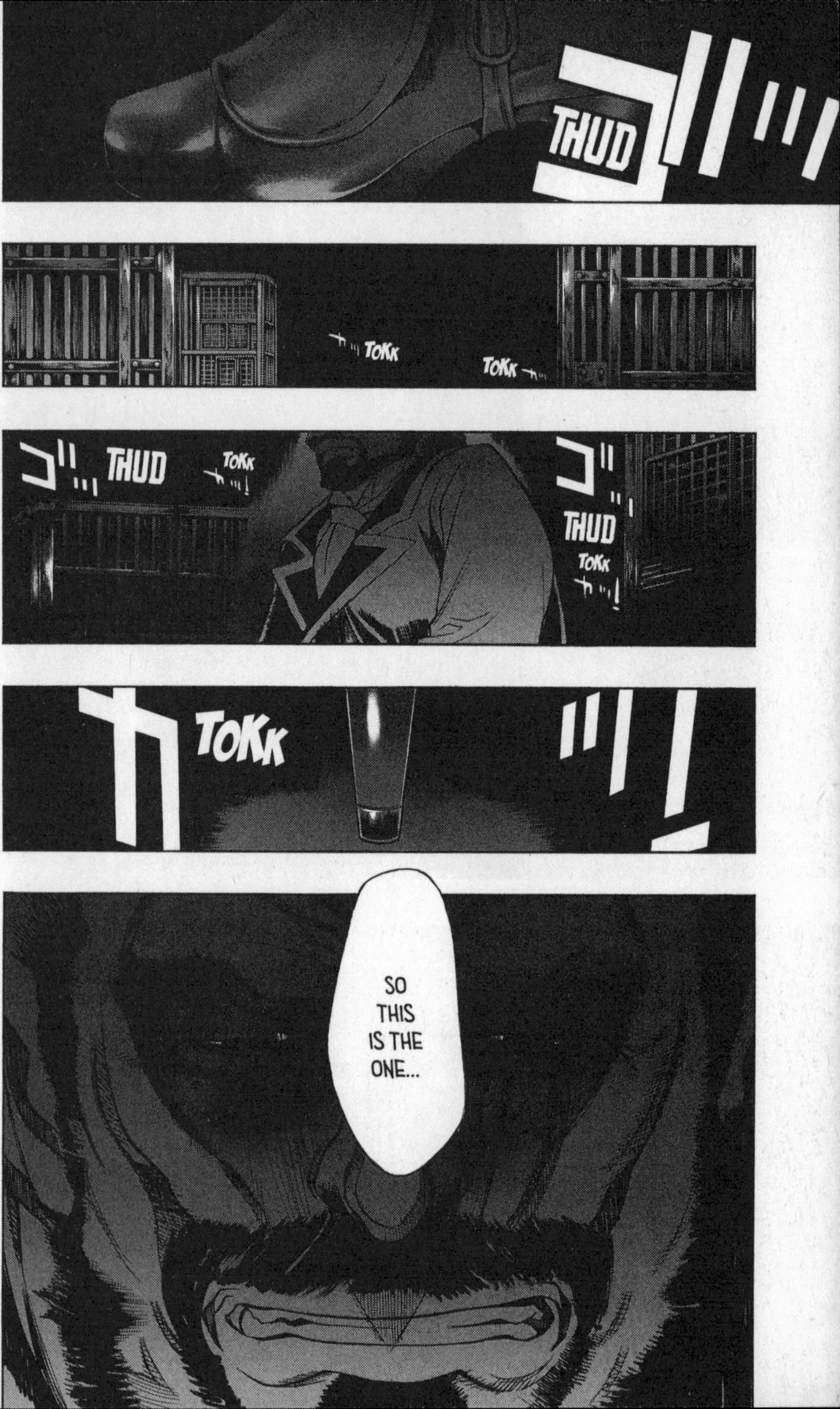
THUD
TOKK
TOKK
THUD
TOKK
THUD
TOKK
TOKK
SO THIS IS THE ONE...

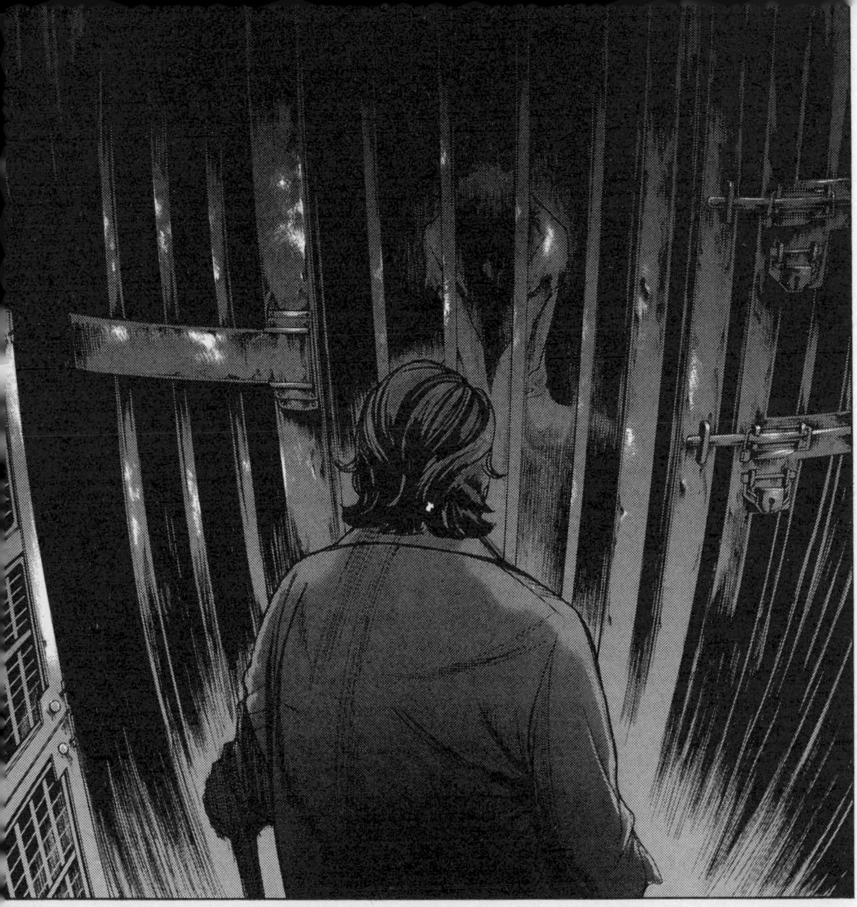
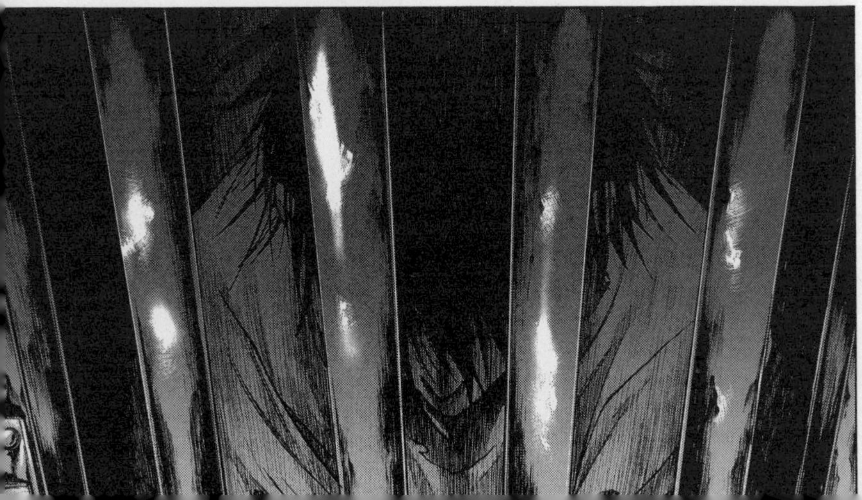

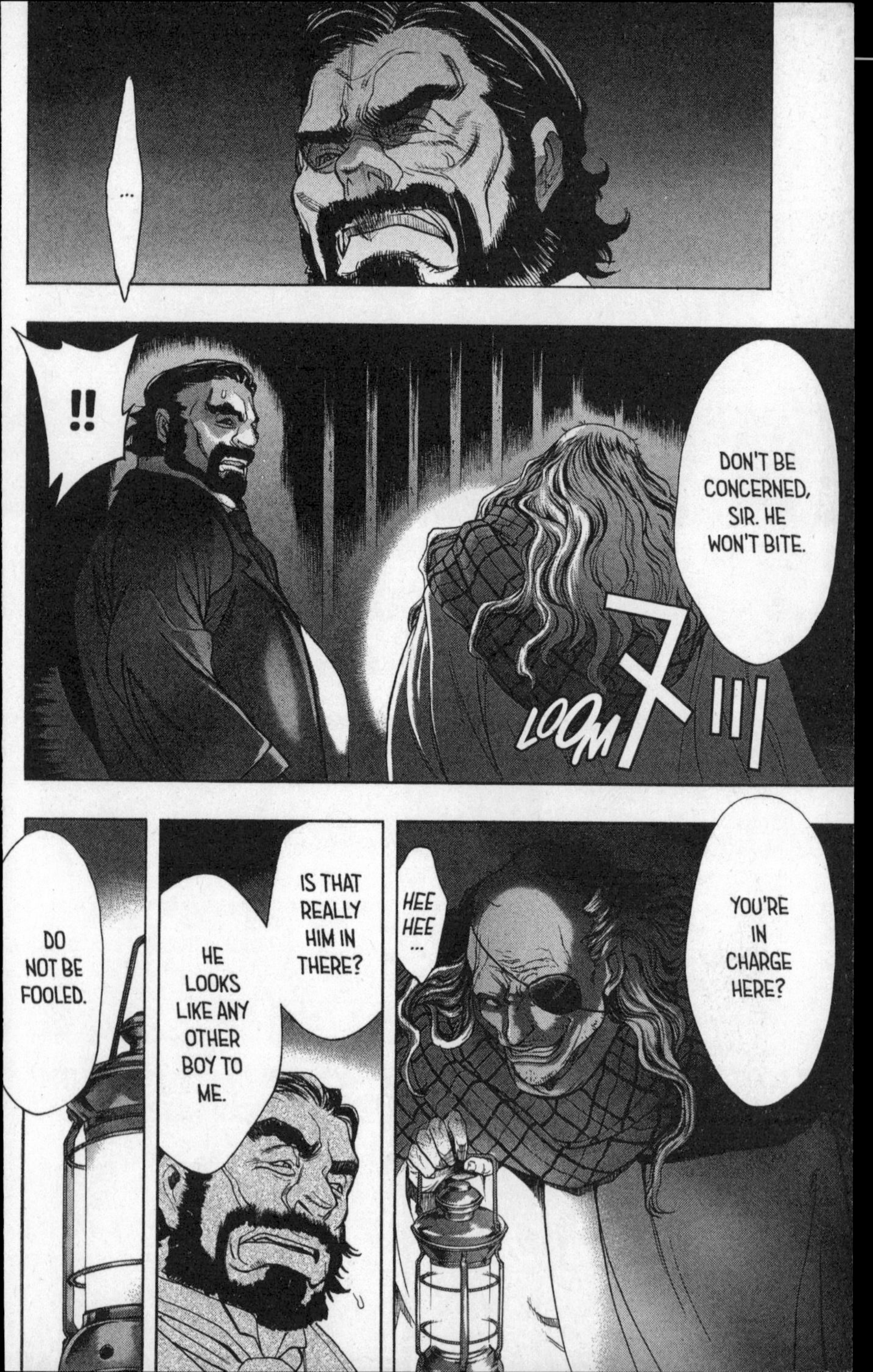
...
DON'T BE CONCERNED, SIR. HE WON'T BITE.
!!
LOOM
YOU'RE IN CHARGE HERE?
HEE HEE ...
IS THAT REALLY HIM IN THERE?
HE LOOKS LIKE ANY OTHER BOY TO ME.
DO NOT BE FOOLED.

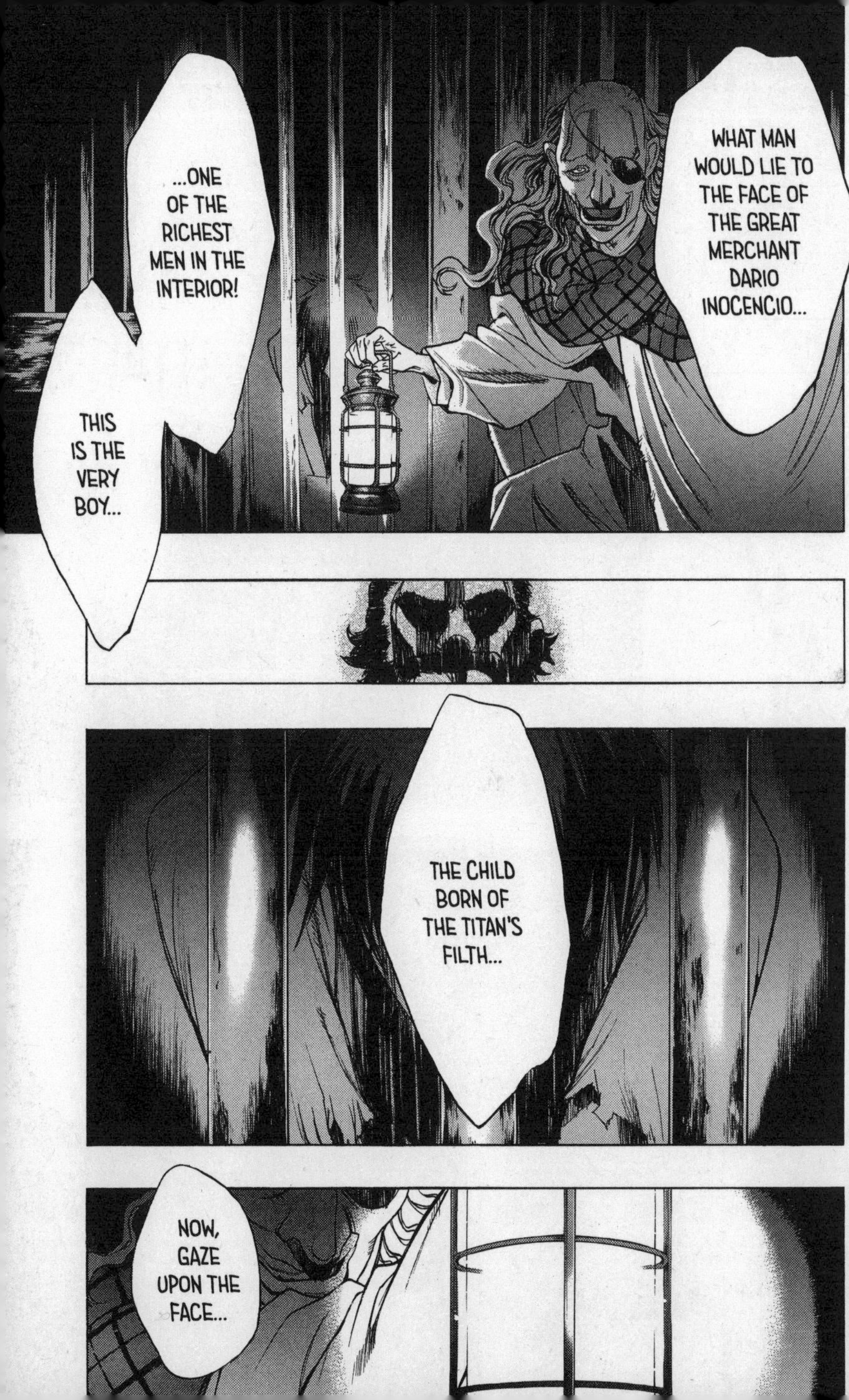
WHAT MAN WOULD LIE TO THE FACE OF THE GREAT MERCHANT DARIO INOCENCIO...
...ONE OF THE RICHEST MEN IN THE INTERIOR!
THIS IS THE VERY BOY...
THE CHILD BORN OF THE TITAN'S FILTH...
NOW, GAZE UPON THE FACE...

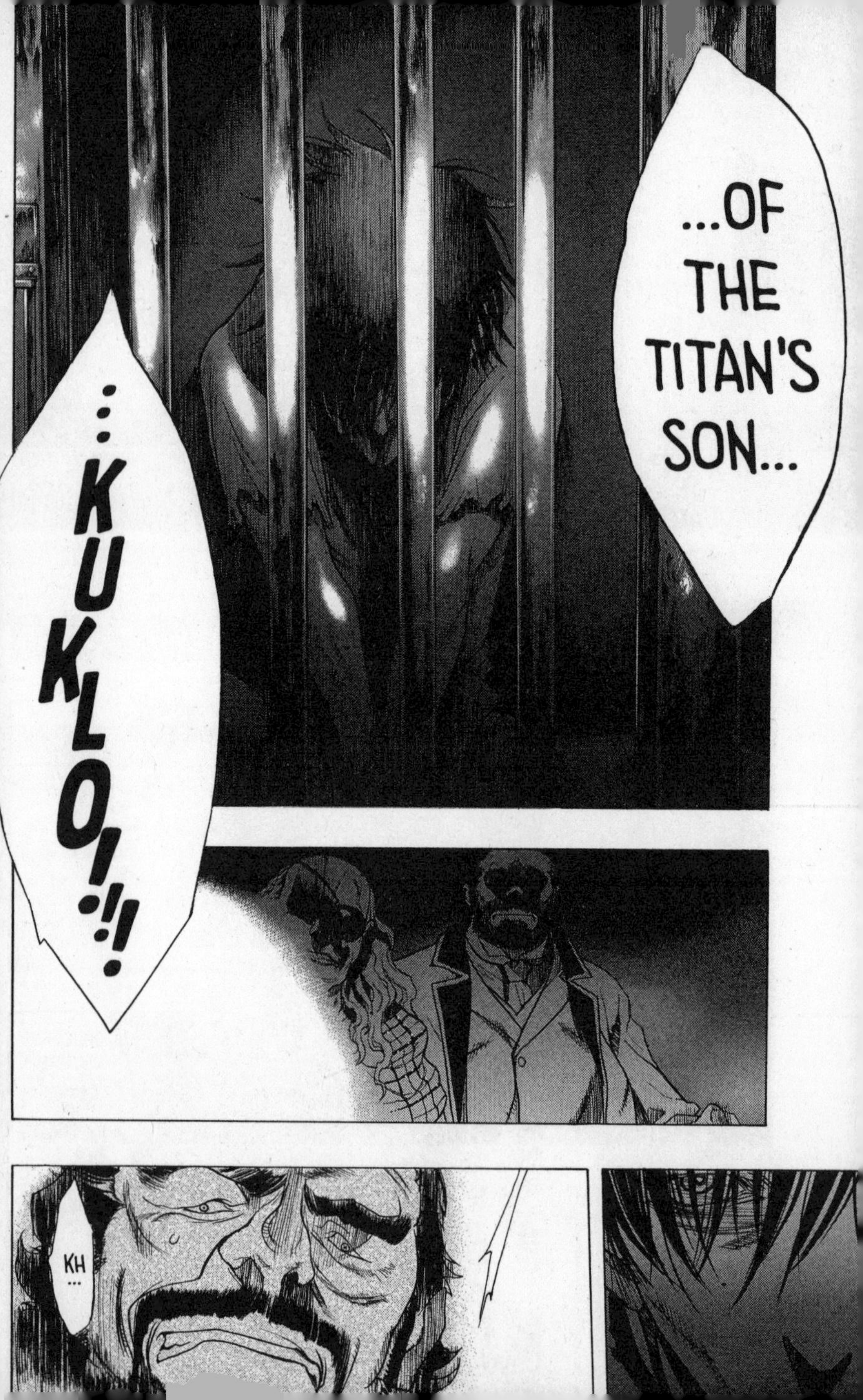
...OF THE TITAN'S SON...
...KUKLO!!!
KH ...

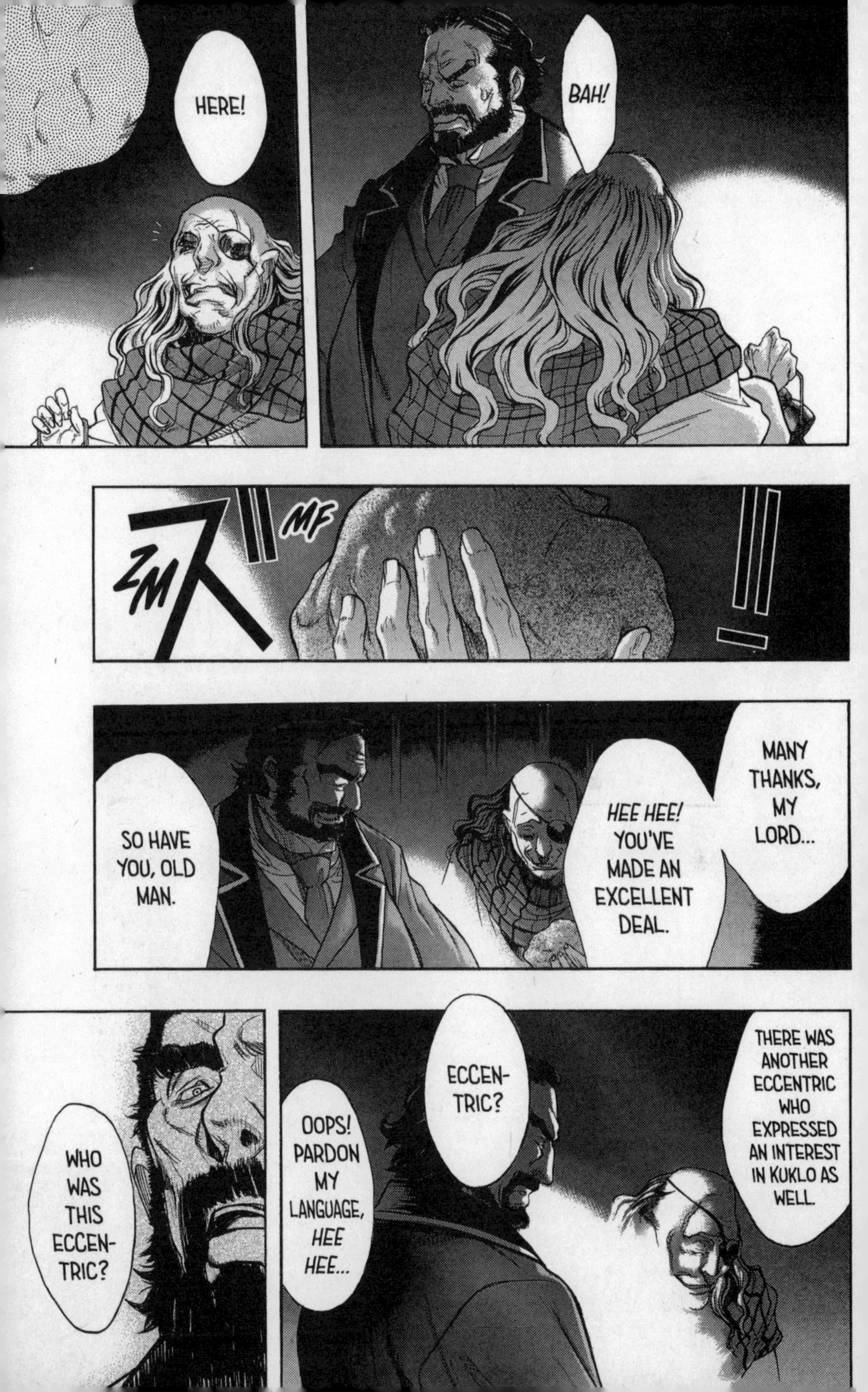
BAH!
HERE!
MF
ZM
MANY THANKS, MY LORD...
HEE HEE! YOU'VE MADE AN EXCELLENT DEAL.
SO HAVE YOU, OLD MAN.
THERE WAS ANOTHER ECCENTRIC WHO EXPRESSED AN INTEREST IN KUKLO AS WELL.
ECCEN-TRIC?
OOPS! PARDON MY LANGUAGE, HEE HEE...
WHO WAS THIS ECCEN-TRIC?

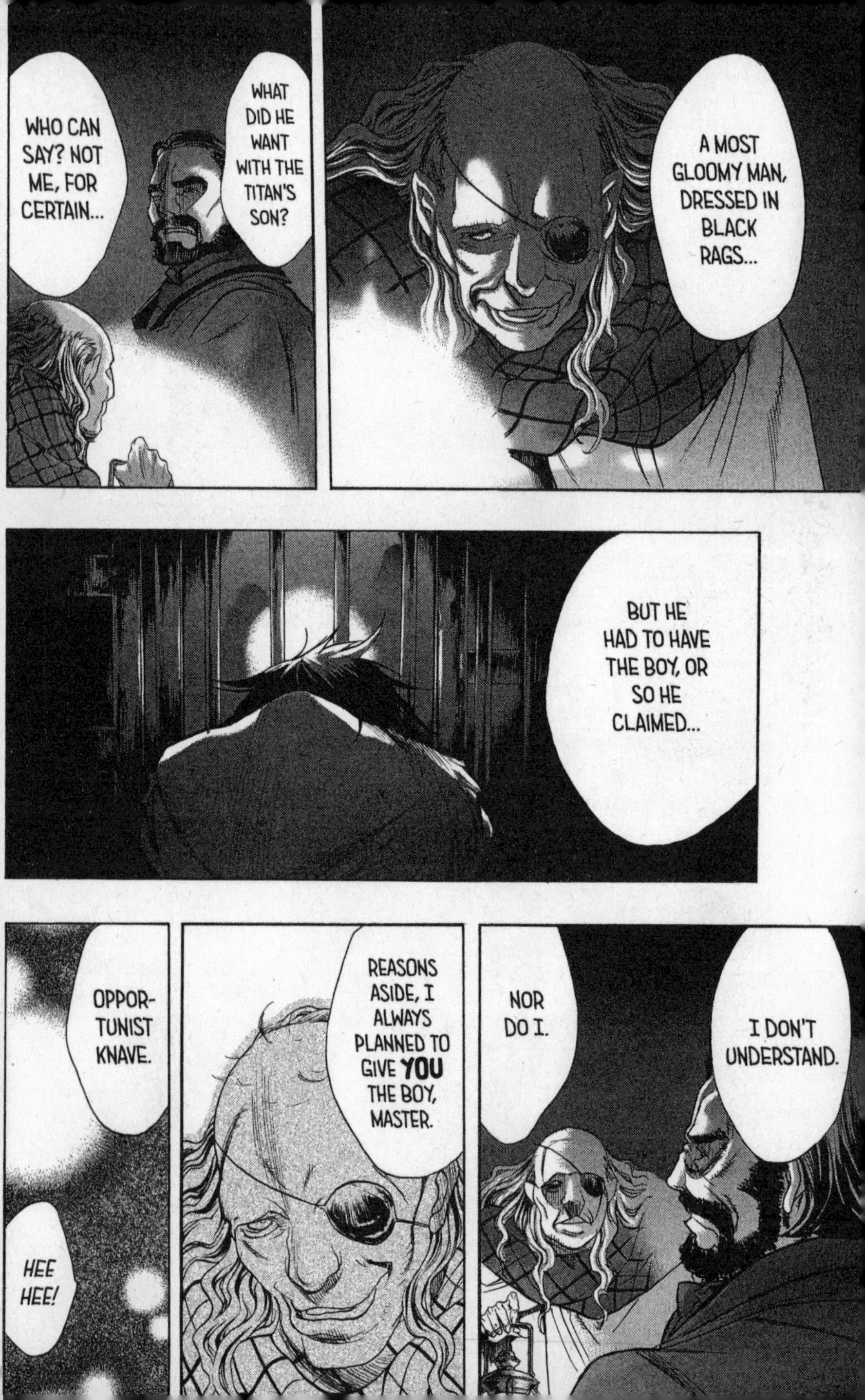
A MOST GLOOMY MAN, DRESSED IN BLACK RAGS...
WHAT DID HE WANT WITH THE TITAN'S SON?
WHO CAN SAY? NOT ME, FOR CERTAIN...
BUT HE HAD TO HAVE THE BOY, OR SO HE CLAIMED...
I DON'T UNDERSTAND.
NOR DO I.
REASONS ASIDE, I ALWAYS PLANNED TO GIVE **YOU** THE BOY, MASTER.
OPPOR-TUNIST KNAVE.
HEE HEE!

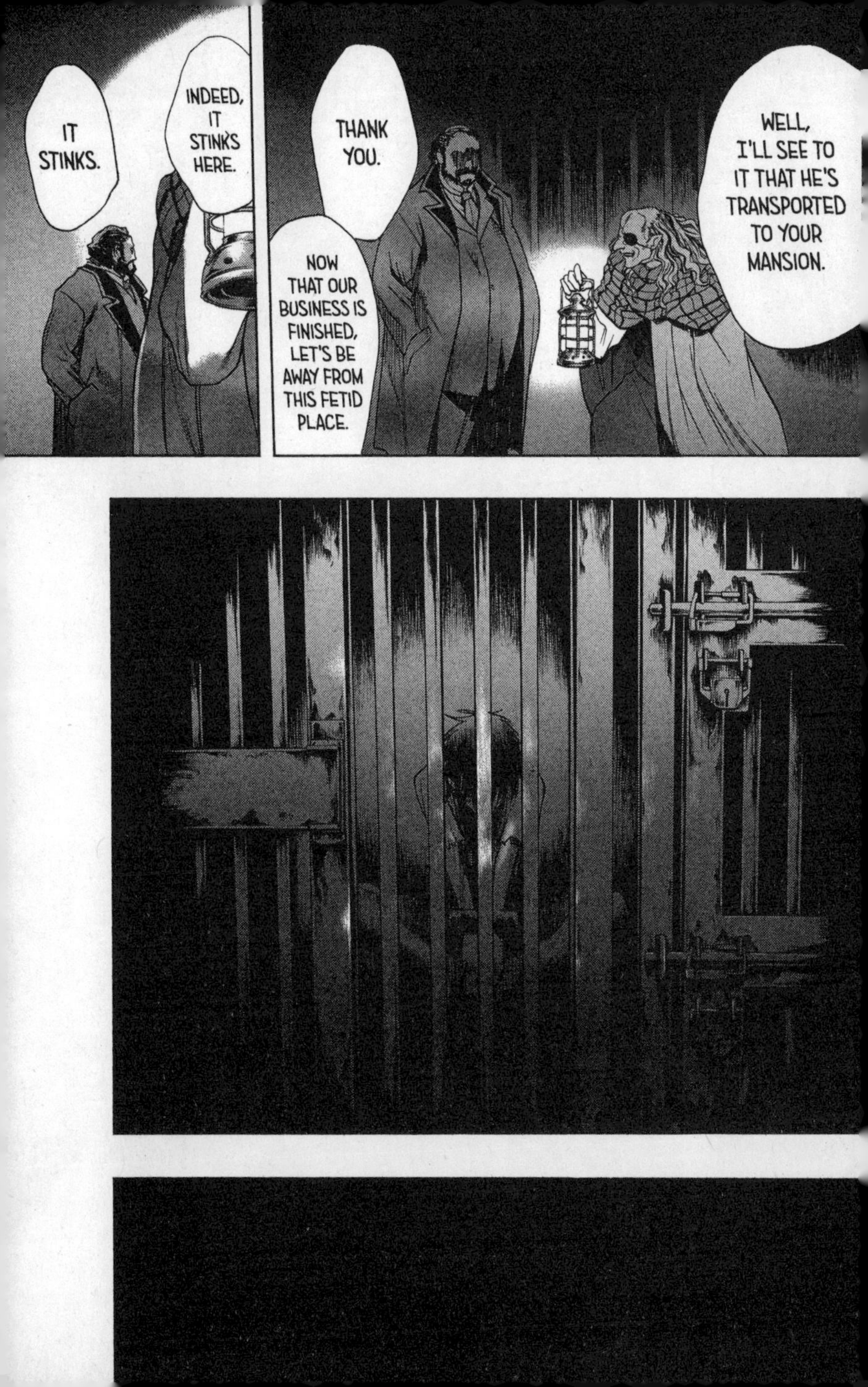
WELL, I'LL SEE TO IT THAT HE'S TRANSPORTED TO YOUR MANSION.
THANK YOU.
NOW THAT OUR BUSINESS IS FINISHED, LET'S BE AWAY FROM THIS FETID PLACE.
INDEED, IT STINKS HERE.
IT STINKS.

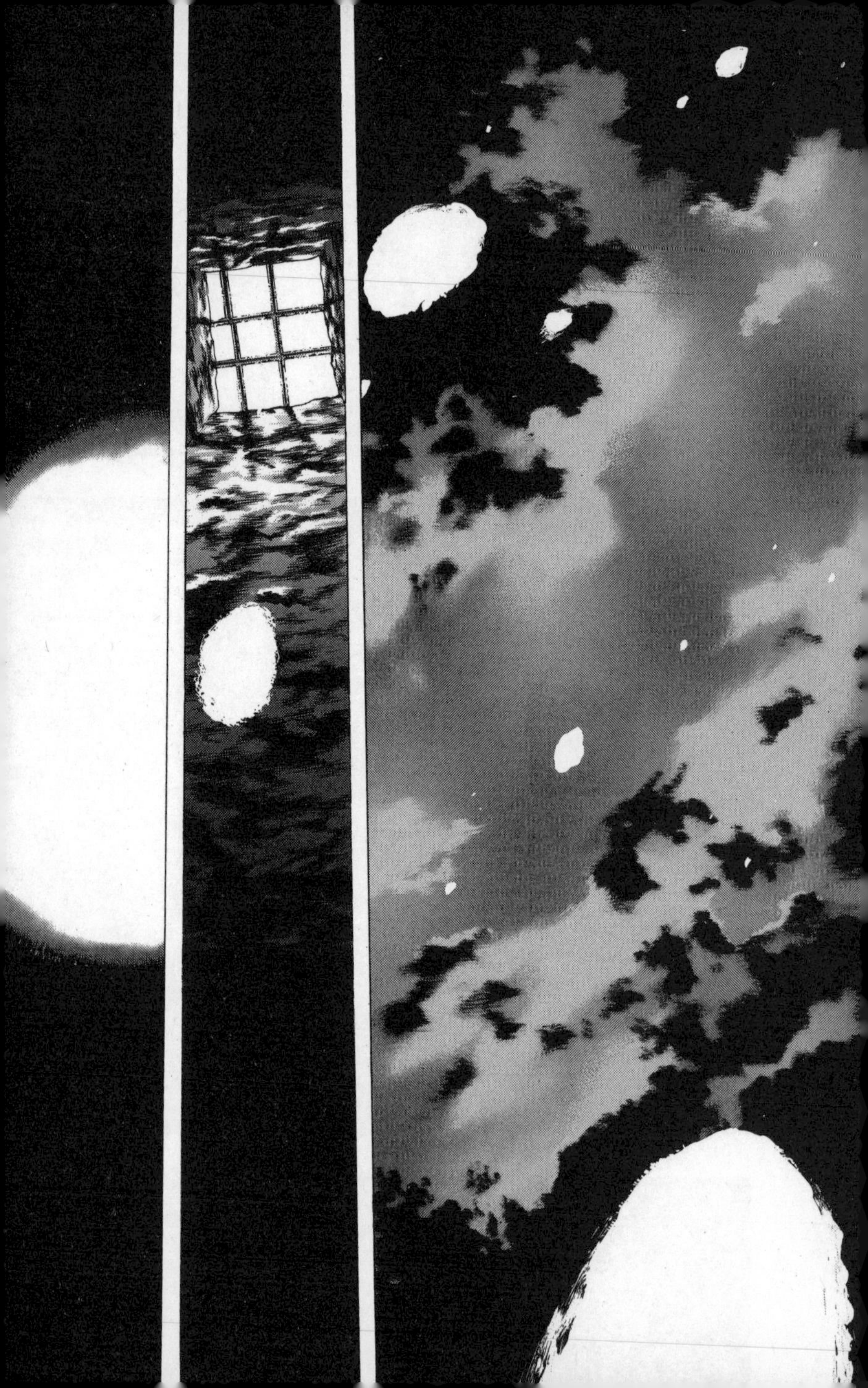

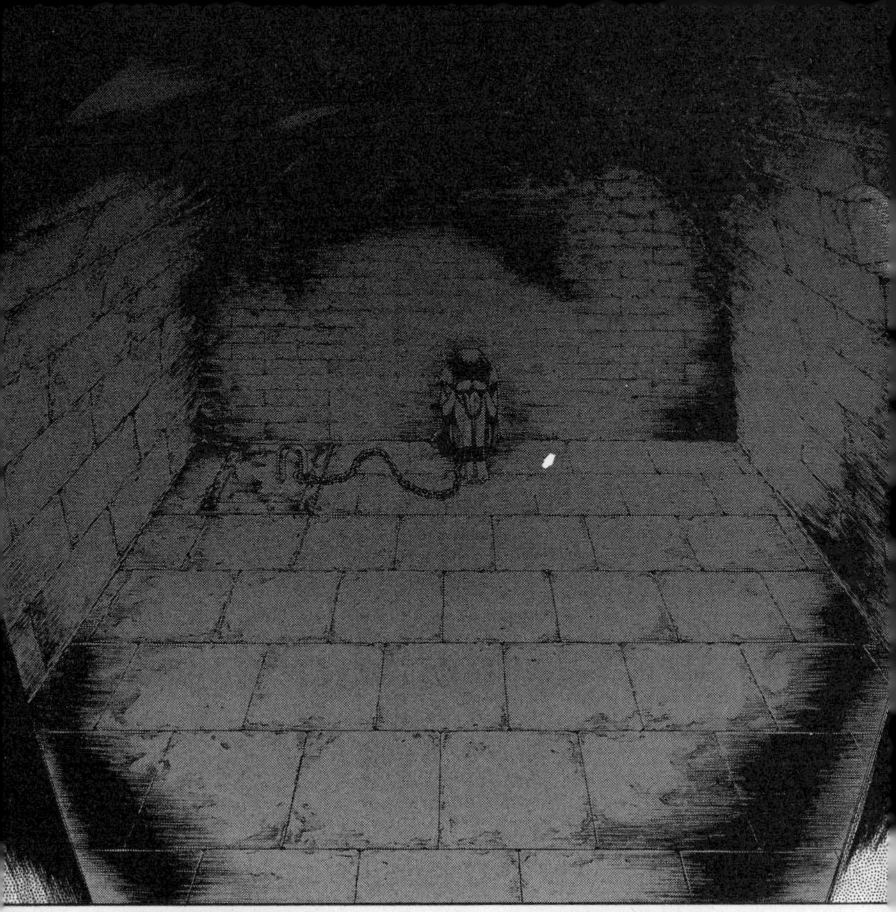
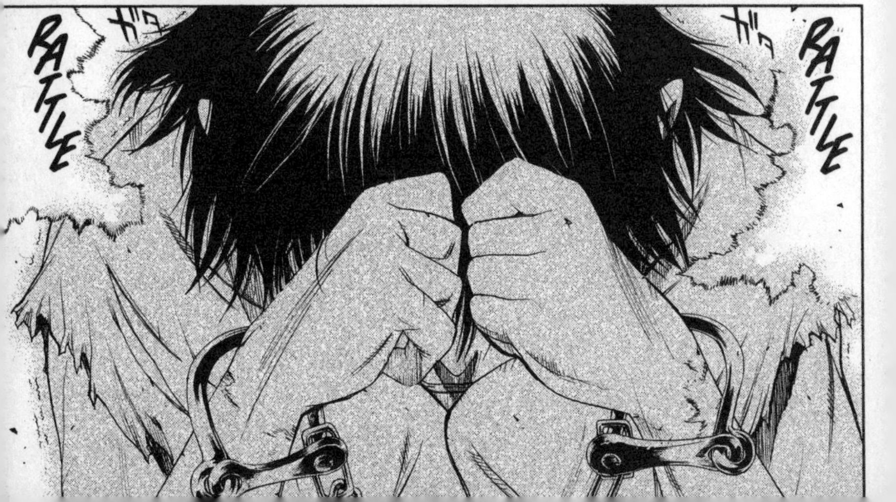
RATTLE
RATTLE

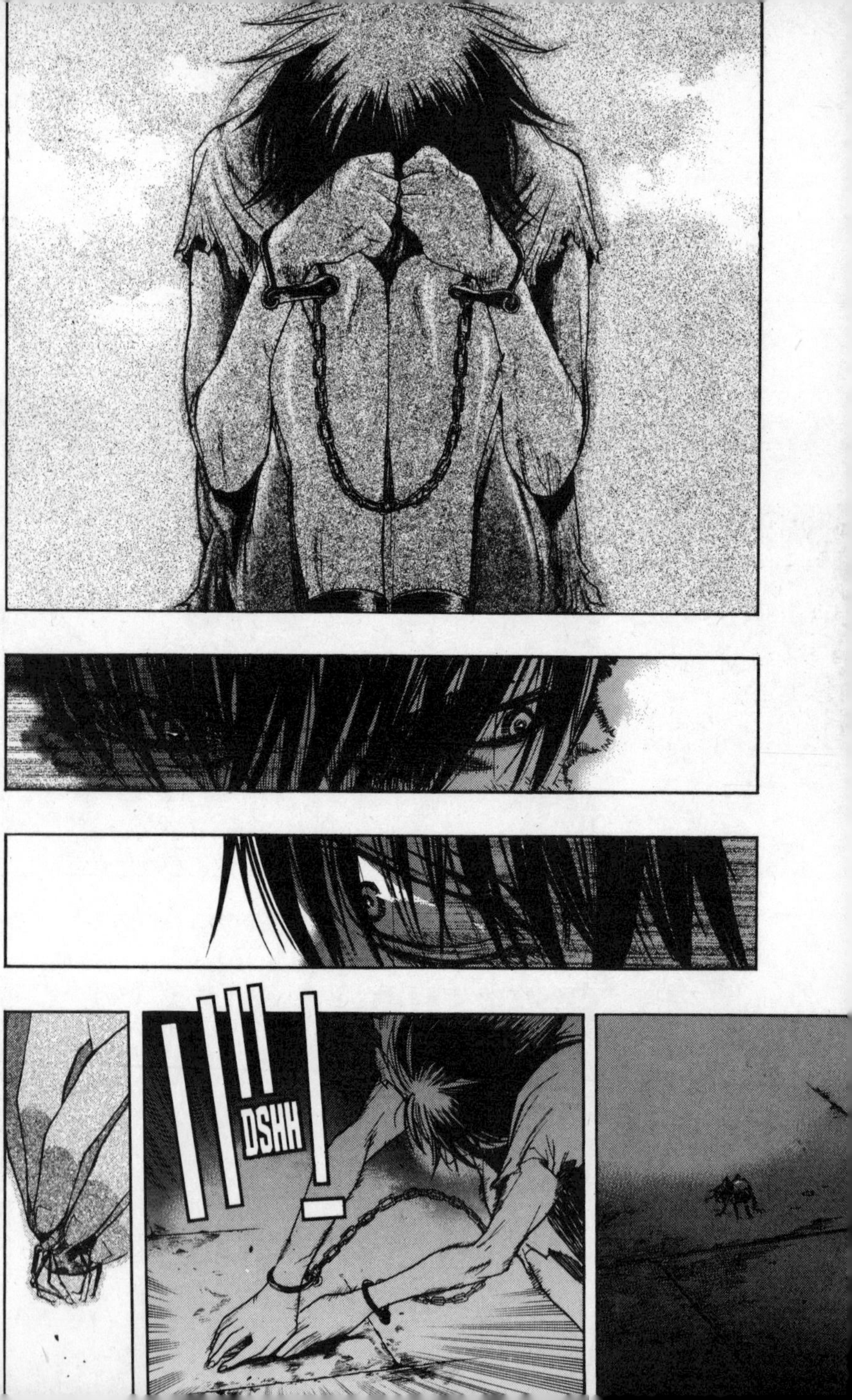
DSHH

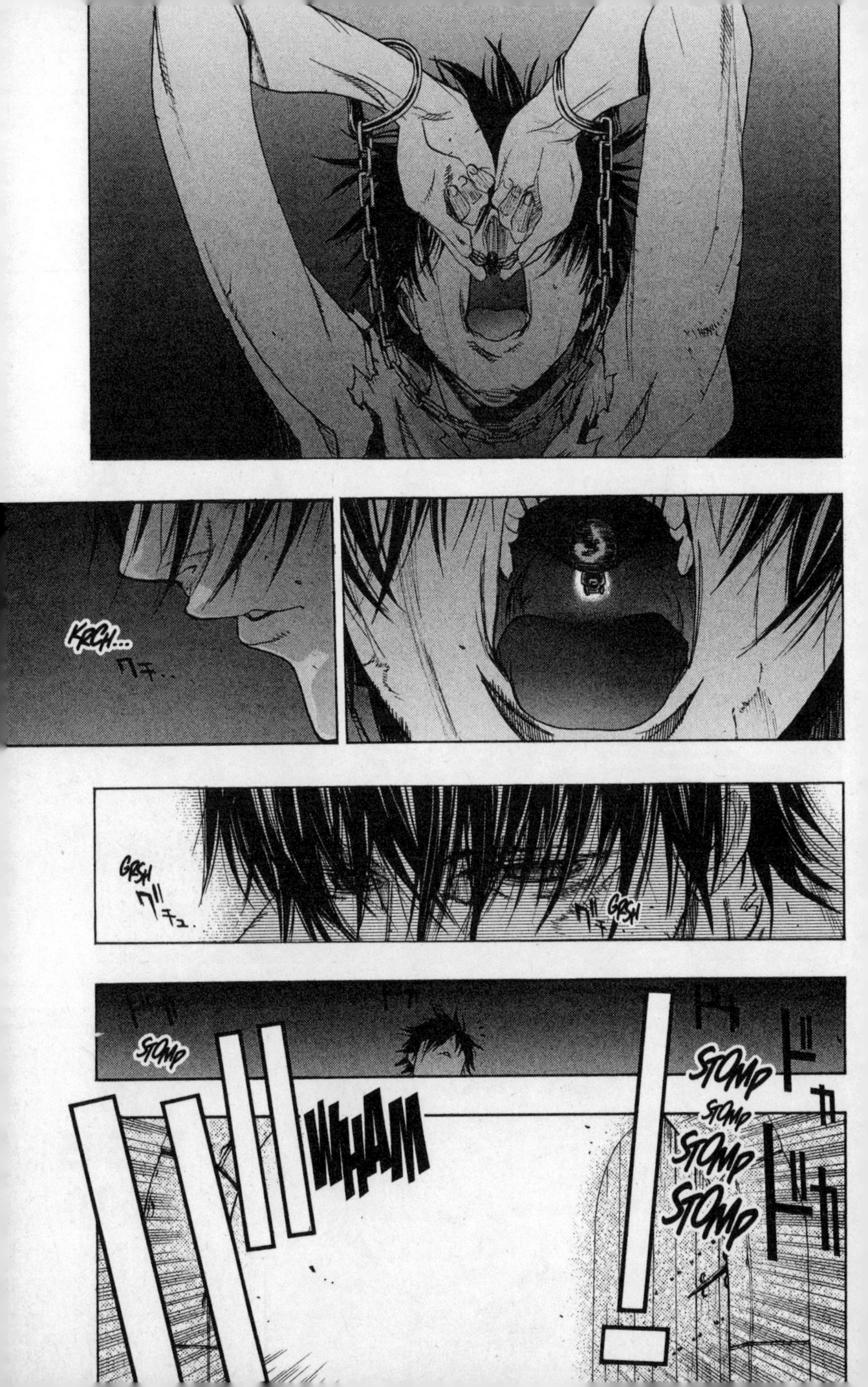
KRCH...
GRSH
GRSH
STOMP
STOMP
STOMP
STOMP
STOMP
WHAM

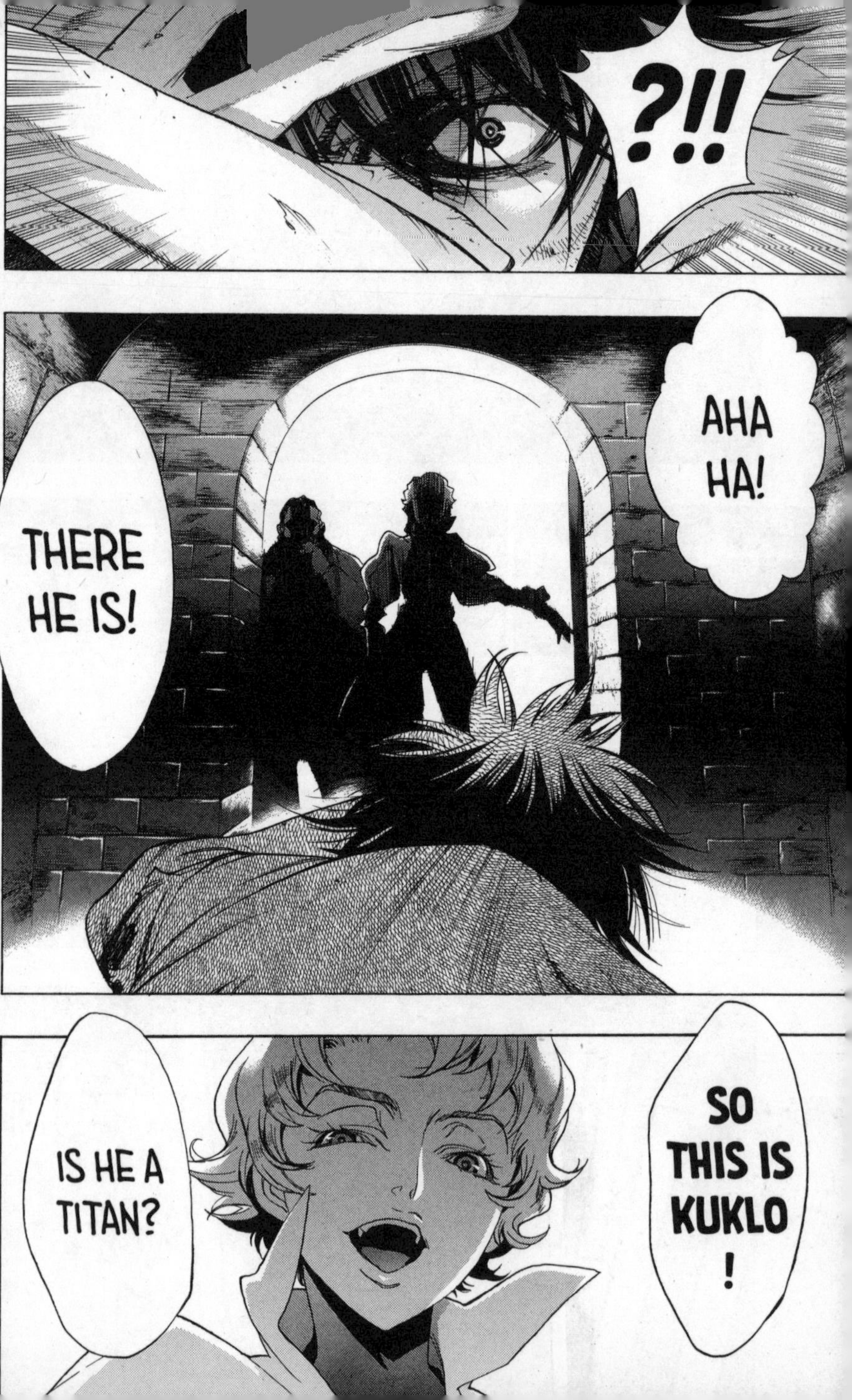
?!!
AHA HA!
THERE HE IS!
SO THIS IS KUKLO !
IS HE A TITAN?

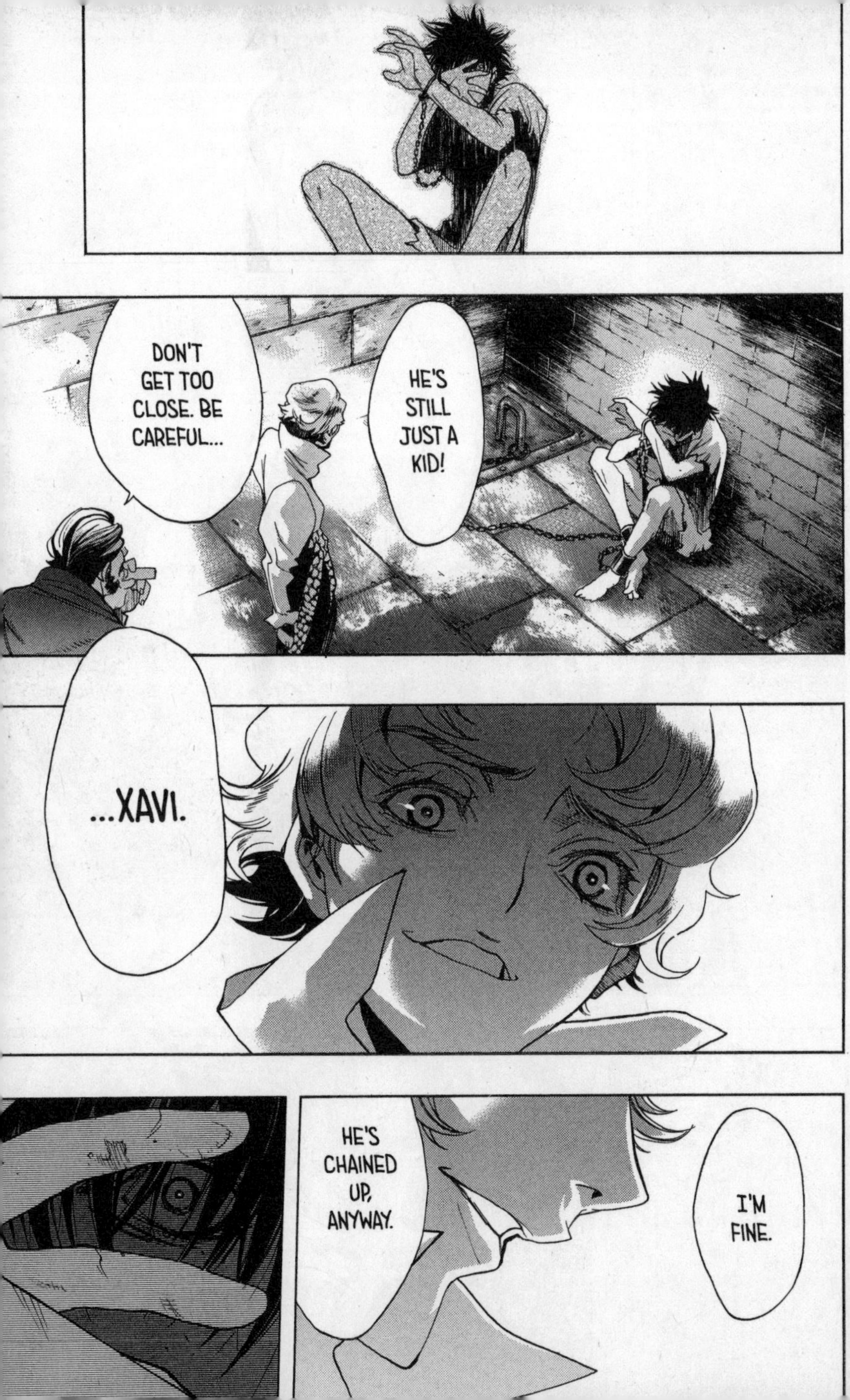
HE'S STILL JUST A KID!
DON'T GET TOO CLOSE. BE CAREFUL...
...XAVI.
I'M FINE.
HE'S CHAINED UP, ANYWAY.

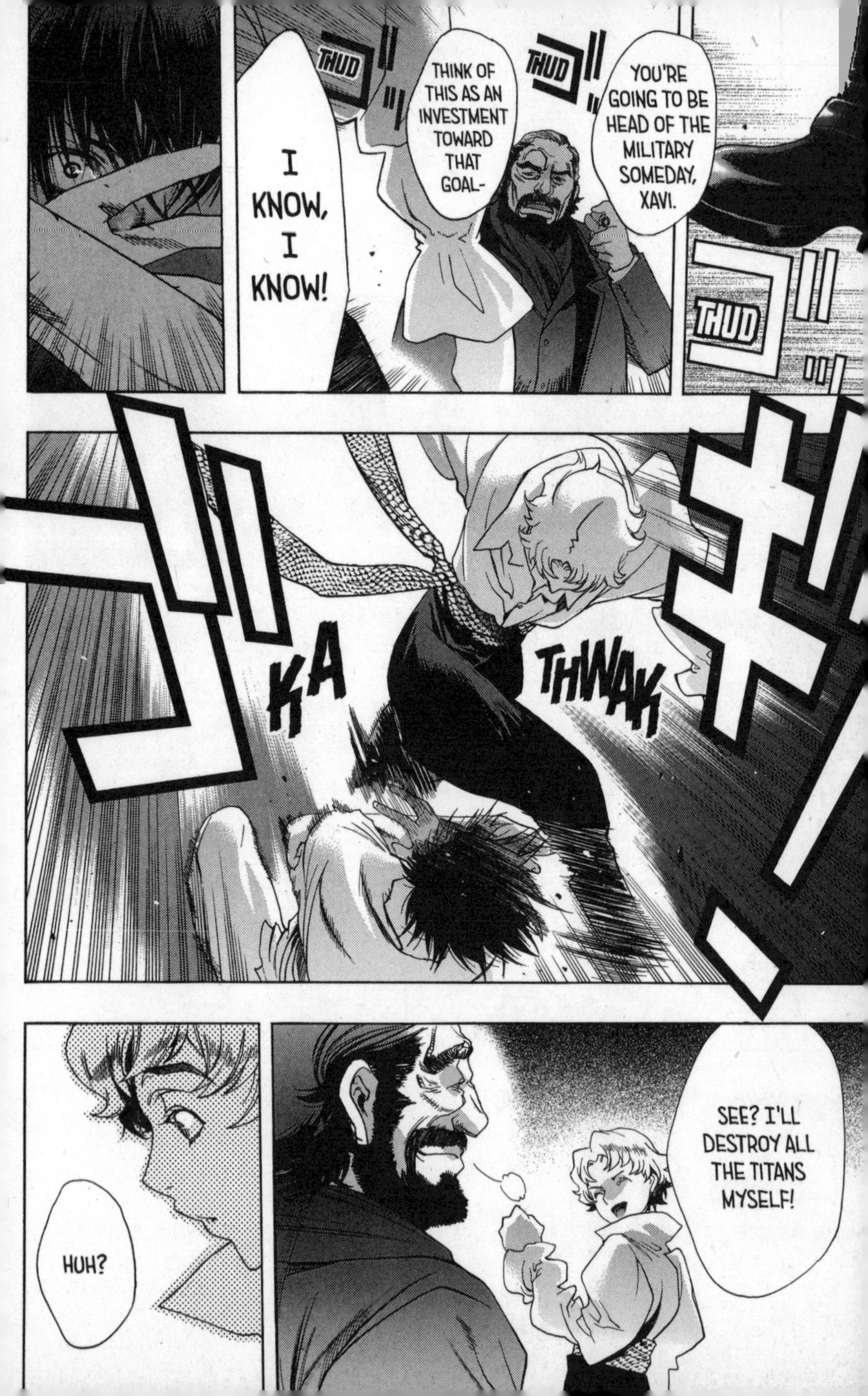
THUD
THUD
YOU'RE GOING TO BE HEAD OF THE MILITARY SOMEDAY, XAVI.
THUD
THINK OF THIS AS AN INVESTMENT TOWARD THAT GOAL-
I KNOW, I KNOW!
KA
THWAK
SEE? I'LL DESTROY ALL THE TITANS MYSELF!
HUH?

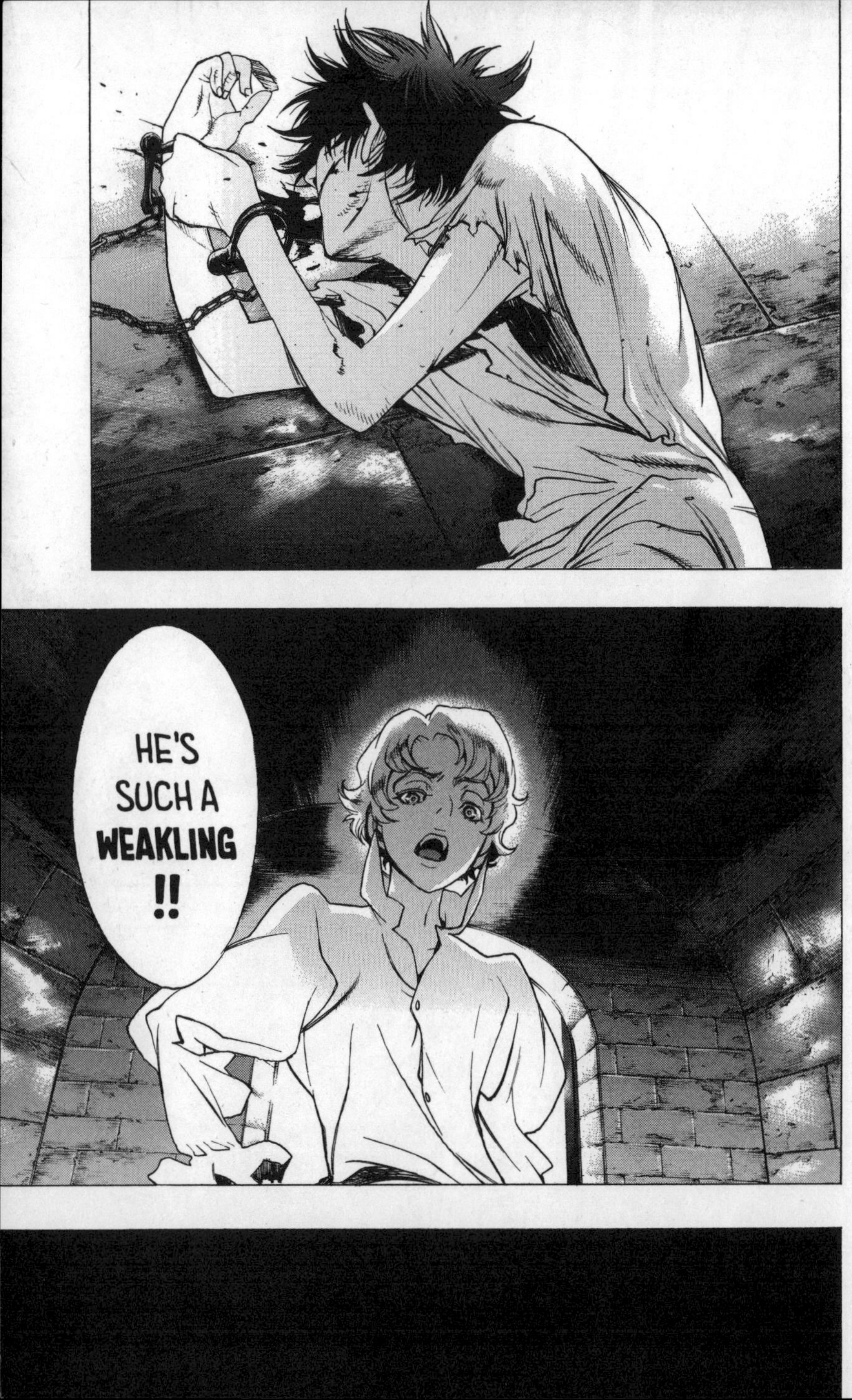
HE'S SUCH A WEAKLING!!

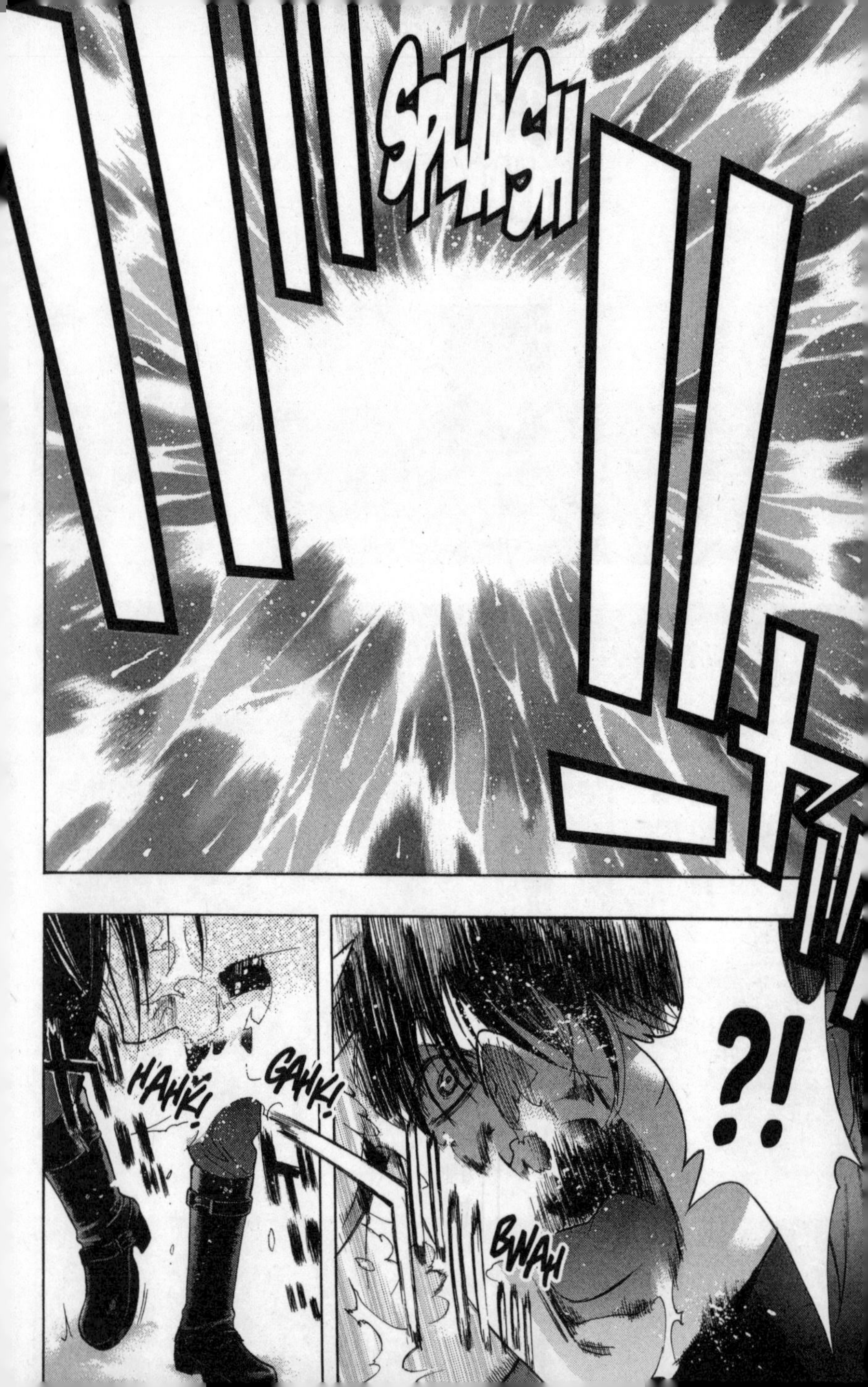
SPLASH
?!
GAHK!
BWAH
HAHK!

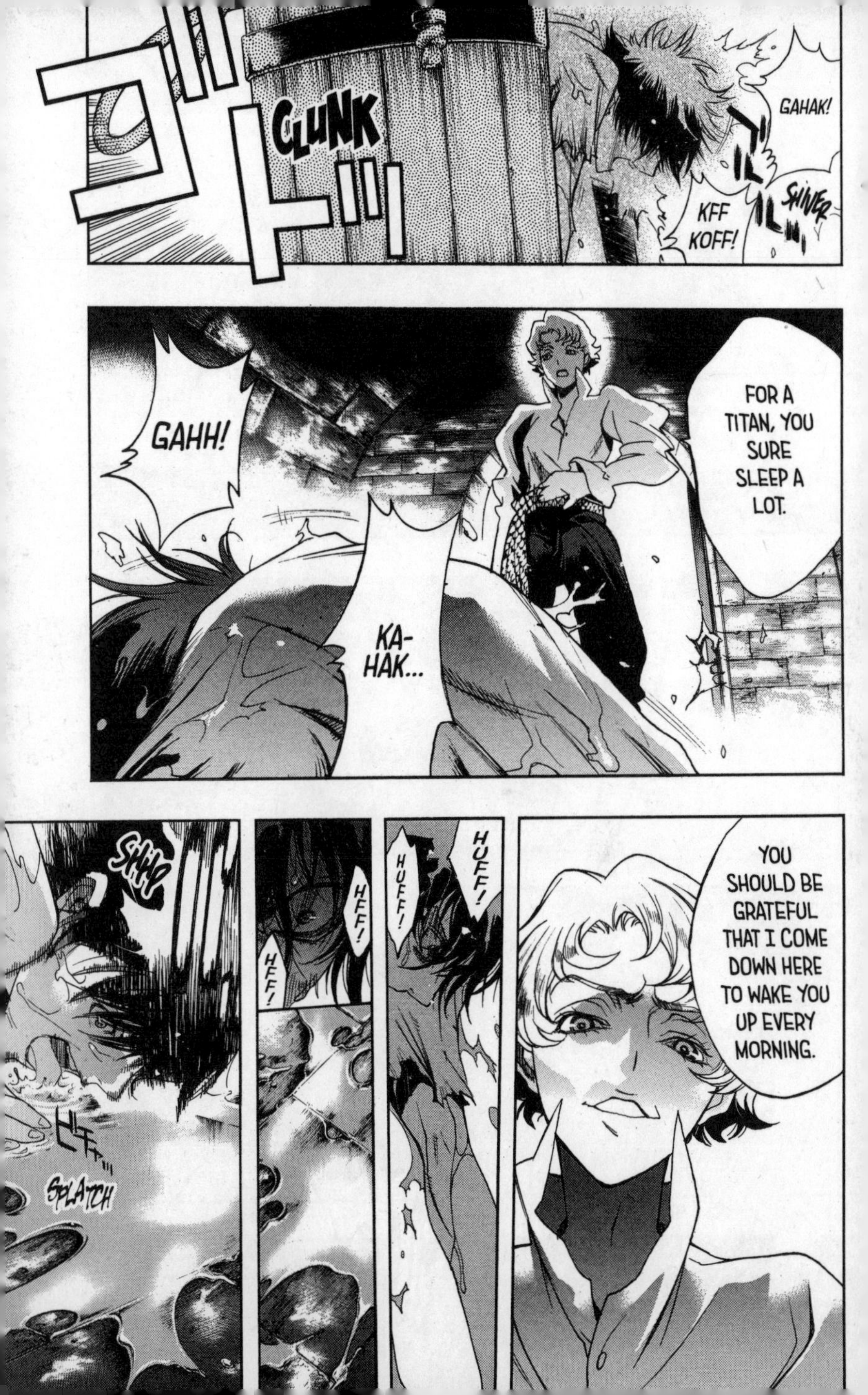
GAHAK!
KFF KOFF!
SHIVER
CLUNK
FOR A TITAN, YOU SURE SLEEP A LOT.
GAHH!
KA-HAK...
YOU SHOULD BE GRATEFUL THAT I COME DOWN HERE TO WAKE YOU UP EVERY MORNING.
HUFF! HUFF!
HFF! HFF!
SPLATCH

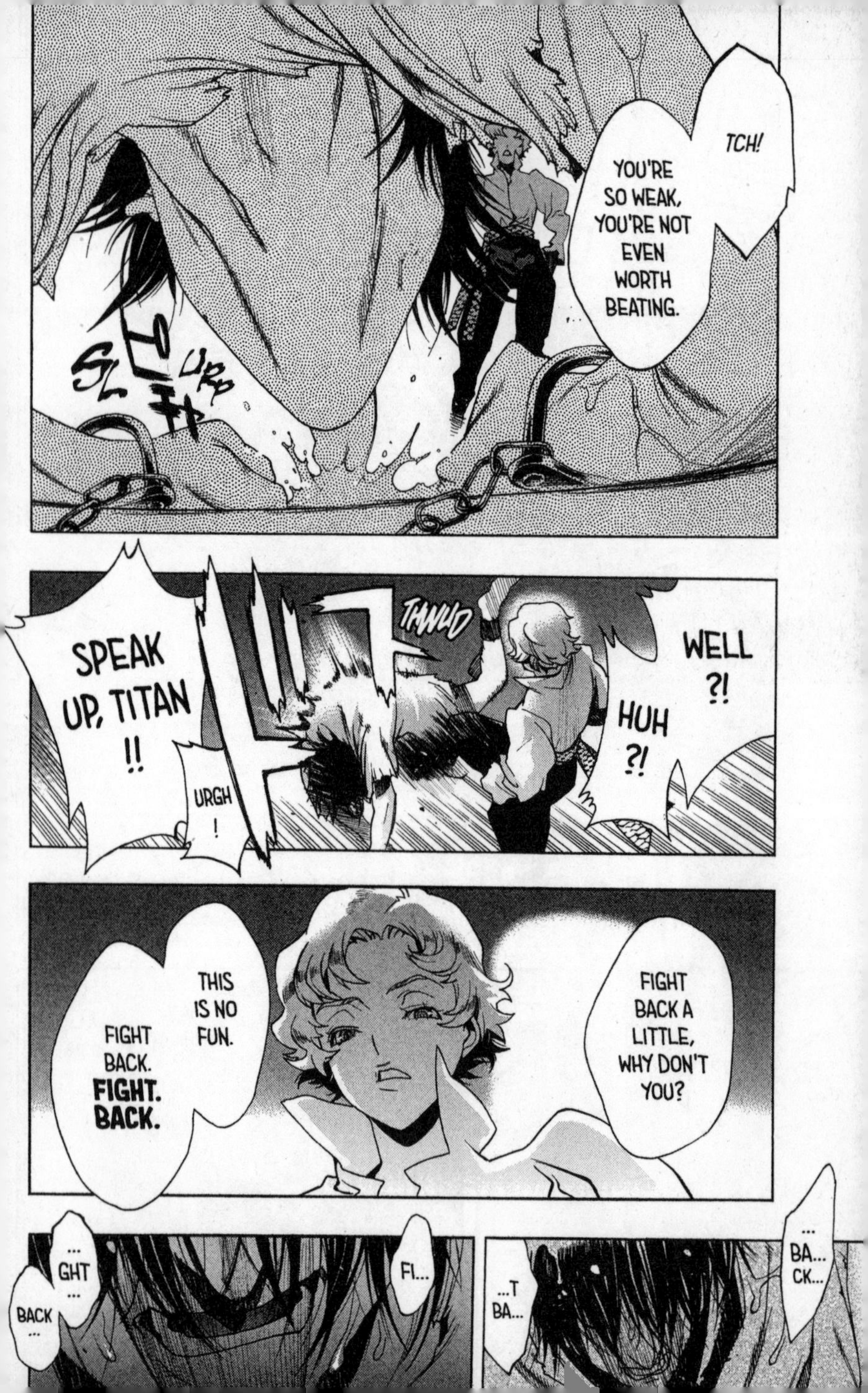
TCH!
YOU'RE SO WEAK, YOU'RE NOT EVEN WORTH BEATING.
WELL ?!
HUH ?!
THWUD
SPEAK UP, TITAN !!
URGH !
FIGHT BACK A LITTLE, WHY DON'T YOU?
THIS IS NO FUN.
FIGHT BACK. **FIGHT. BACK.**
... BA... CK...
...T BA...
FI...
... GHT ...
BACK ...

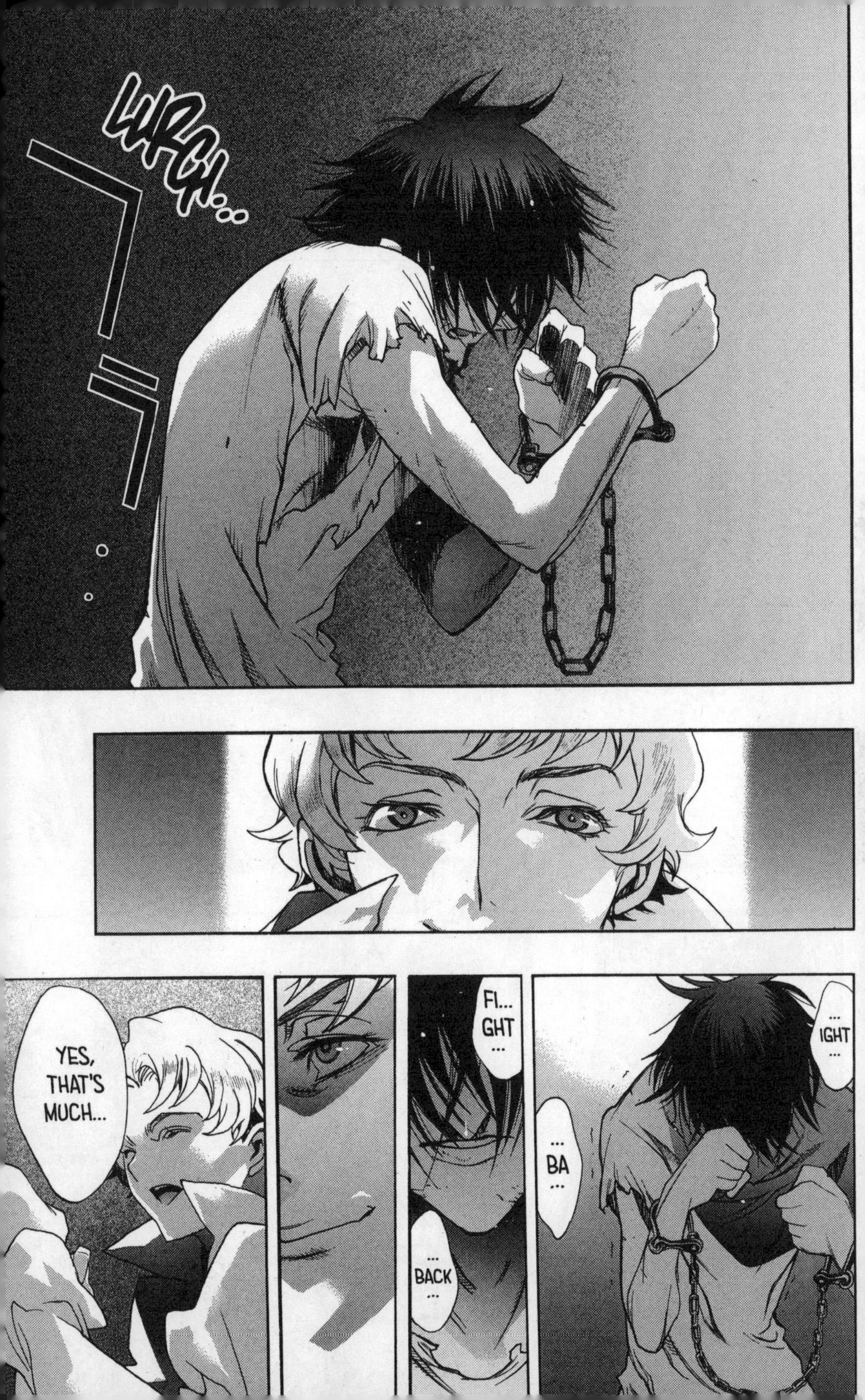
URGH...
...IGHT...
FI... GHT...
...BA...
...BACK...
YES, THAT'S MUCH...

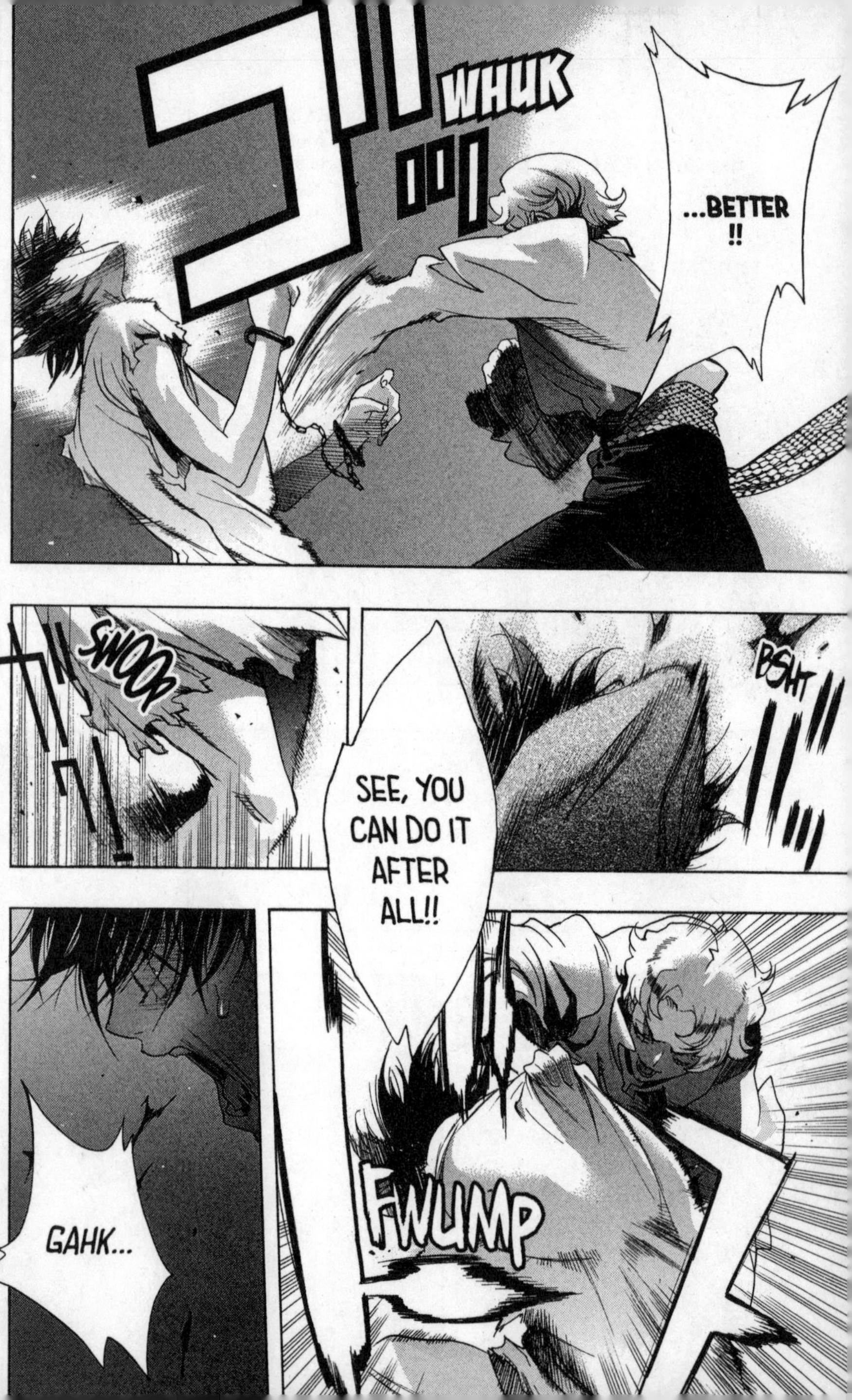
WHUK
...BETTER !!
BSHT
SEE, YOU CAN DO IT AFTER ALL!!
FWUMP
GAHK...

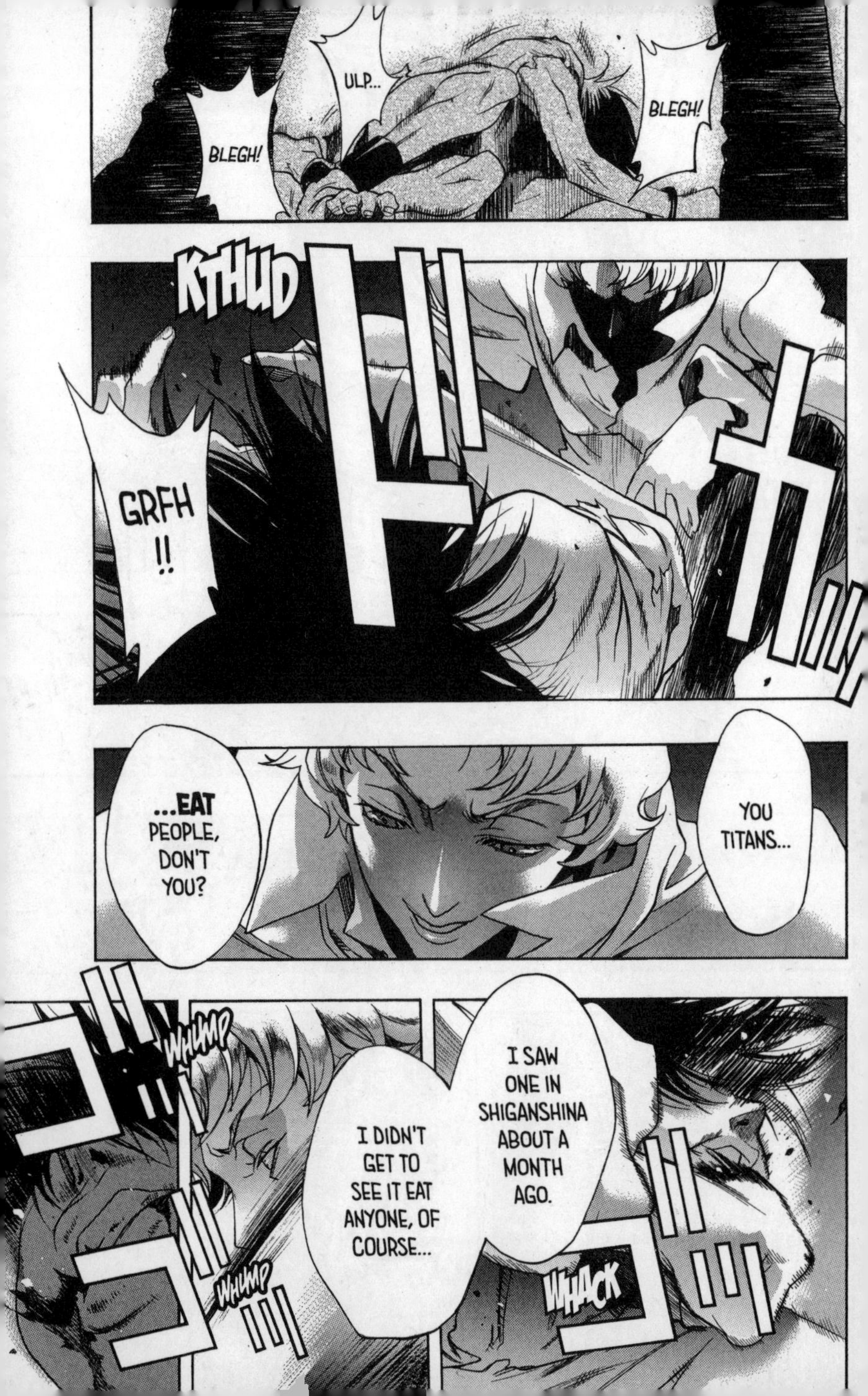
BLEGH!
ULP...
BLEGH!
KTHUD
GRFH !!
YOU TITANS...
...EAT PEOPLE, DON'T YOU?
I SAW ONE IN SHIGANSHINA ABOUT A MONTH AGO.
WHACK
WHUMP
I DIDN'T GET TO SEE IT EAT ANYONE, OF COURSE...
WHUMP

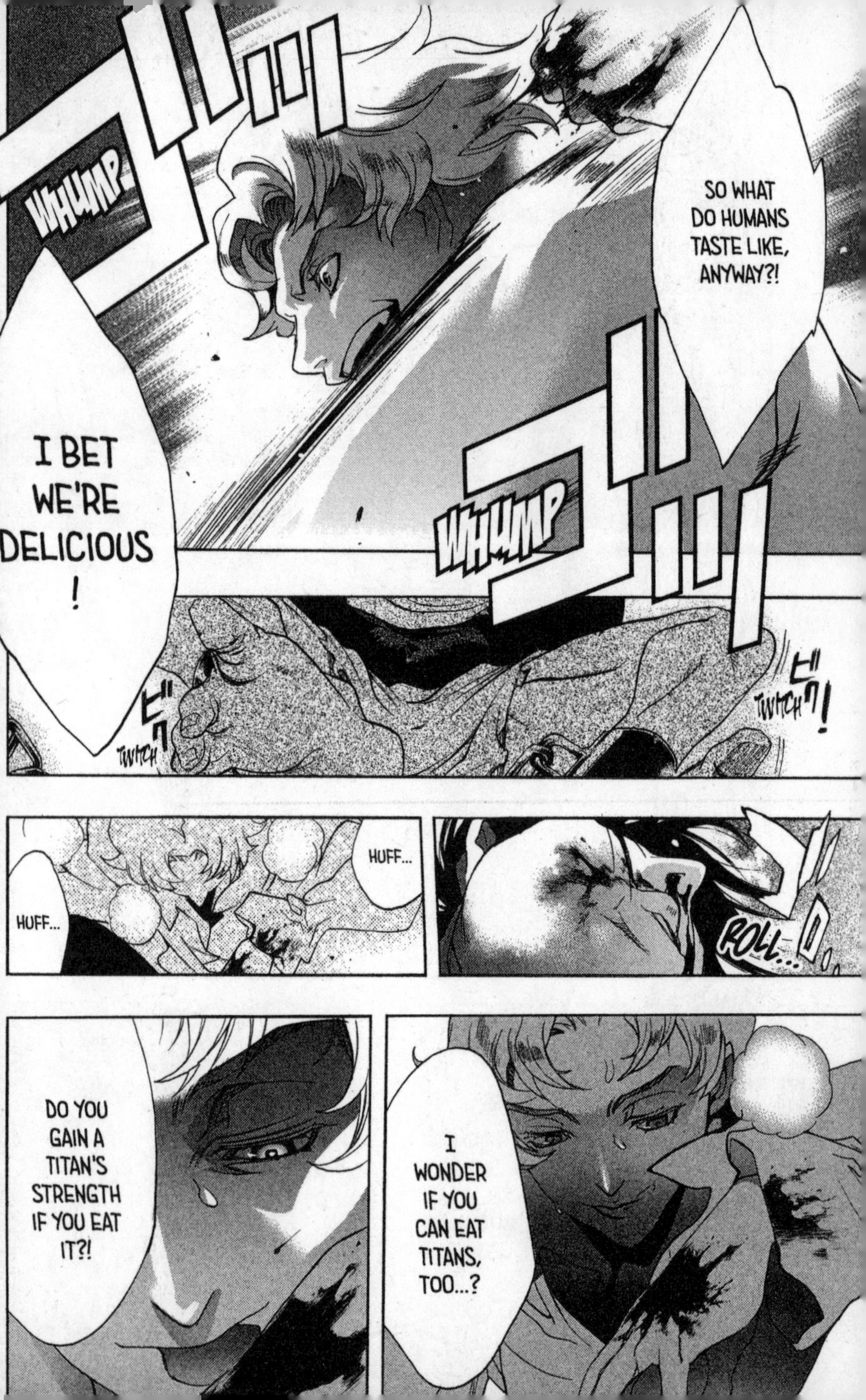

SO WHAT DO HUMANS TASTE LIKE, ANYWAY?!
WHUMP.
I BET WE'RE DELICIOUS!
WHUMP
TWITCH
TWITCH
ROLL...
HUFF...
HUFF...
I WONDER IF YOU CAN EAT TITANS, TOO...?
DO YOU GAIN A TITAN'S STRENGTH IF YOU EAT IT?!

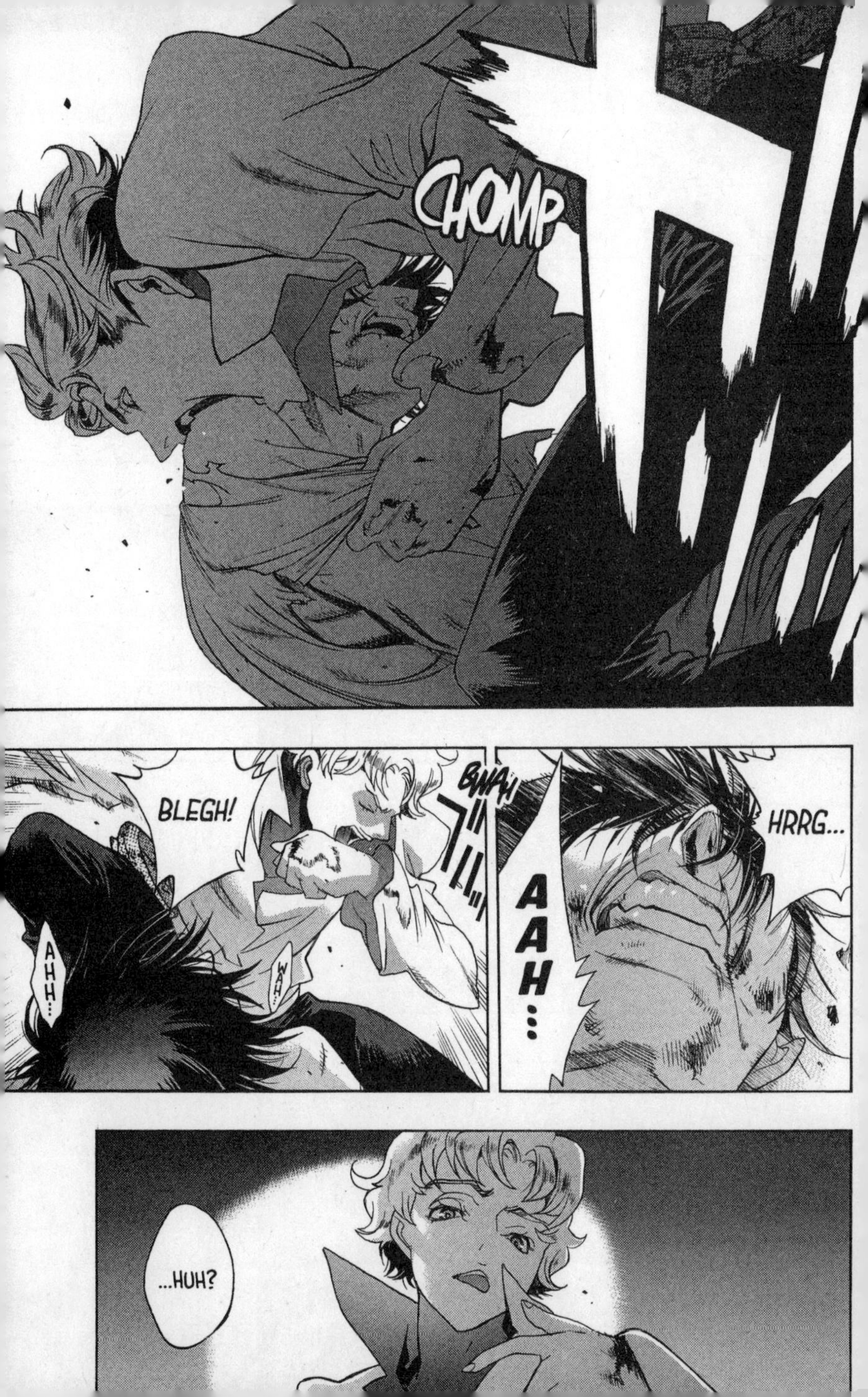
CHOMP
HRRG...
AAAH...
BWAH!
BLEGH!
WAH...
AHH...
...HUH?

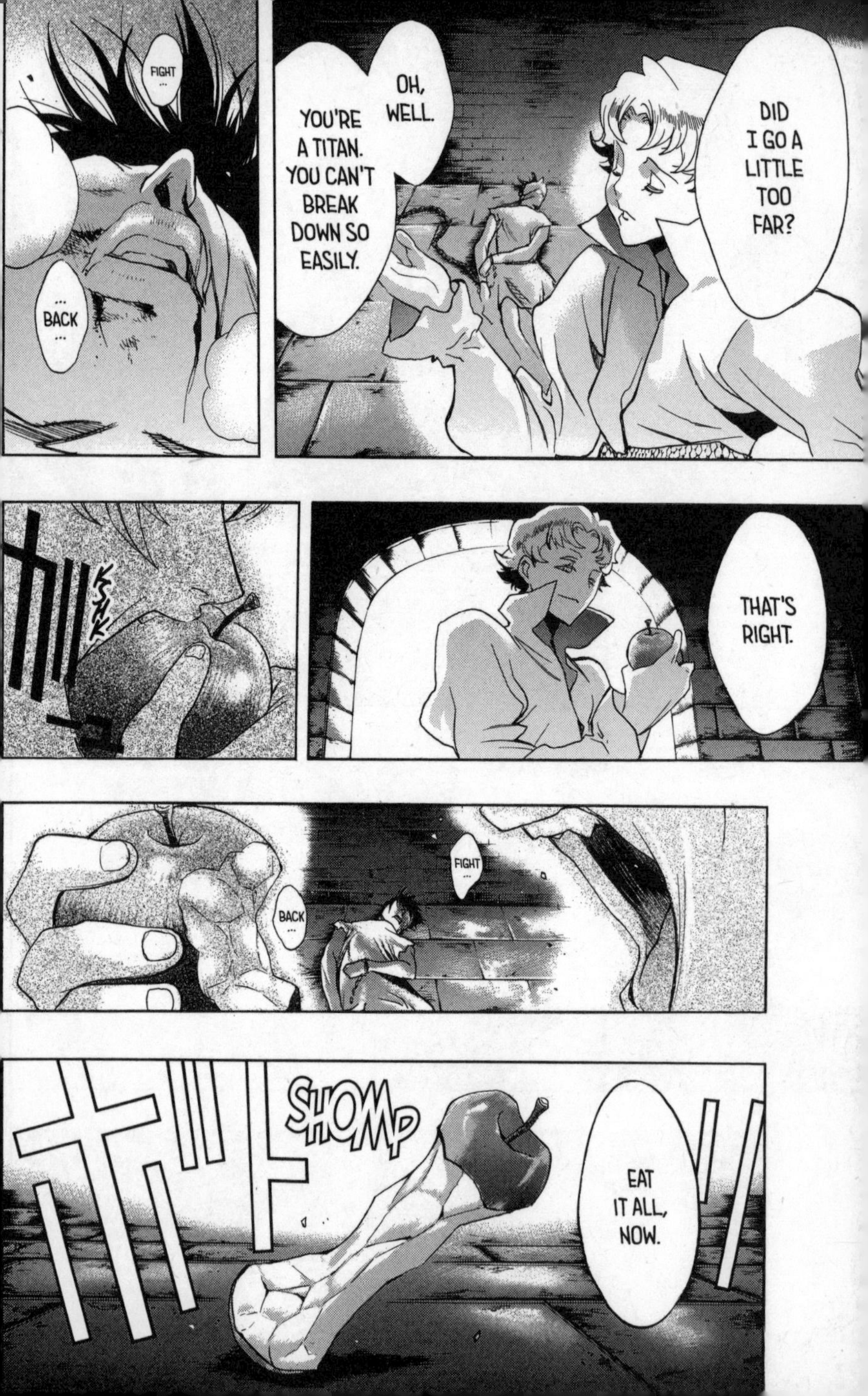
DID I GO A LITTLE TOO FAR?
OH, WELL.
YOU'RE A TITAN. YOU CAN'T BREAK DOWN SO EASILY.
FIGHT ...
... BACK ...
THAT'S RIGHT.
KSHK
FIGHT ...
BACK ...
EAT IT ALL, NOW.
SHOMP

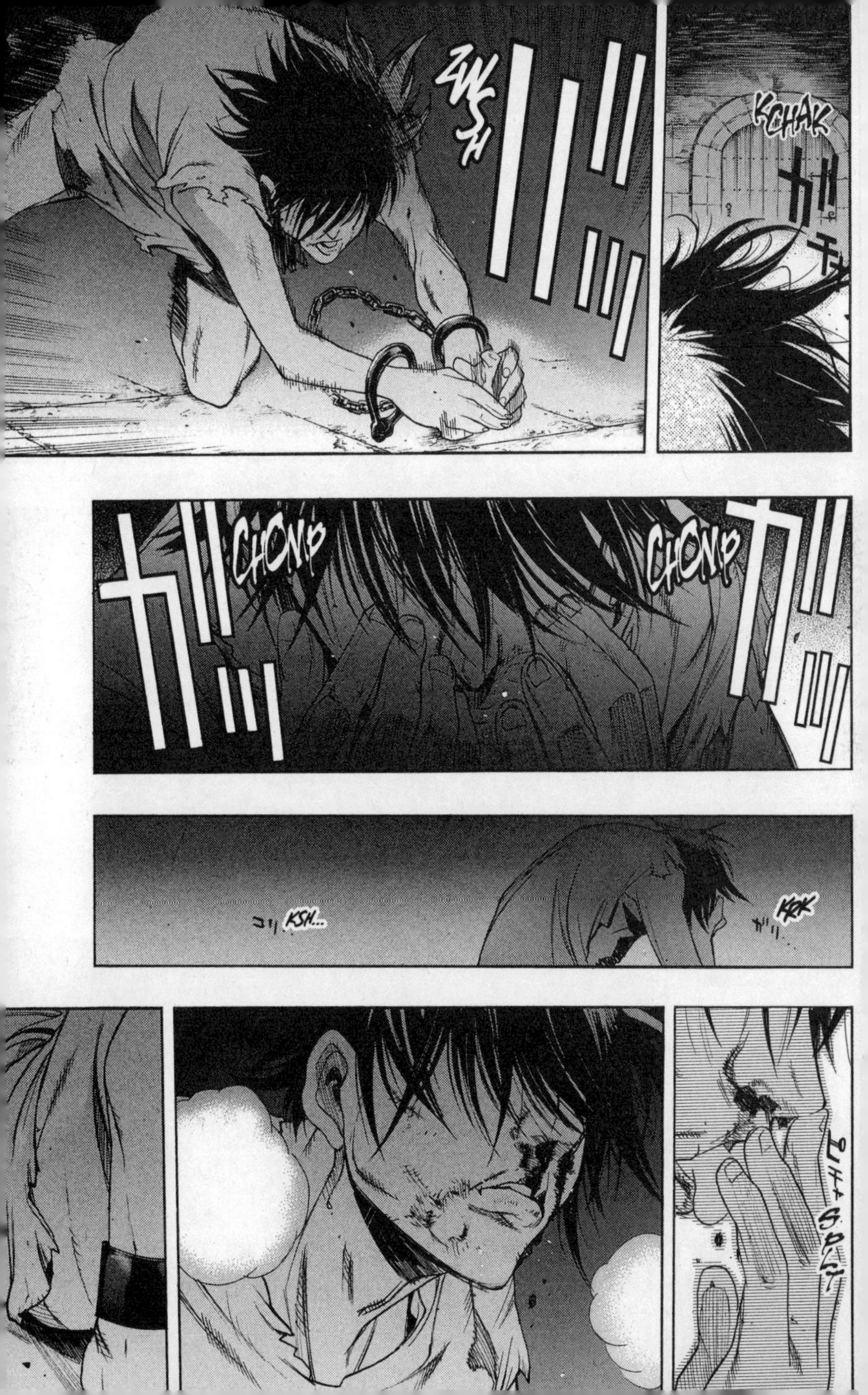
KCHAK
ZWISH
CHOMP
CHOMP
KRK
KSH...
SPLT

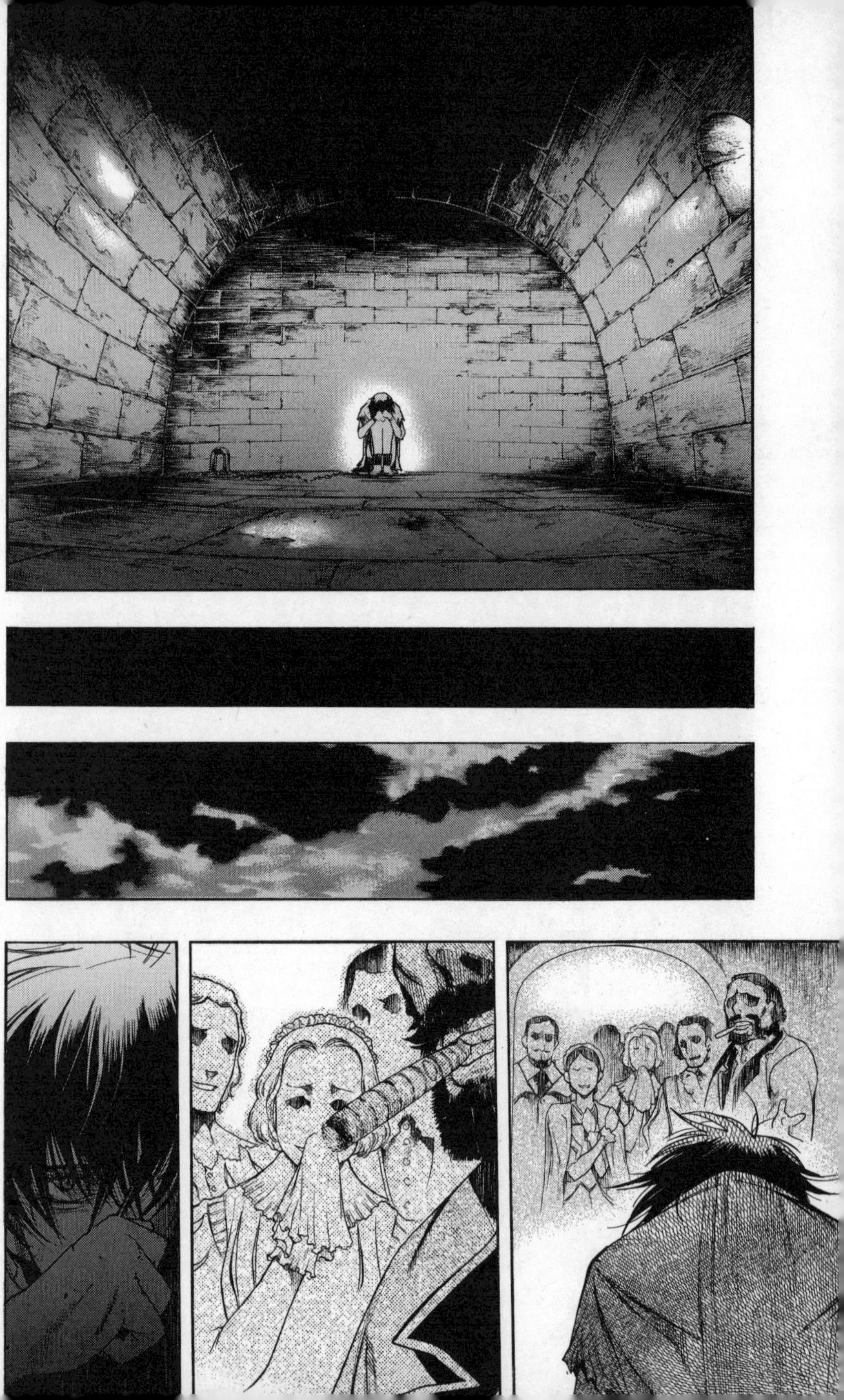

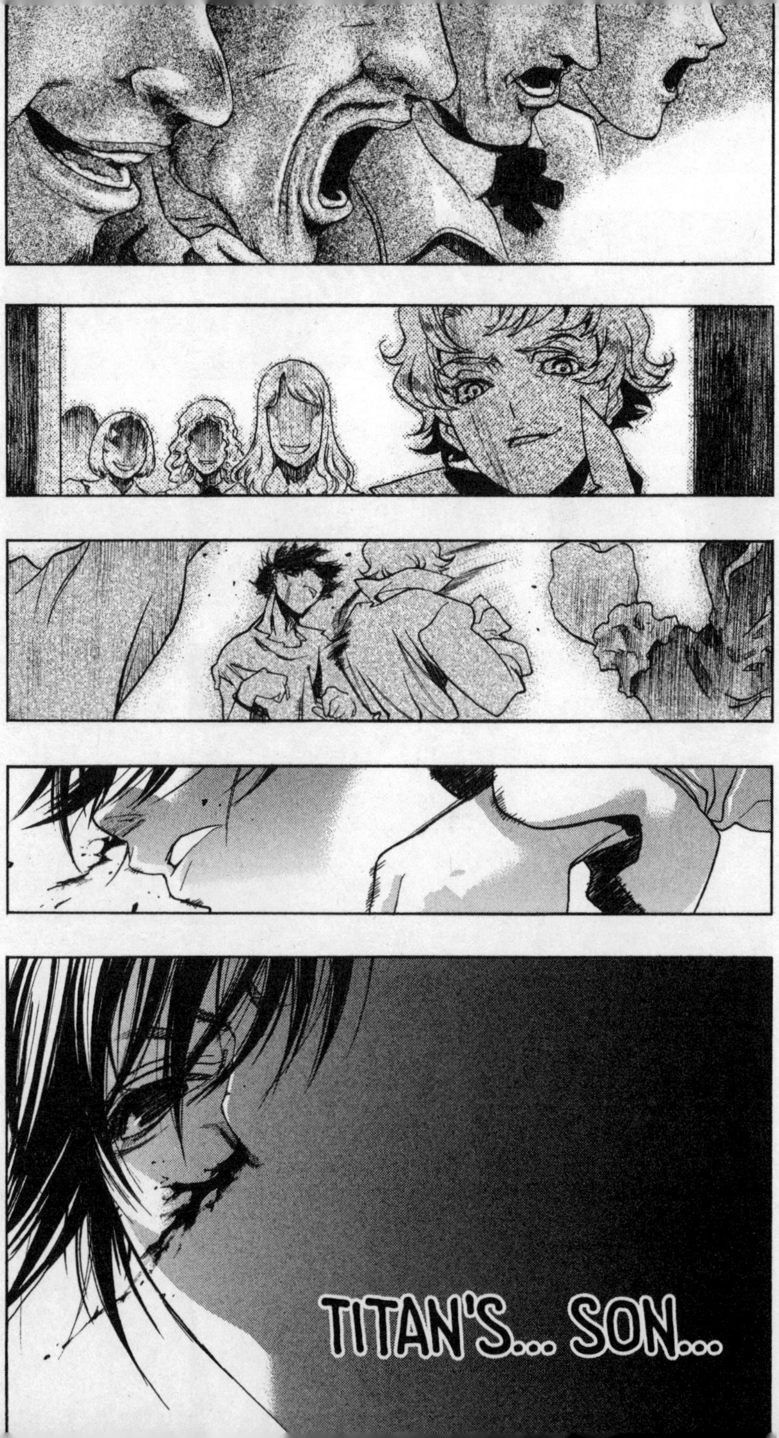
TITAN'S... SON...

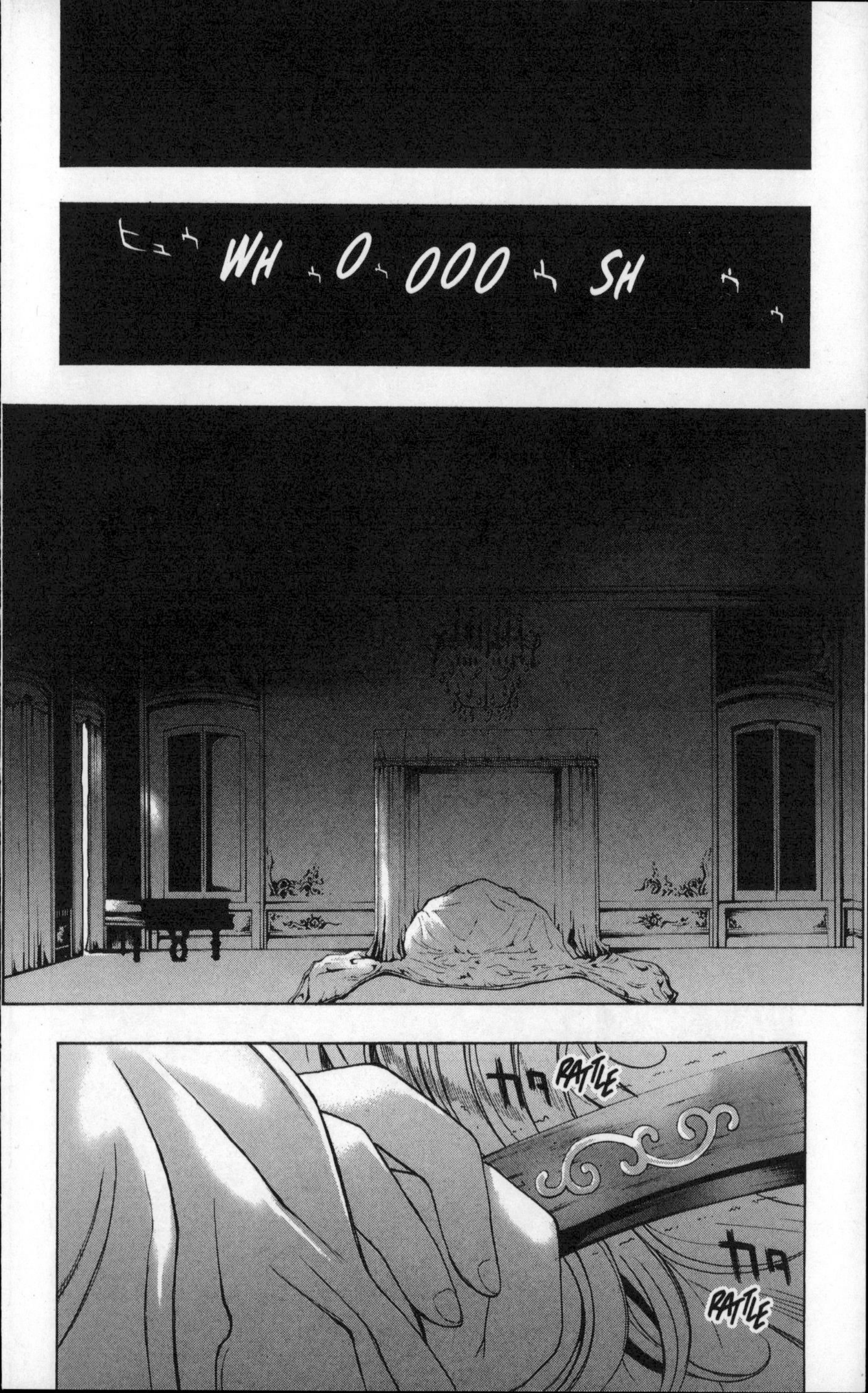
WH O OOO SH
カタ RATTLE
カタ RATTLE

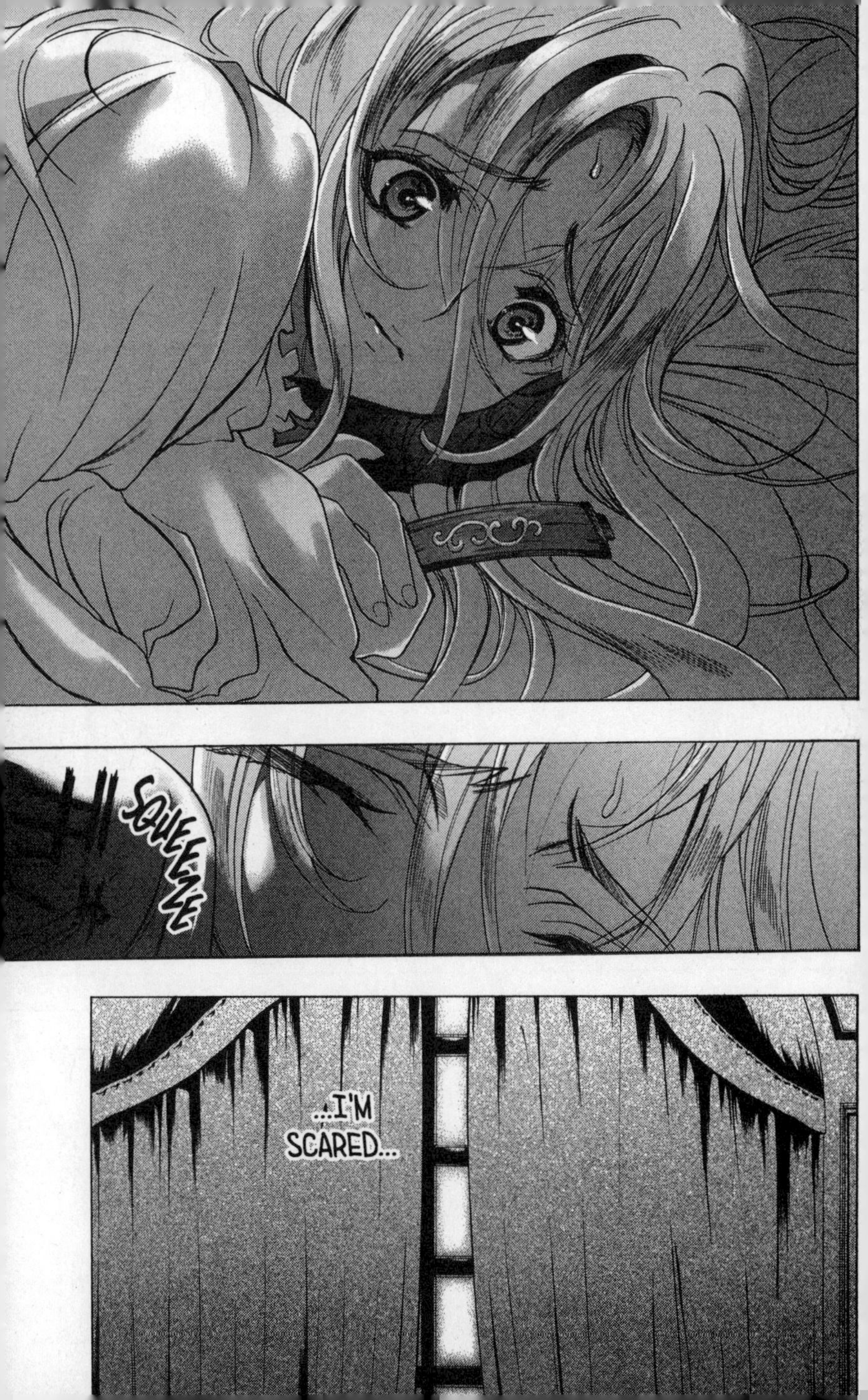
SQUEEZE
...I'M SCARED...

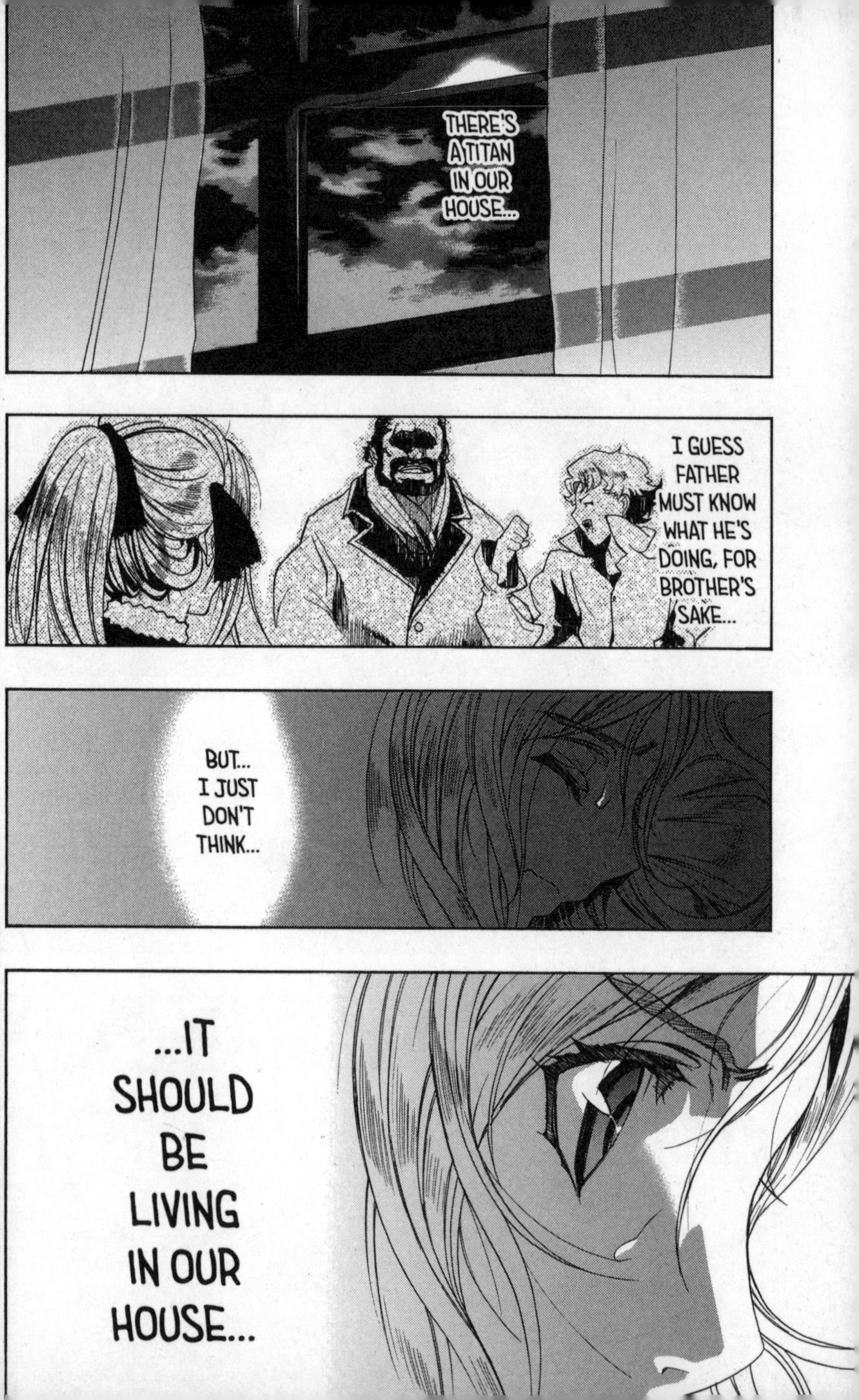
THERE'S A TITAN IN OUR HOUSE...
I GUESS FATHER MUST KNOW WHAT HE'S DOING, FOR BROTHER'S SAKE...
BUT... I JUST DON'T THINK...
...IT SHOULD BE LIVING IN OUR HOUSE...

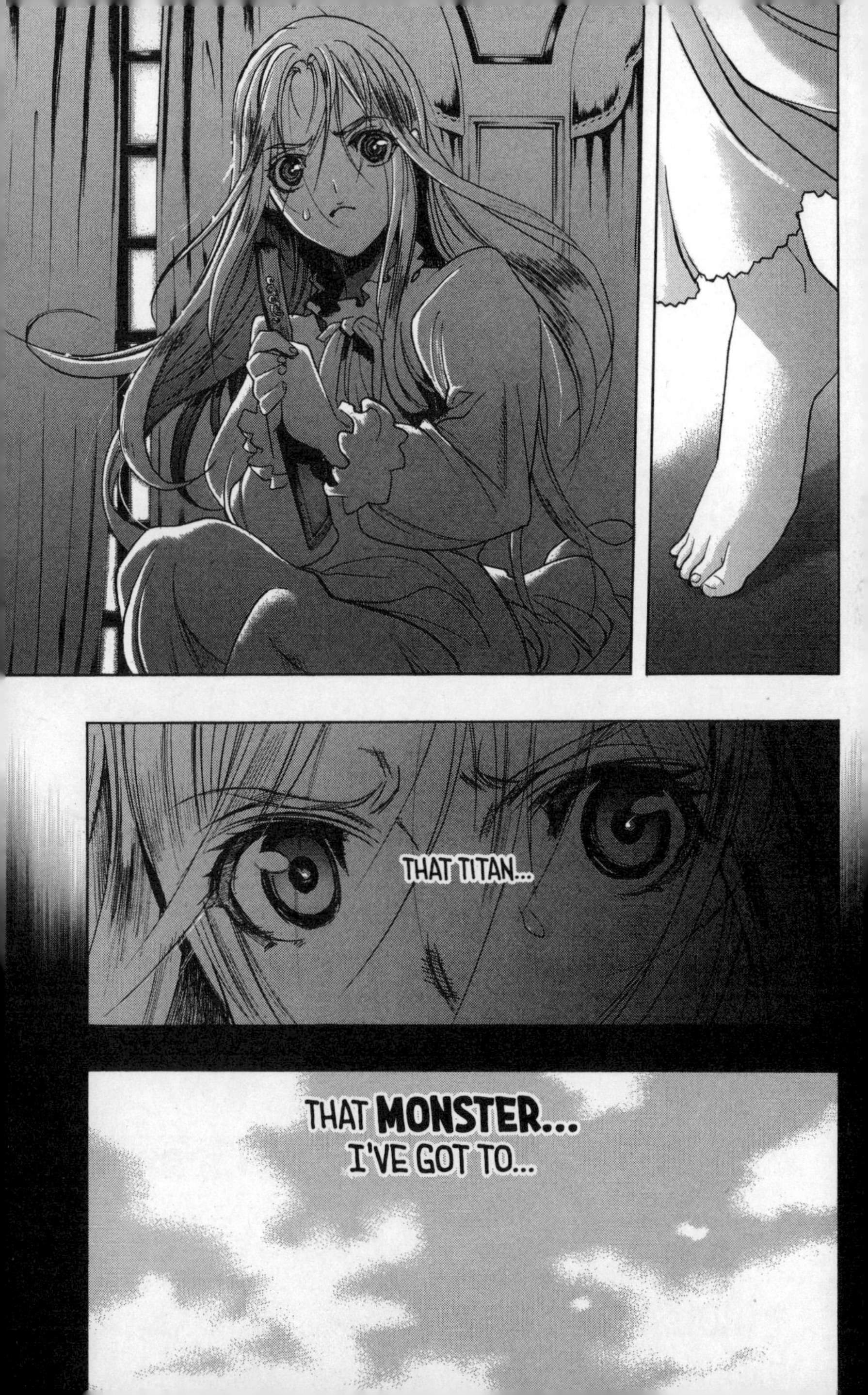
THAT TITAN...
THAT MONSTER...
I'VE GOT TO...

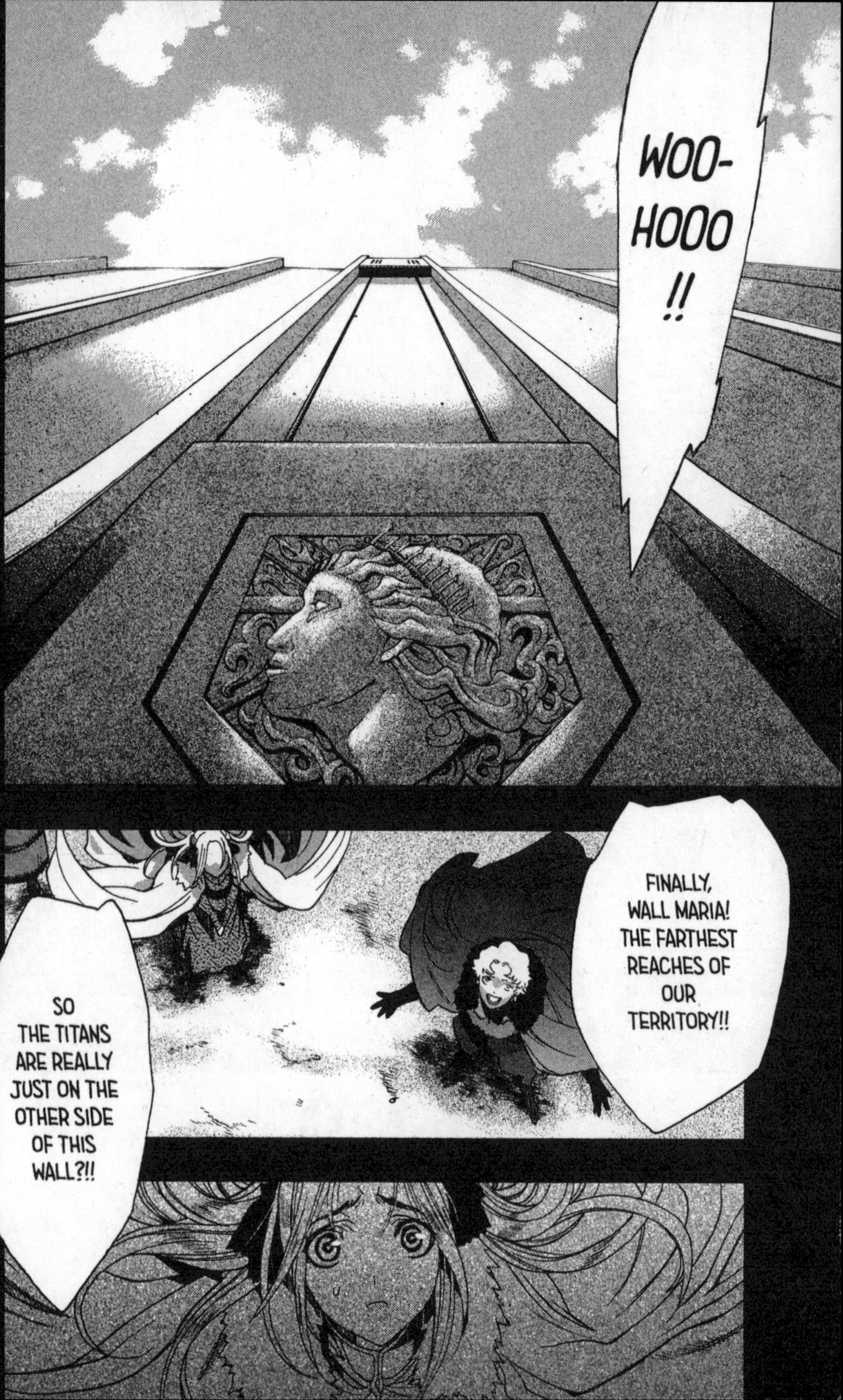
WOO-HOOO!!
FINALLY, WALL MARIA! THE FARTHEST REACHES OF OUR TERRITORY!!
SO THE TITANS ARE REALLY JUST ON THE OTHER SIDE OF THIS WALL?!!

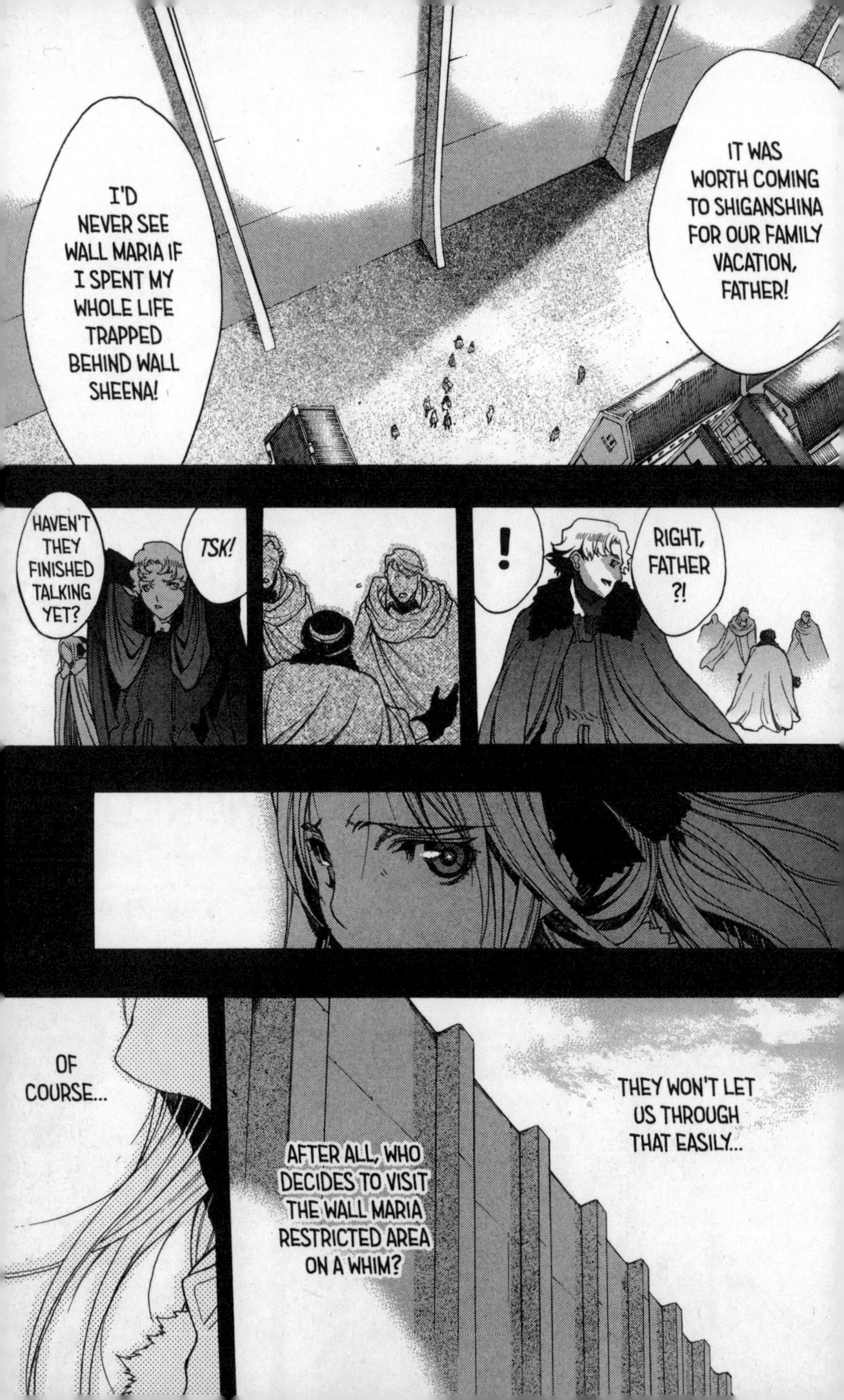
IT WAS WORTH COMING TO SHIGANSHINA FOR OUR FAMILY VACATION, FATHER!
I'D NEVER SEE WALL MARIA IF I SPENT MY WHOLE LIFE TRAPPED BEHIND WALL SHEENA!
RIGHT, FATHER?!
!
TSK!
HAVEN'T THEY FINISHED TALKING YET?
THEY WON'T LET US THROUGH THAT EASILY...
AFTER ALL, WHO DECIDES TO VISIT THE WALL MARIA RESTRICTED AREA ON A WHIM?
OF COURSE...

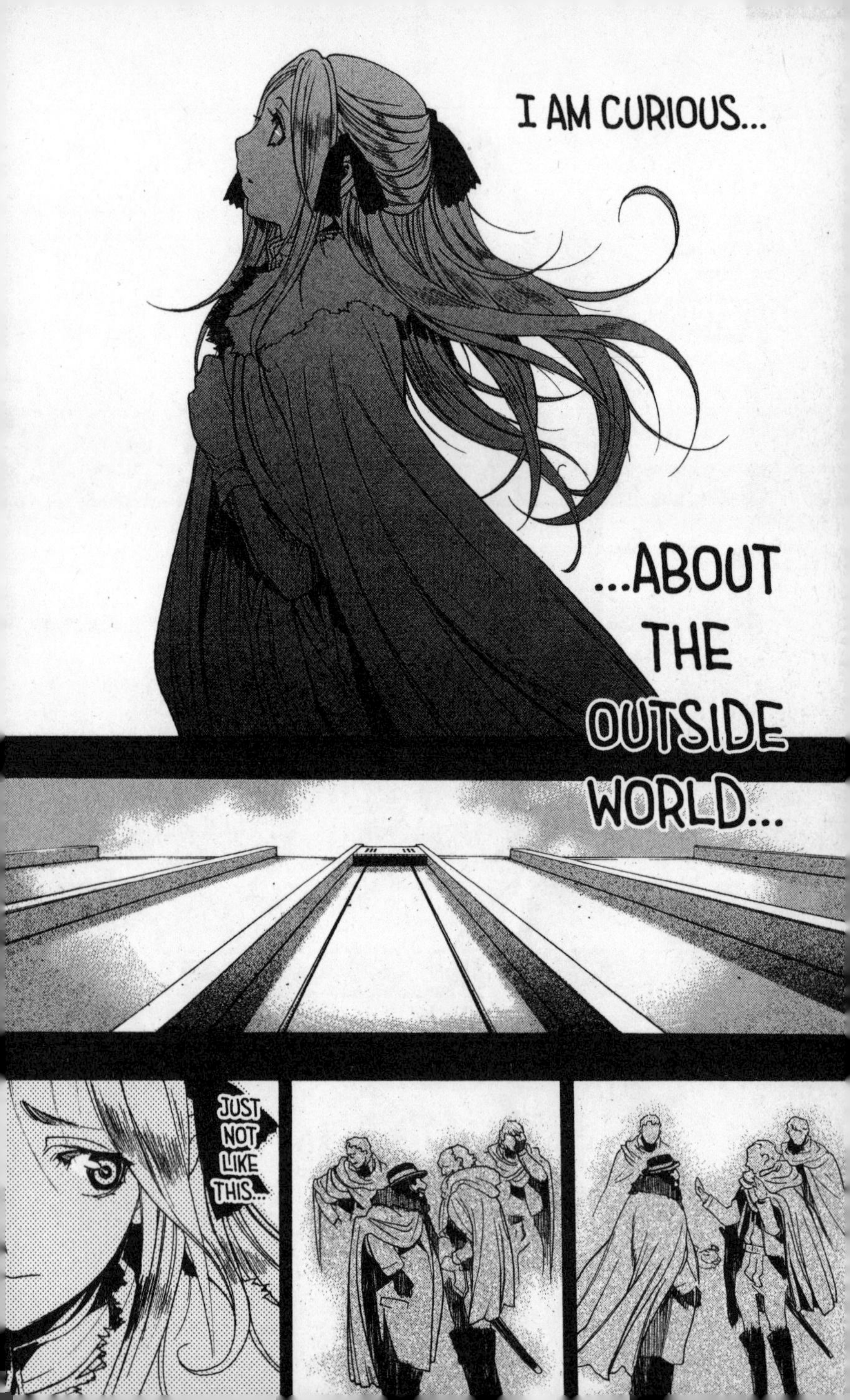
I AM CURIOUS...
...ABOUT THE OUTSIDE WORLD...
JUST NOT LIKE THIS...

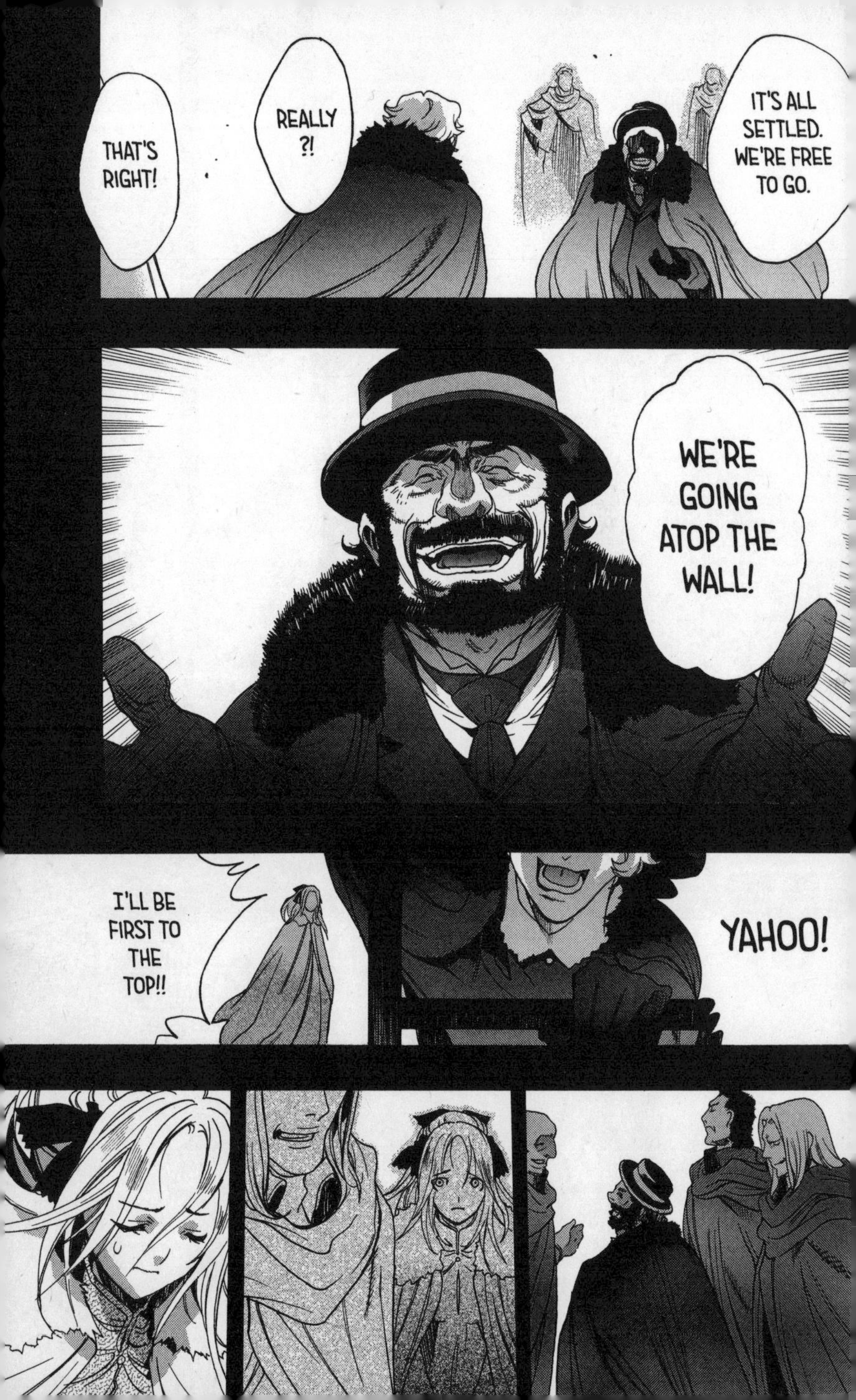
IT'S ALL SETTLED. WE'RE FREE TO GO.
REALLY ?!
THAT'S RIGHT!
WE'RE GOING ATOP THE WALL!
YAHOO!
I'LL BE FIRST TO THE TOP!!

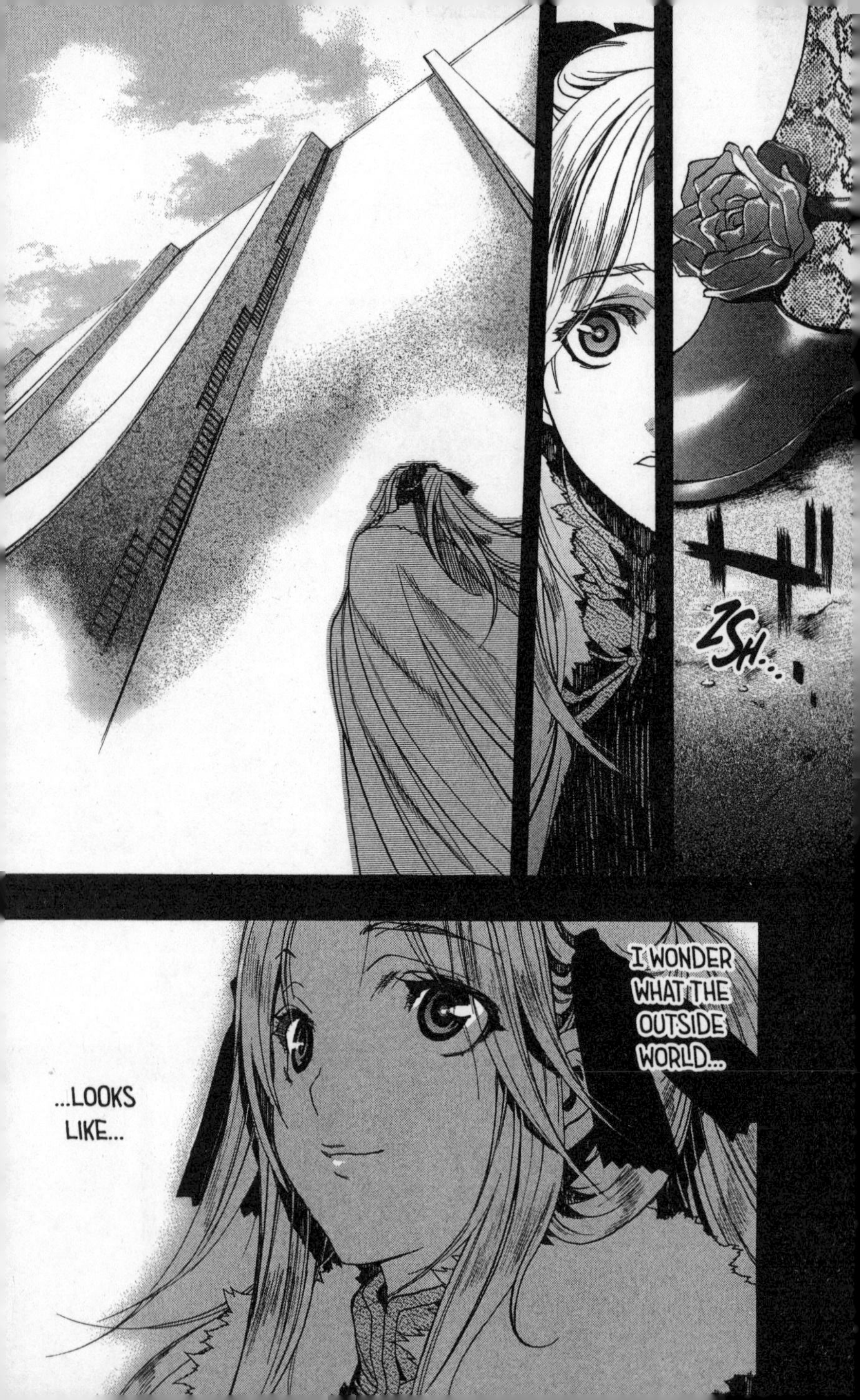
ZSH...
I WONDER WHAT THE OUTSIDE WORLD...
...LOOKS LIKE...

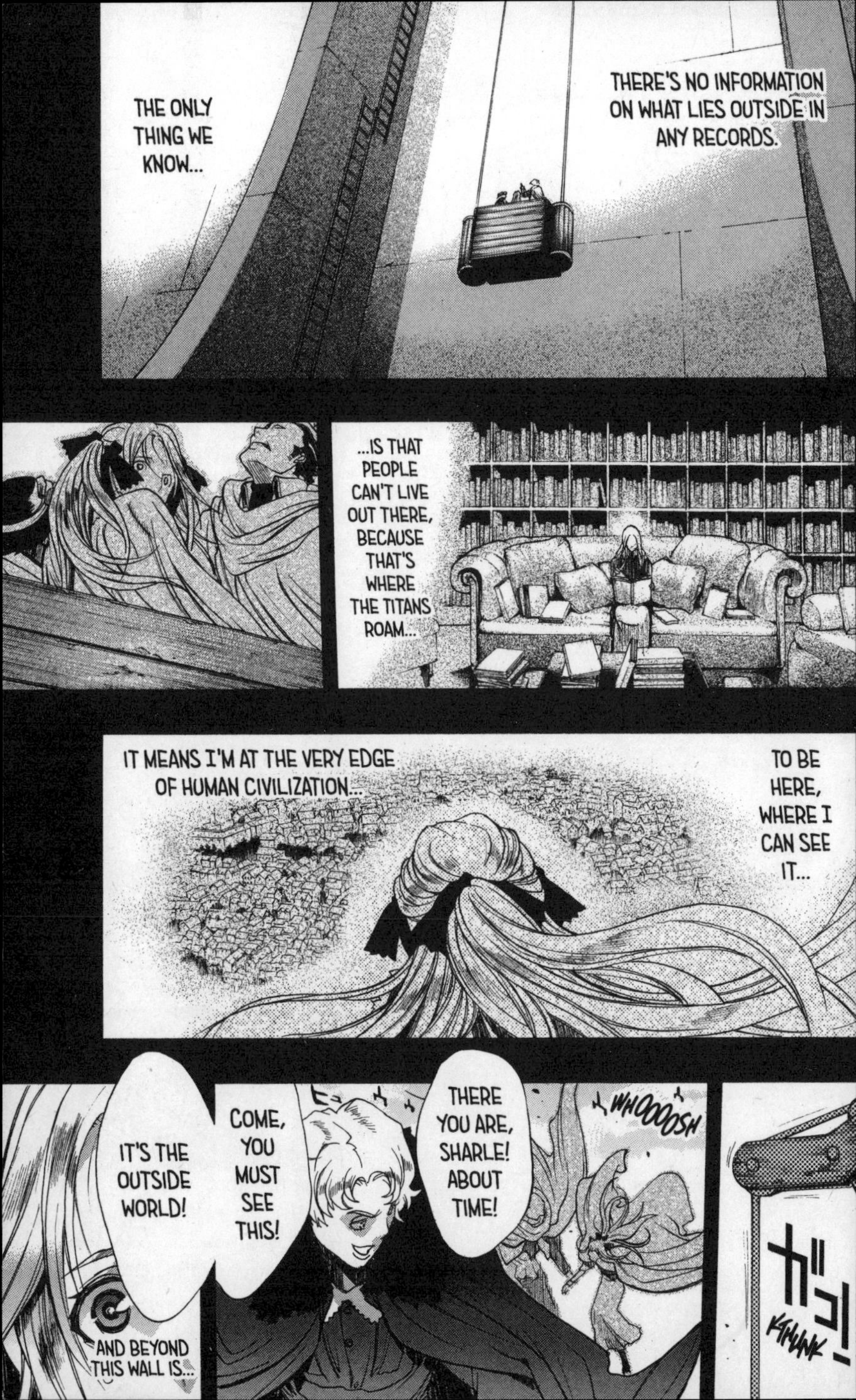
THERE'S NO INFORMATION ON WHAT LIES OUTSIDE IN ANY RECORDS.
THE ONLY THING WE KNOW...
...IS THAT PEOPLE CAN'T LIVE OUT THERE, BECAUSE THAT'S WHERE THE TITANS ROAM...
TO BE HERE, WHERE I CAN SEE IT...
IT MEANS I'M AT THE VERY EDGE OF HUMAN CIVILIZATION...
ガコ!
KACHUNK
WHOOOOSH
THERE YOU ARE, SHARLE! ABOUT TIME!
COME, YOU MUST SEE THIS!
IT'S THE OUTSIDE WORLD!
AND BEYOND THIS WALL IS...

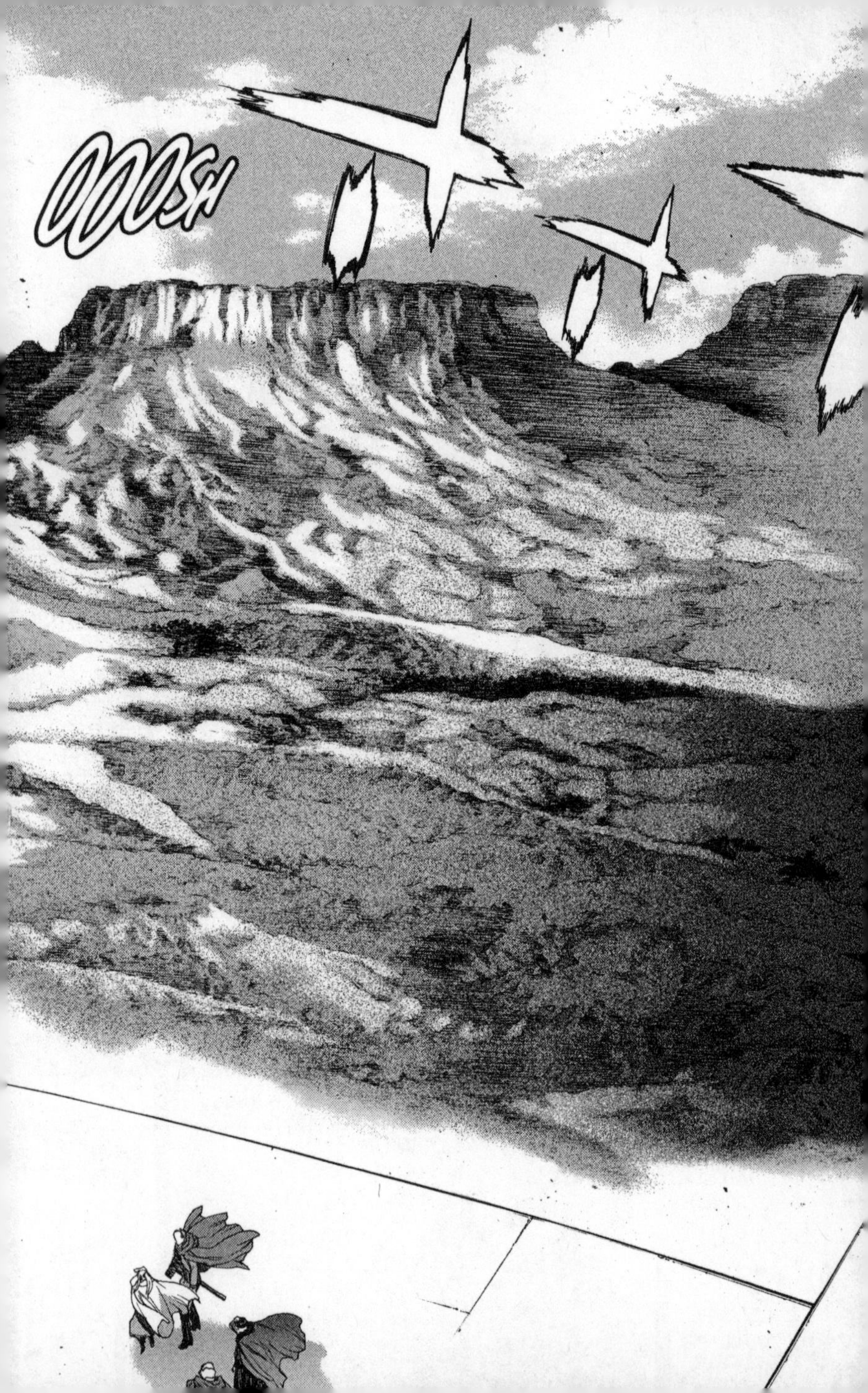
OOOSH

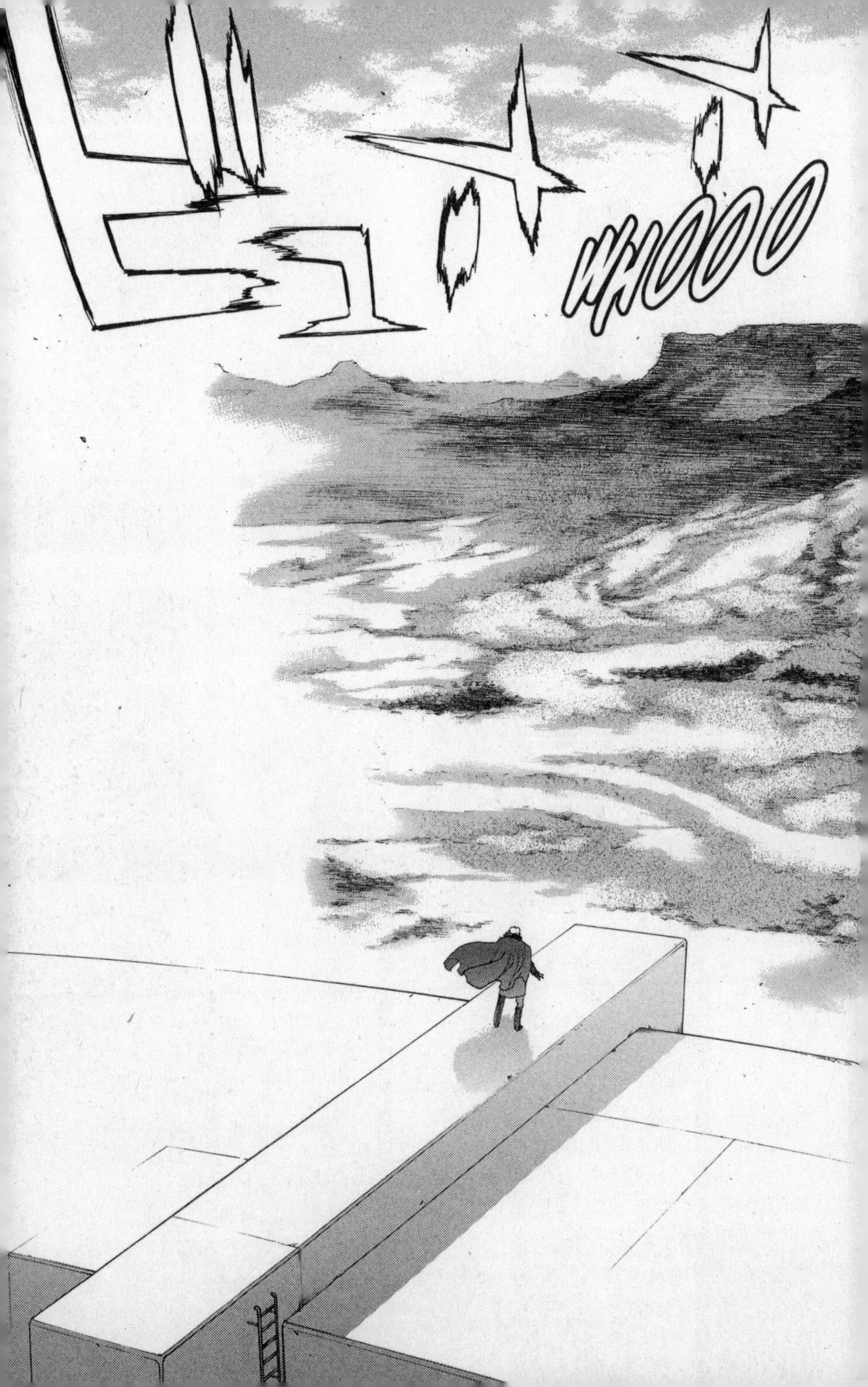
WHOOOO

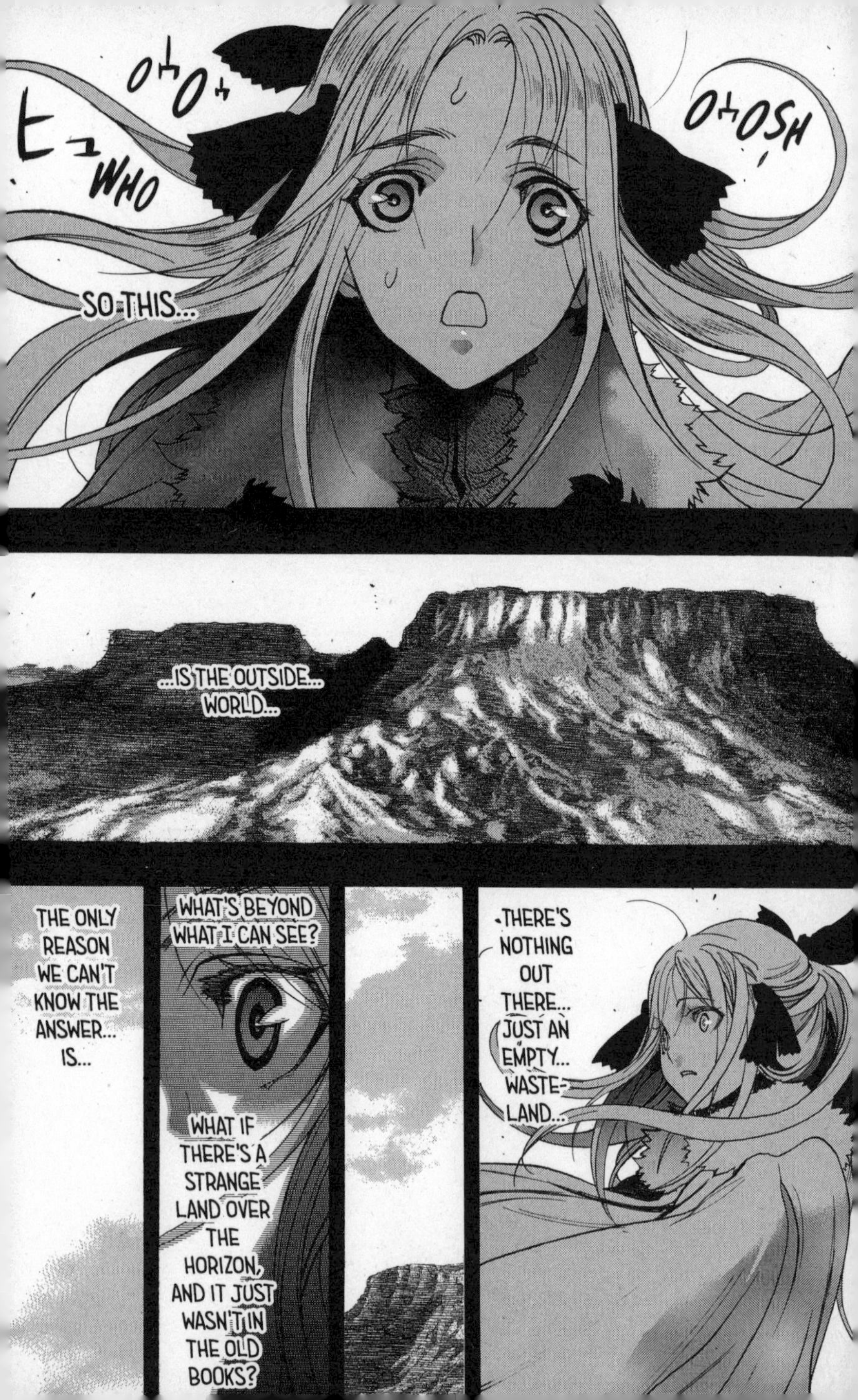
WHO
OSH
SO THIS...
...IS THE OUTSIDE... WORLD...
THERE'S NOTHING OUT THERE... JUST AN EMPTY... WASTE-LAND...
WHAT'S BEYOND WHAT I CAN SEE?
WHAT IF THERE'S A STRANGE LAND OVER THE HORIZON, AND IT JUST WASN'T IN THE OLD BOOKS?
THE ONLY REASON WE CAN'T KNOW THE ANSWER... IS...

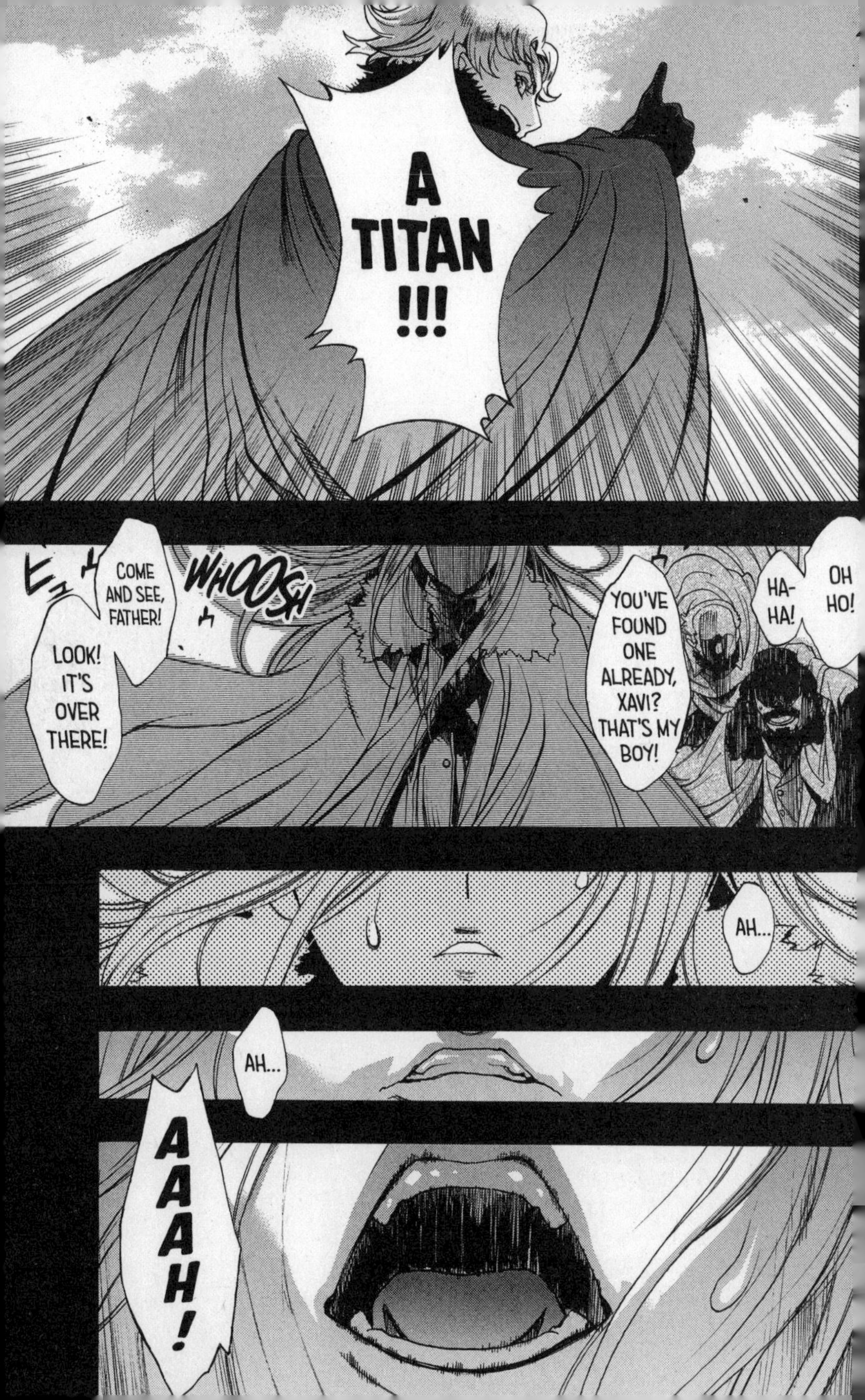
A TITAN!!!
OH HO!
HA-HA!
YOU'VE FOUND ONE ALREADY, XAVI? THAT'S MY BOY!
WHOOSH
COME AND SEE, FATHER!
LOOK! IT'S OVER THERE!
AH...
AH...
AAAAH!

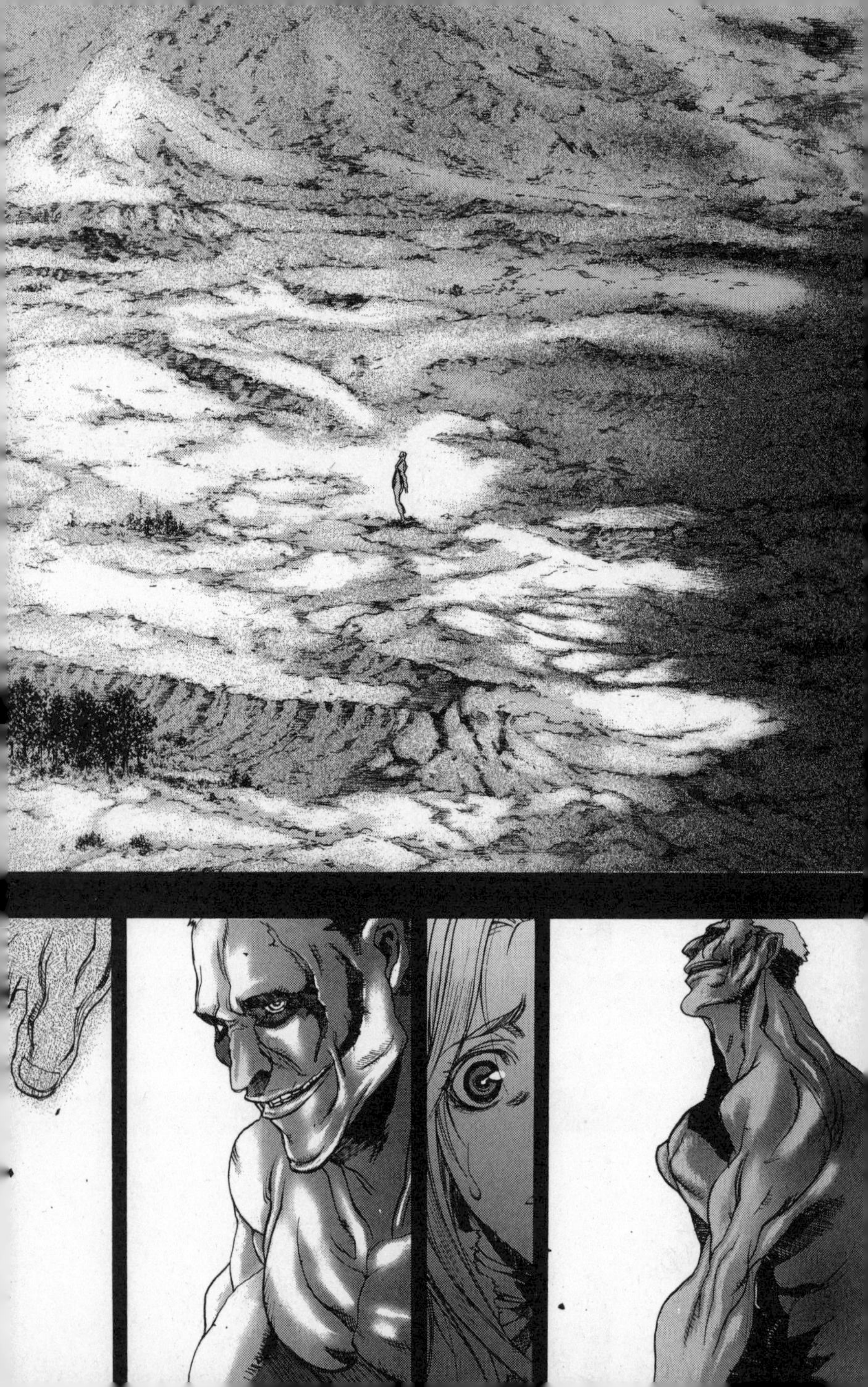

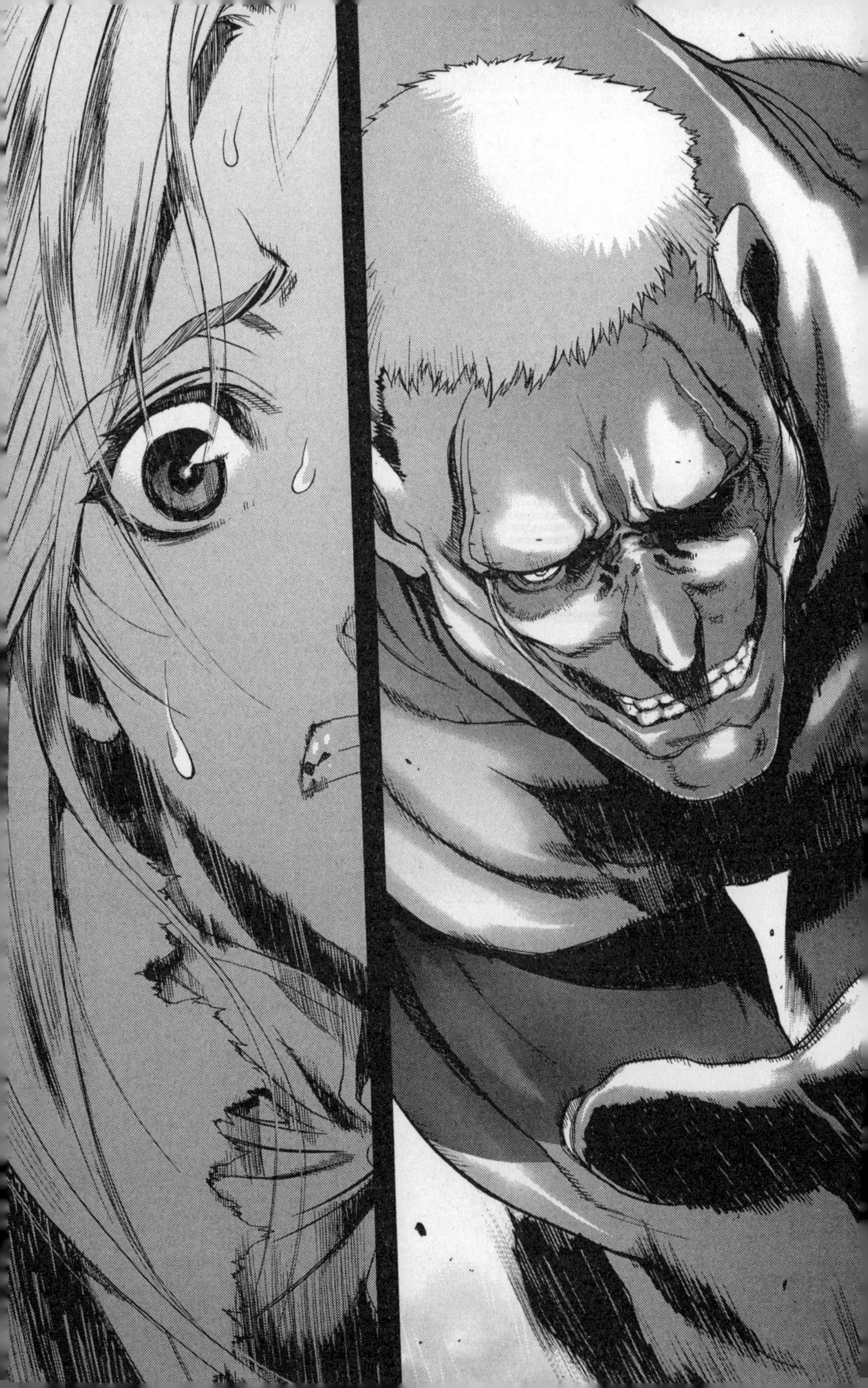

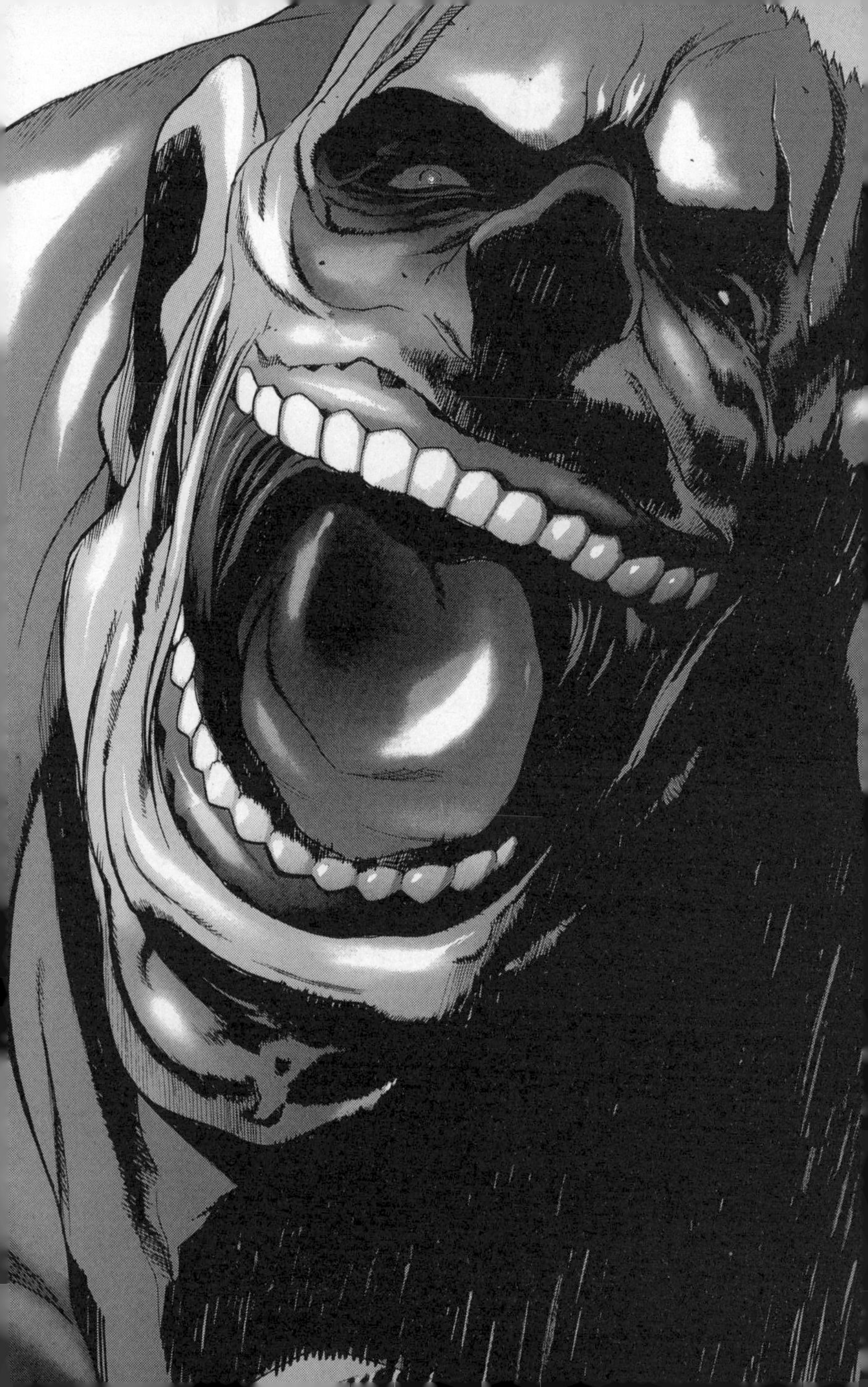

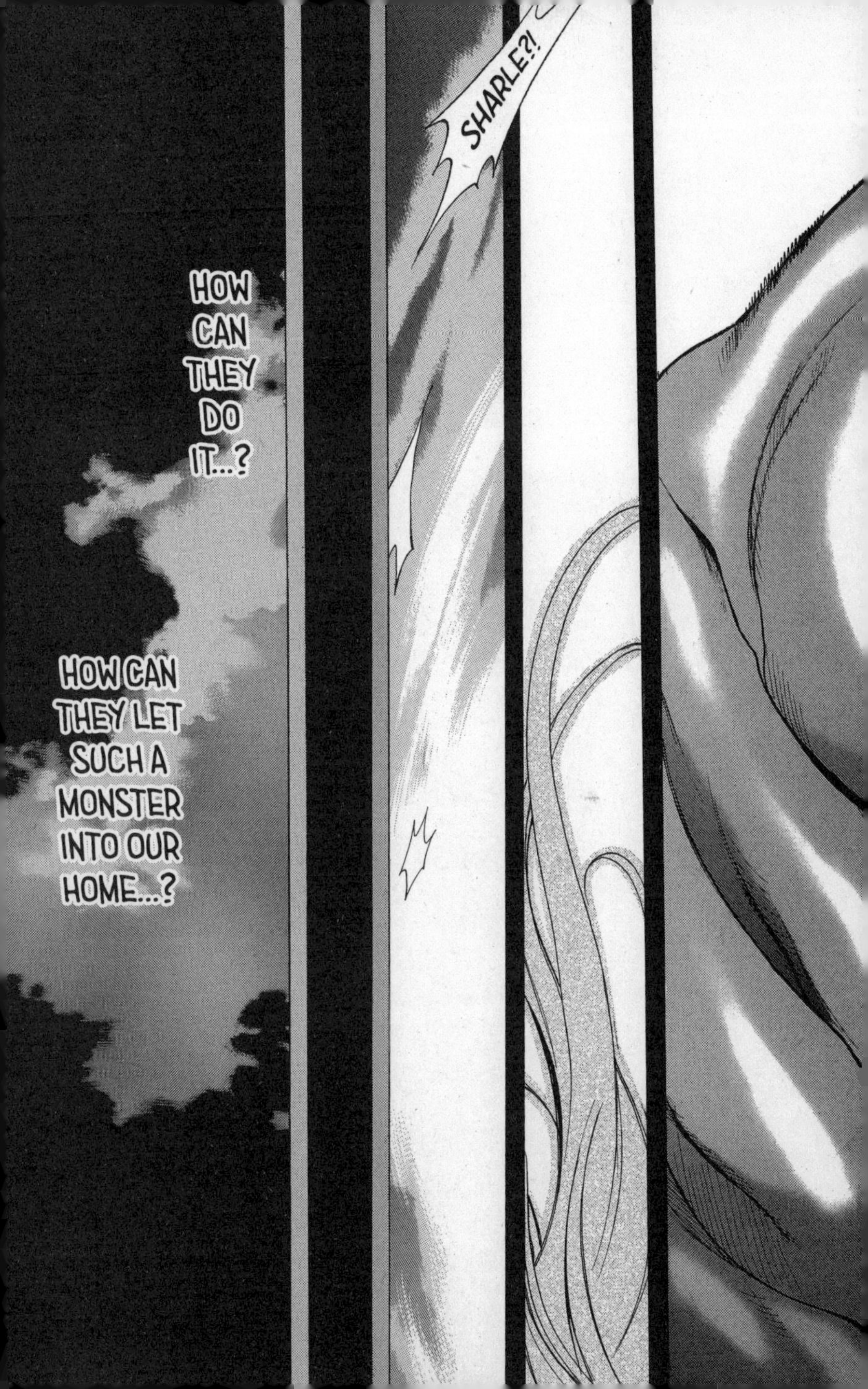
SHARLE?!
HOW CAN THEY DO IT...?
HOW CAN THEY LET SUCH A MONSTER INTO OUR HOME...?

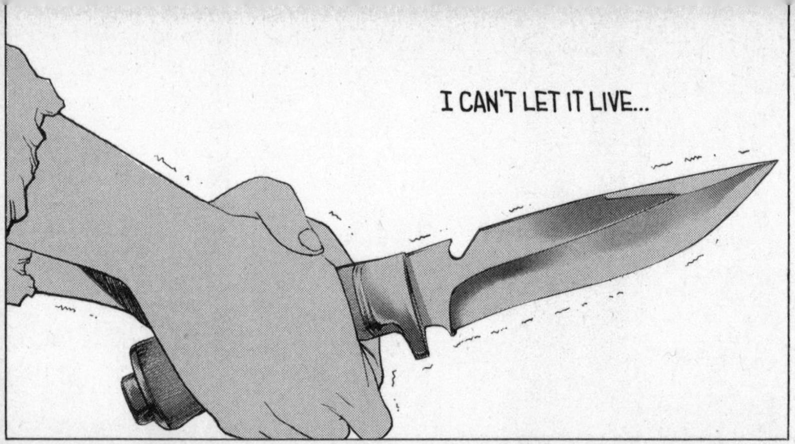
I CAN'T LET IT LIVE...

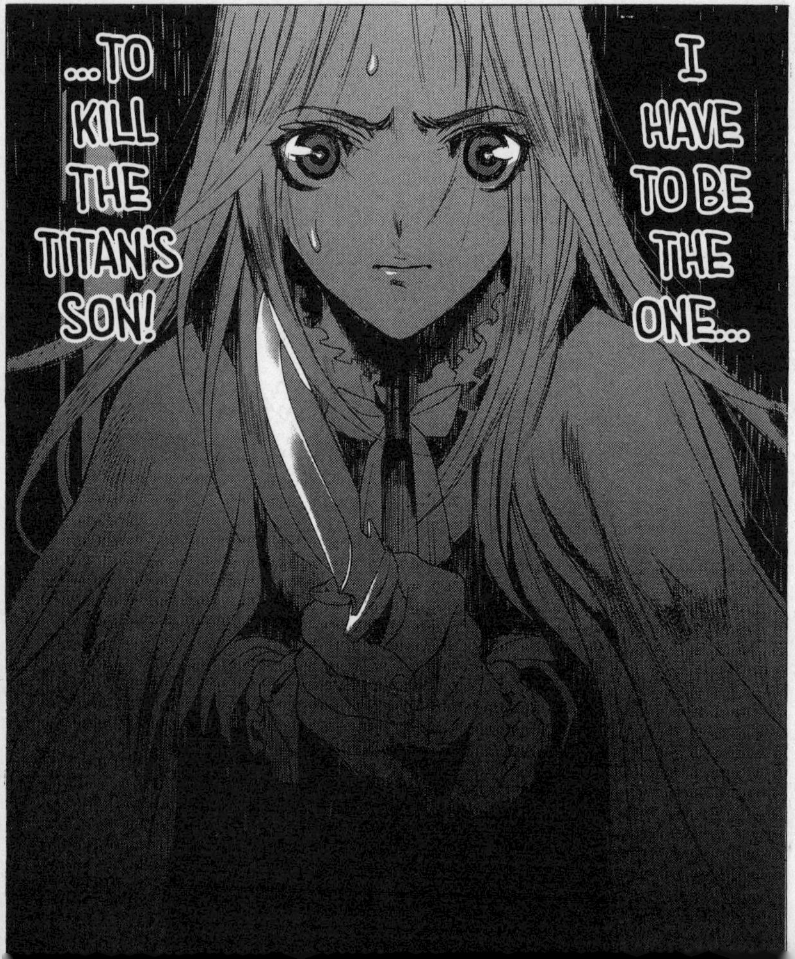
I HAVE TO BE THE ONE...
...TO KILL THE TITAN'S SON!

Chapter 2: Her Determination END

ATTACK on TITAN

BEFORE THE FALL

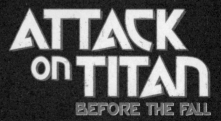

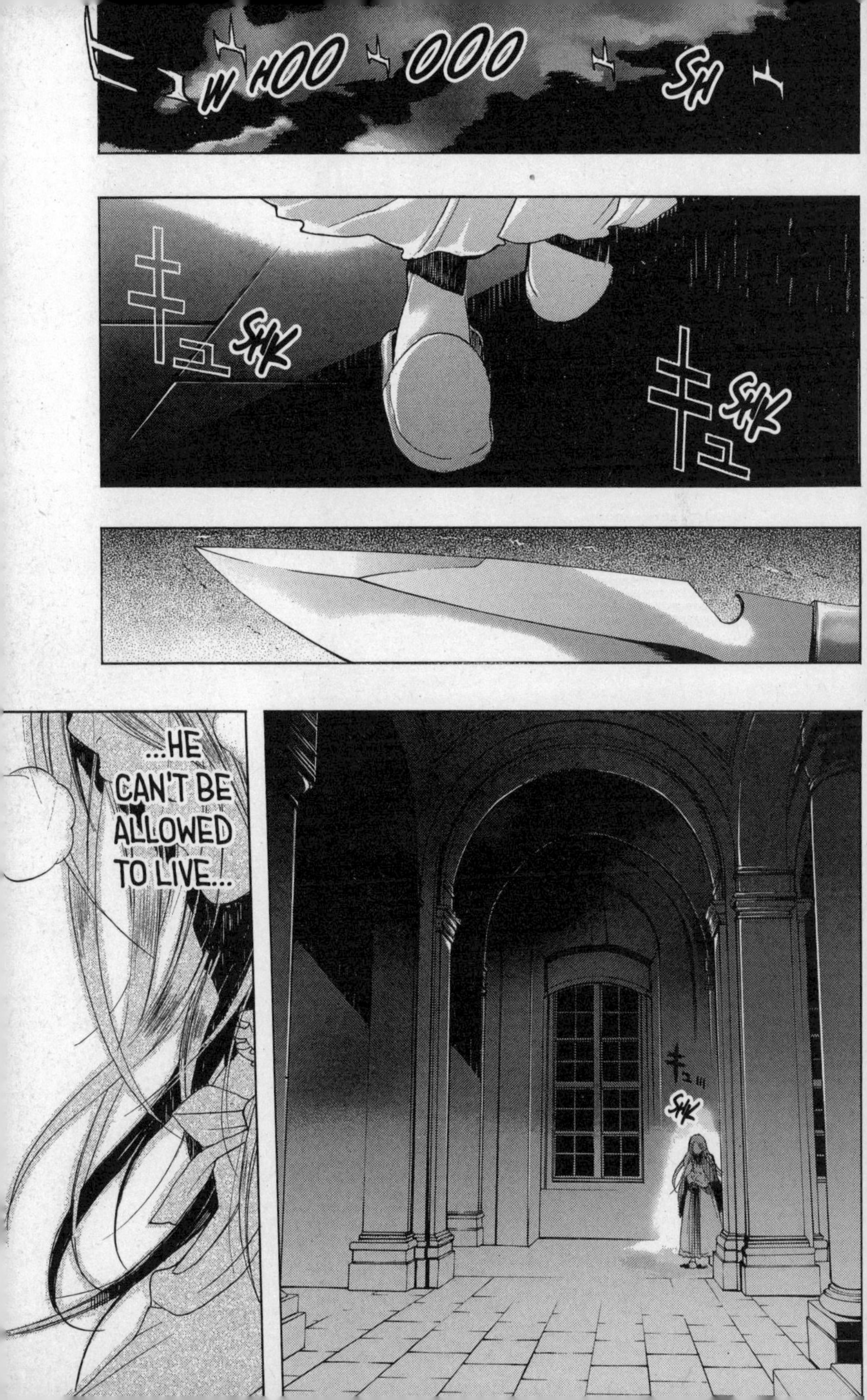
WHOOOOOSH
SHK
SHK
SHK
...HE CAN'T BE ALLOWED TO LIVE...

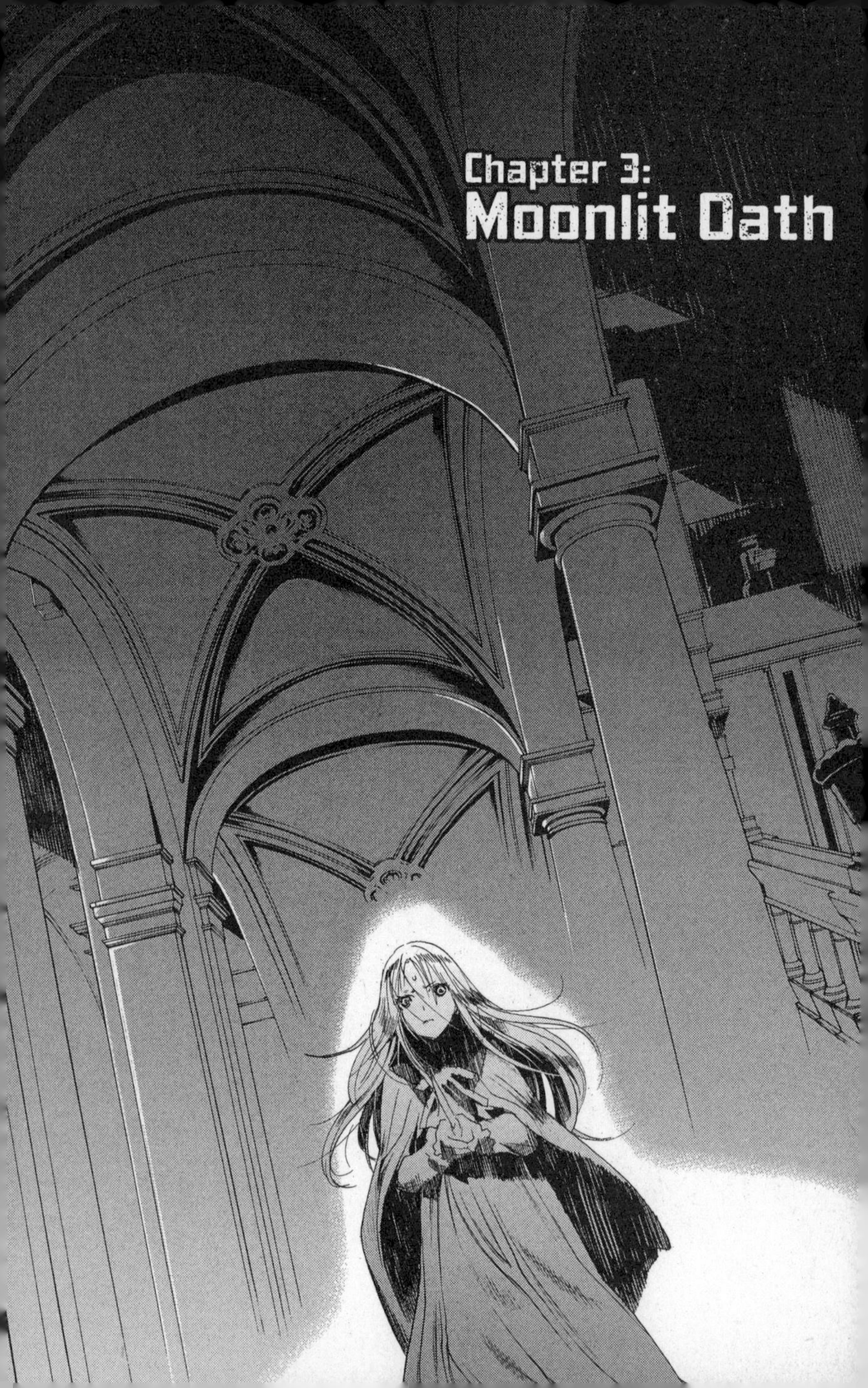
Chapter 3:
Moonlit Oath

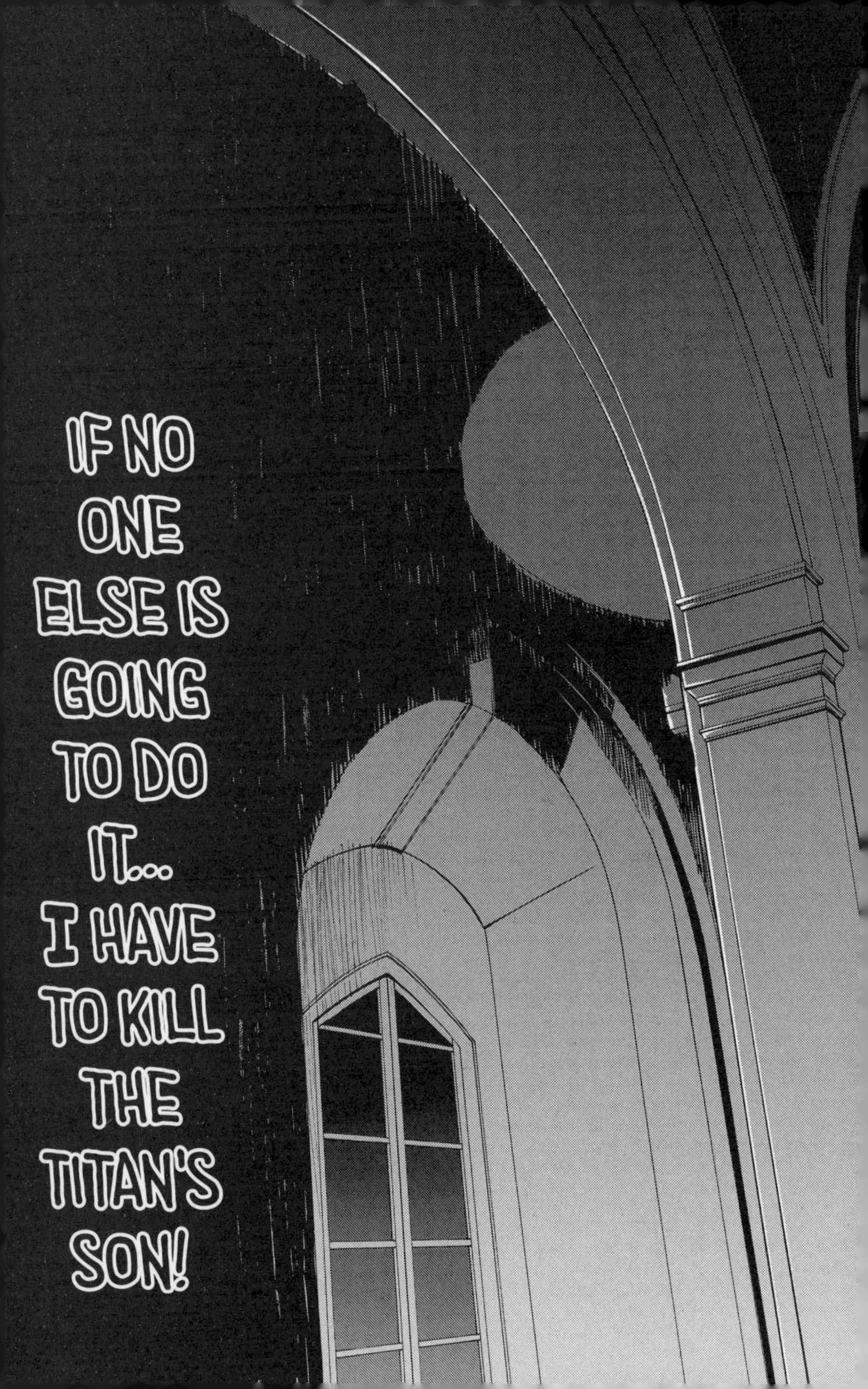
IF NO ONE ELSE IS GOING TO DO IT... I HAVE TO KILL THE TITAN'S SON!

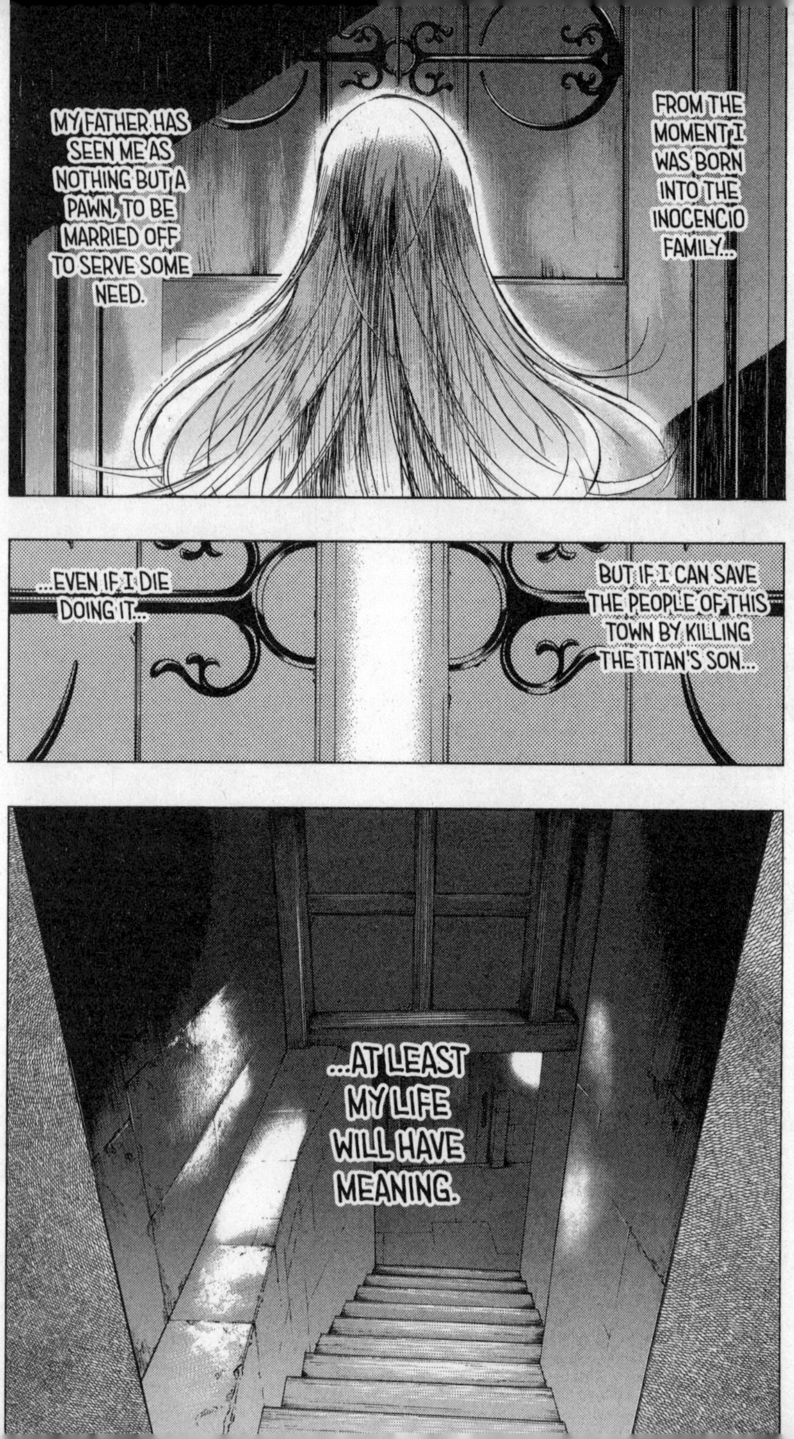
FROM THE MOMENT I WAS BORN INTO THE INOCENCIO FAMILY...
MY FATHER HAS SEEN ME AS NOTHING BUT A PAWN, TO BE MARRIED OFF TO SERVE SOME NEED.
BUT IF I CAN SAVE THE PEOPLE OF THIS TOWN BY KILLING THE TITAN'S SON...
...EVEN IF I DIE DOING IT...
...AT LEAST MY LIFE WILL HAVE MEANING.

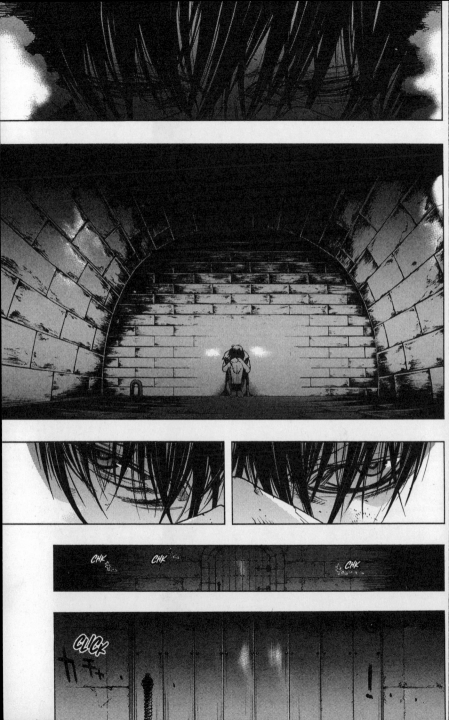

CHK   CHK

CHK

CLICK

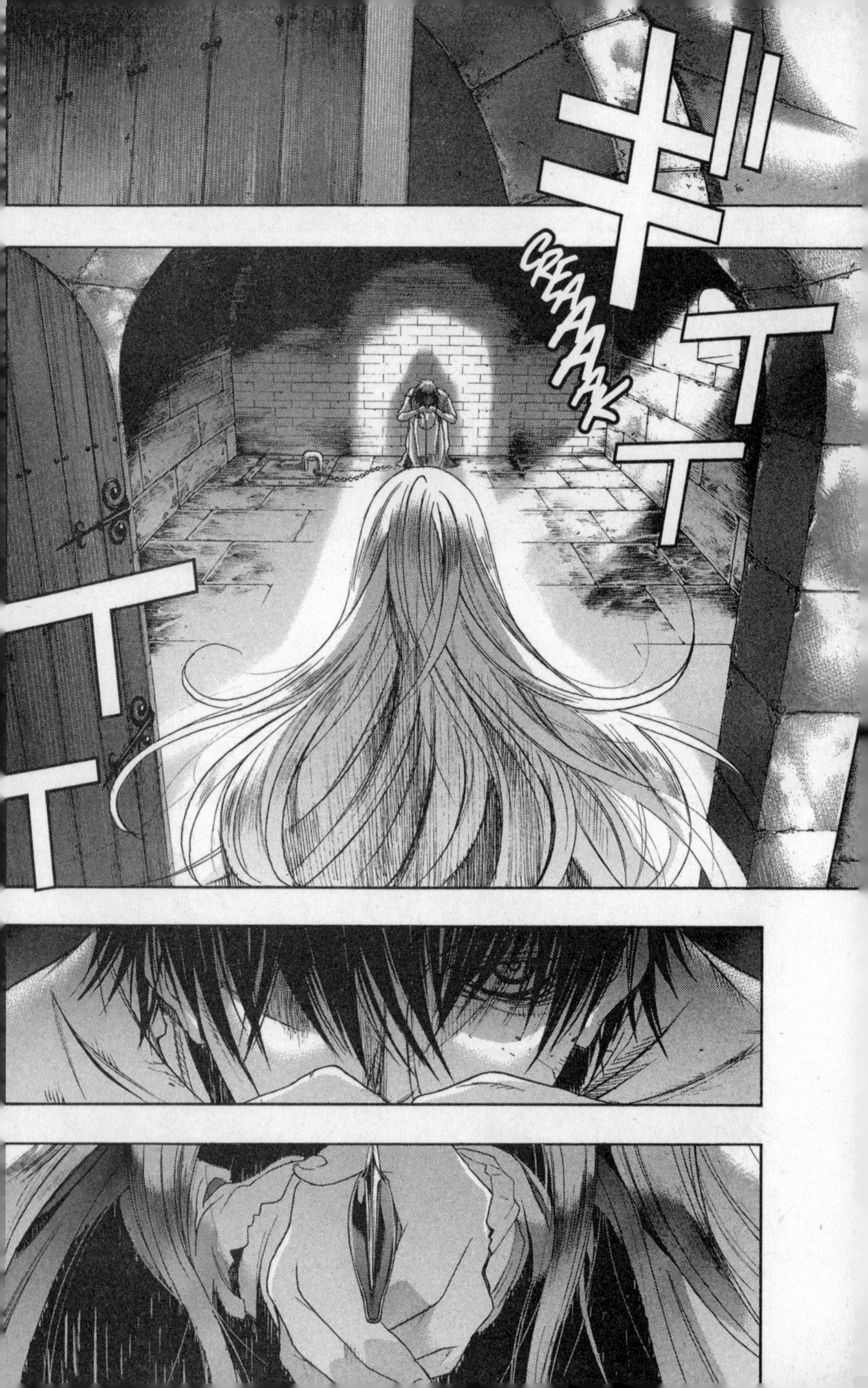
CREAAAAK

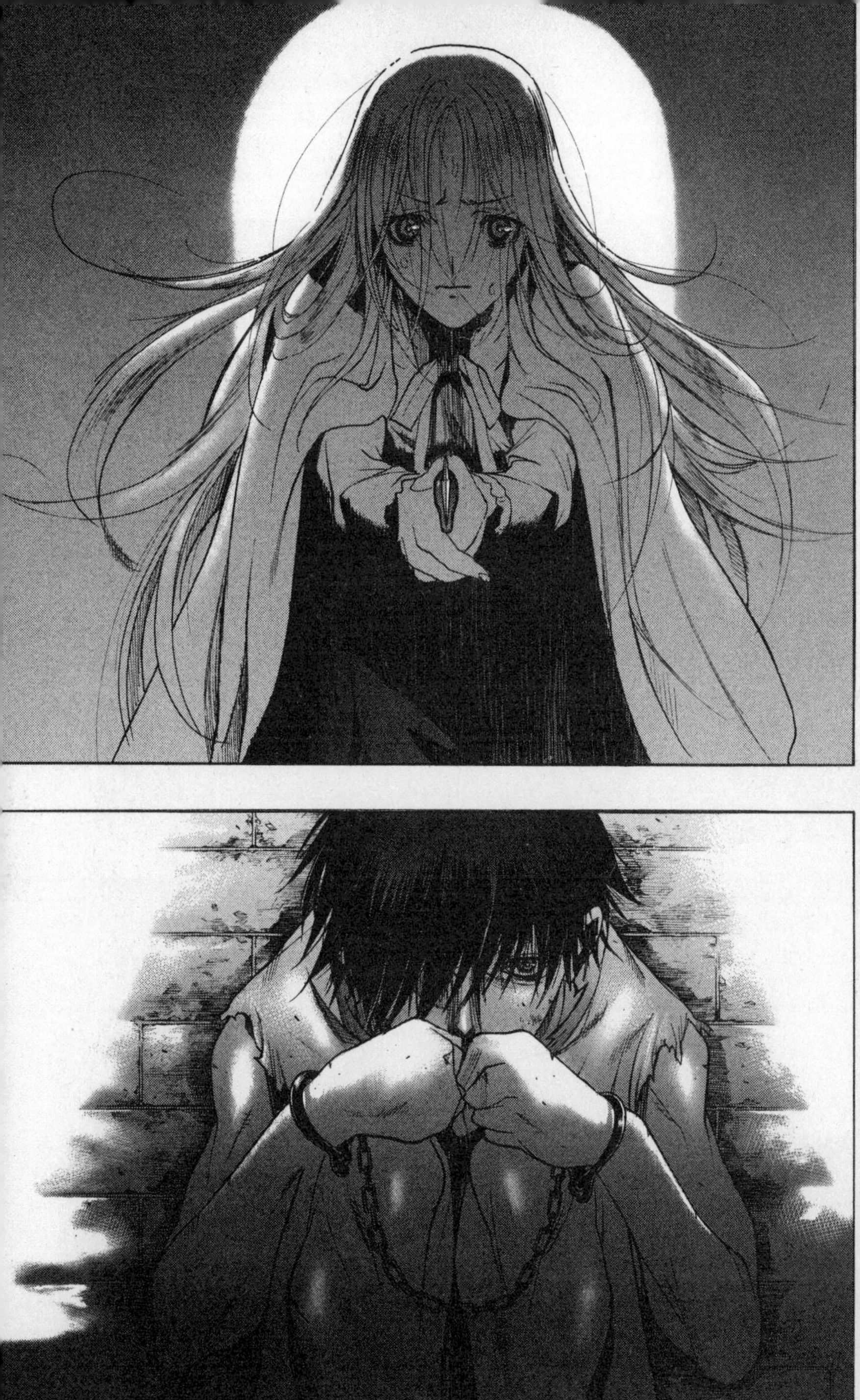

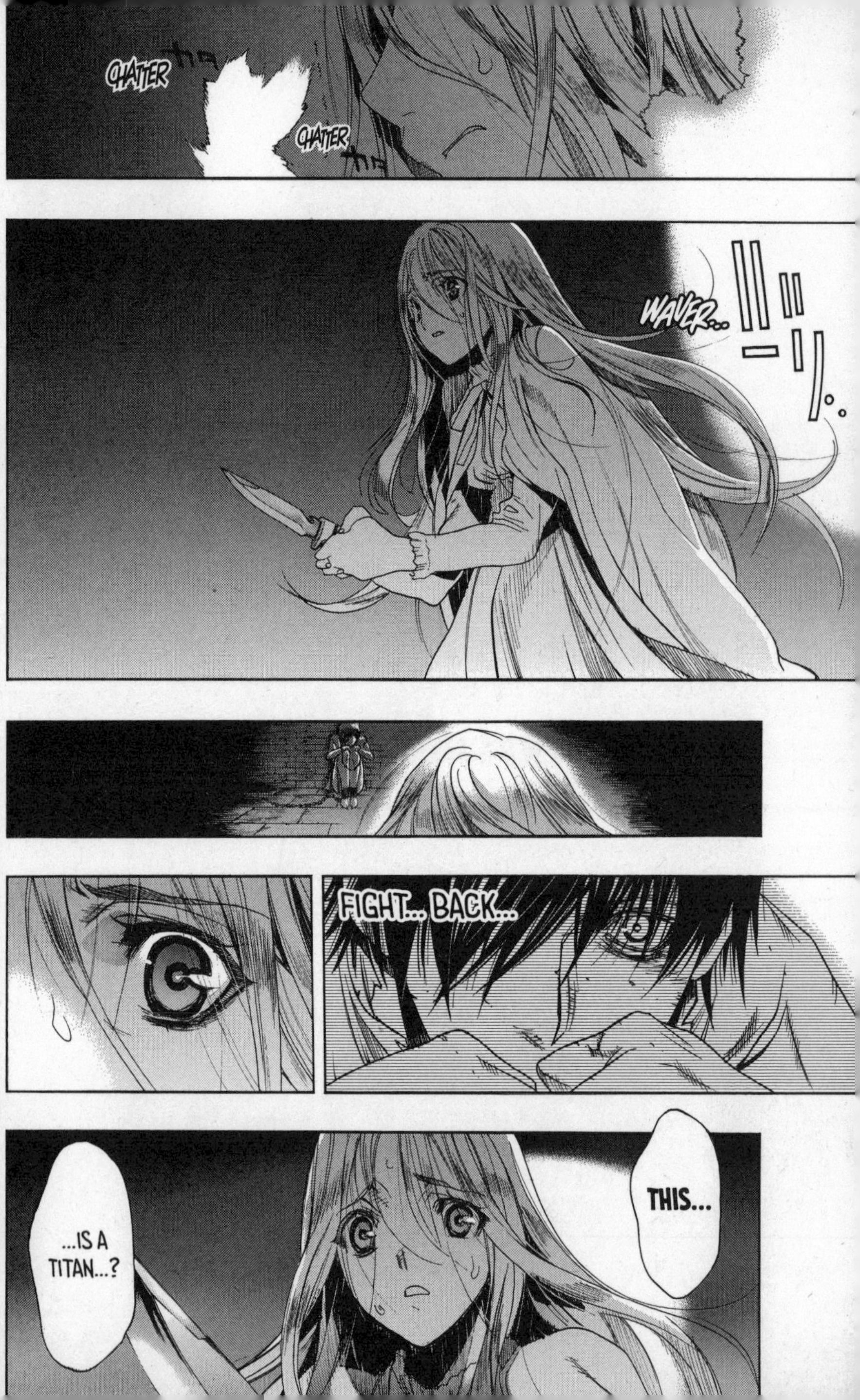
CHATTER
CHATTER
WAVER...
FIGHT... BACK...
THIS...
...IS A TITAN...?

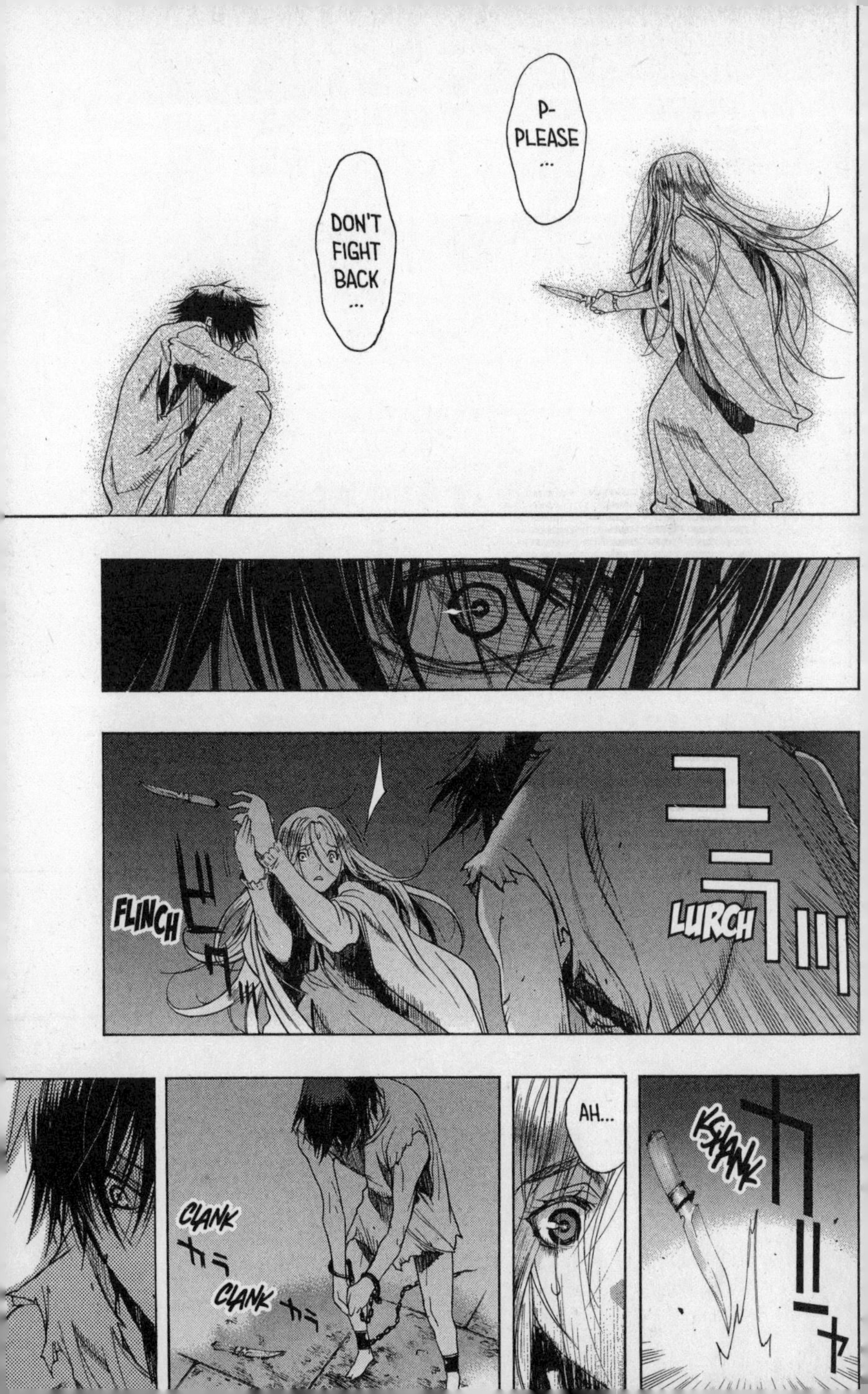
P- PLEASE ...
DON'T FIGHT BACK ...
LURCH
FLINCH
K-SHANK
AH...
CLANK
CLANK

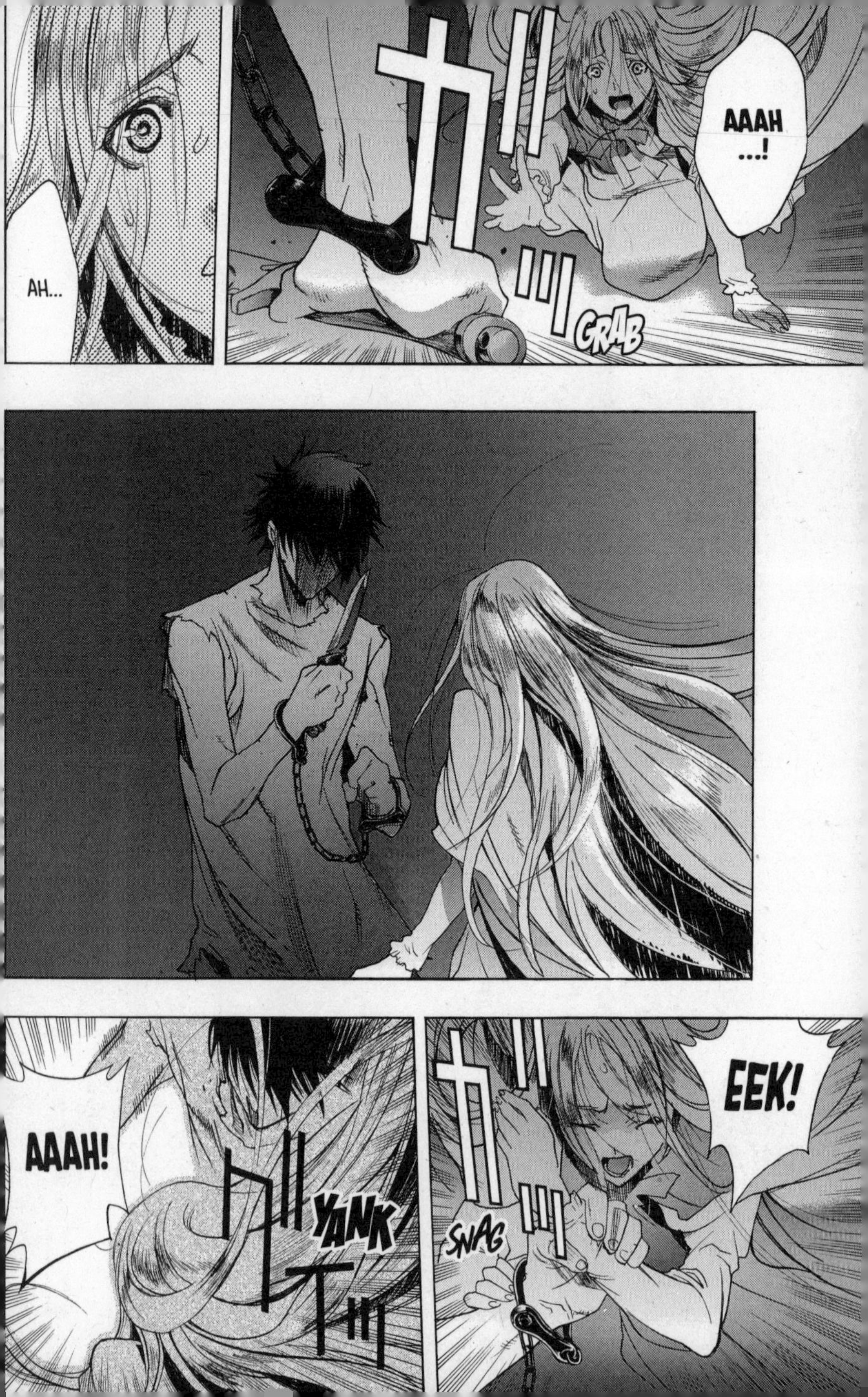
AAAH ...!
GRAB
AH...
EEK!
SNAG
AAAH!
YANK

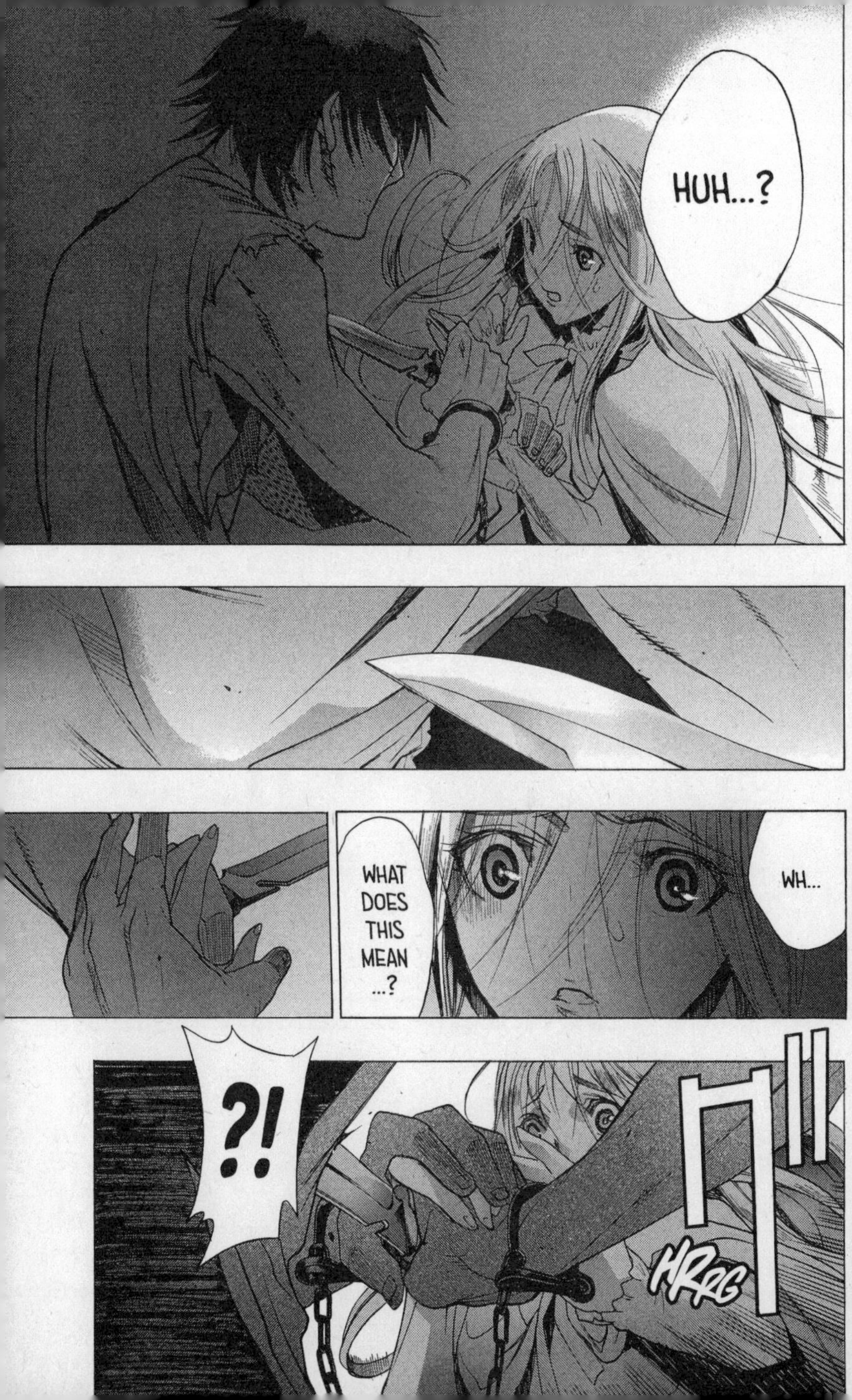
HUH...?
WH...
WHAT DOES THIS MEAN ...?
?!
HRRG

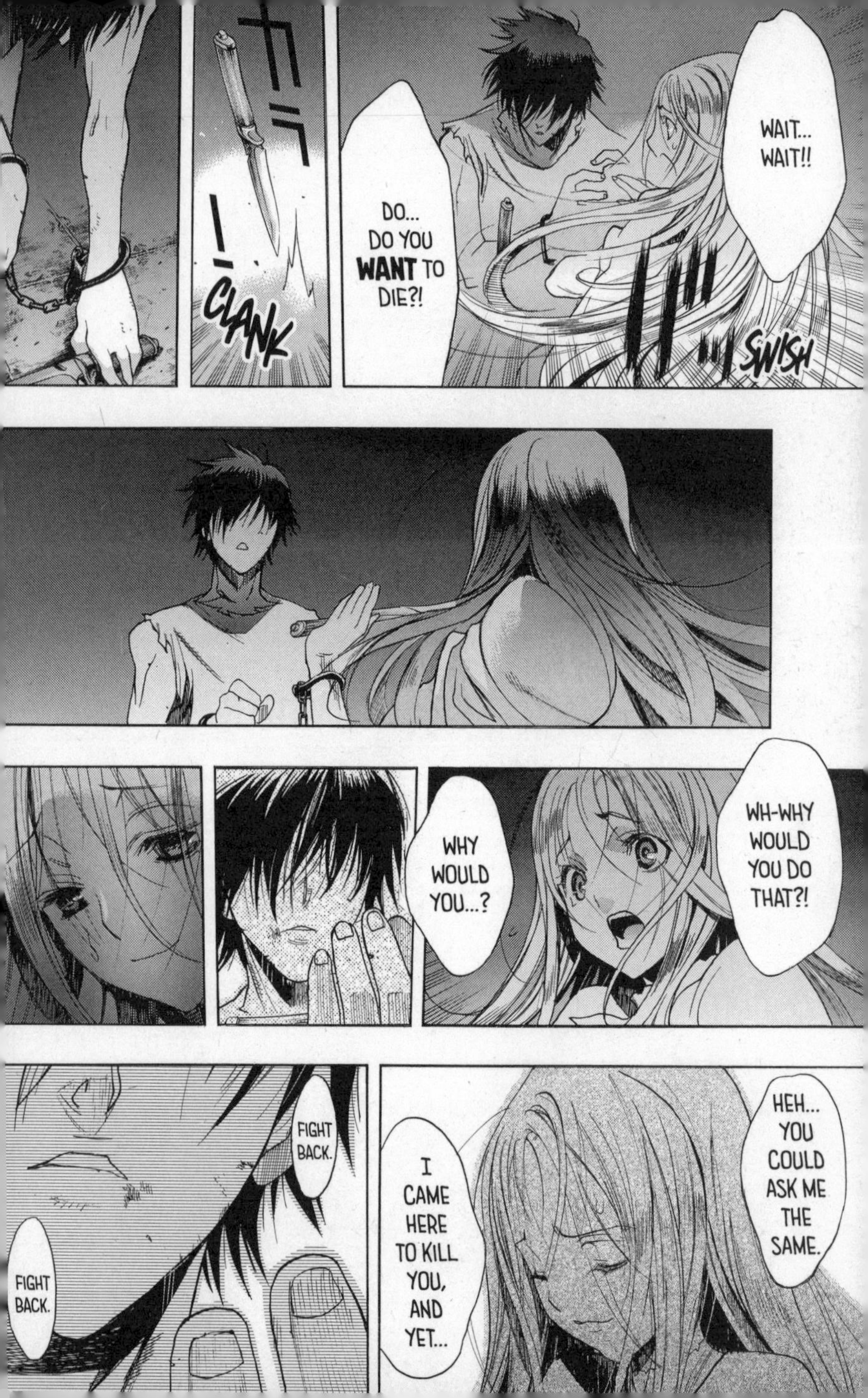
WAIT... WAIT!!
DO... DO YOU WANT TO DIE?!
SWISH
CLANK
WH-WHY WOULD YOU DO THAT?!
WHY WOULD YOU...?
HEH... YOU COULD ASK ME THE SAME.
I CAME HERE TO KILL YOU, AND YET...
FIGHT BACK.
FIGHT BACK.

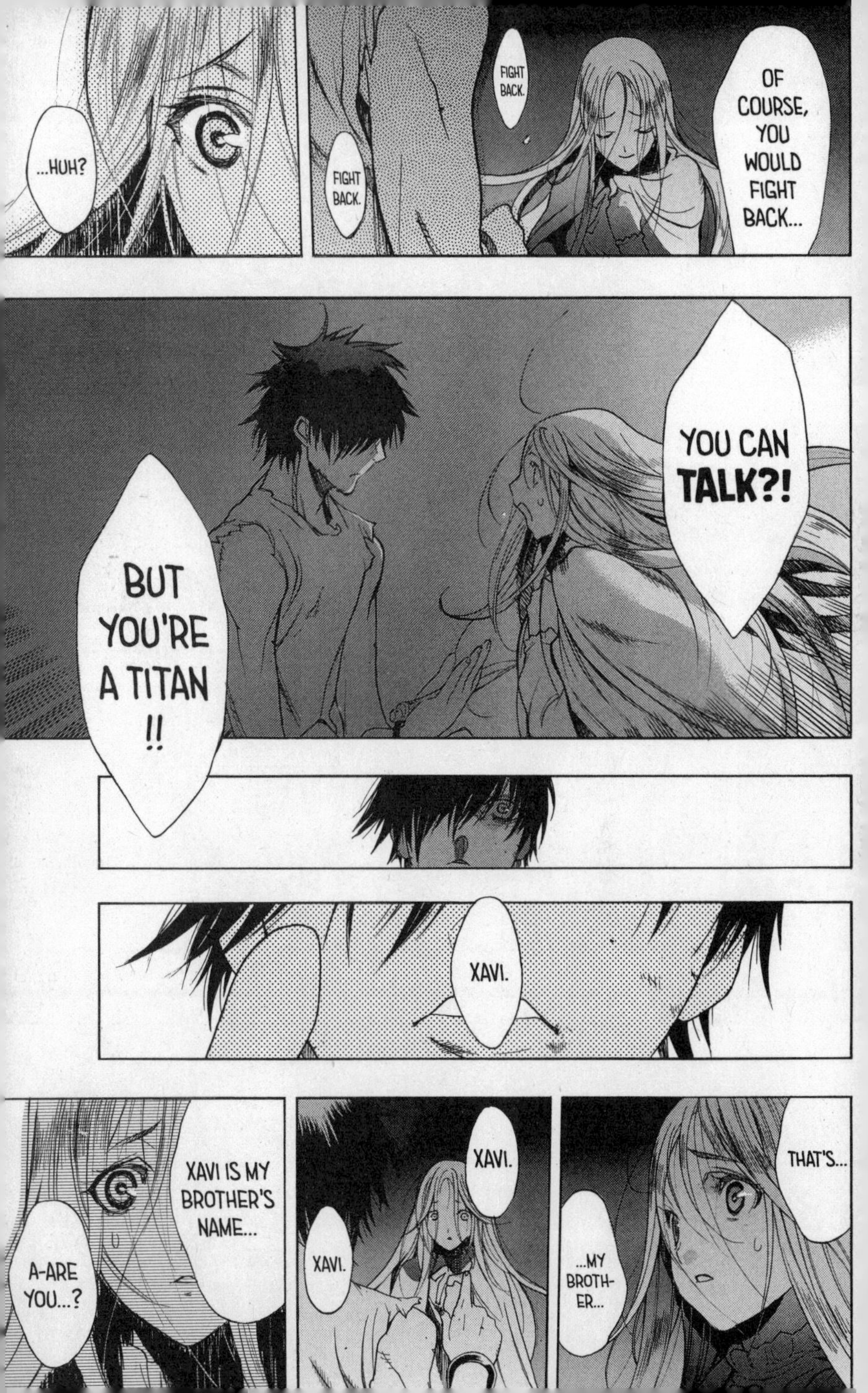
OF COURSE, YOU WOULD FIGHT BACK...
FIGHT BACK.
FIGHT BACK.
...HUH?
YOU CAN **TALK?!**
BUT YOU'RE A TITAN !!
XAVI.
THAT'S...
...MY BROTH-ER...
XAVI.
XAVI.
XAVI IS MY BROTHER'S NAME...
A-ARE YOU...?

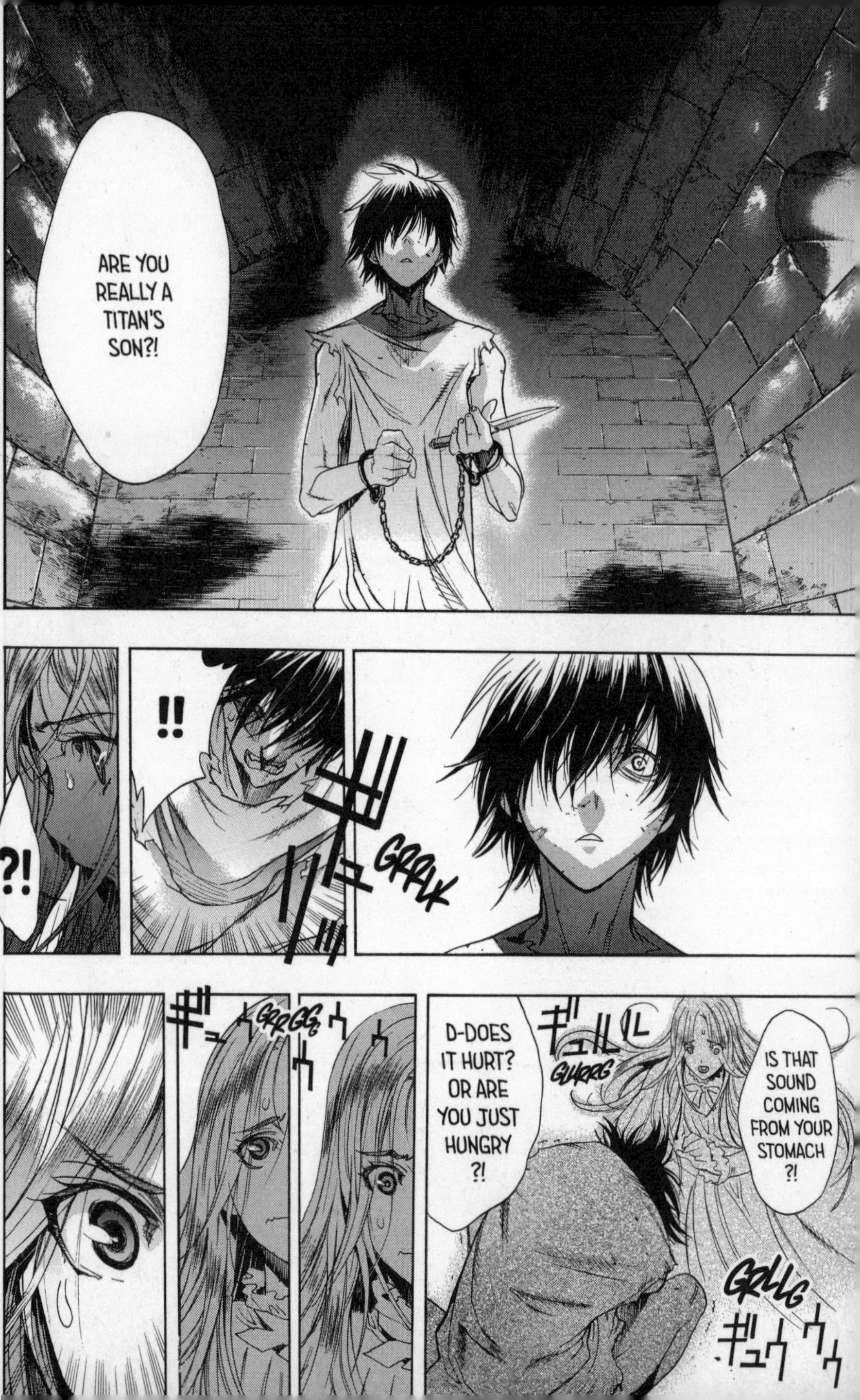
ARE YOU REALLY A TITAN'S SON?!
GRRLK
!!
?!
IS THAT SOUND COMING FROM YOUR STOMACH ?!
GURRG
D-DOES IT HURT? OR ARE YOU JUST HUNGRY ?!
GRLLG
GRRGG

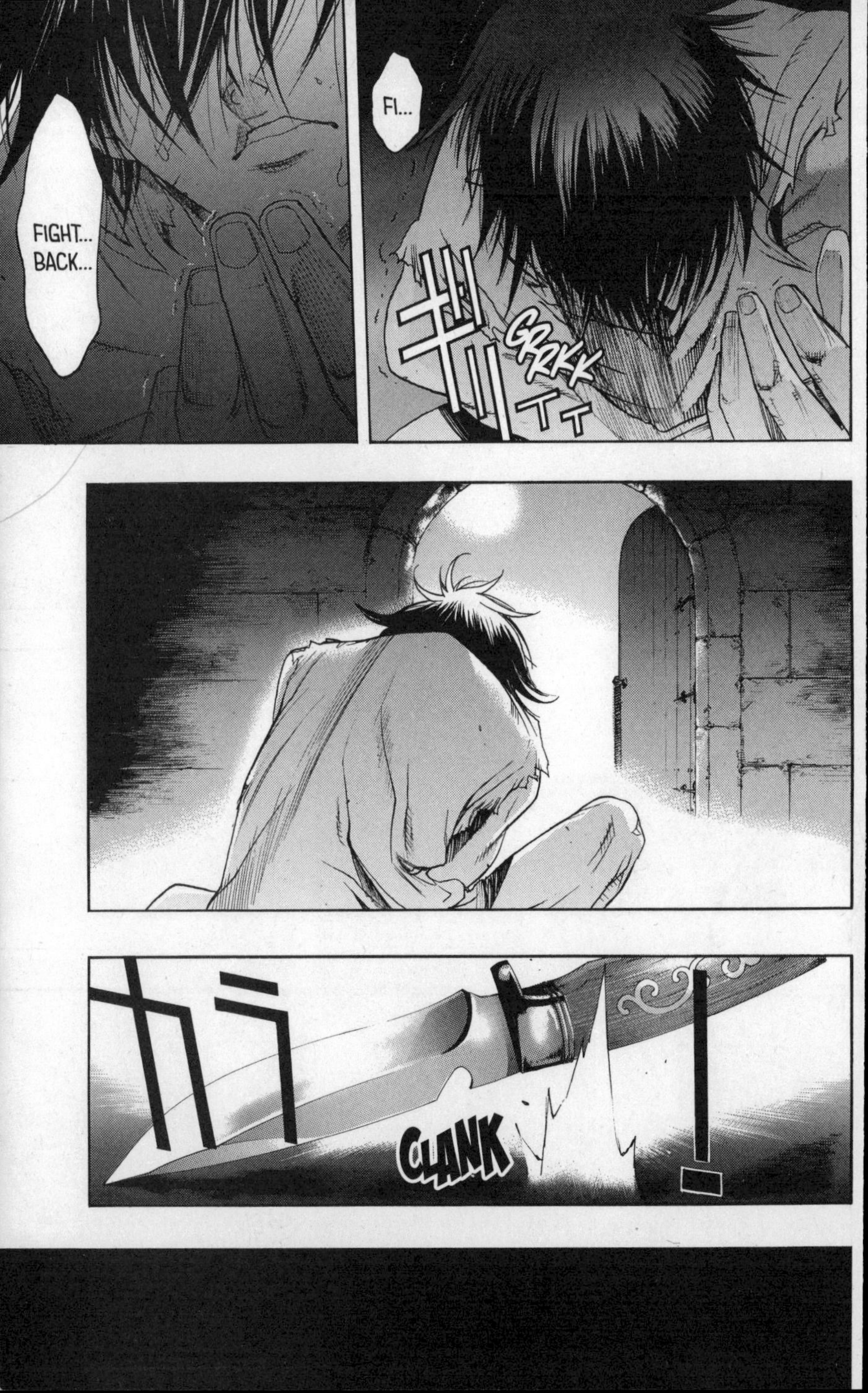
FI...
GRRKK
FIGHT... BACK...
CLANK

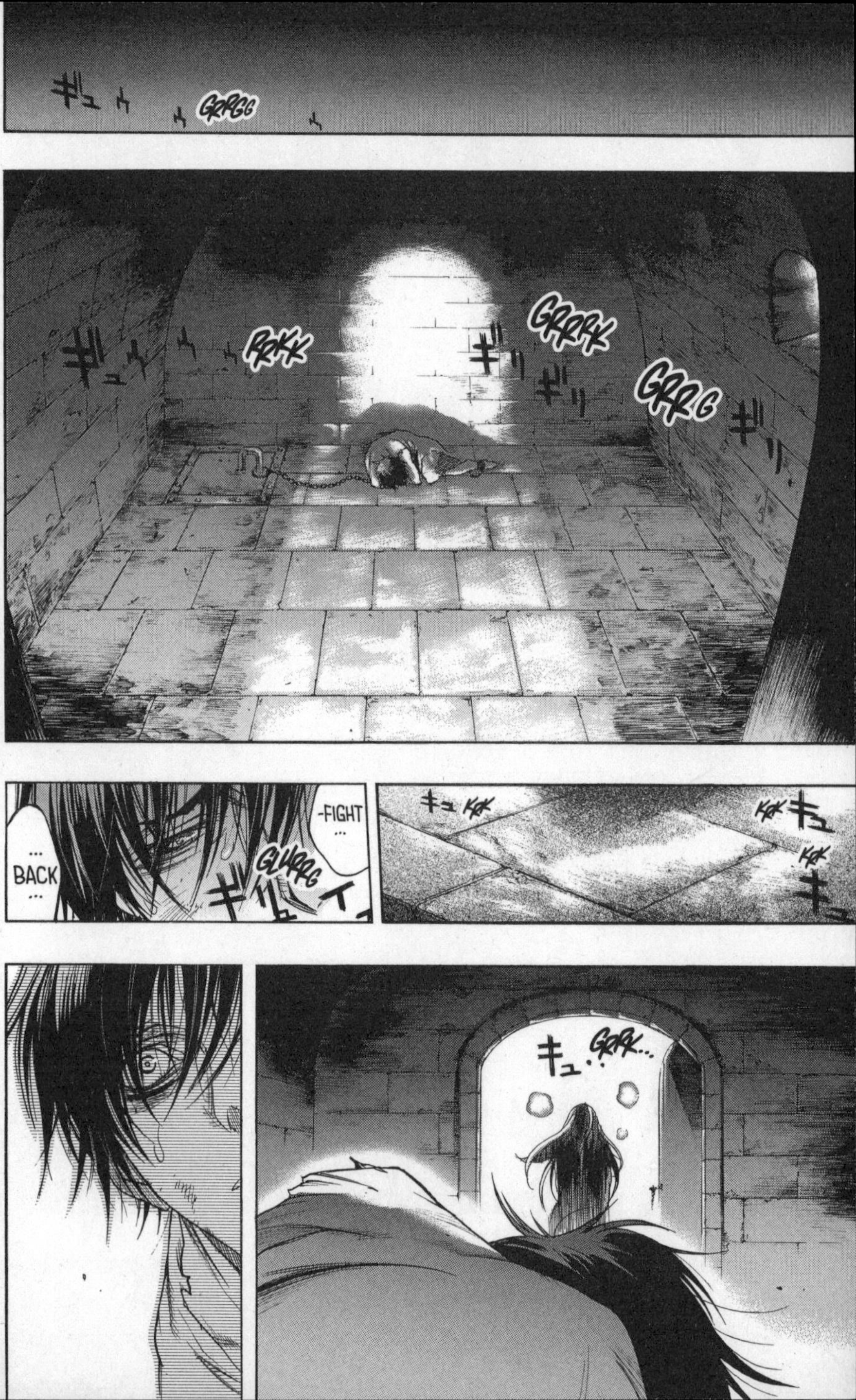
GRRGG
GRRRK
GRRG
RRKK
KRK
KRK
KRK
-FIGHT ...
GLURRG
... BACK ...
GRRK...

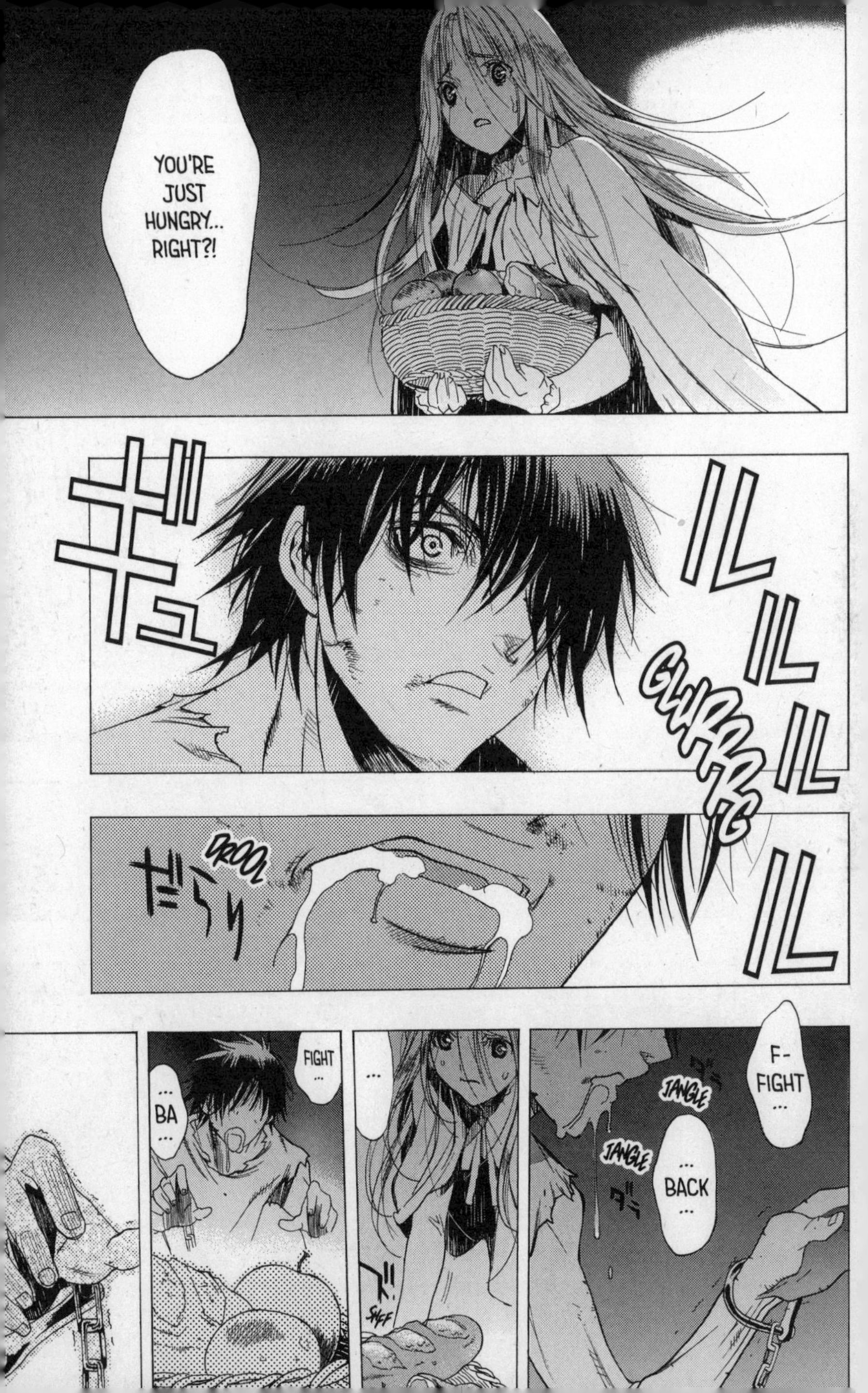
YOU'RE JUST HUNGRY... RIGHT?!
GURRRG
DROOL
F-FIGHT ...
JANGLE
JANGLE
... BACK ...
...
FIGHT ...
... BA ...

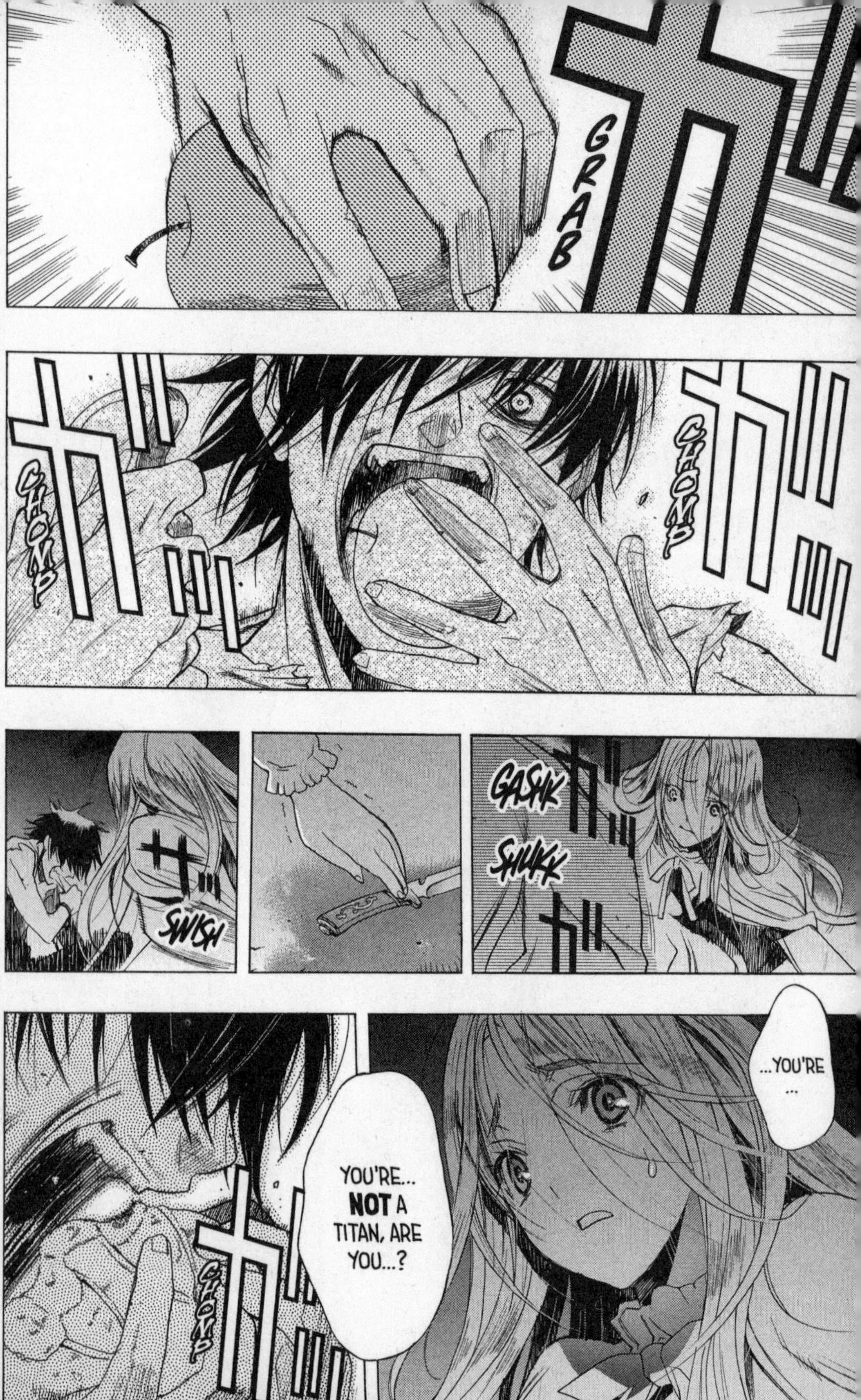
GRAB
CHOMP
CHOMP
GASHK
SHUKK
SWISH
...YOU'RE ...
YOU'RE... **NOT** A TITAN, ARE YOU...?
CHOMP

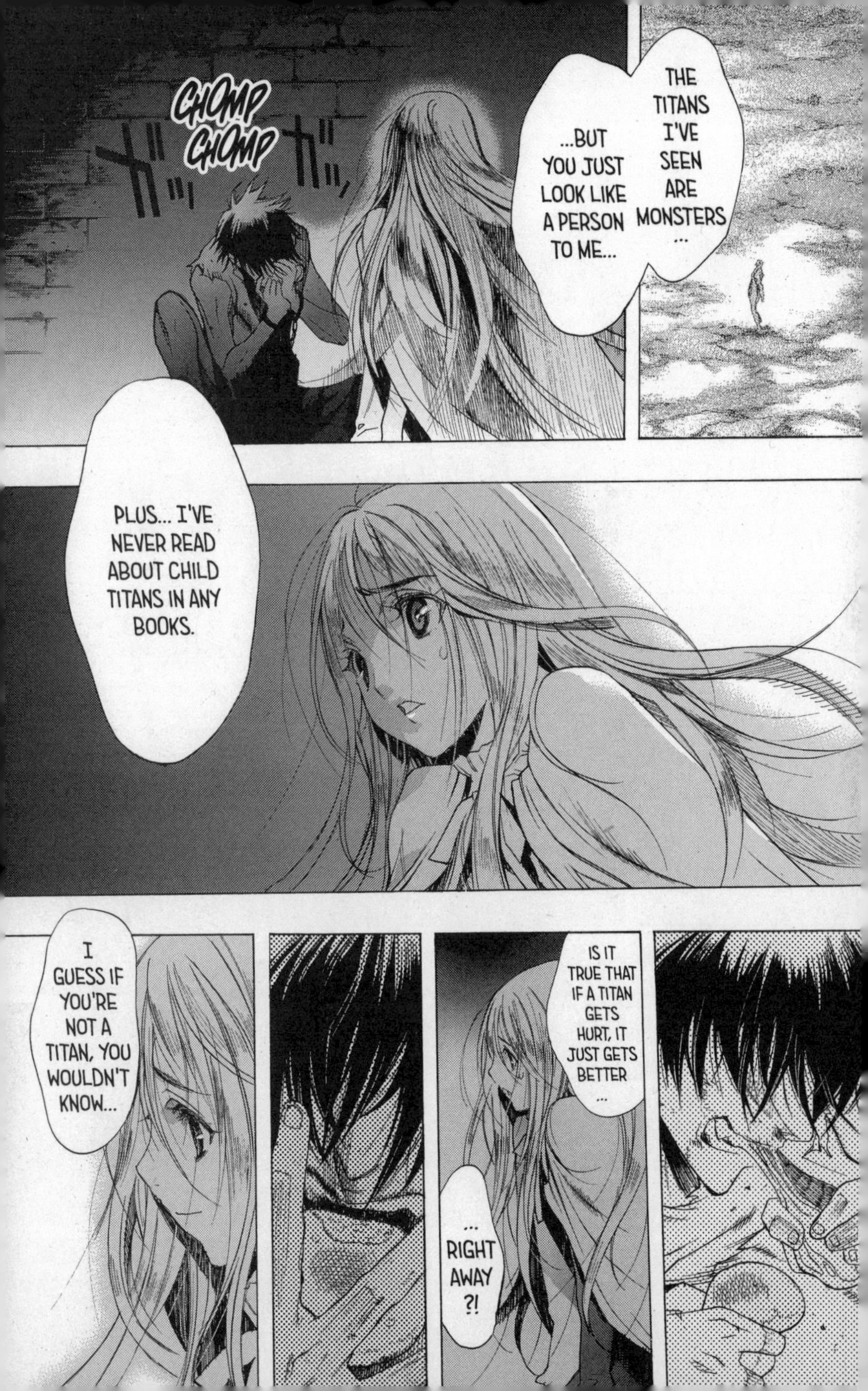
THE TITANS I'VE SEEN ARE MONSTERS...
CHOMP CHOMP
...BUT YOU JUST LOOK LIKE A PERSON TO ME...
PLUS... I'VE NEVER READ ABOUT CHILD TITANS IN ANY BOOKS.
IS IT TRUE THAT IF A TITAN GETS HURT, IT JUST GETS BETTER...
...RIGHT AWAY?!
I GUESS IF YOU'RE NOT A TITAN, YOU WOULDN'T KNOW...

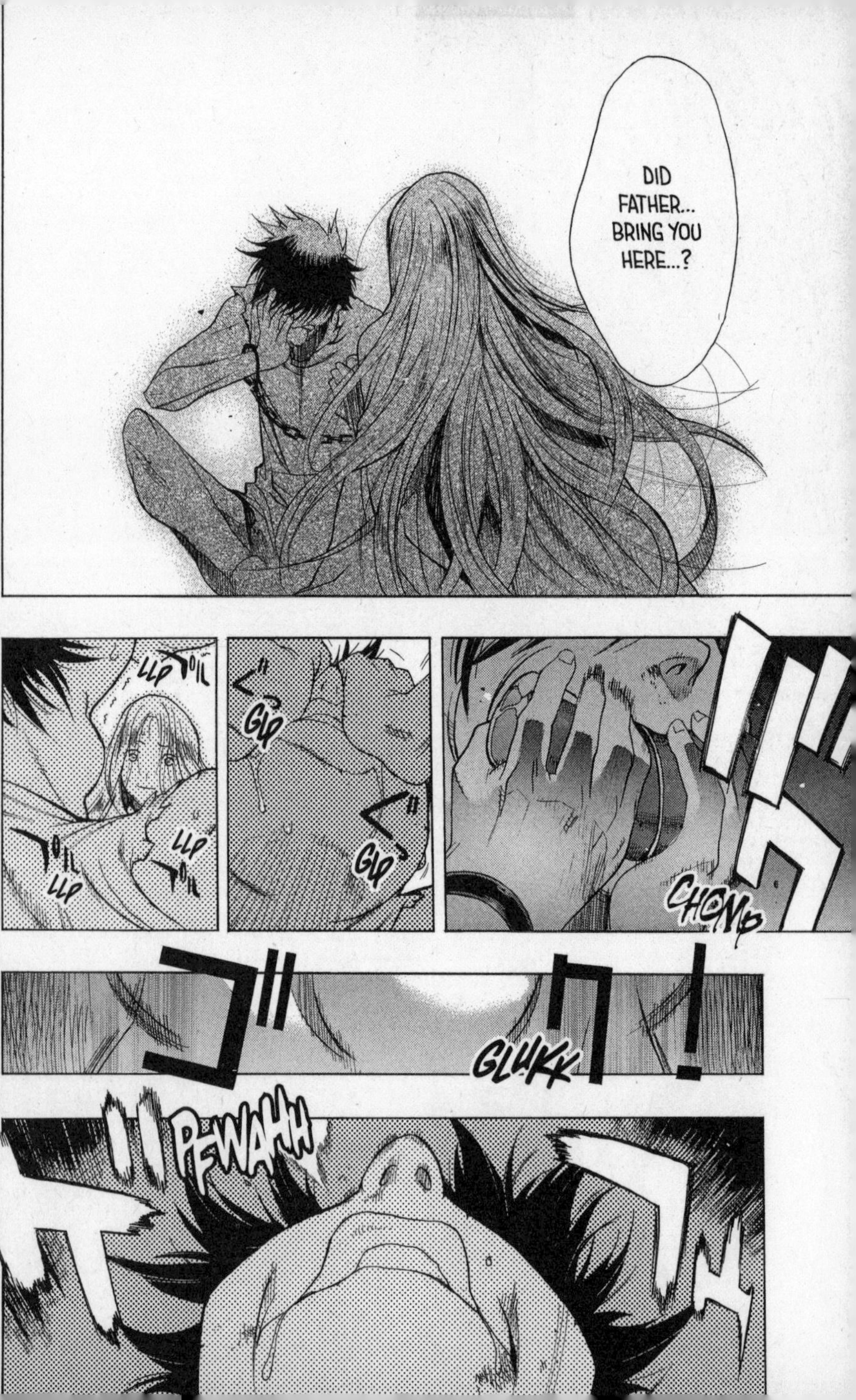
DID FATHER... BRING YOU HERE...?
CHOMP
GLP
GLP
LLP
LLP
LLP
GLUKK
PFWAHH

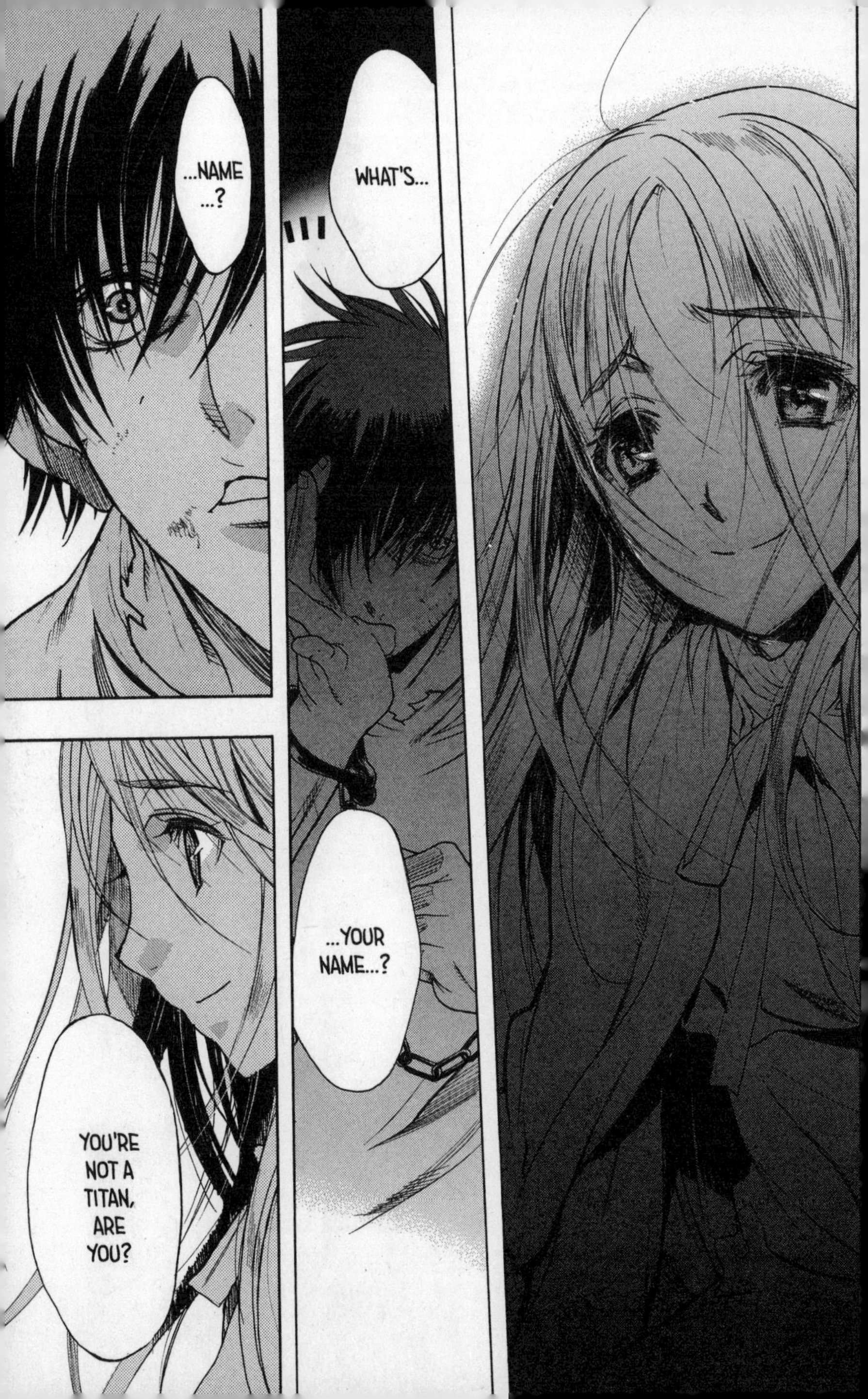
WHAT'S...
...YOUR NAME...?
...NAME ...?
YOU'RE NOT A TITAN, ARE YOU?

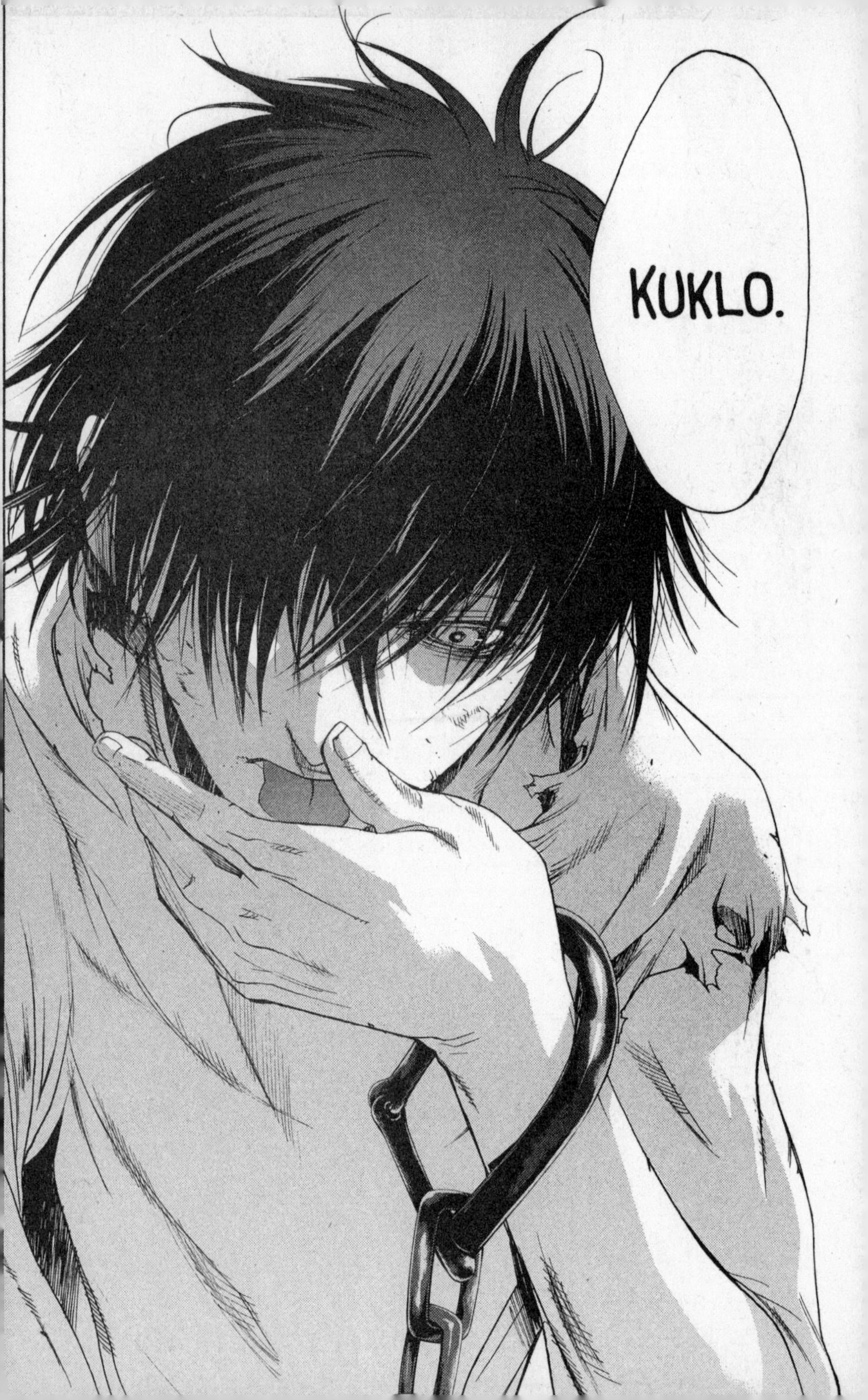
KUKLO.

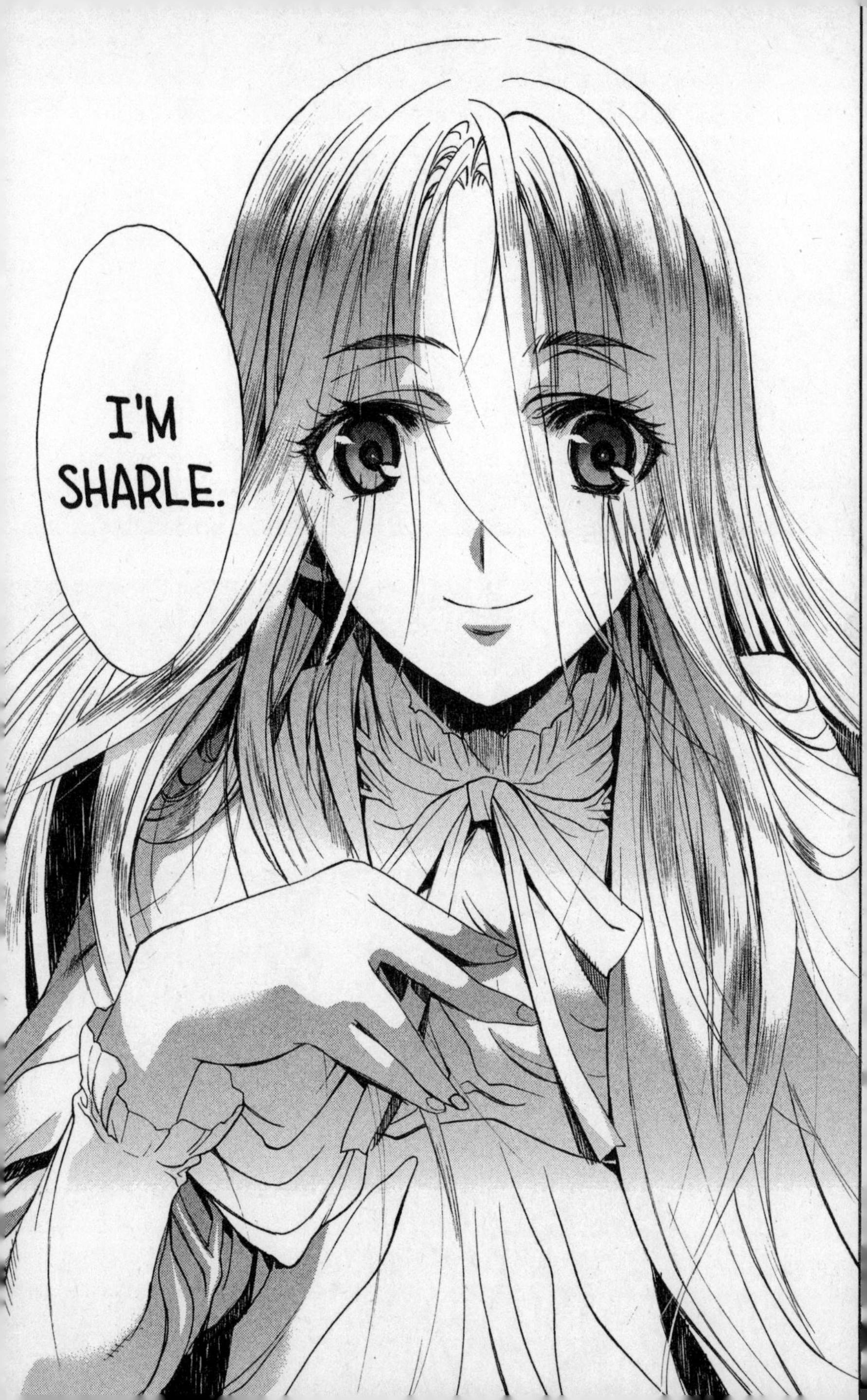
I'M SHARLE.

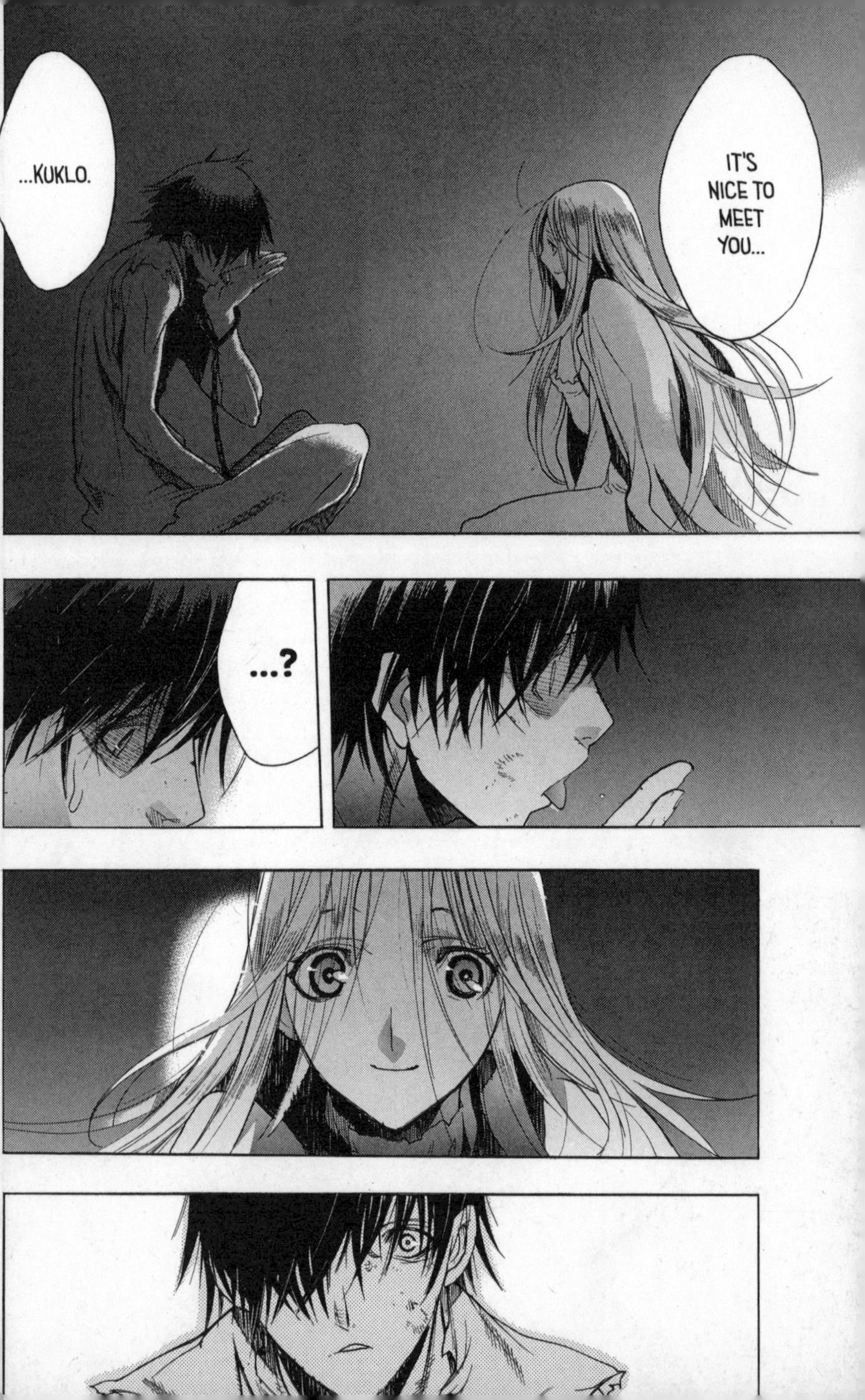
IT'S NICE TO MEET YOU...
...KUKLO.
...?

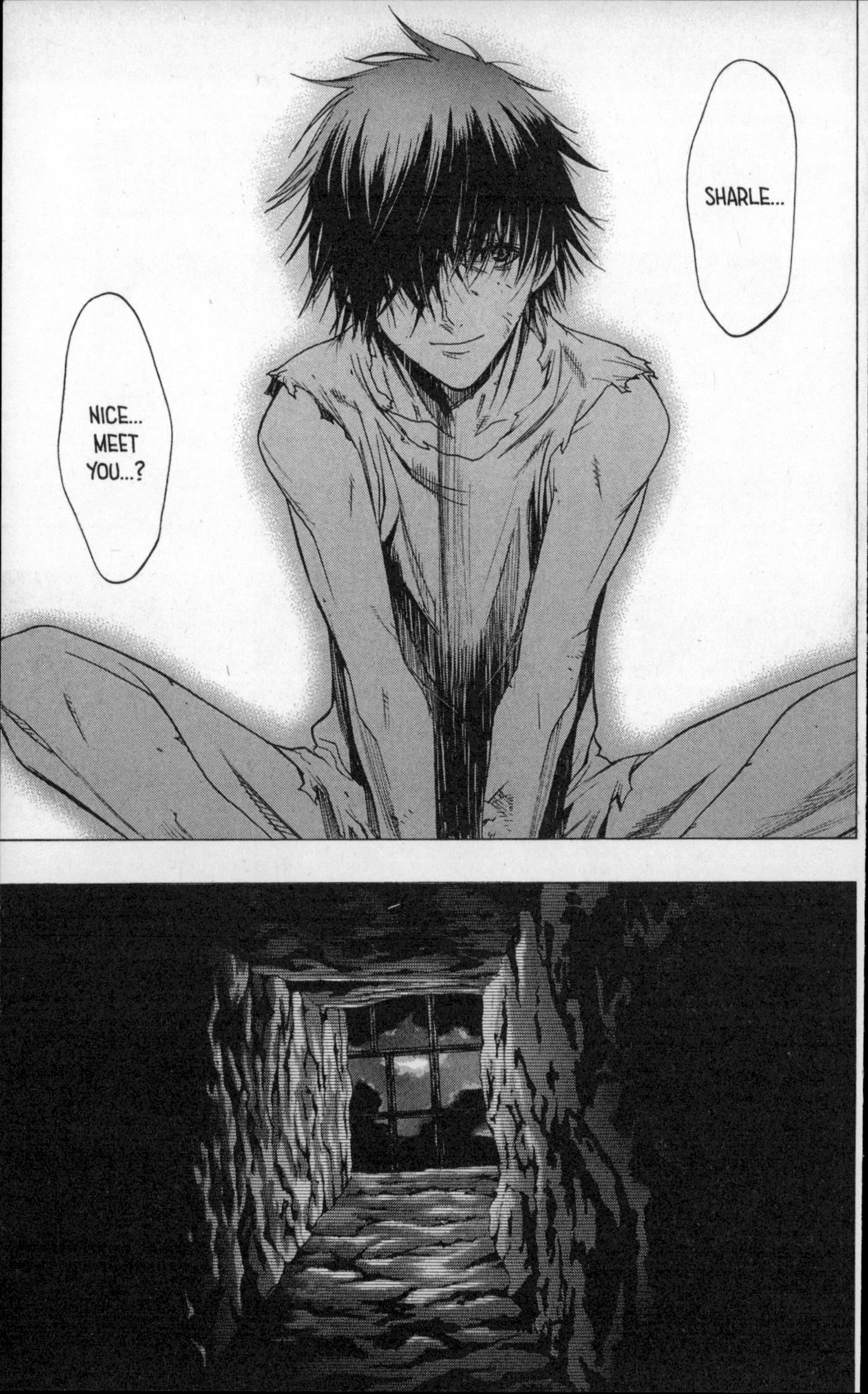
SHARLE...
NICE... MEET YOU...?

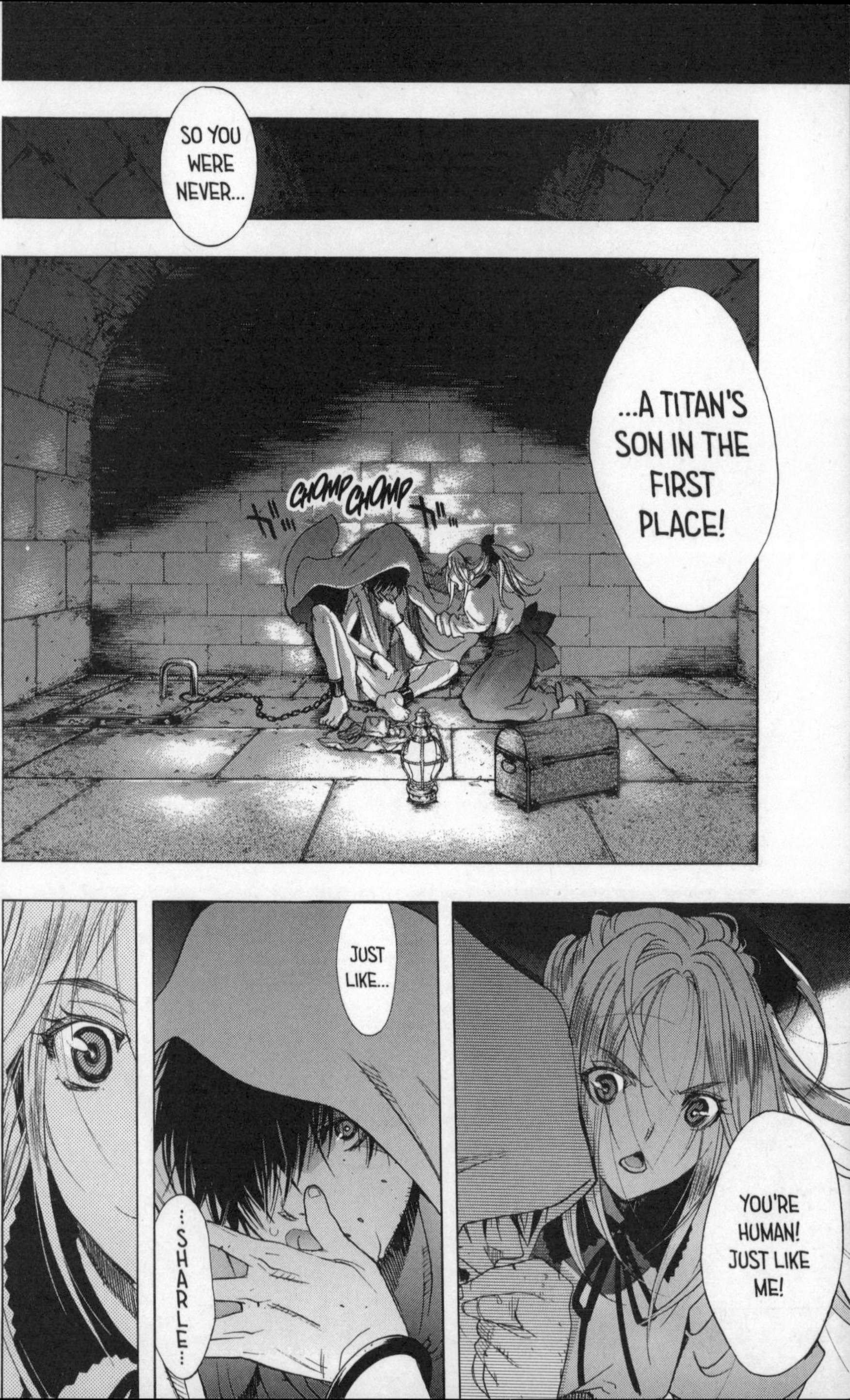
SO YOU WERE NEVER...
...A TITAN'S SON IN THE FIRST PLACE!
CHOMP CHOMP
YOU'RE HUMAN! JUST LIKE ME!
JUST LIKE...
...SHARLE...

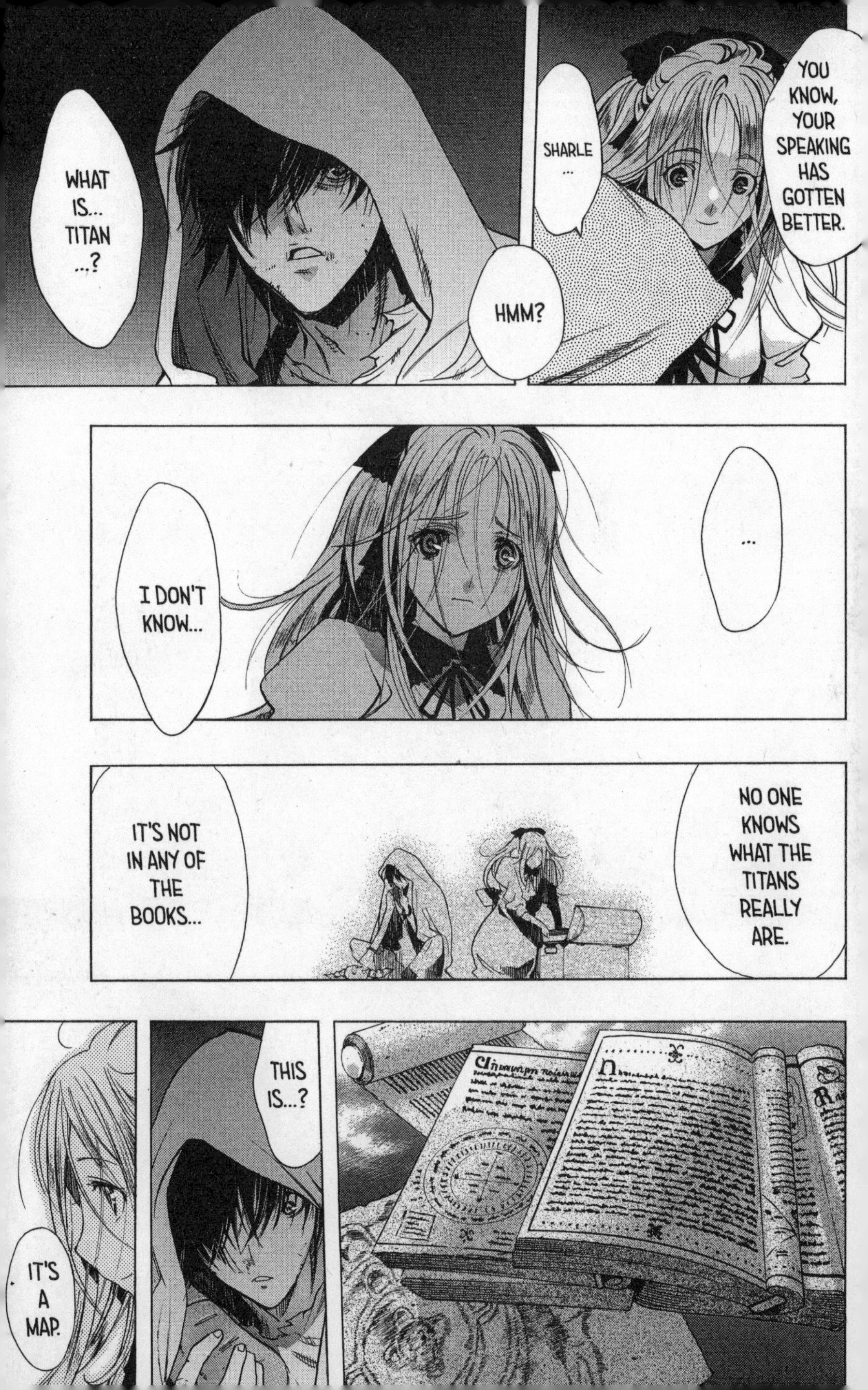
YOU KNOW, YOUR SPEAKING HAS GOTTEN BETTER.
SHARLE ...
HMM?
WHAT IS... TITAN ...?
...
I DON'T KNOW...
NO ONE KNOWS WHAT THE TITANS REALLY ARE.
IT'S NOT IN ANY OF THE BOOKS...
THIS IS...?
IT'S A MAP.

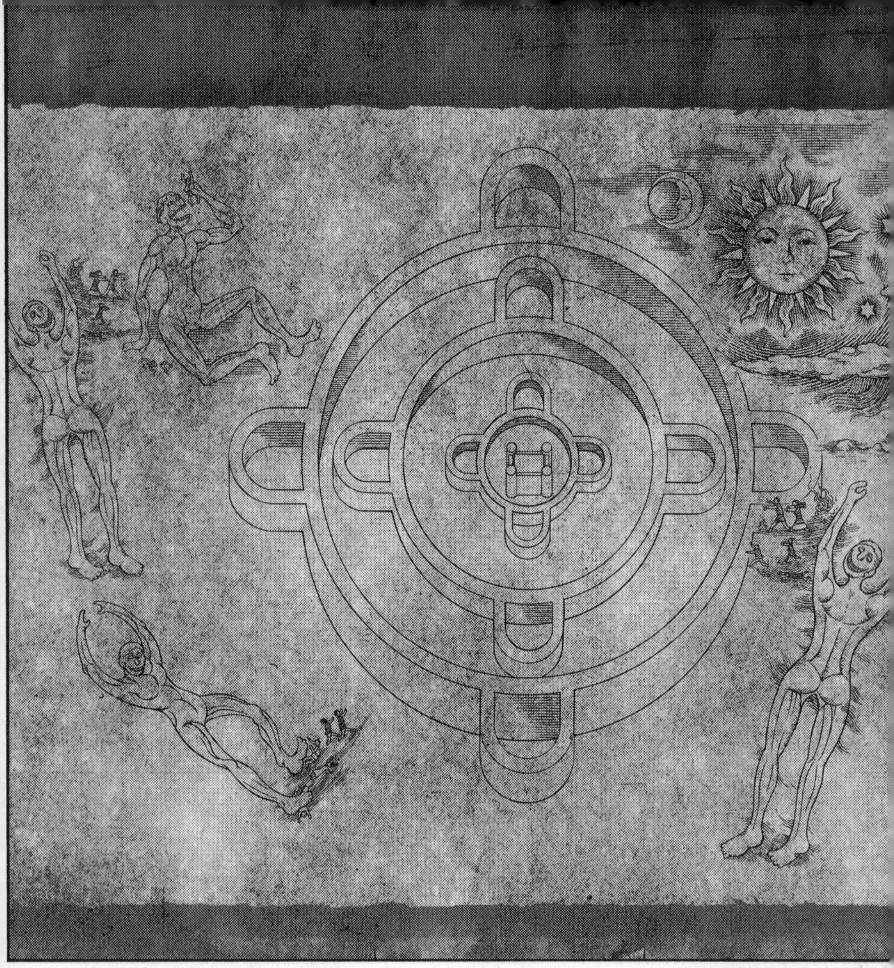

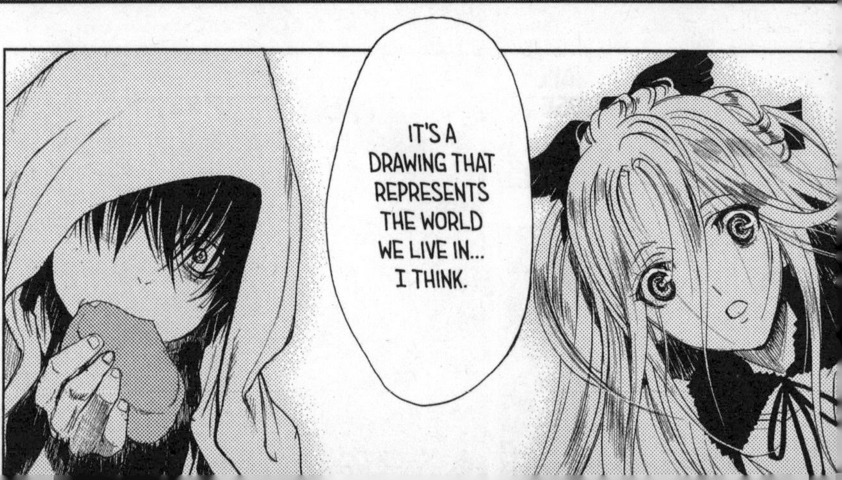
IT'S A DRAWING THAT REPRESENTS THE WORLD WE LIVE IN... I THINK.

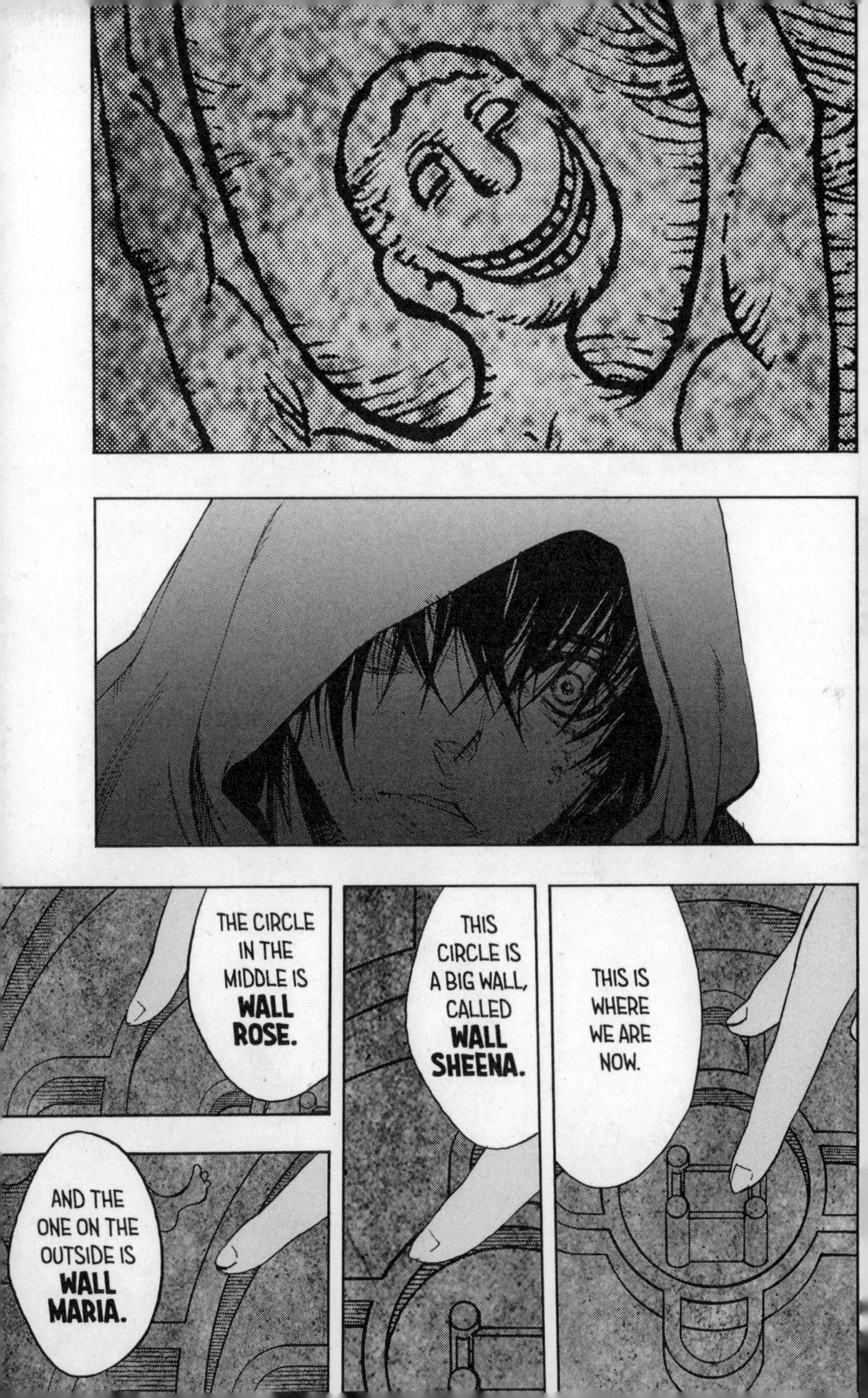
THIS IS WHERE WE ARE NOW.
THIS CIRCLE IS A BIG WALL, CALLED WALL SHEENA.
THE CIRCLE IN THE MIDDLE IS WALL ROSE.
AND THE ONE ON THE OUTSIDE IS WALL MARIA.

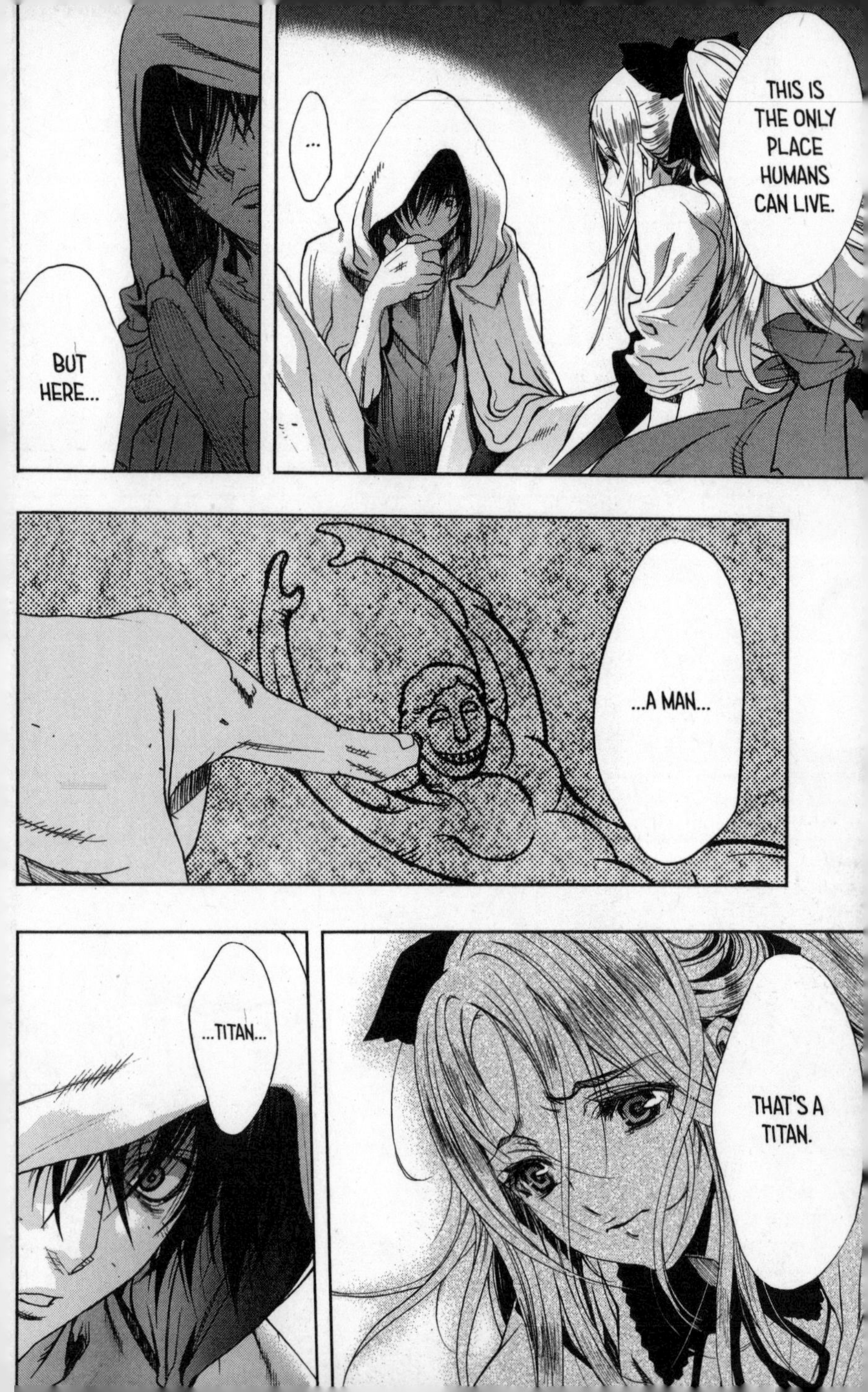
THIS IS THE ONLY PLACE HUMANS CAN LIVE.
...
BUT HERE...
...A MAN...
THAT'S A TITAN.
...TITAN...

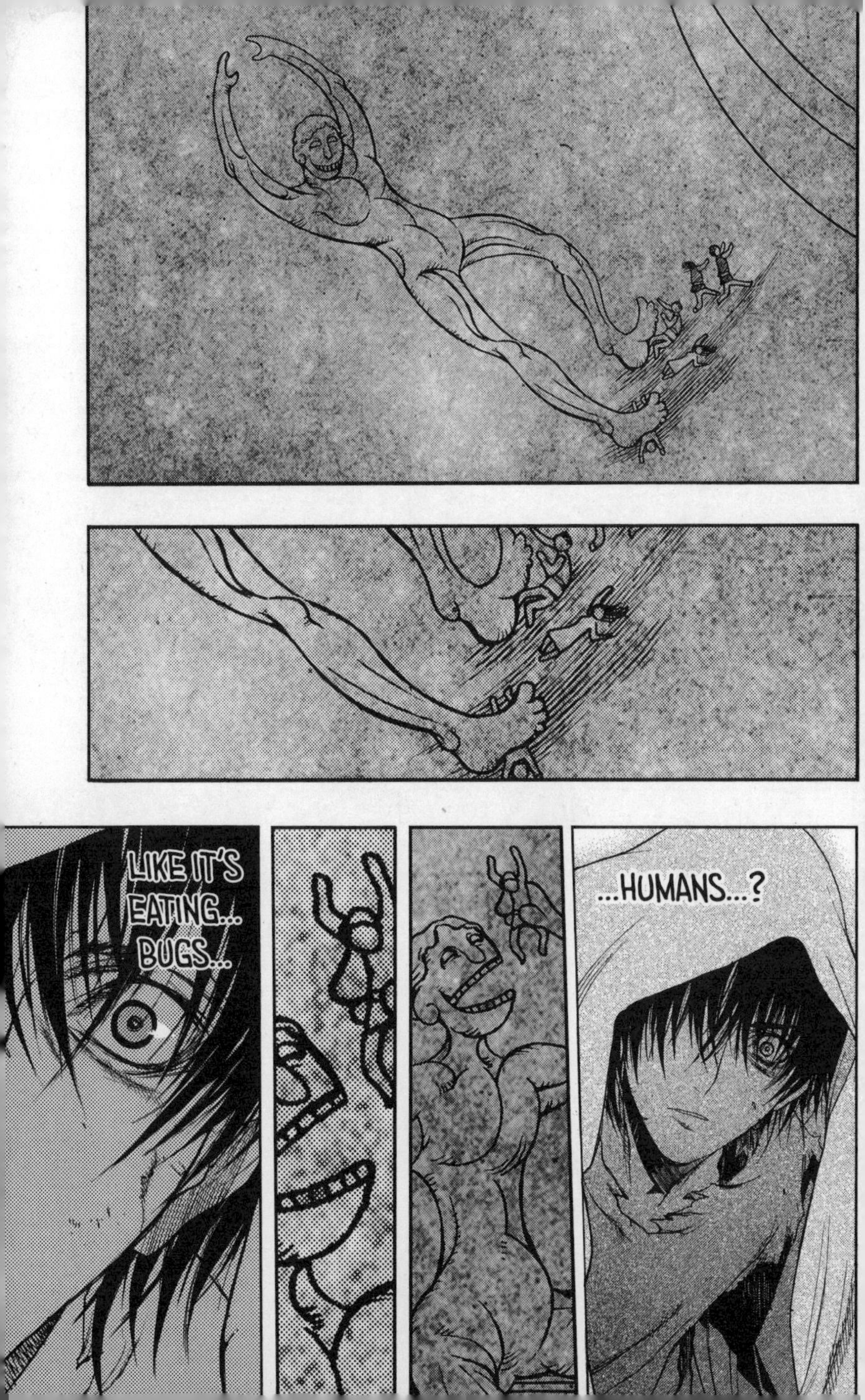
...HUMANS...?
LIKE IT'S EATING... BUGS...

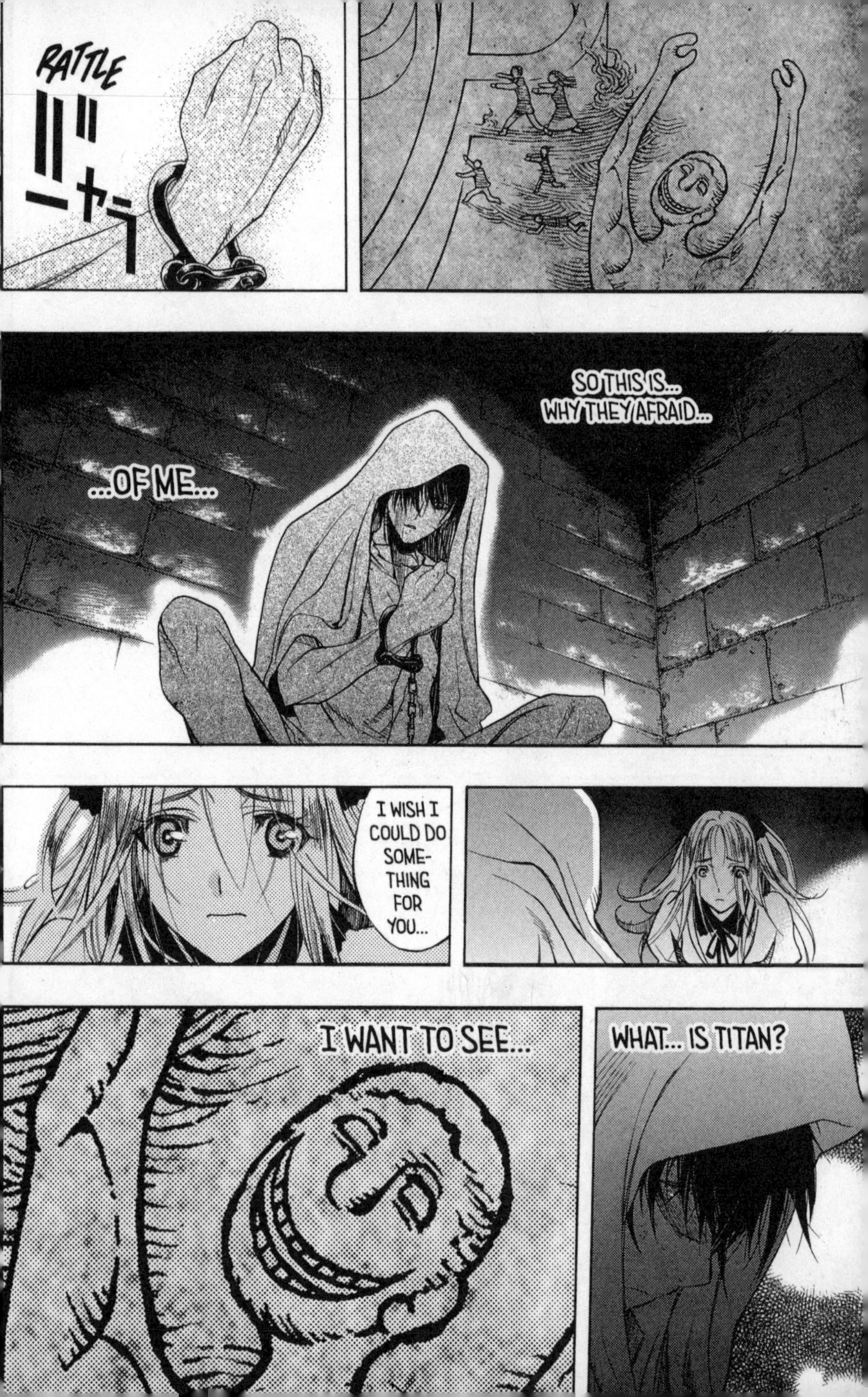
RATTLE
ジャラ
SO THIS IS... WHY THEY AFRAID...
...OF ME...
I WISH I COULD DO SOME-THING FOR YOU...
WHAT... IS TITAN?
I WANT TO SEE...

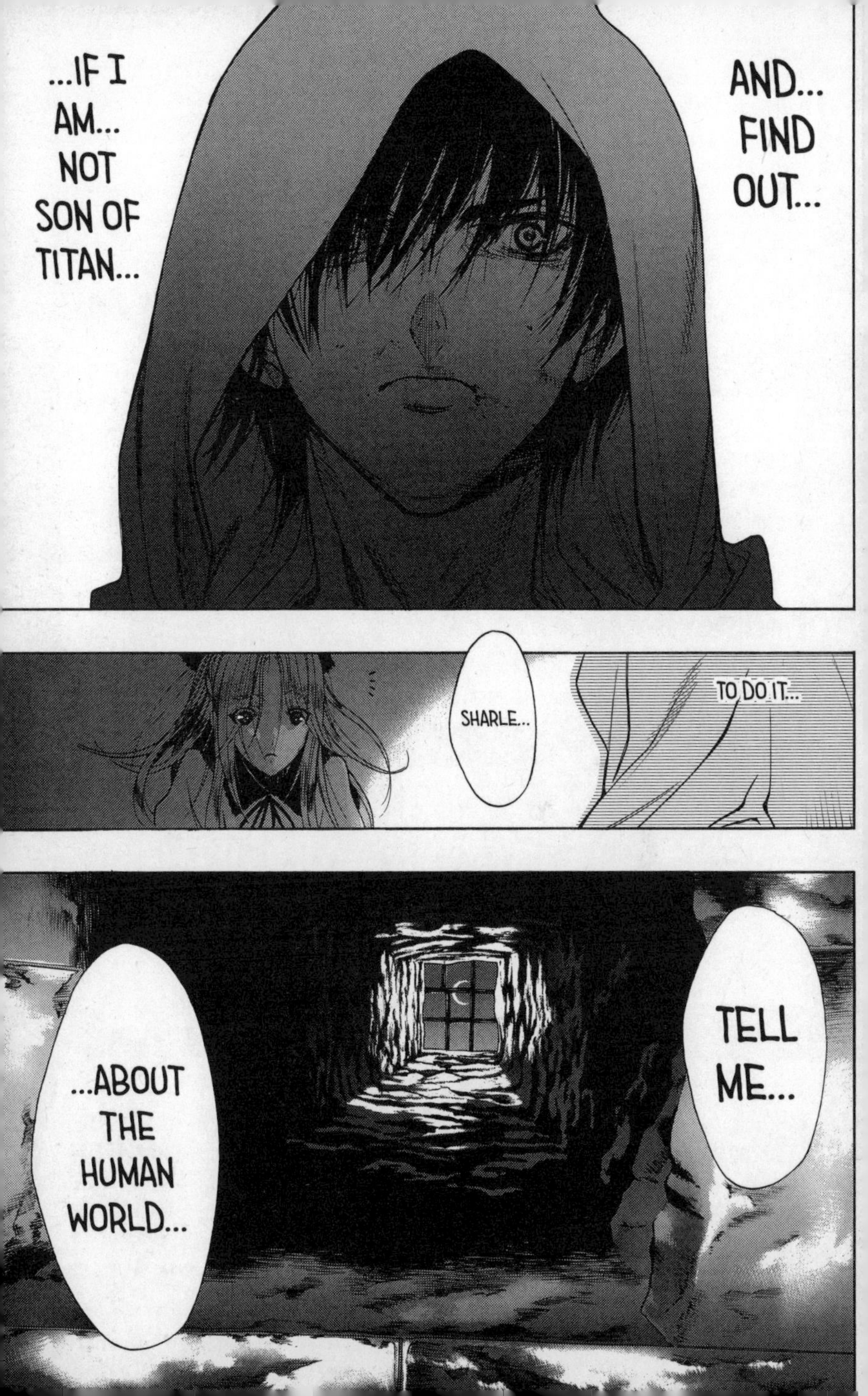
AND... FIND OUT...
...IF I AM... NOT SON OF TITAN...
TO DO IT...
SHARLE...
TELL ME...
...ABOUT THE HUMAN WORLD...

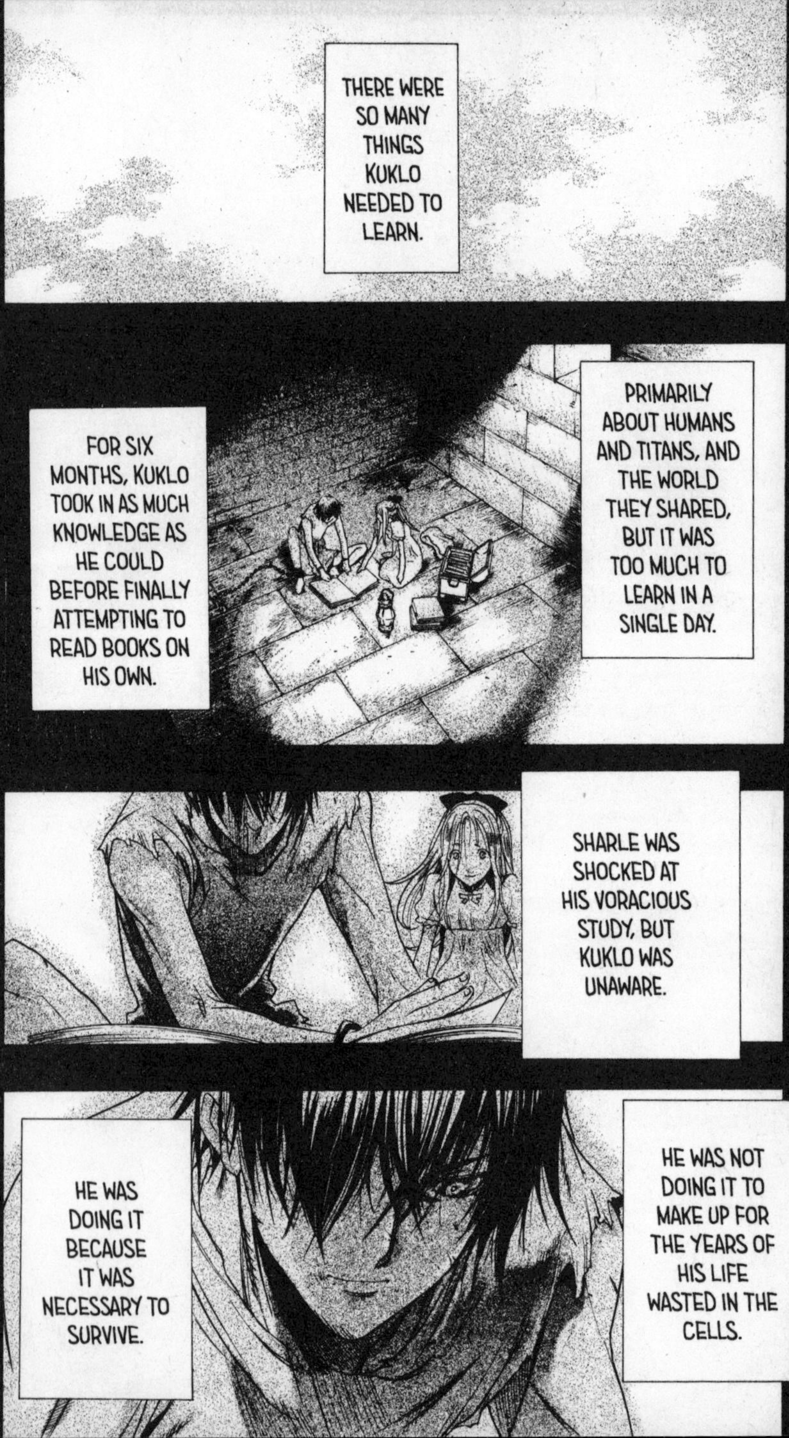
THERE WERE SO MANY THINGS KUKLO NEEDED TO LEARN.
PRIMARILY ABOUT HUMANS AND TITANS, AND THE WORLD THEY SHARED, BUT IT WAS TOO MUCH TO LEARN IN A SINGLE DAY.
FOR SIX MONTHS, KUKLO TOOK IN AS MUCH KNOWLEDGE AS HE COULD BEFORE FINALLY ATTEMPTING TO READ BOOKS ON HIS OWN.
SHARLE WAS SHOCKED AT HIS VORACIOUS STUDY, BUT KUKLO WAS UNAWARE.
HE WAS NOT DOING IT TO MAKE UP FOR THE YEARS OF HIS LIFE WASTED IN THE CELLS.
HE WAS DOING IT BECAUSE IT WAS NECESSARY TO SURVIVE.

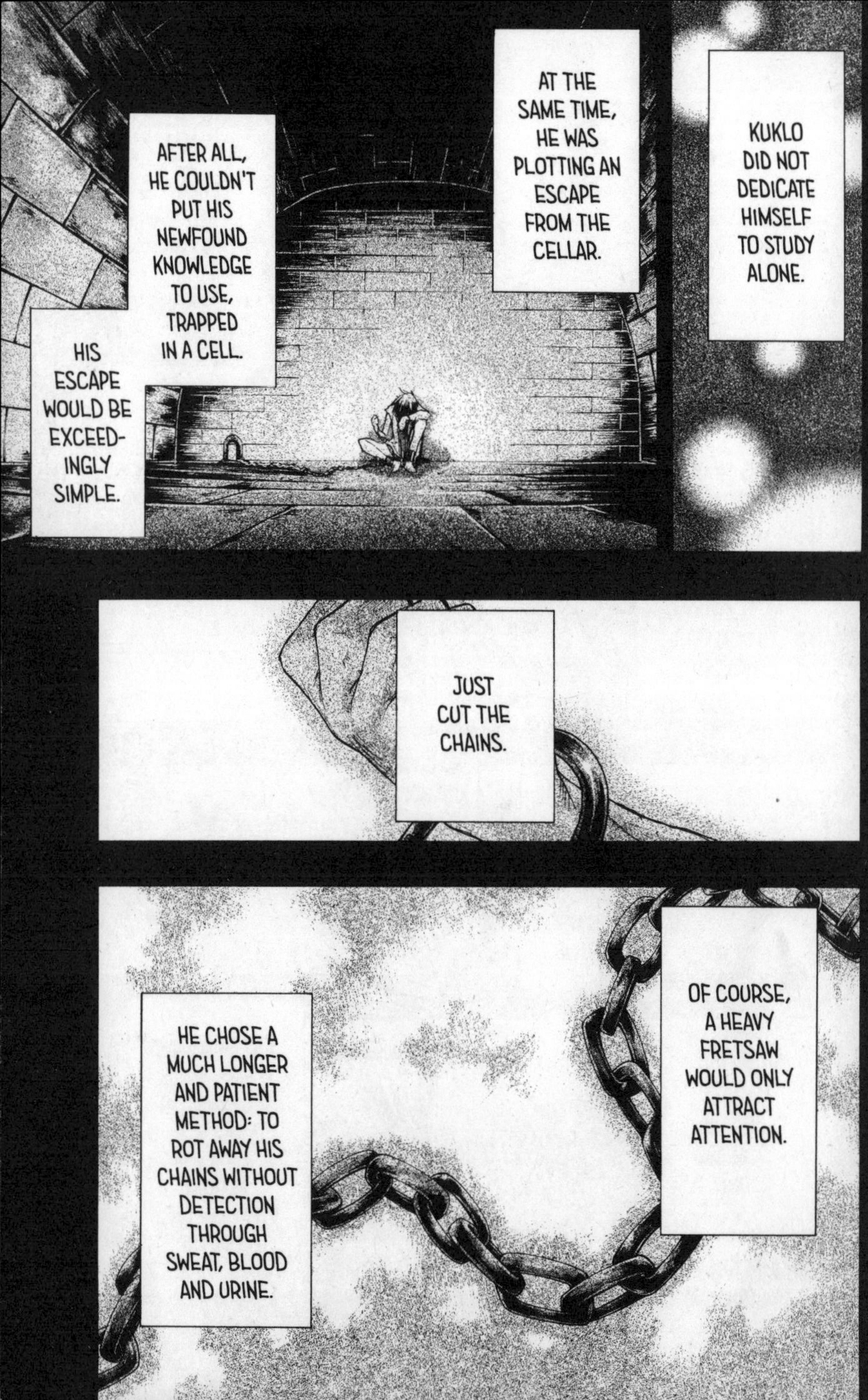
KUKLO DID NOT DEDICATE HIMSELF TO STUDY ALONE.
AT THE SAME TIME, HE WAS PLOTTING AN ESCAPE FROM THE CELLAR.
AFTER ALL, HE COULDN'T PUT HIS NEWFOUND KNOWLEDGE TO USE, TRAPPED IN A CELL.
HIS ESCAPE WOULD BE EXCEED-INGLY SIMPLE.
JUST CUT THE CHAINS.
OF COURSE, A HEAVY FRETSAW WOULD ONLY ATTRACT ATTENTION.
HE CHOSE A MUCH LONGER AND PATIENT METHOD: TO ROT AWAY HIS CHAINS WITHOUT DETECTION THROUGH SWEAT, BLOOD AND URINE.

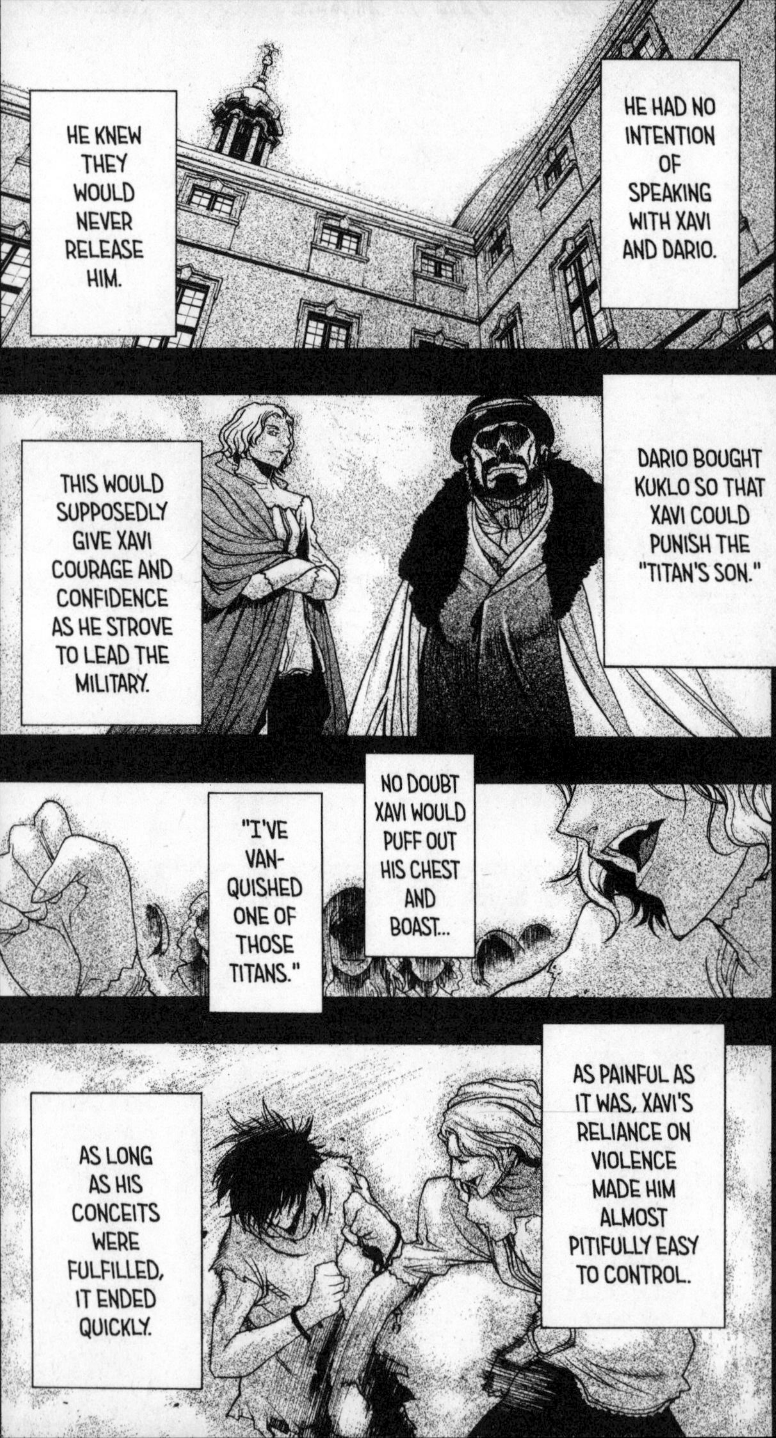
HE HAD NO INTENTION OF SPEAKING WITH XAVI AND DARIO.
HE KNEW THEY WOULD NEVER RELEASE HIM.
DARIO BOUGHT KUKLO SO THAT XAVI COULD PUNISH THE "TITAN'S SON."
THIS WOULD SUPPOSEDLY GIVE XAVI COURAGE AND CONFIDENCE AS HE STROVE TO LEAD THE MILITARY.
NO DOUBT XAVI WOULD PUFF OUT HIS CHEST AND BOAST...
"I'VE VAN-QUISHED ONE OF THOSE TITANS."
AS PAINFUL AS IT WAS, XAVI'S RELIANCE ON VIOLENCE MADE HIM ALMOST PITIFULLY EASY TO CONTROL.
AS LONG AS HIS CONCEITS WERE FULFILLED, IT ENDED QUICKLY.

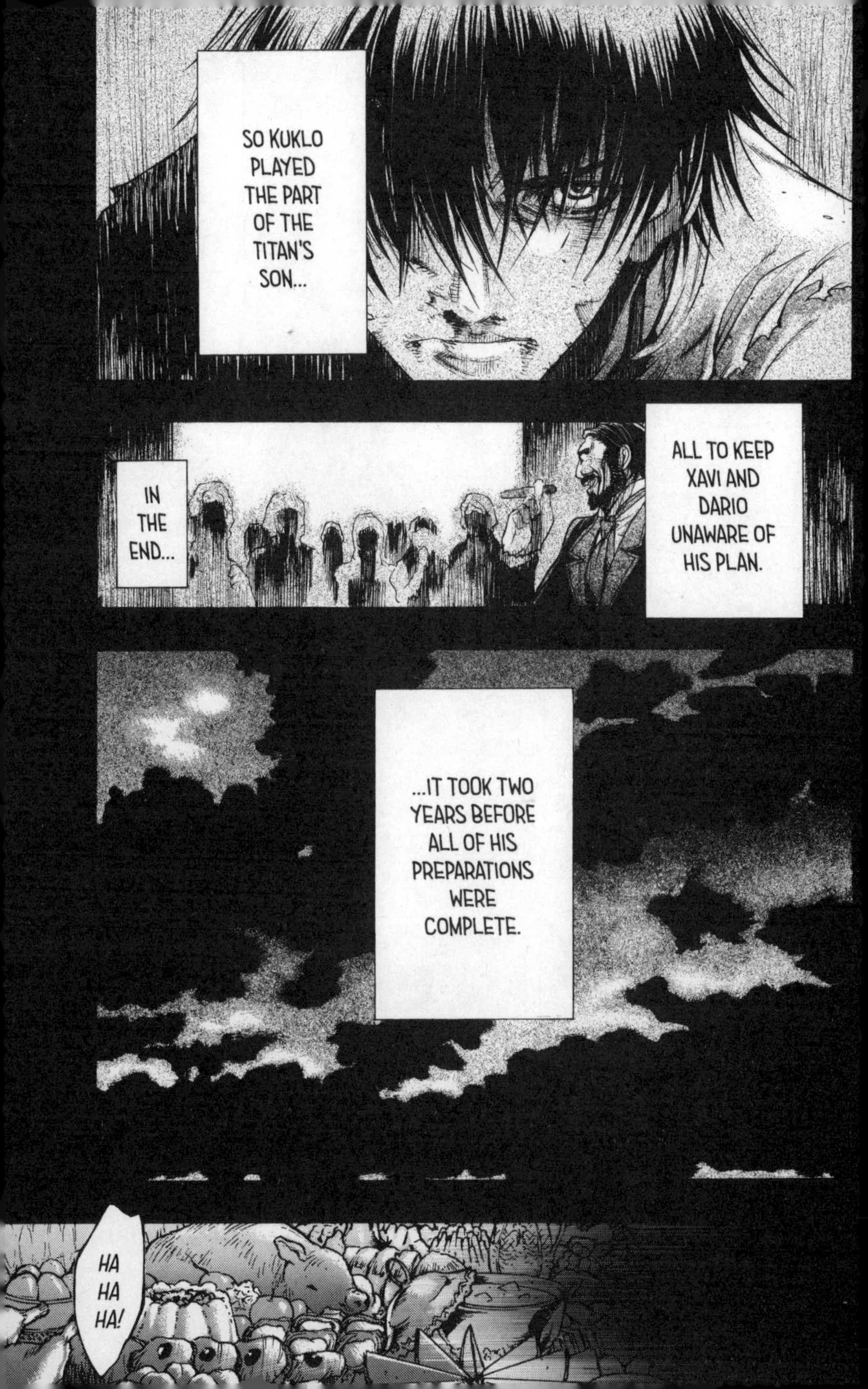
SO KUKLO PLAYED THE PART OF THE TITAN'S SON...
ALL TO KEEP XAVI AND DARIO UNAWARE OF HIS PLAN.
IN THE END...
...IT TOOK TWO YEARS BEFORE ALL OF HIS PREPARATIONS WERE COMPLETE.
HA HA HA!

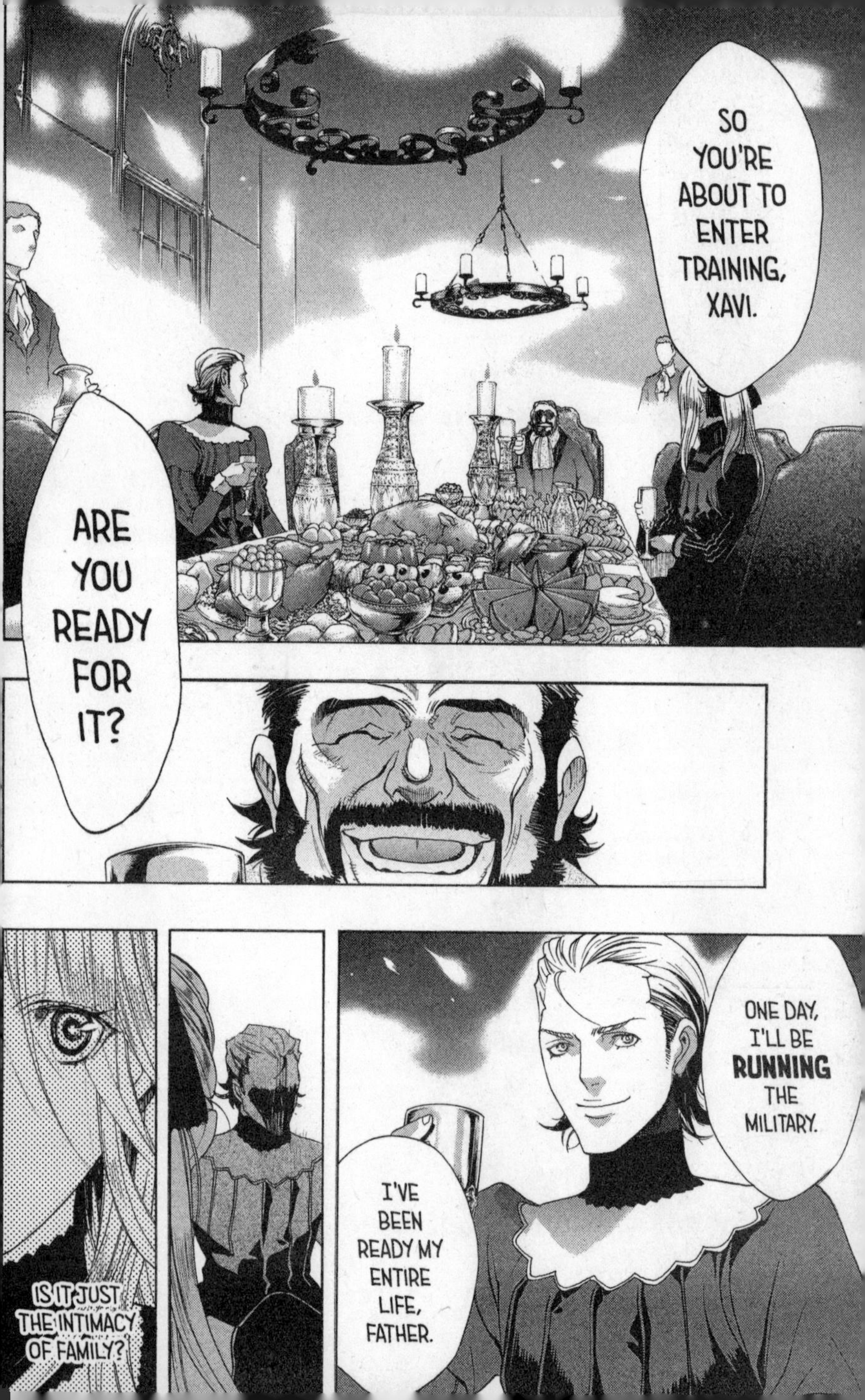
SO YOU'RE ABOUT TO ENTER TRAINING, XAVI.
ARE YOU READY FOR IT?
ONE DAY, I'LL BE **RUNNING** THE MILITARY.
I'VE BEEN READY MY ENTIRE LIFE, FATHER.
IS IT JUST THE INTIMACY OF FAMILY?

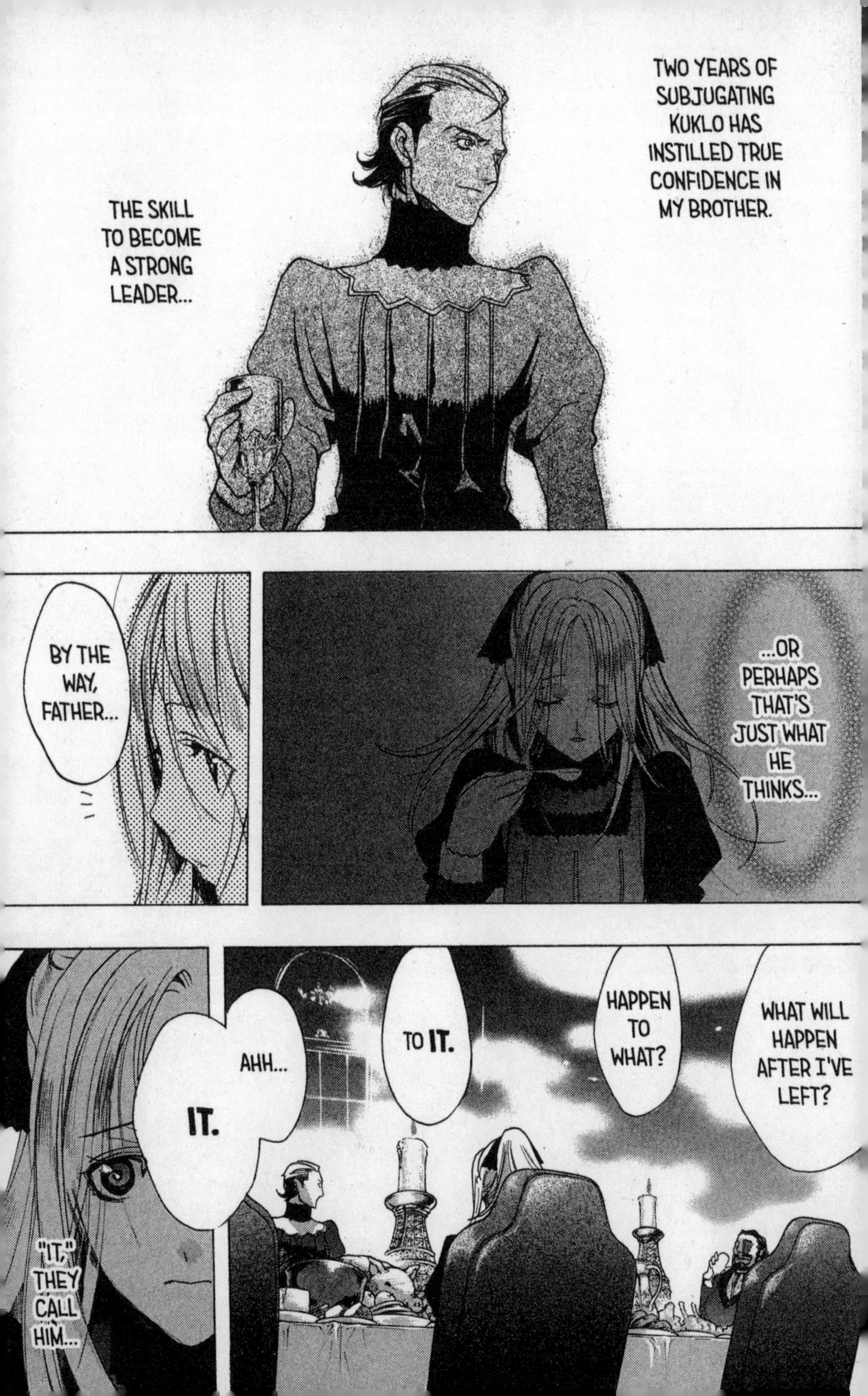
TWO YEARS OF SUBJUGATING KUKLO HAS INSTILLED TRUE CONFIDENCE IN MY BROTHER.
THE SKILL TO BECOME A STRONG LEADER...
...OR PERHAPS THAT'S JUST WHAT HE THINKS...
BY THE WAY, FATHER...
WHAT WILL HAPPEN AFTER I'VE LEFT?
HAPPEN TO WHAT?
TO IT.
AHH...
IT.
"IT," THEY CALL HIM...

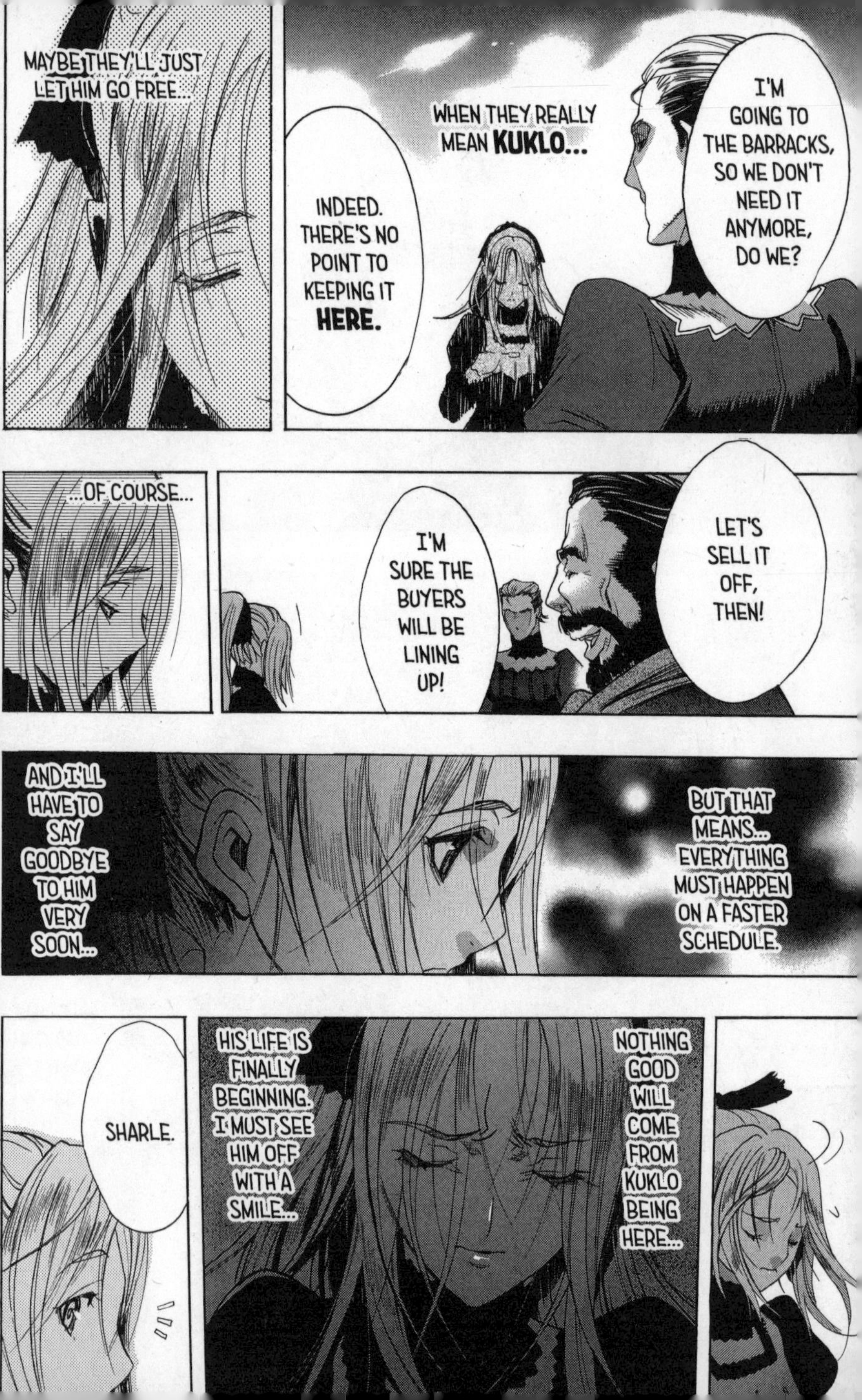
I'M GOING TO THE BARRACKS, SO WE DON'T NEED IT ANYMORE, DO WE?
WHEN THEY REALLY MEAN KUKLO...
INDEED. THERE'S NO POINT TO KEEPING IT HERE.
MAYBE THEY'LL JUST LET HIM GO FREE...
LET'S SELL IT OFF, THEN!
I'M SURE THE BUYERS WILL BE LINING UP!
...OF COURSE...
BUT THAT MEANS... EVERYTHING MUST HAPPEN ON A FASTER SCHEDULE.
AND I'LL HAVE TO SAY GOODBYE TO HIM VERY SOON...
NOTHING GOOD WILL COME FROM KUKLO BEING HERE...
HIS LIFE IS FINALLY BEGINNING. I MUST SEE HIM OFF WITH A SMILE...
SHARLE.

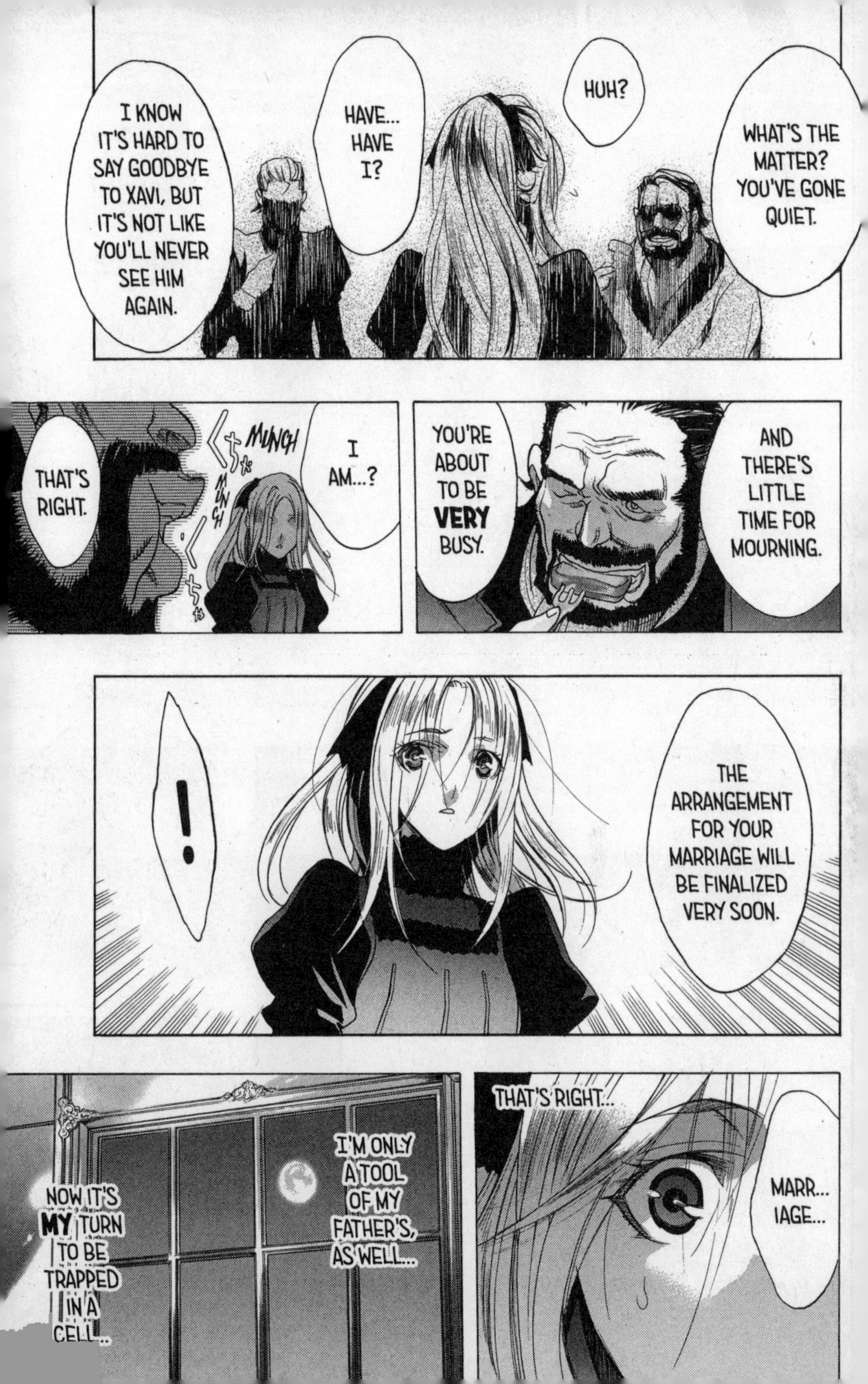
WHAT'S THE MATTER? YOU'VE GONE QUIET.
HUH?
HAVE... HAVE I?
I KNOW IT'S HARD TO SAY GOODBYE TO XAVI, BUT IT'S NOT LIKE YOU'LL NEVER SEE HIM AGAIN.
AND THERE'S LITTLE TIME FOR MOURNING.
YOU'RE ABOUT TO BE VERY BUSY.
I AM...?
MUNCH
MUNCH
THAT'S RIGHT.
THE ARRANGEMENT FOR YOUR MARRIAGE WILL BE FINALIZED VERY SOON.
!
MARR... IAGE...
THAT'S RIGHT...
I'M ONLY A TOOL OF MY FATHER'S, AS WELL...
NOW IT'S MY TURN TO BE TRAPPED IN A CELL...

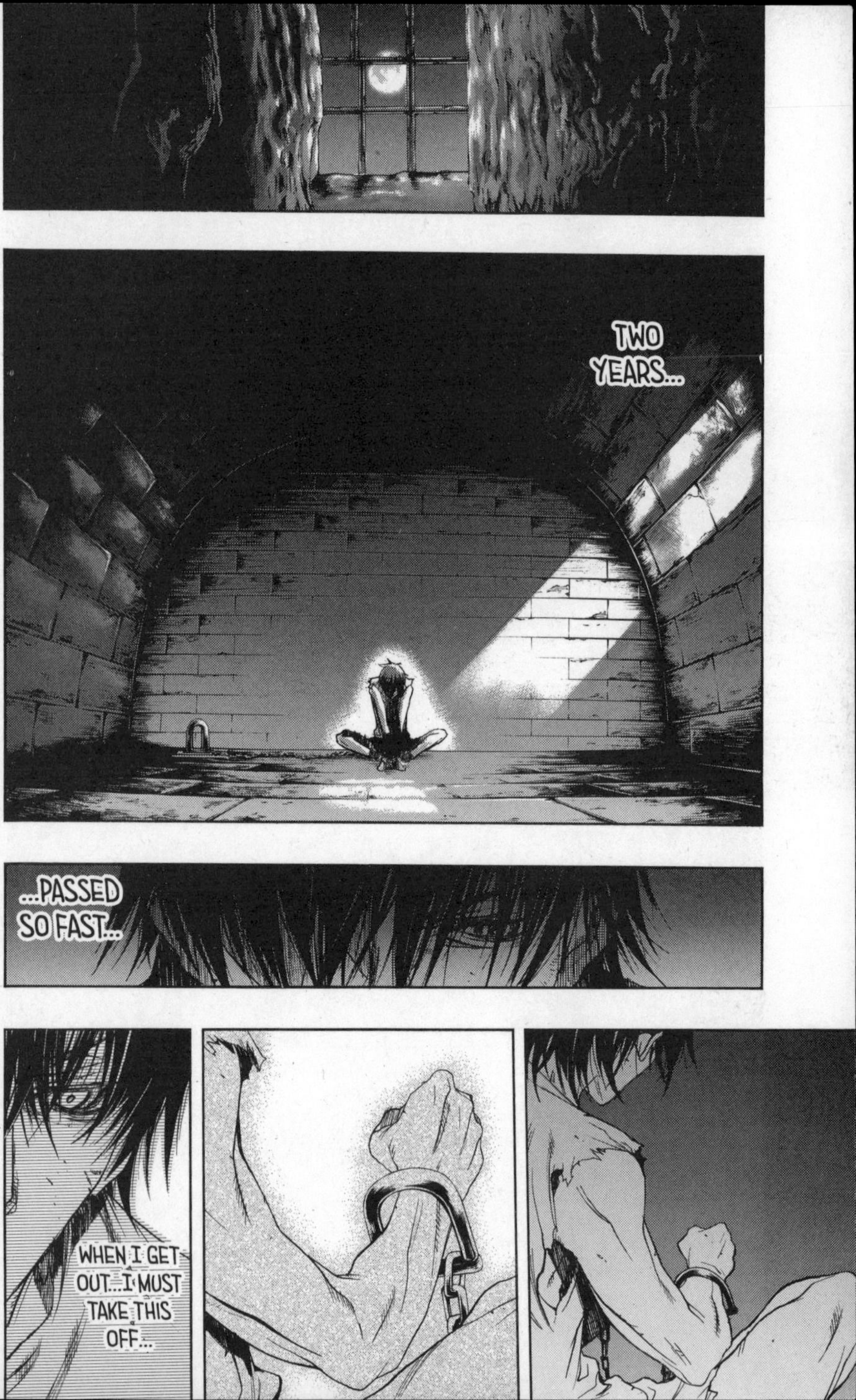
TWO YEARS...
...PASSED SO FAST...
WHEN I GET OUT...I MUST TAKE THIS OFF...

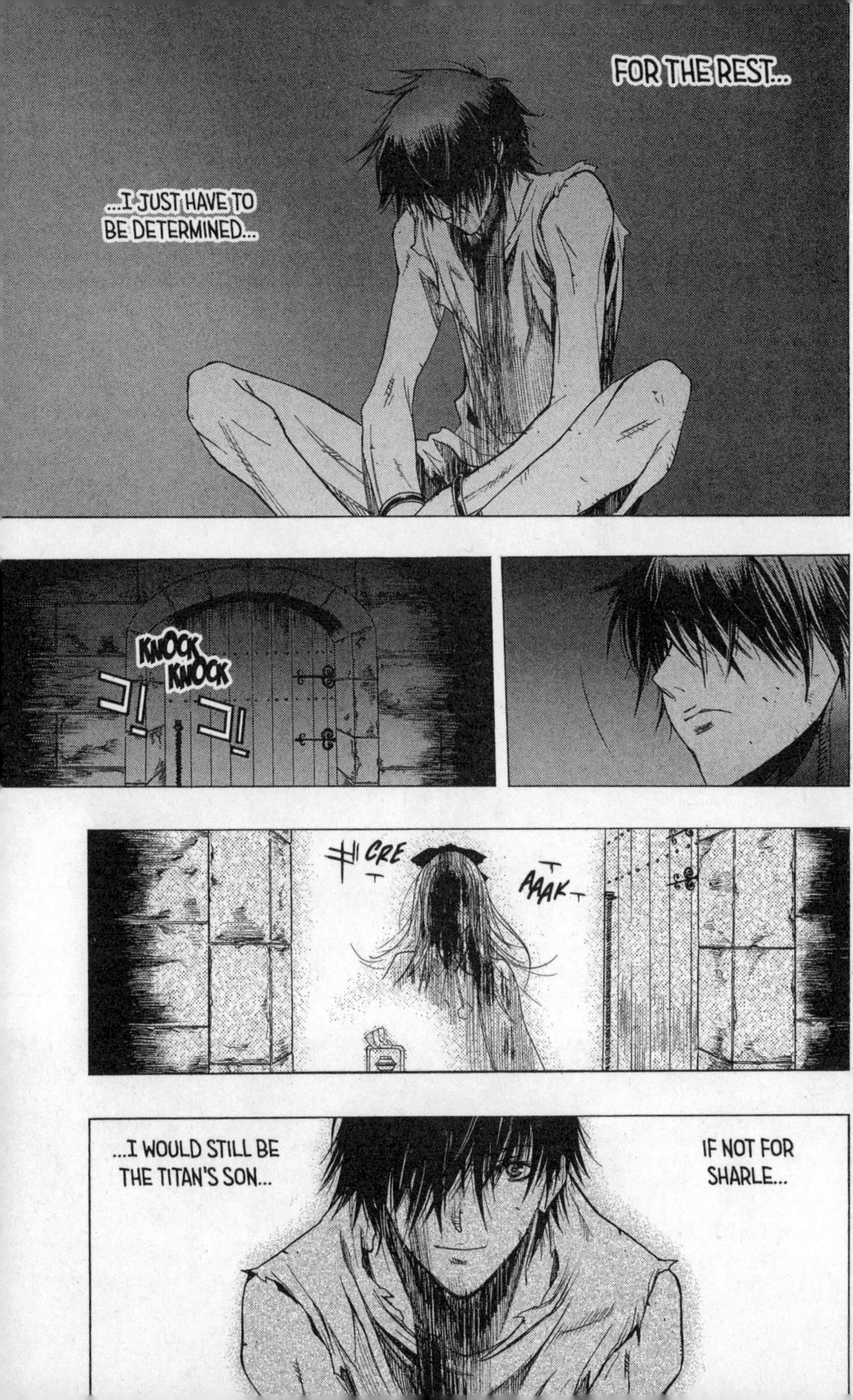
FOR THE REST...
...I JUST HAVE TO BE DETERMINED...
KNOCK KNOCK
CRE AAAK
IF NOT FOR SHARLE...
...I WOULD STILL BE THE TITAN'S SON...

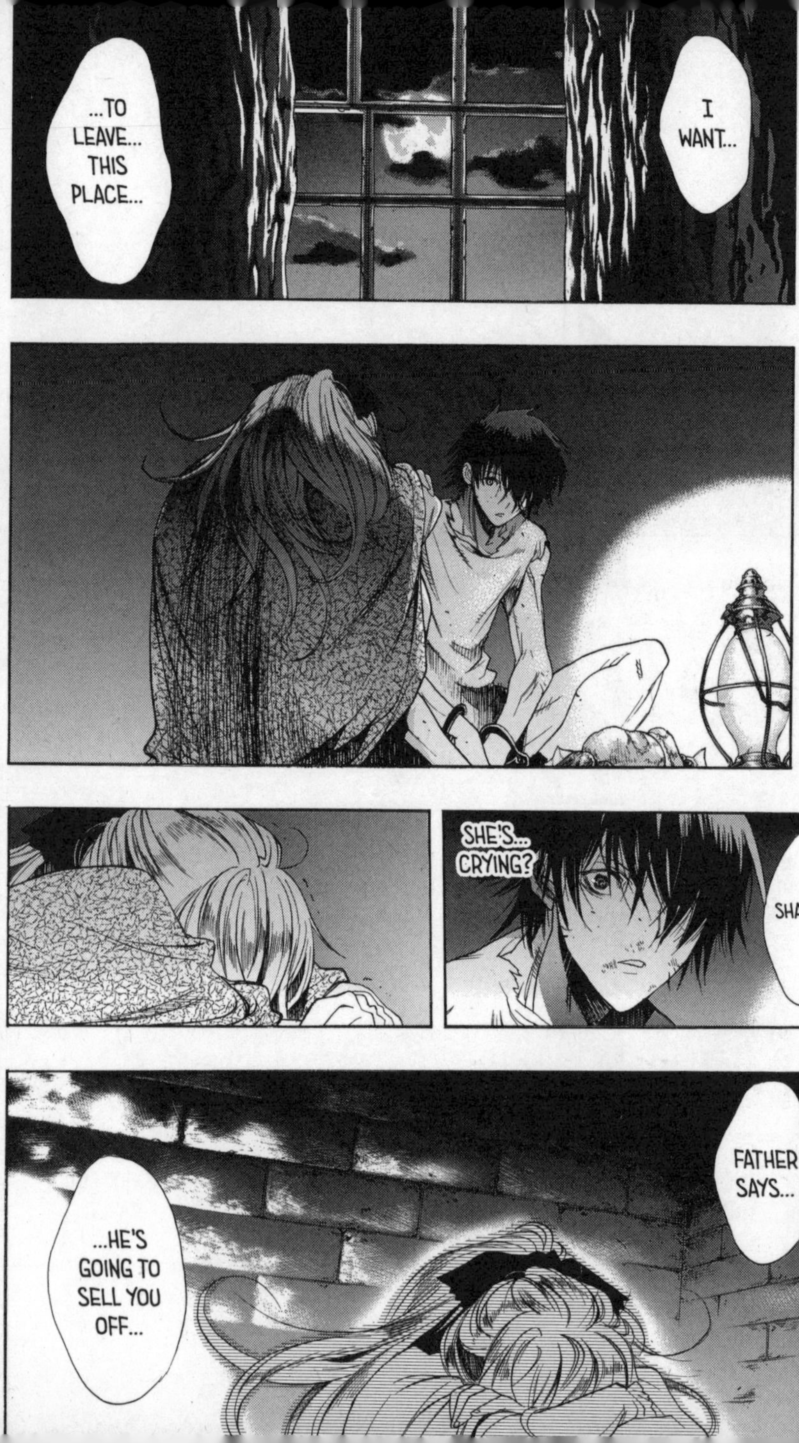
I WANT...
...TO LEAVE... THIS PLACE...
SHARLE...
SHE'S... CRYING?
FATHER SAYS...
...HE'S GOING TO SELL YOU OFF...

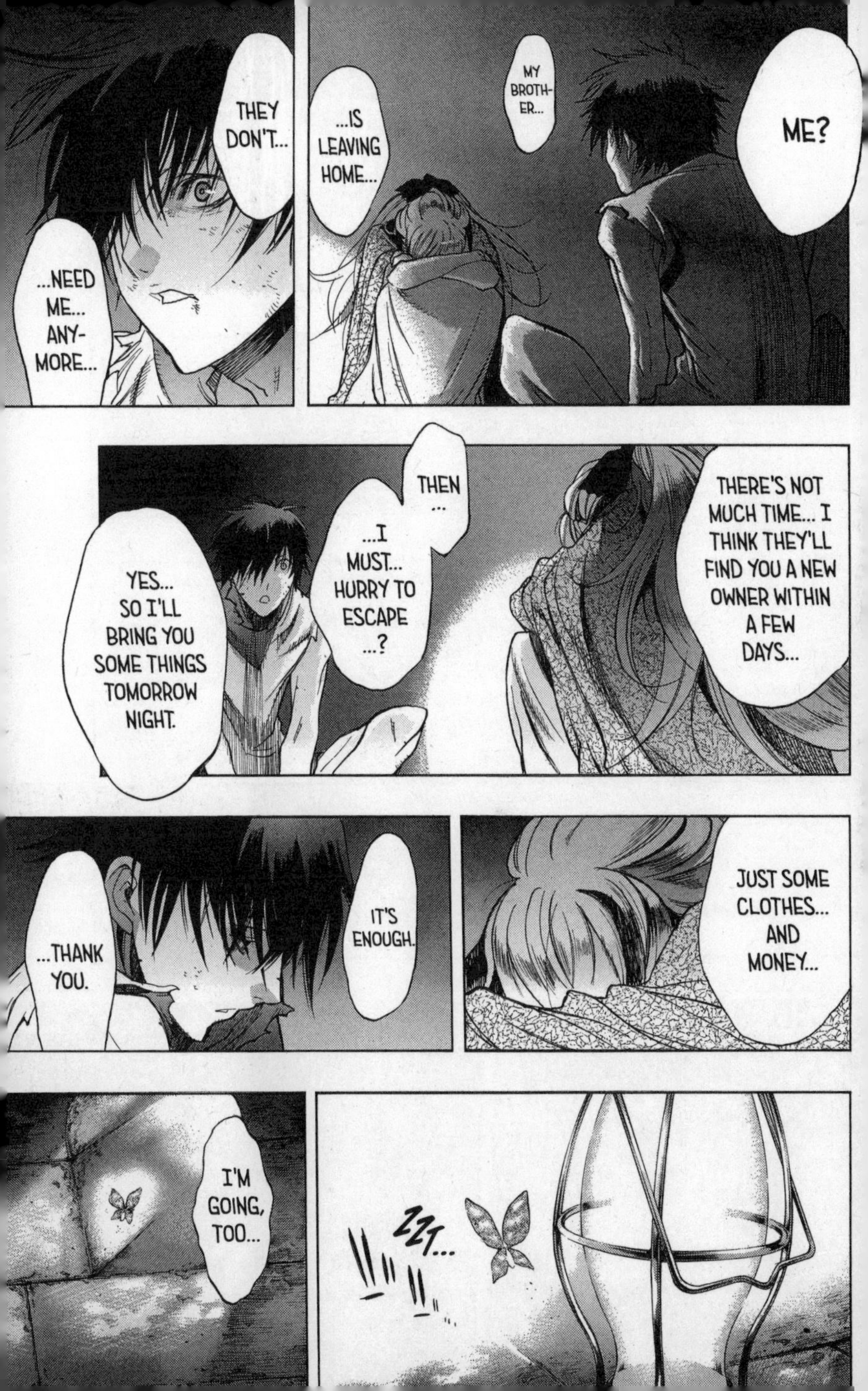
ME?
MY BROTHER-ER...
...IS LEAVING HOME...
THEY DON'T...
...NEED ME... ANYMORE...
THERE'S NOT MUCH TIME... I THINK THEY'LL FIND YOU A NEW OWNER WITHIN A FEW DAYS...
THEN ...
...I MUST... HURRY TO ESCAPE ...?
YES... SO I'LL BRING YOU SOME THINGS TOMORROW NIGHT.
JUST SOME CLOTHES... AND MONEY...
IT'S ENOUGH.
...THANK YOU.
ZZT...
I'M GOING, TOO...

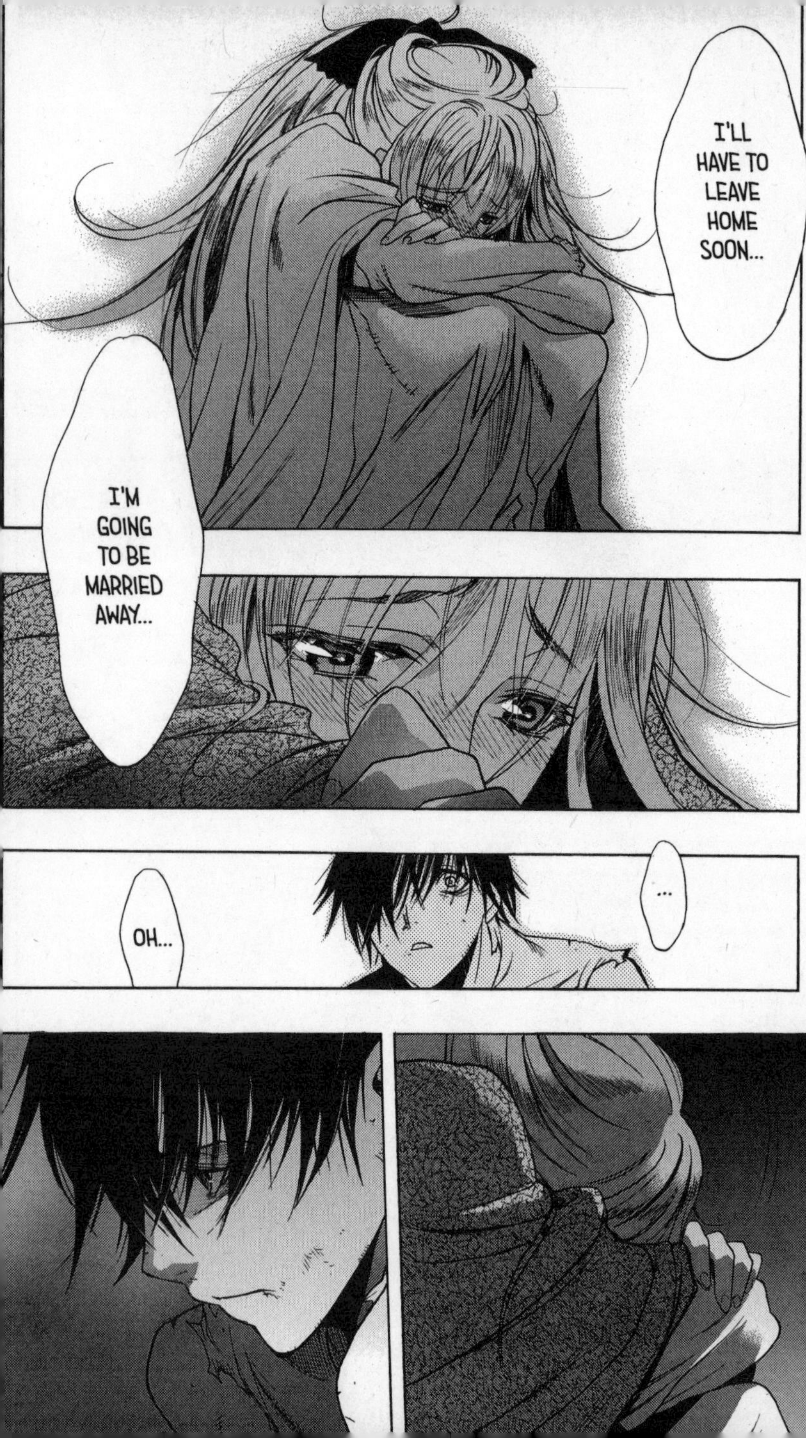
I'LL HAVE TO LEAVE HOME SOON...
I'M GOING TO BE MARRIED AWAY...
...
OH...

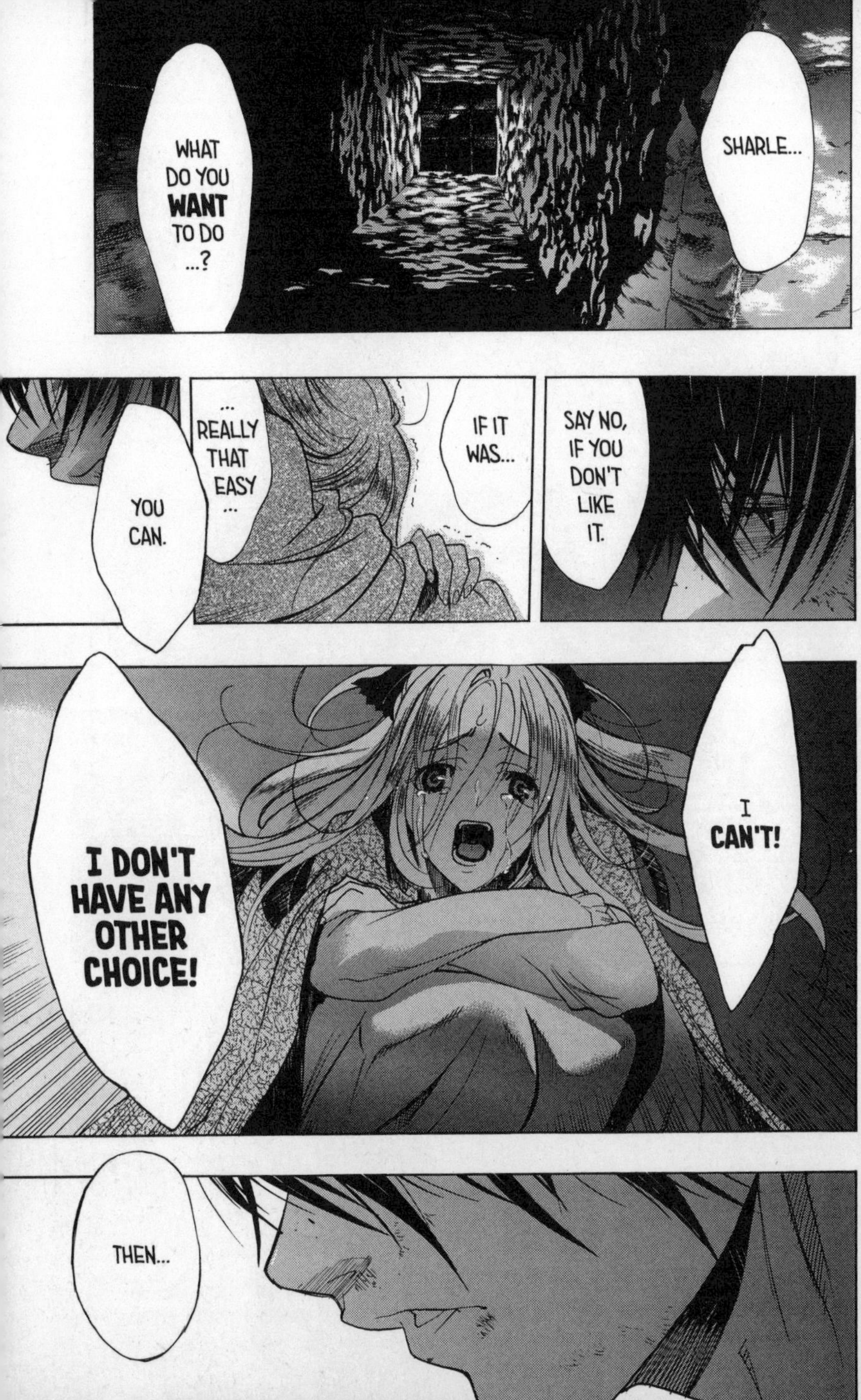
SHARLE...
WHAT DO YOU **WANT** TO DO ...?
SAY NO, IF YOU DON'T LIKE IT.
IF IT WAS...
... REALLY THAT EASY ...
YOU CAN.
I **CAN'T!**
I DON'T HAVE ANY OTHER CHOICE!
THEN...

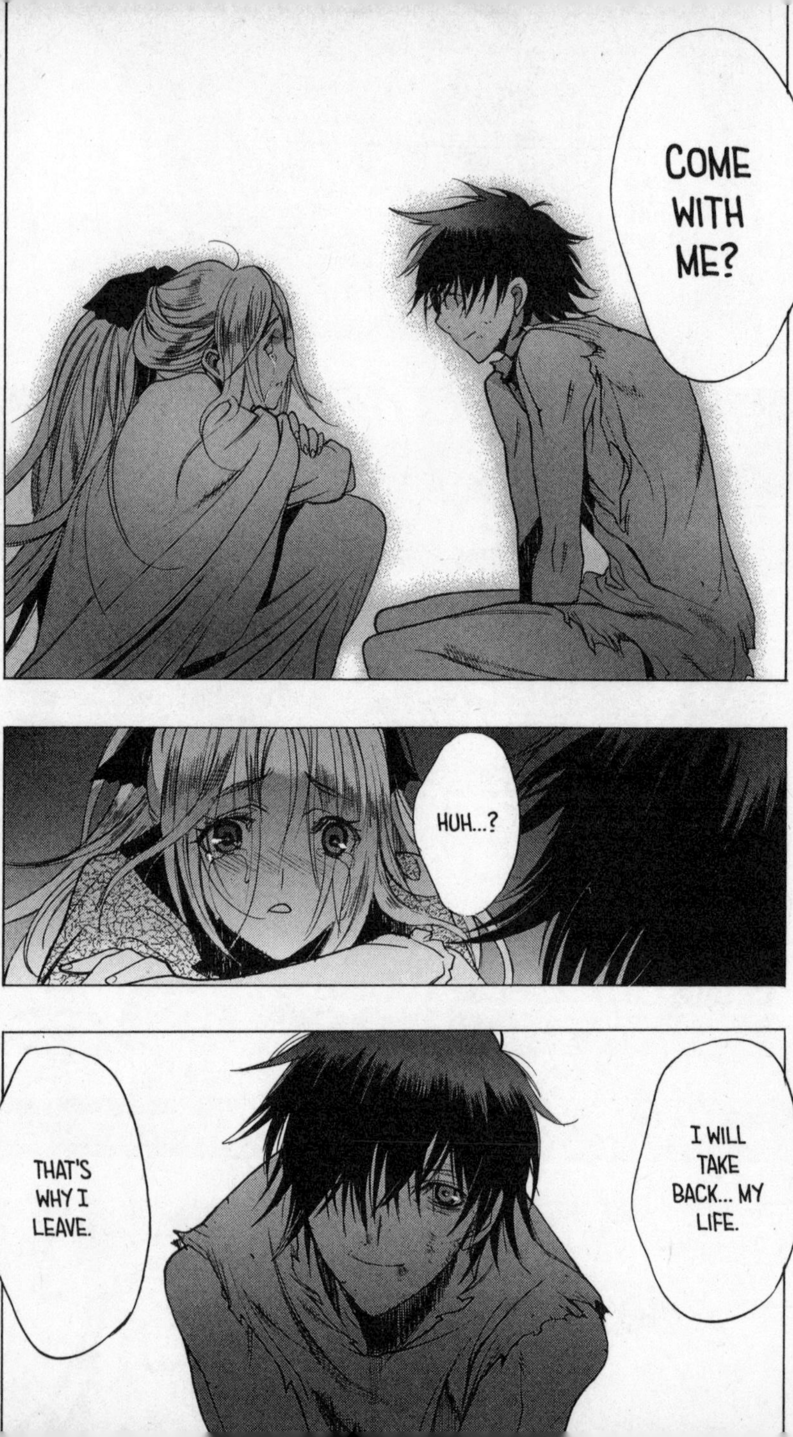
COME WITH ME?
HUH...?
I WILL TAKE BACK... MY LIFE.
THAT'S WHY I LEAVE.

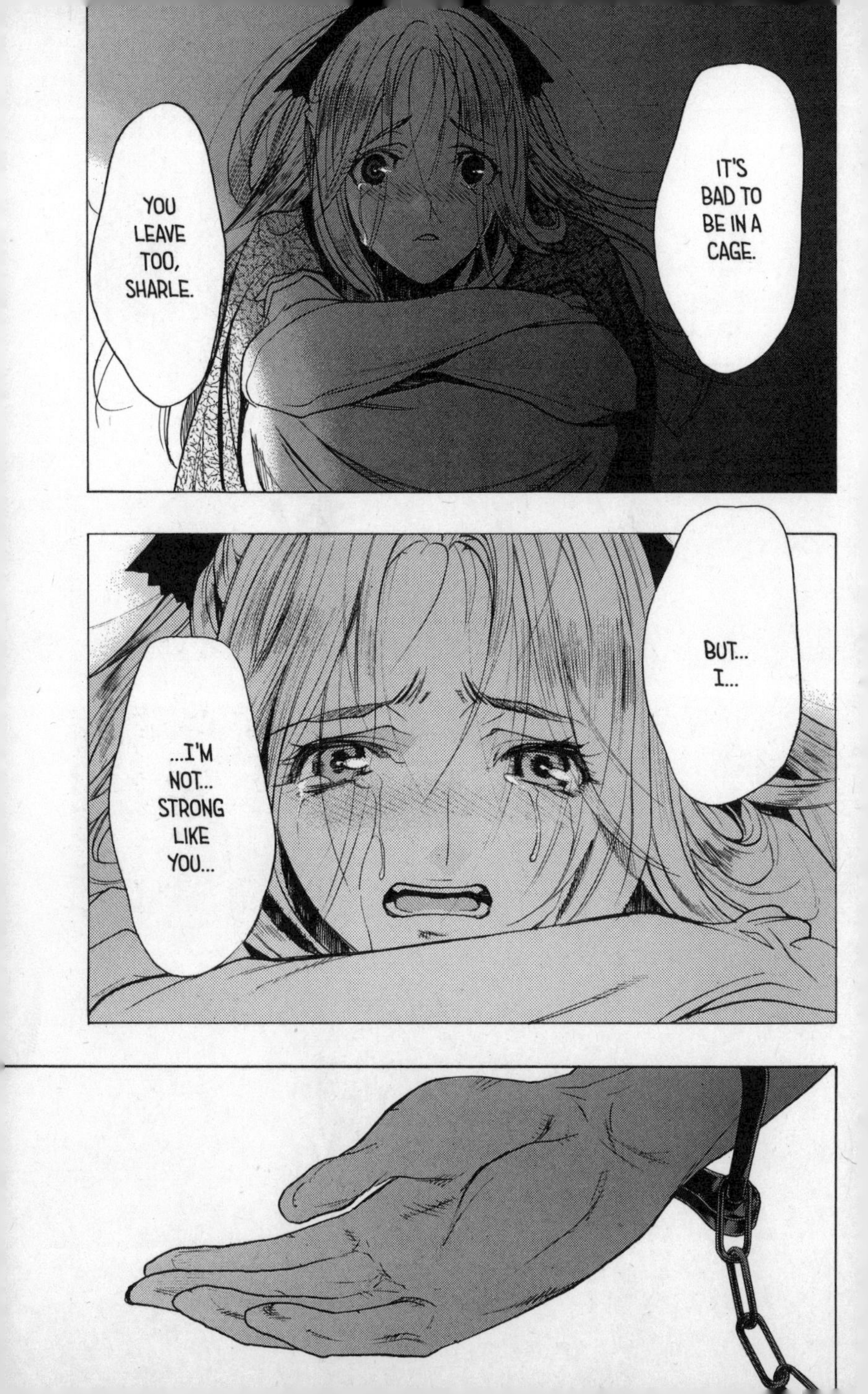
IT'S BAD TO BE IN A CAGE.
YOU LEAVE TOO, SHARLE.
BUT... I...
...I'M NOT... STRONG LIKE YOU...

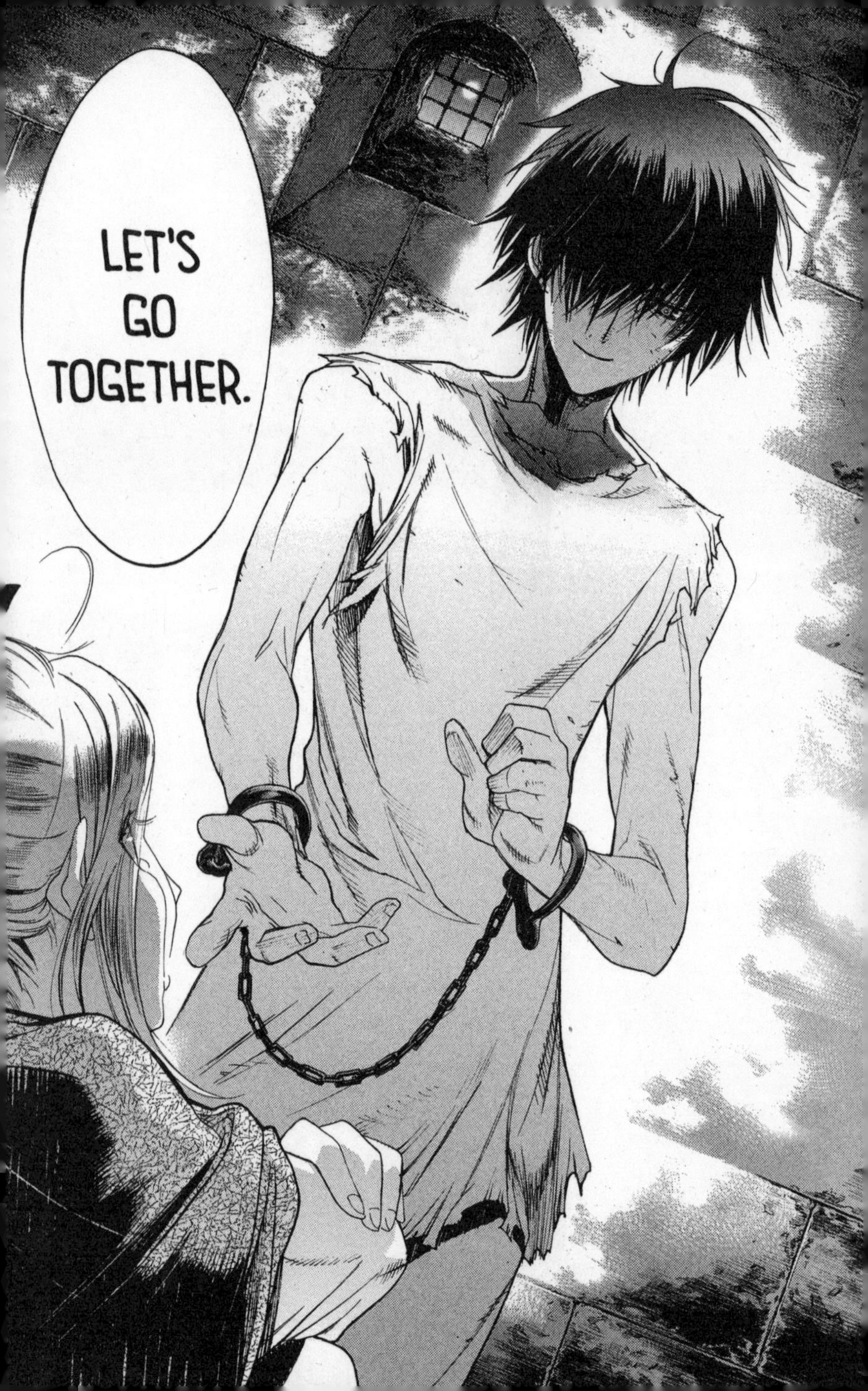
LET'S GO TOGETHER.

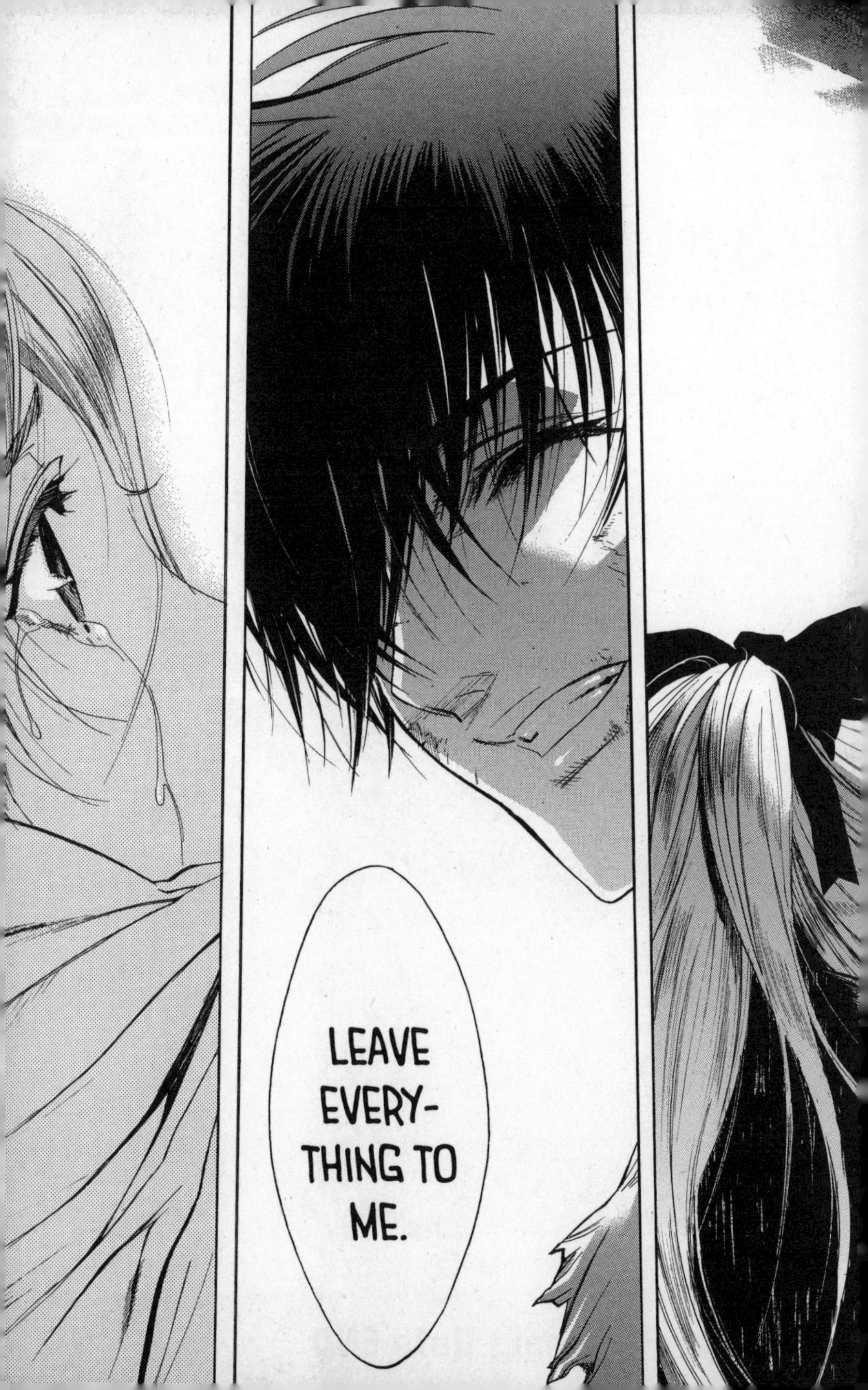
LEAVE EVERY-THING TO ME.

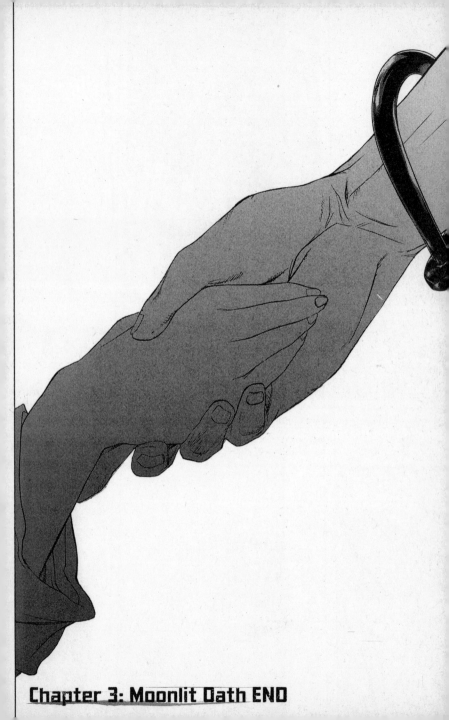

Chapter 3: Moonlit Oath END

ATTACK on TITAN
BEFORE THE FALL

TO BE CONTINUED

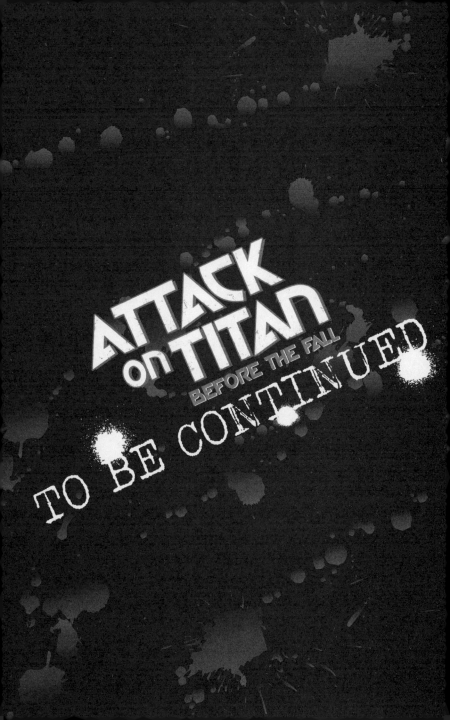

The following 12-page story, "Attack on Titan: Before the Fall: Trailer," is something like a pilot version of this story that was originally run in the magazine as a prologue. Because of this, some events may differ from the finished story.

THE FALL OF WALL MARIA.

THE FATEFUL DAY...

...ON WHICH HUMANITY LOST...

...A THIRD OF ITS SAFE HARBOR...

BUT FEW KNEW OF THE FACT THAT **THEY** ONCE BREACHED OUR WALLS 70 YEARS AGO...

...FOR DESPITE THE MANY VICTIMS OF THAT DISASTER, THE ROYAL GOVERNMENT FORBADE THE PEOPLE TO SPEAK OF IT, AND ERASED ALL TRACES OF IT FROM RECORD...

BUT IT REALLY DID HAPPEN.

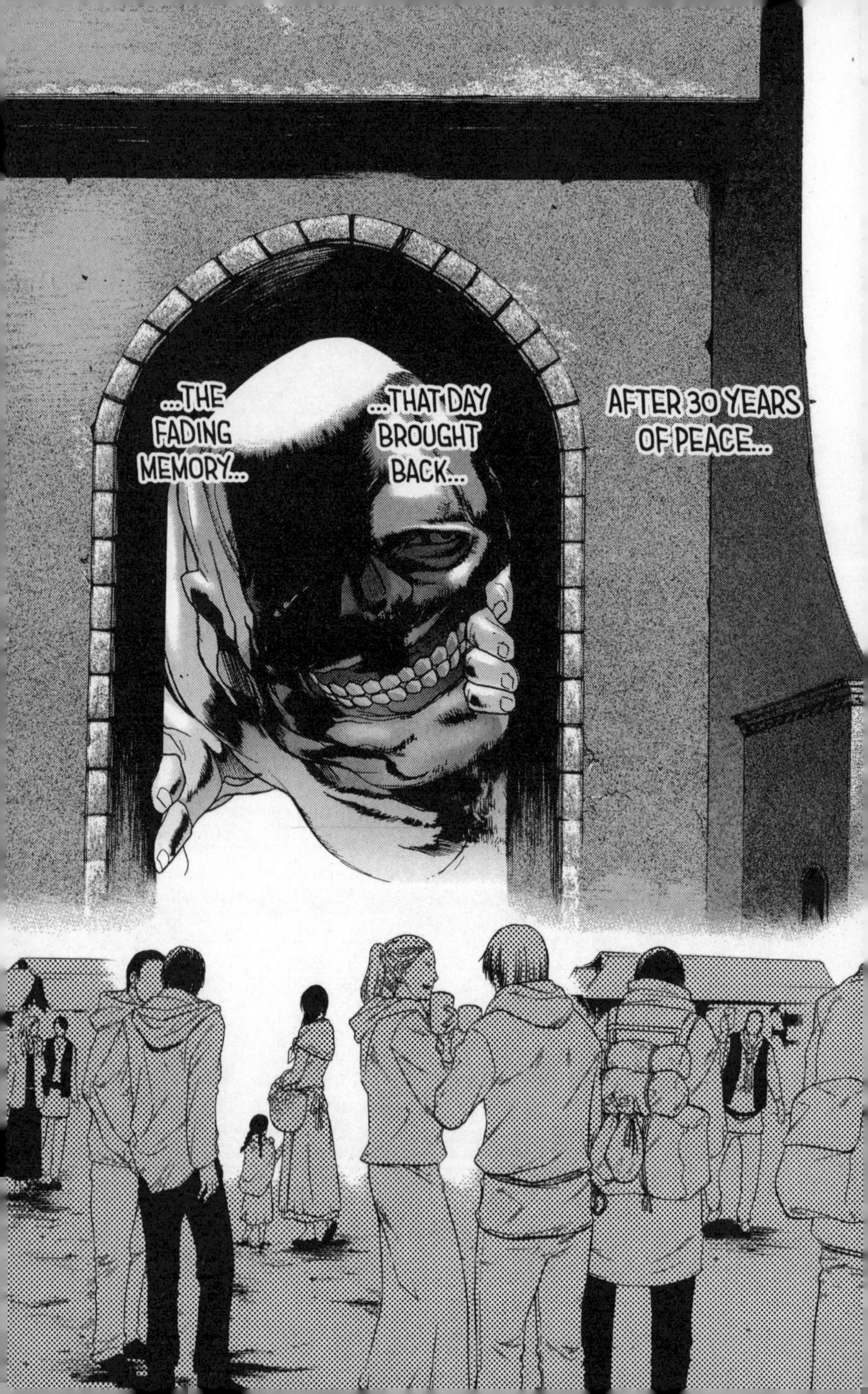
AFTER 30 YEARS OF PEACE...
...THAT DAY BROUGHT BACK...
...THE FADING MEMORY...

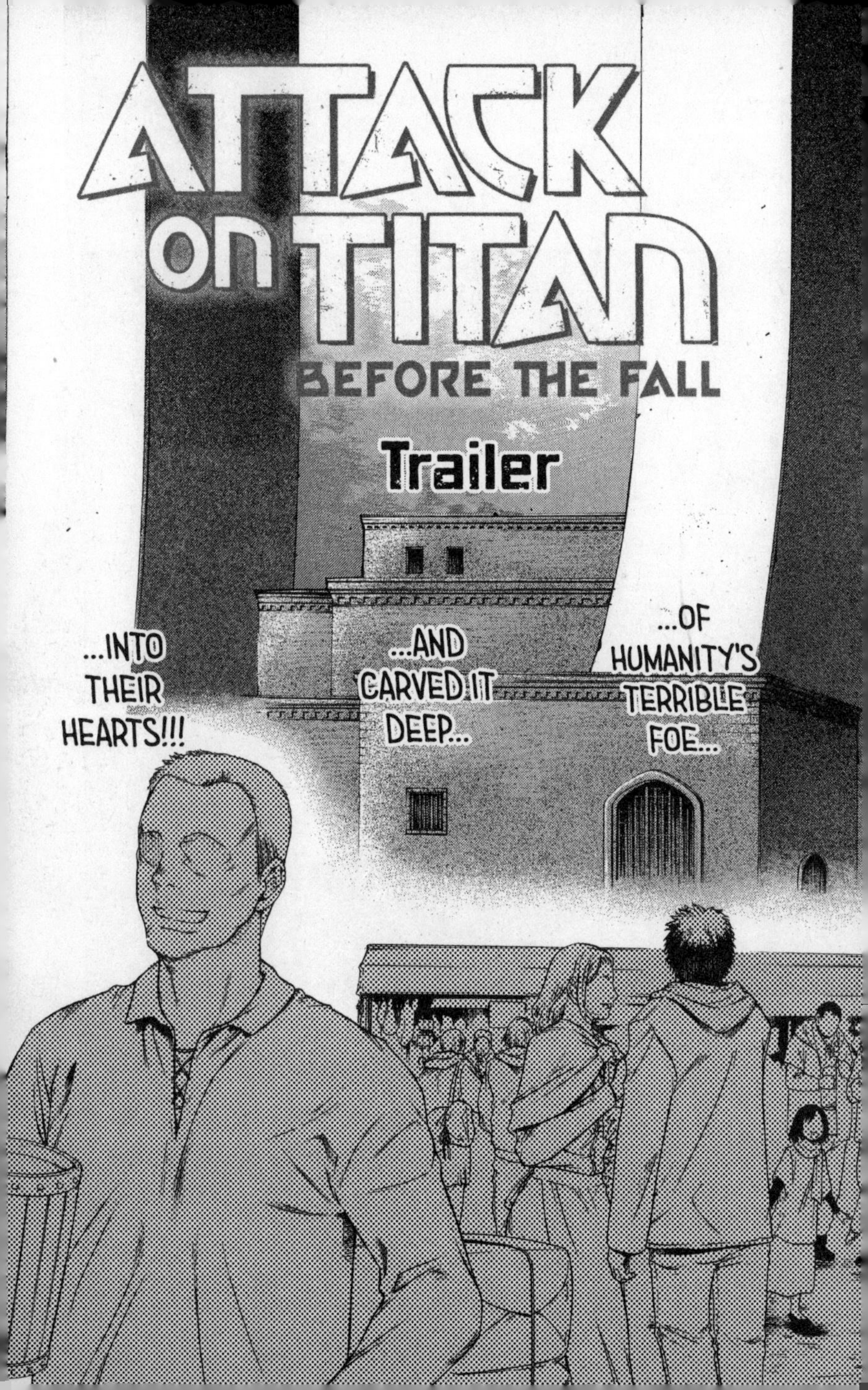
ATTACK on TITAN
BEFORE THE FALL
Trailer
...OF HUMANITY'S TERRIBLE FOE...
...AND CARVED IT DEEP...
...INTO THEIR HEARTS!!!

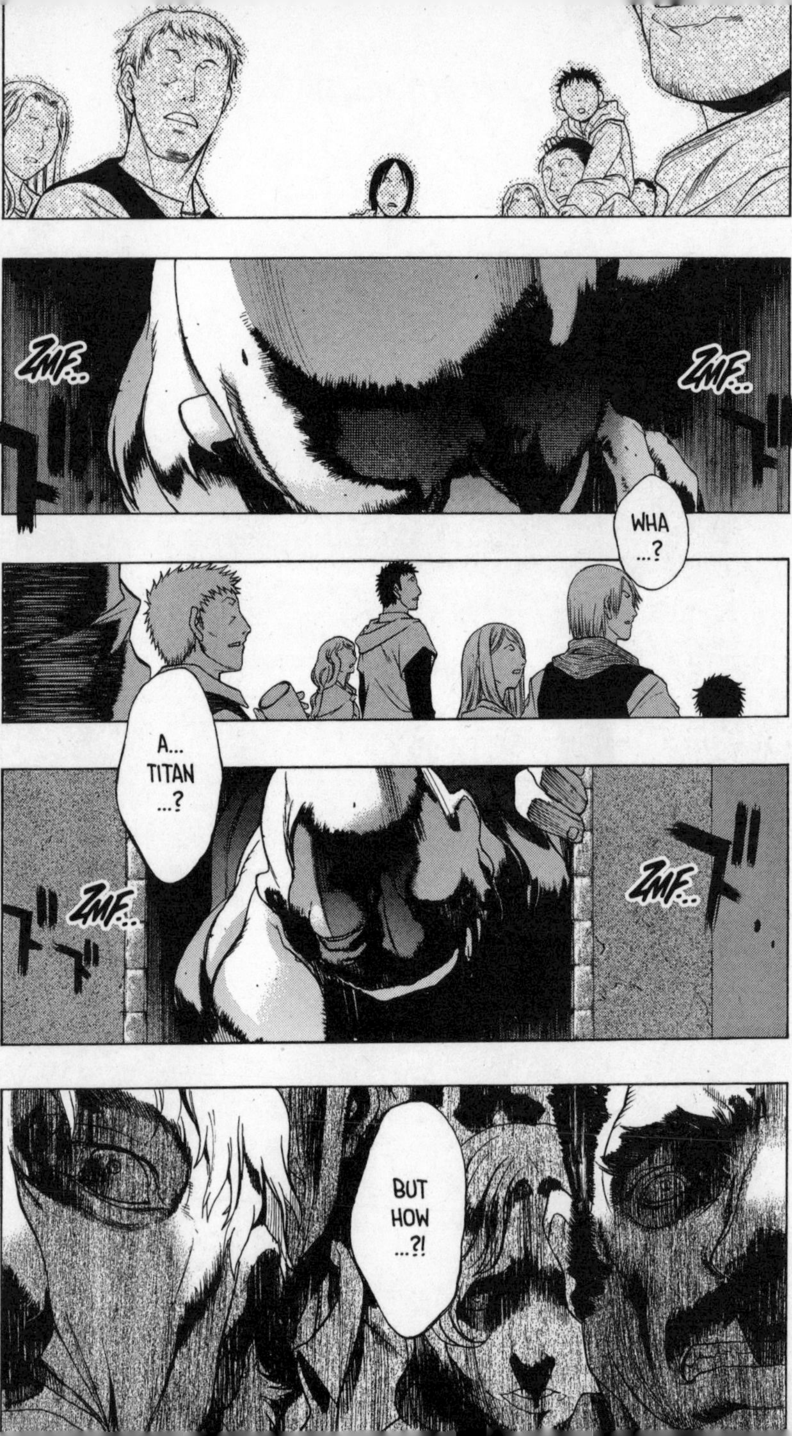
ZMF..
ZMF..
WHA ...?
A... TITAN ...?
ZMF..
ZMF..
BUT HOW ...?!

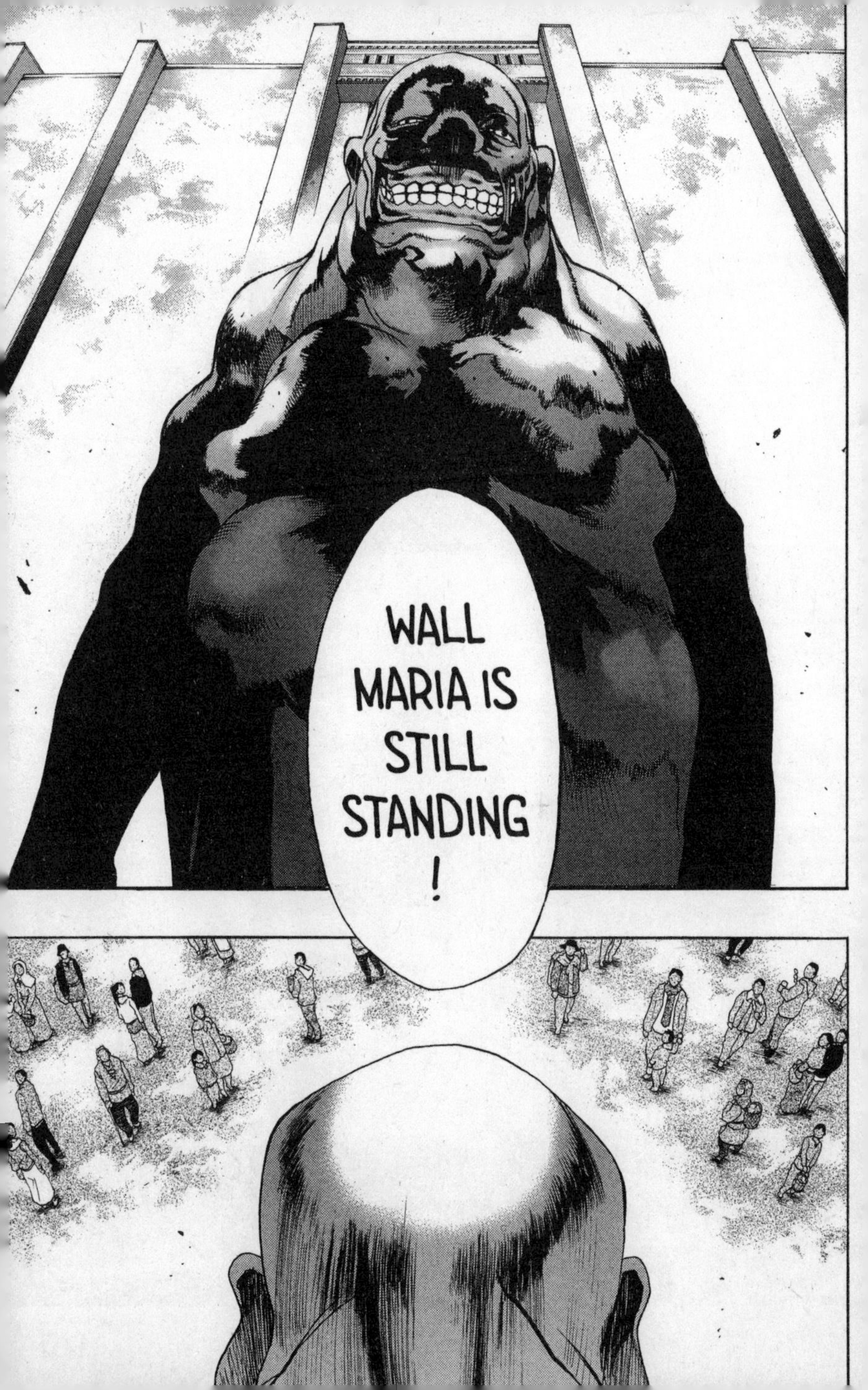
WALL MARIA IS STILL STANDING!

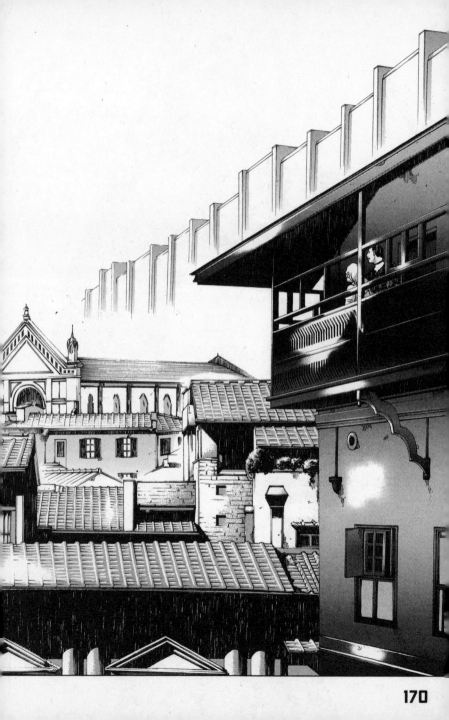

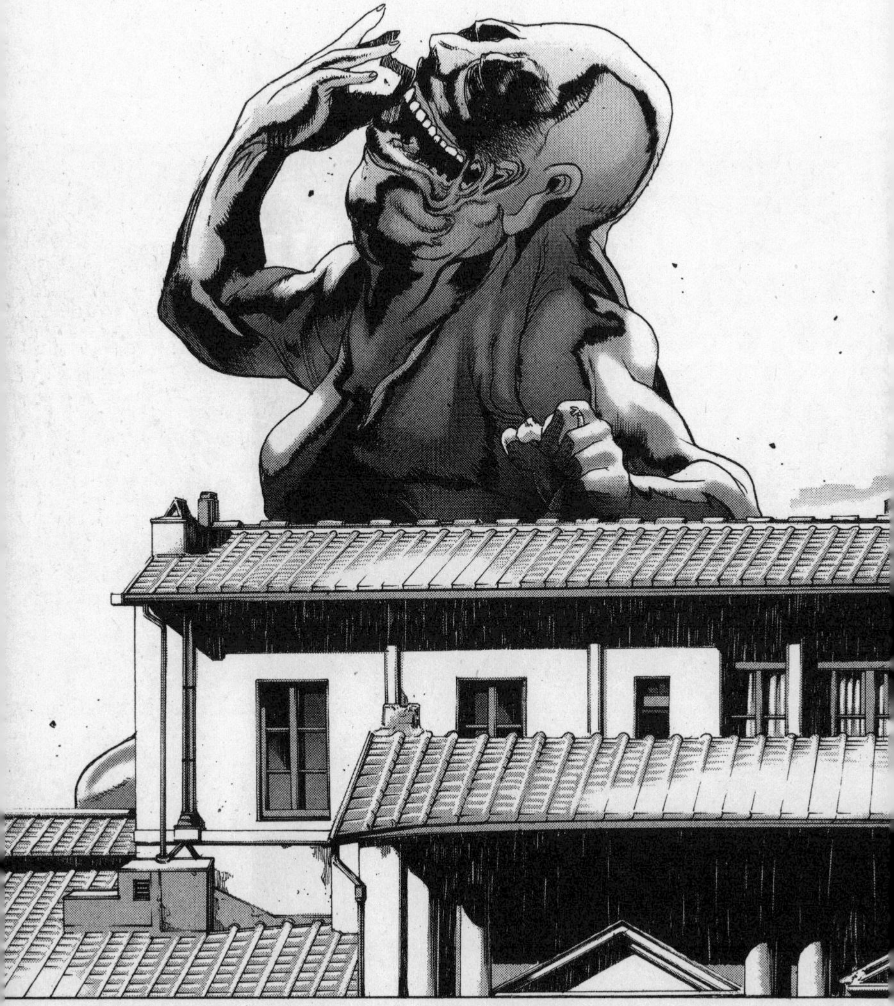

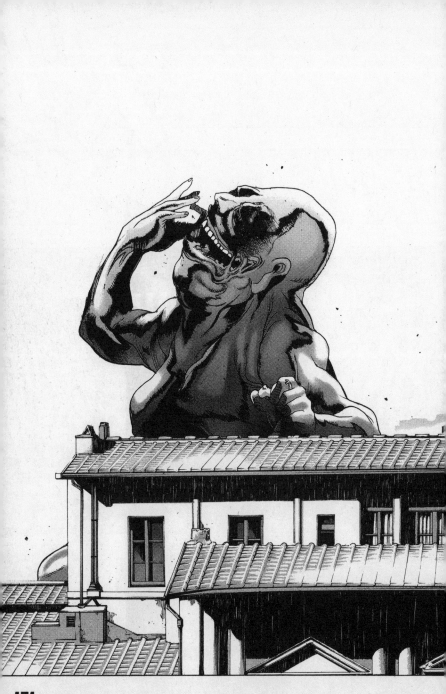

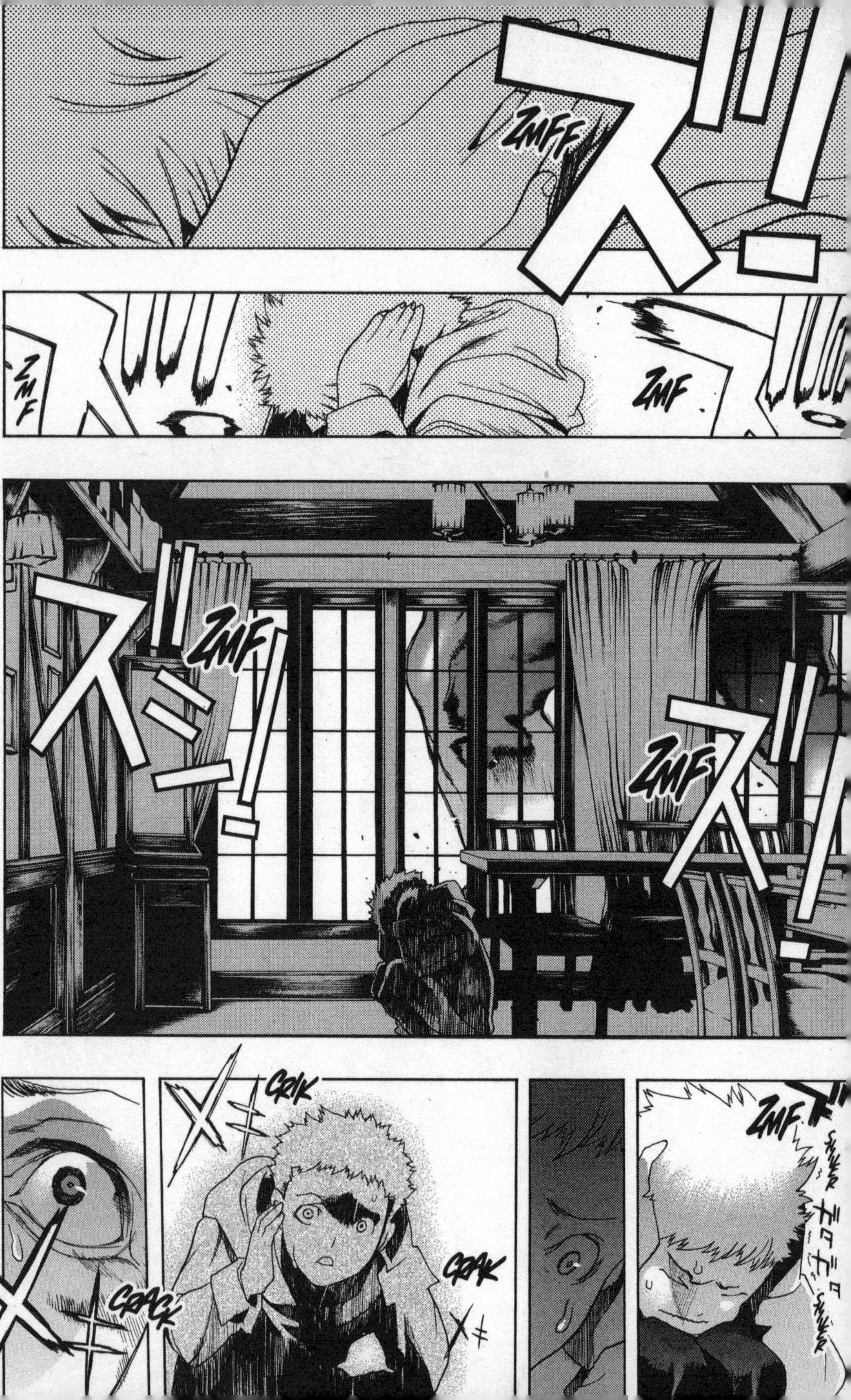
ズ!!
ZMFF
ZMF
ZMF
ZMF
ZMF
ZMF
SHIVER
SHIVER
CRIK
CRAK
CRACK

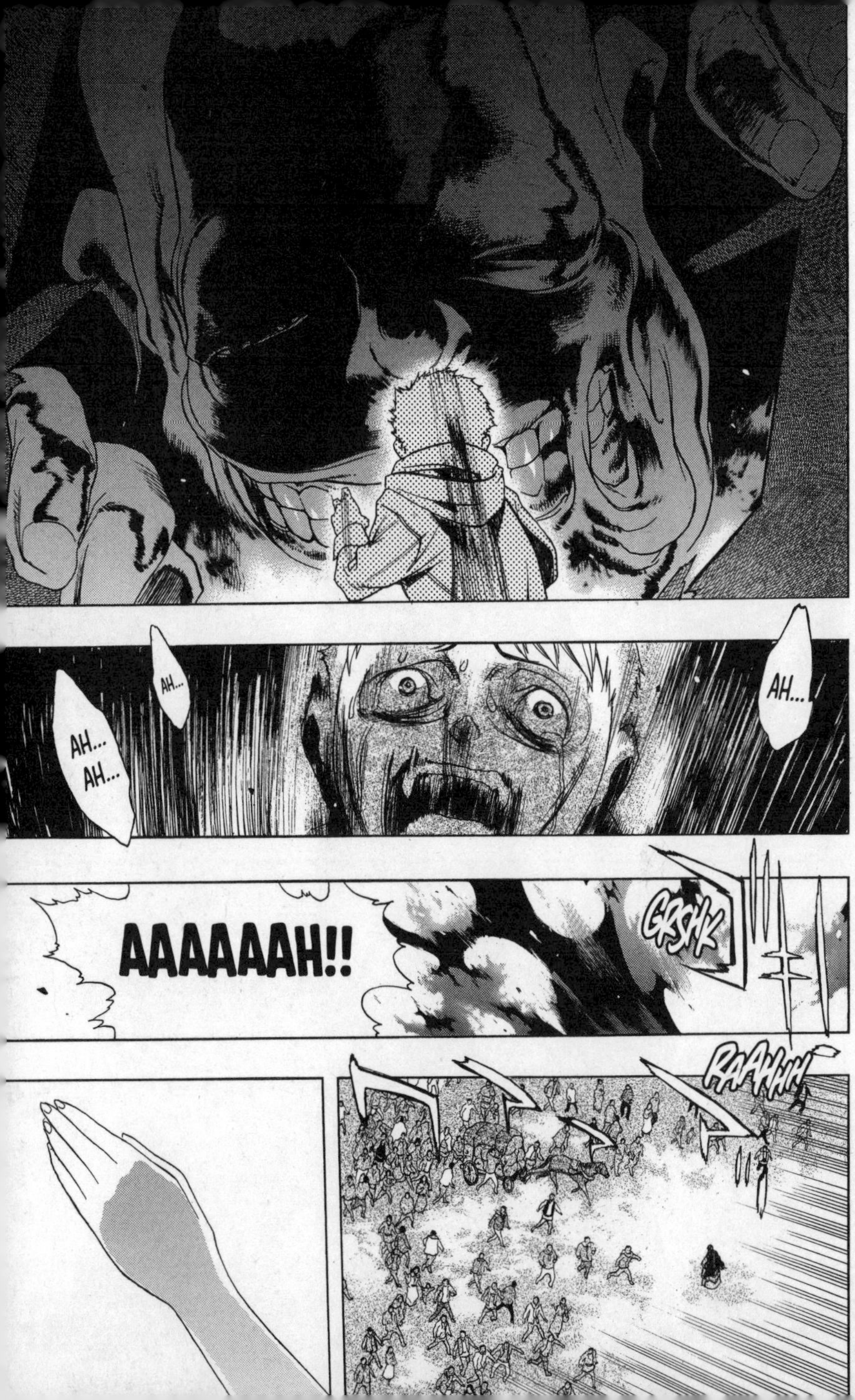
AH...
AH...
AH... AH...
GRSHK
AAAAAAH!!
RAAAHH

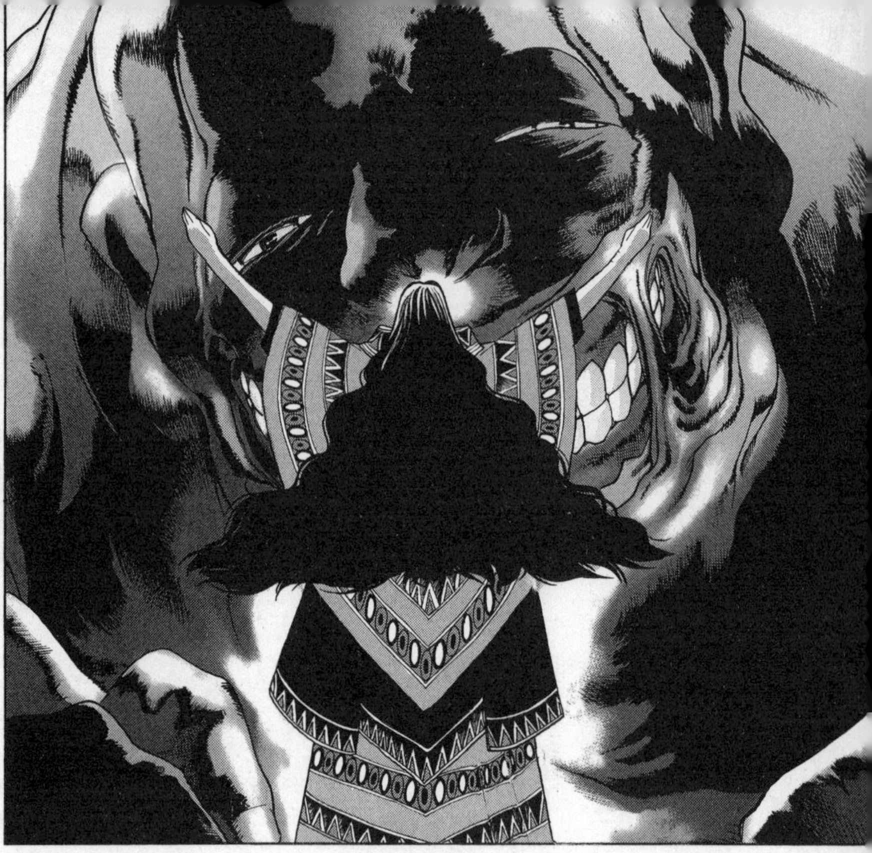

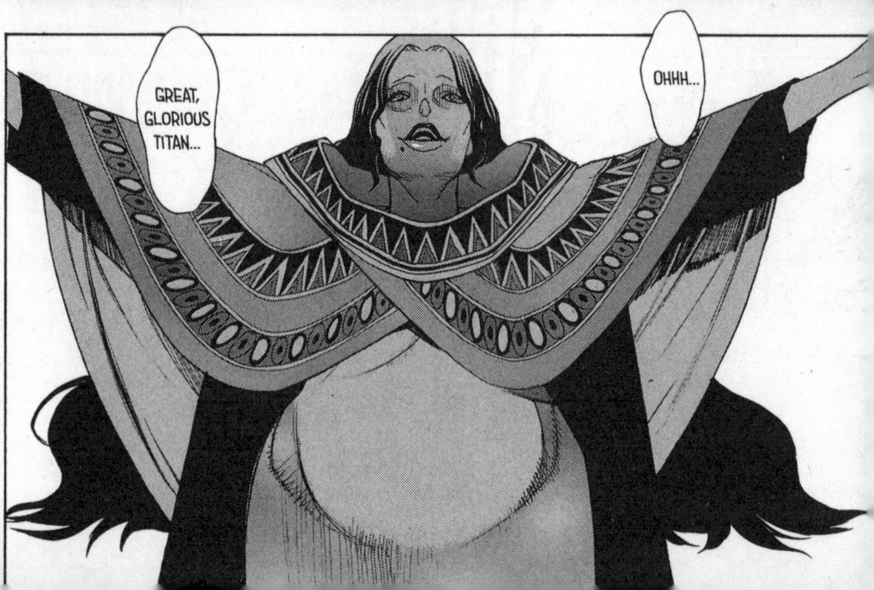
OHHH...
GREAT, GLORIOUS TITAN...

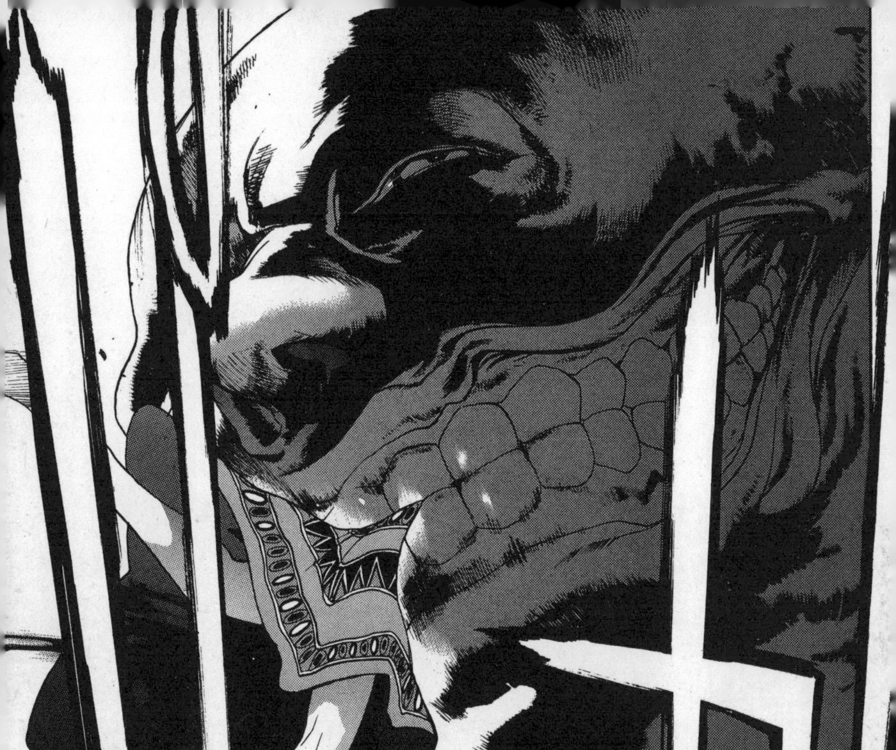
KSHUNK
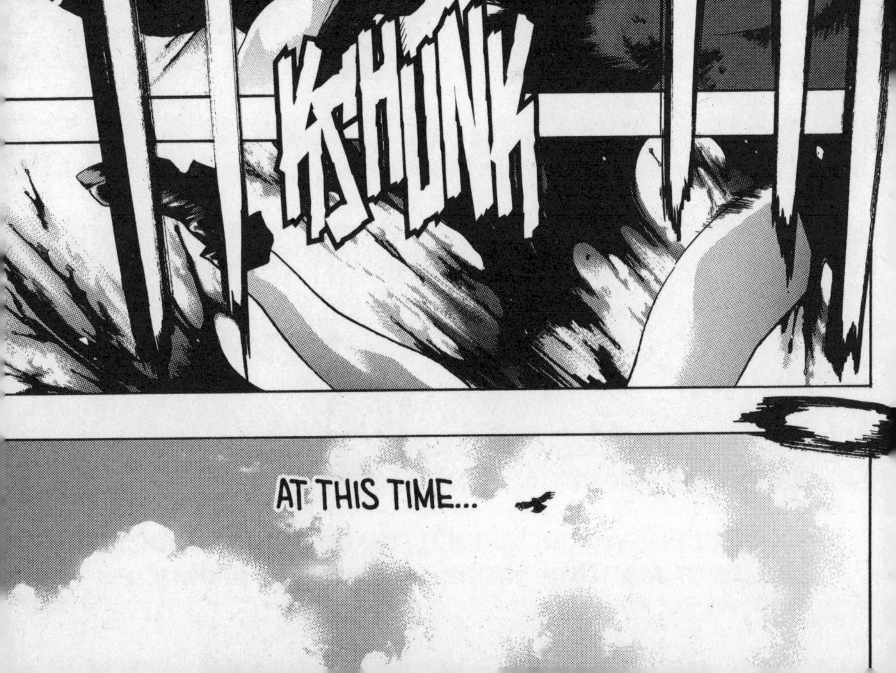
AT THIS TIME...

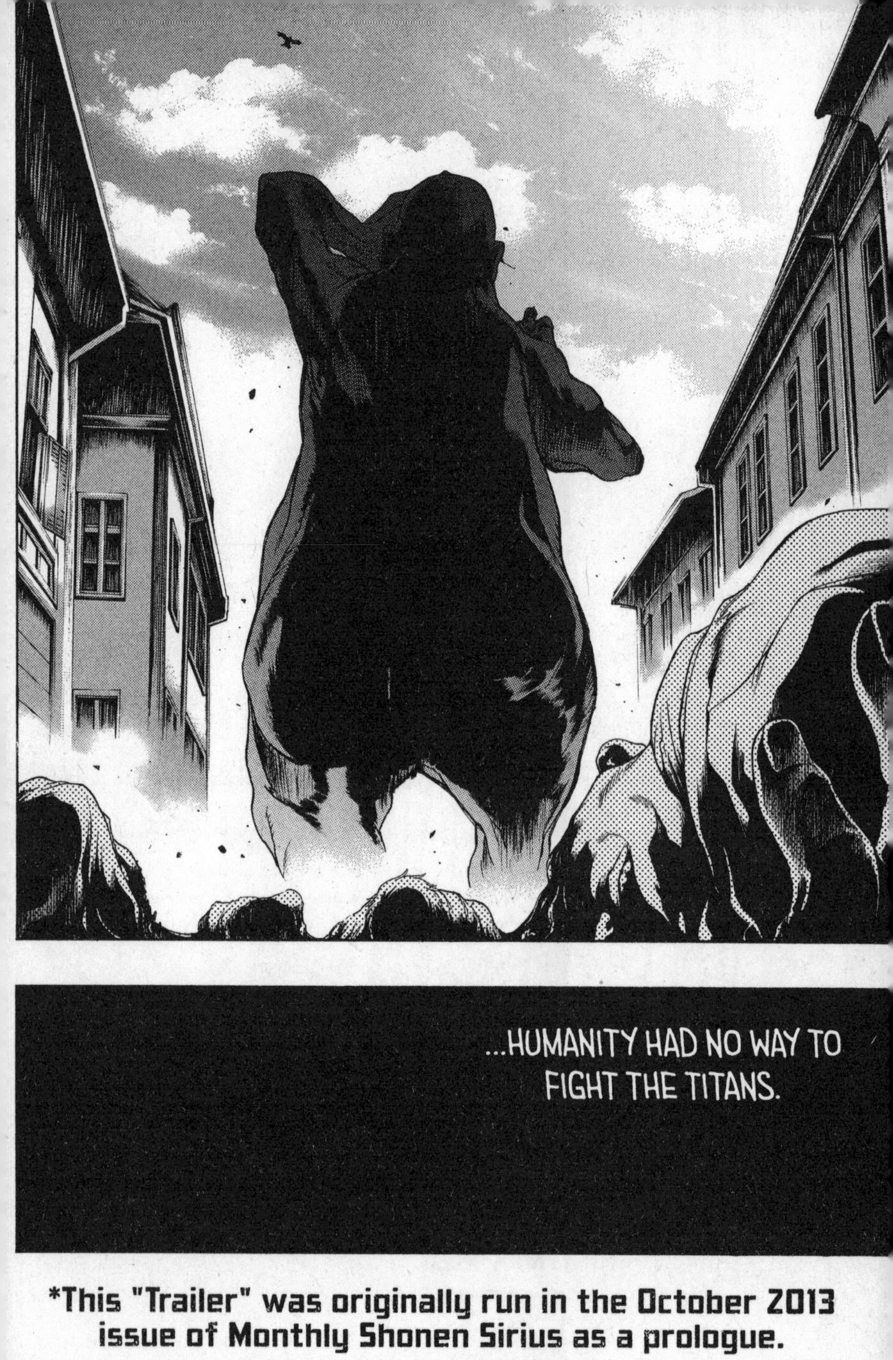

...HUMANITY HAD NO WAY TO FIGHT THE TITANS.

*This "Trailer" was originally run in the October 2013 issue of Monthly Shonen Sirius as a prologue.

ATTACK on TITAN

BEFORE THE FALL

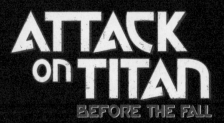

WANT MORE TITAN?
The following pages contain a preview of "Attack on Titan: Junior High," a parody spin-off of "Attack on Titan" that recasts your favorite characters as junior high students! Vol. 1 includes over 300 pages of Titanic comedy!
ATTACK on TITAN
JUNIOR HIGH
Vol. 1 available now from Kodansha Comics!

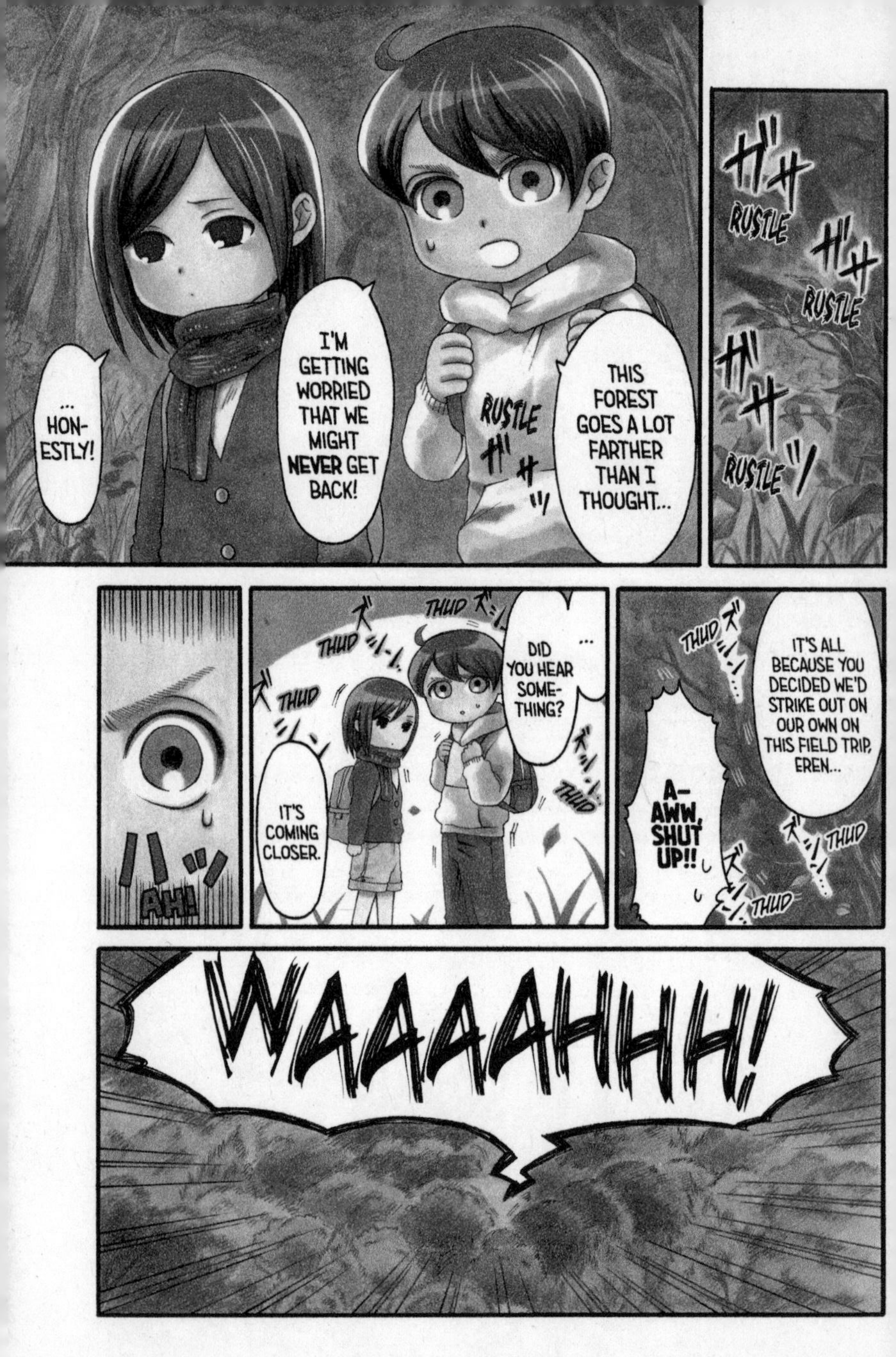
RUSTLE
RUSTLE
RUSTLE
THIS FOREST GOES A LOT FARTHER THAN I THOUGHT...
RUSTLE
I'M GETTING WORRIED THAT WE MIGHT **NEVER** GET BACK!
... HONESTLY!
IT'S ALL BECAUSE YOU DECIDED WE'D STRIKE OUT ON OUR OWN ON THIS FIELD TRIP, EREN...
THUD
A-AWW, SHUT UP!!
THUD
THUD
... DID YOU HEAR SOMETHING?
THUD
THUD
THUD
THUD
IT'S COMING CLOSER.
AH!
WAAAAHHH!

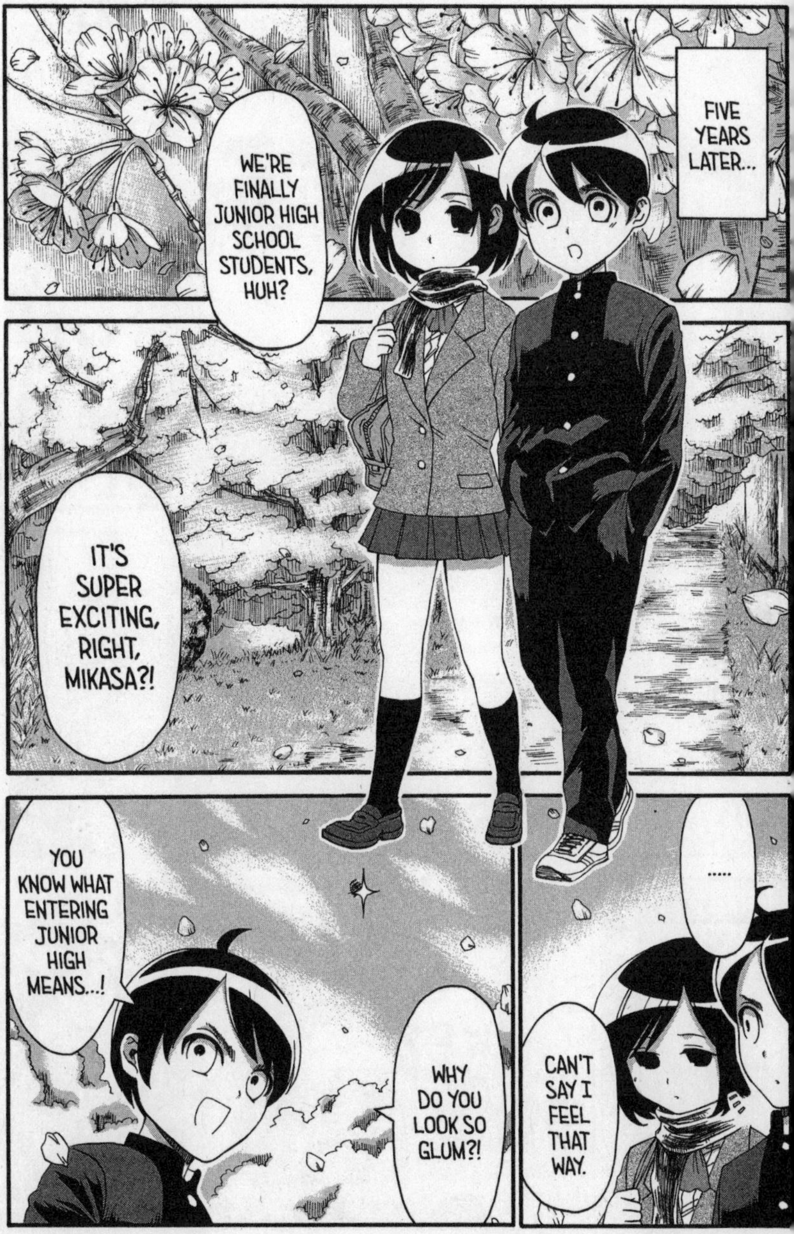
FIVE YEARS LATER...
WE'RE FINALLY JUNIOR HIGH SCHOOL STUDENTS, HUH?
IT'S SUPER EXCITING, RIGHT, MIKASA?!
.....
CAN'T SAY I FEEL THAT WAY.
WHY DO YOU LOOK SO GLUM?!
YOU KNOW WHAT ENTERING JUNIOR HIGH MEANS...!

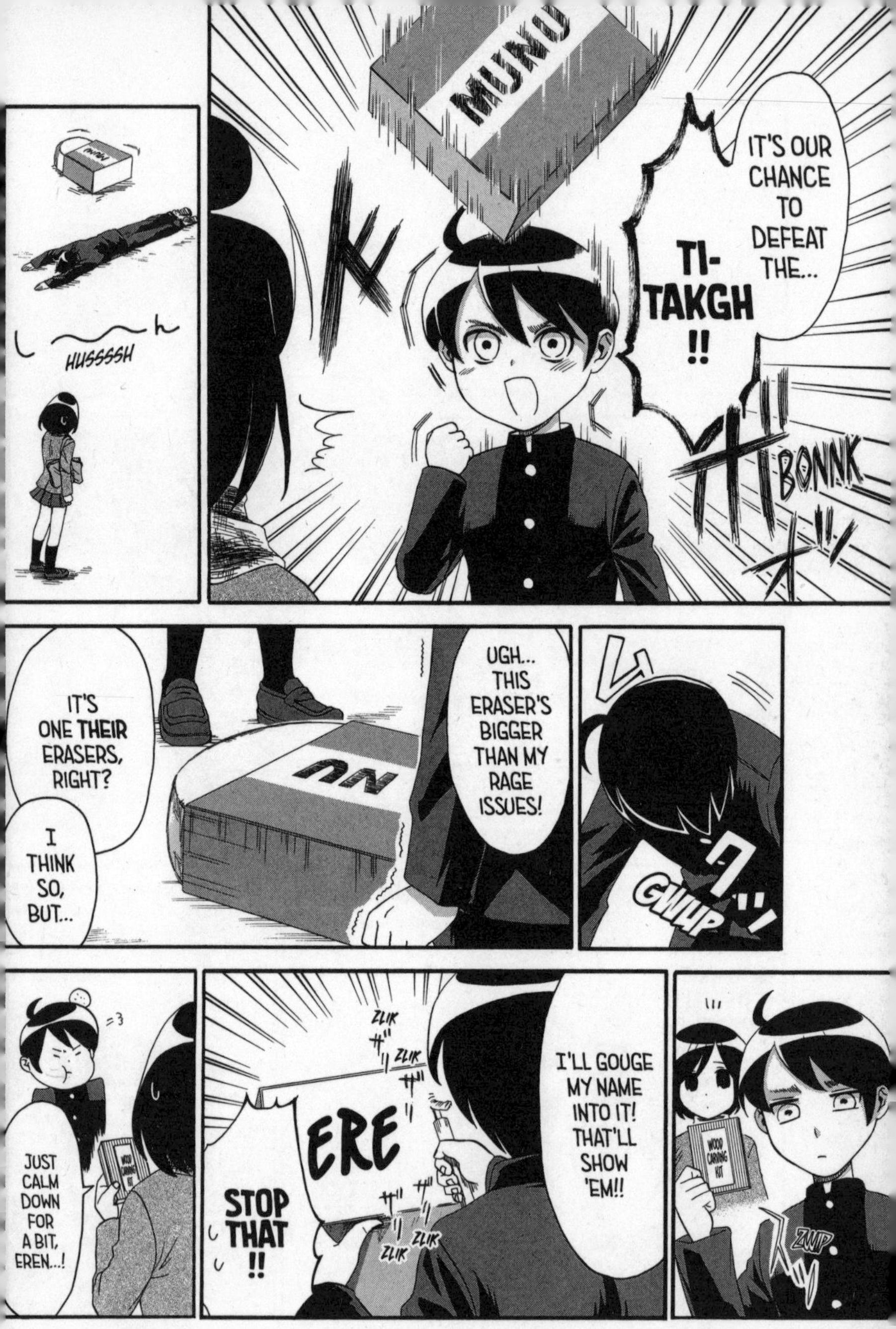
MUNU
IT'S OUR CHANCE TO DEFEAT THE...
TI-TAKGH!!
BONNK
HUSSSSH
GWUP
UGH... THIS ERASER'S BIGGER THAN MY RAGE ISSUES!
NU
IT'S ONE THEIR ERASERS, RIGHT?
I THINK SO, BUT...
WOOD CARVING KIT
ZWIP
I'LL GOUGE MY NAME INTO IT! THAT'LL SHOW 'EM!!
ZLIK
ZLIK
ERE
STOP THAT!!
ZLIK
ZLIK
JUST CALM DOWN FOR A BIT, EREN...!
WOOD CARVING KIT

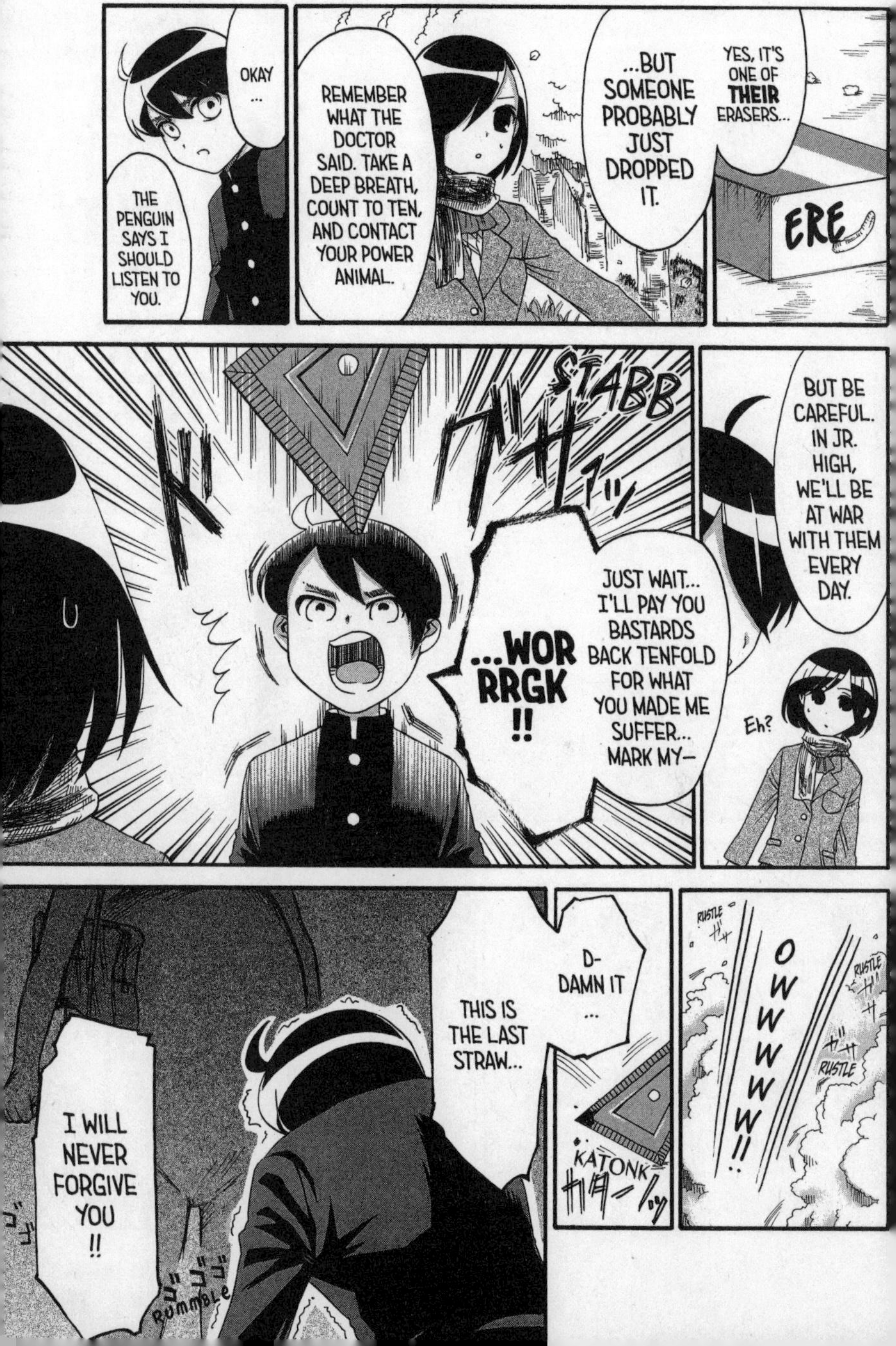
YES, IT'S ONE OF **THEIR** ERASERS...
ERE
...BUT SOMEONE PROBABLY JUST DROPPED IT.
REMEMBER WHAT THE DOCTOR SAID. TAKE A DEEP BREATH, COUNT TO TEN, AND CONTACT YOUR POWER ANIMAL.
OKAY ...
THE PENGUIN SAYS I SHOULD LISTEN TO YOU.
BUT BE CAREFUL. IN JR. HIGH, WE'LL BE AT WAR WITH THEM EVERY DAY.
Eh?
JUST WAIT... I'LL PAY YOU BASTARDS BACK TENFOLD FOR WHAT YOU MADE ME SUFFER... MARK MY—
STABB
...WORRRGK !!
RUSTLE
RUSTLE
RUSTLE
OWWWWWW!!
D-DAMN IT ...
THIS IS THE LAST STRAW...
KATONK
I WILL NEVER FORGIVE YOU !!
RUMMBLE

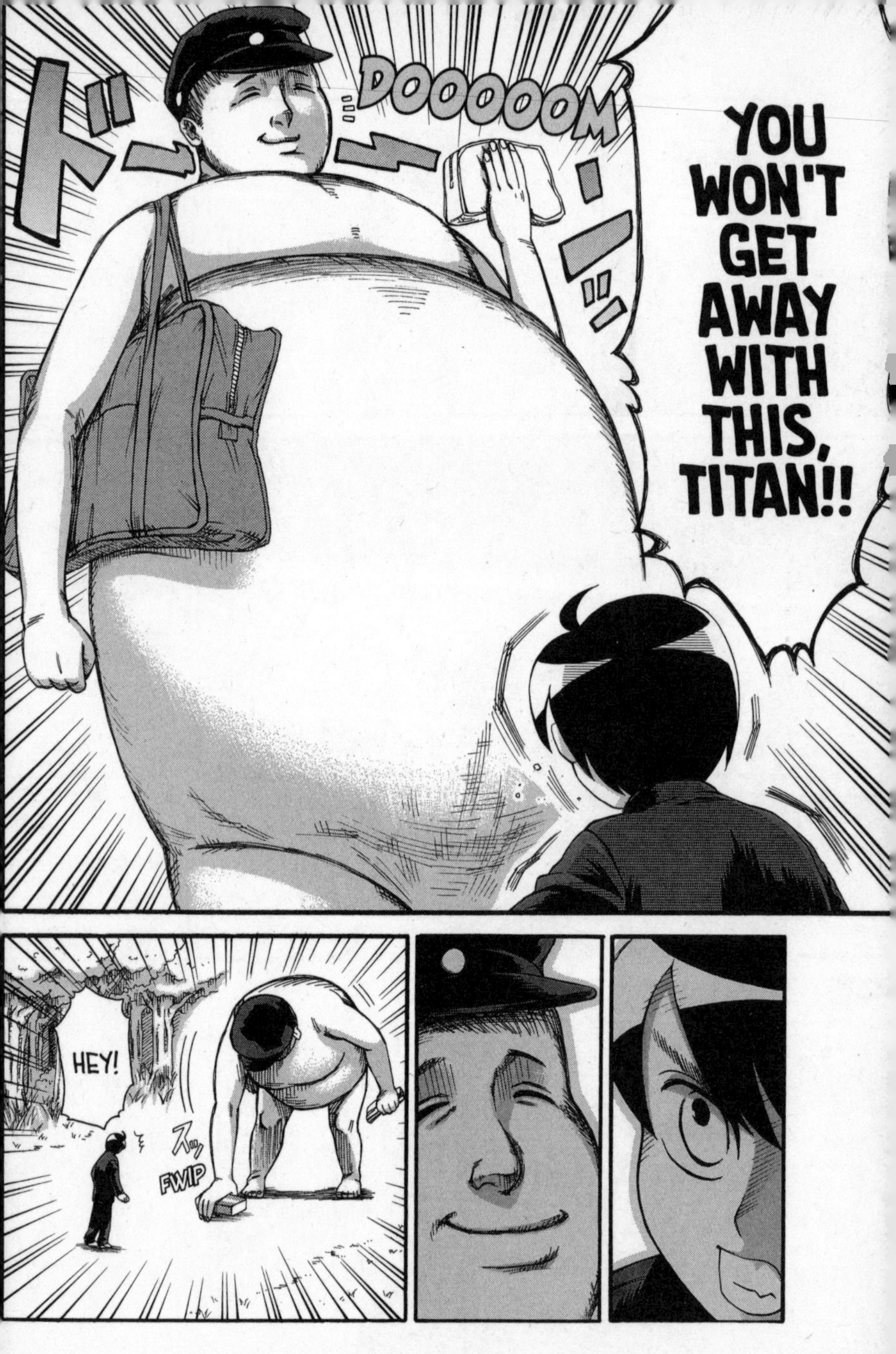
ドーン
DOOOOOM
YOU WON'T GET AWAY WITH THIS, TITAN!!
HEY!
スッ
FWIP

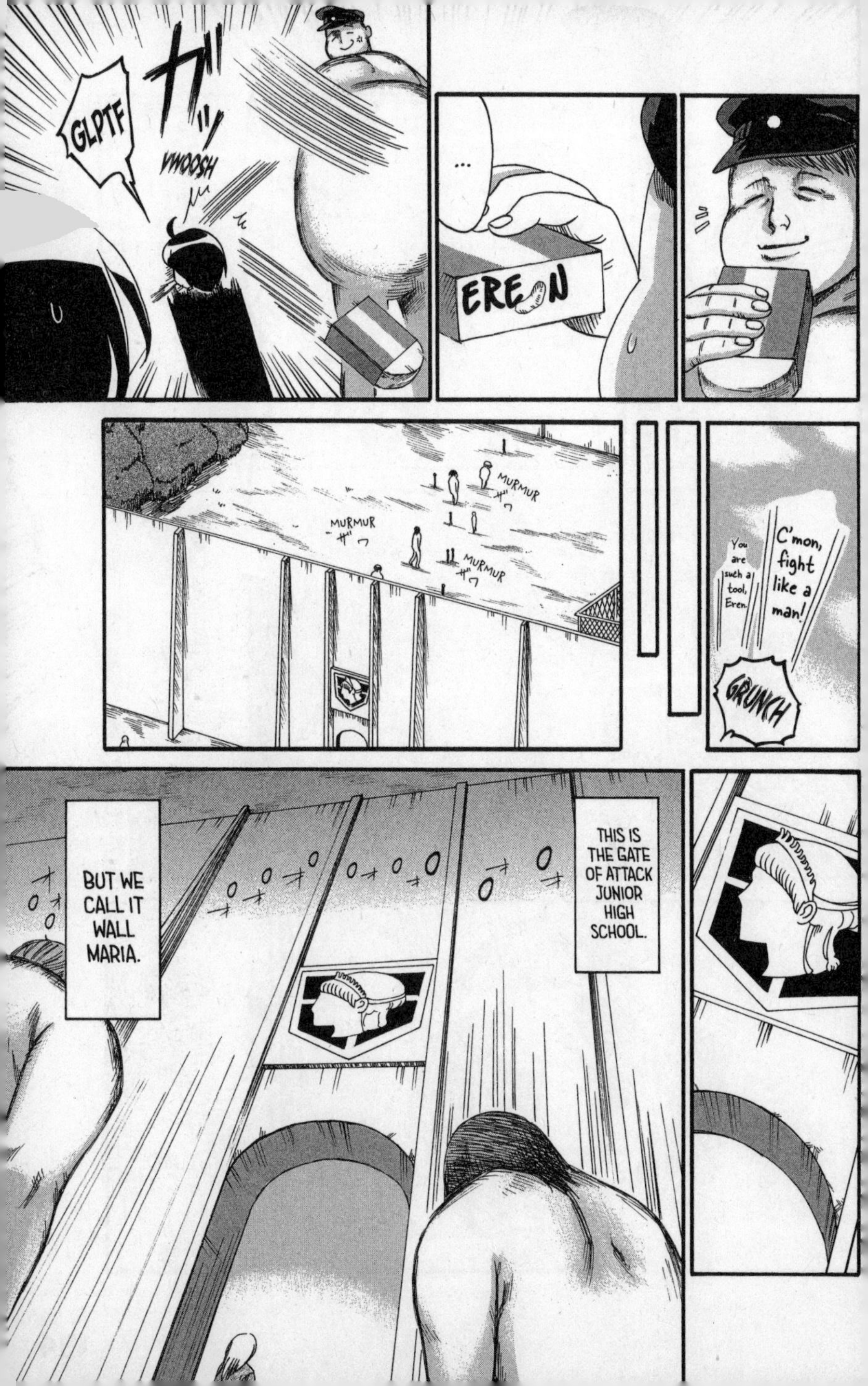
...
EREN
GLPTF
VWOOSH
C'mon, fight like a man!
You are such a tool, Eren.
GRUNCH
MURMUR
MURMUR
MURMUR
THIS IS THE GATE OF ATTACK JUNIOR HIGH SCHOOL.
BUT WE CALL IT WALL MARIA.

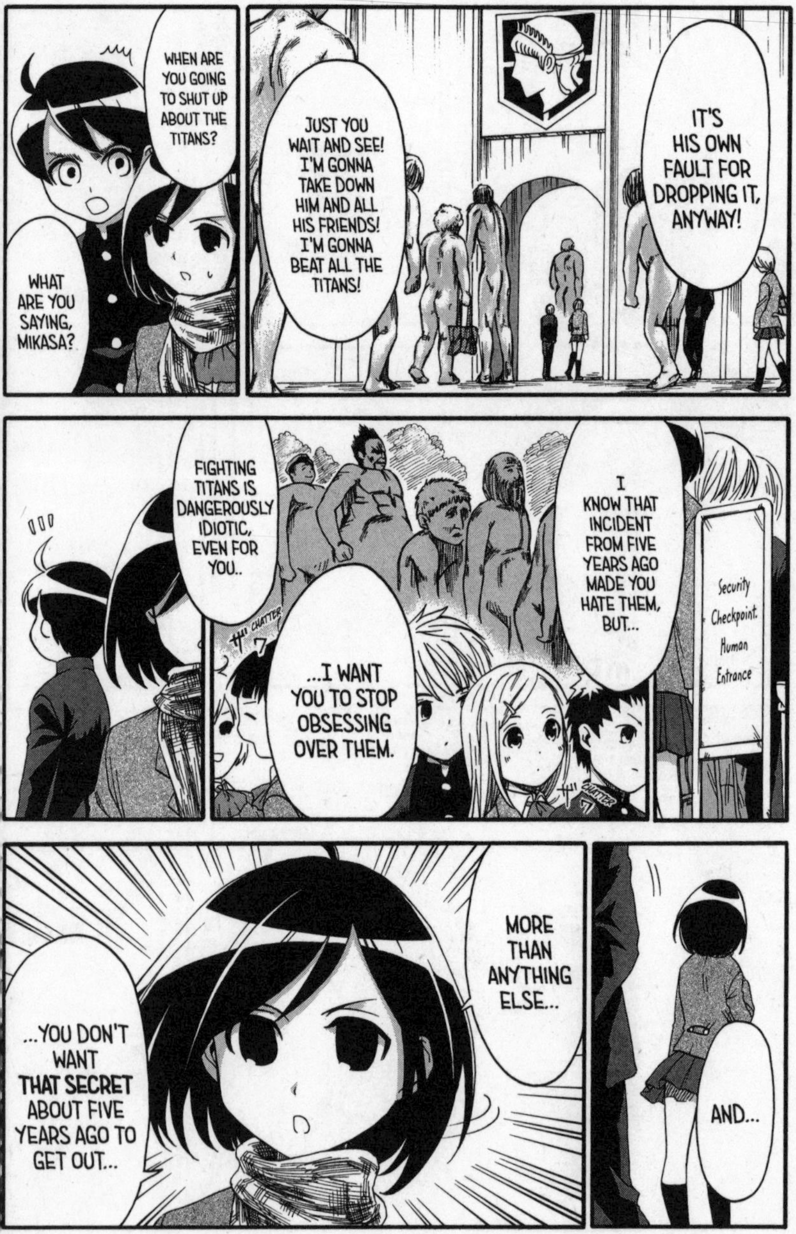
IT'S HIS OWN FAULT FOR DROPPING IT, ANYWAY!
JUST YOU WAIT AND SEE! I'M GONNA TAKE DOWN HIM AND ALL HIS FRIENDS! I'M GONNA BEAT ALL THE TITANS!
WHEN ARE YOU GOING TO SHUT UP ABOUT THE TITANS?
WHAT ARE YOU SAYING, MIKASA?
Security Checkpoint. Human Entrance
I KNOW THAT INCIDENT FROM FIVE YEARS AGO MADE YOU HATE THEM, BUT...
FIGHTING TITANS IS DANGEROUSLY IDIOTIC, EVEN FOR YOU..
CHATTER
...I WANT YOU TO STOP OBSESSING OVER THEM.
CHATTER
AND...
MORE THAN ANYTHING ELSE...
...YOU DON'T WANT THAT SECRET ABOUT FIVE YEARS AGO TO GET OUT...

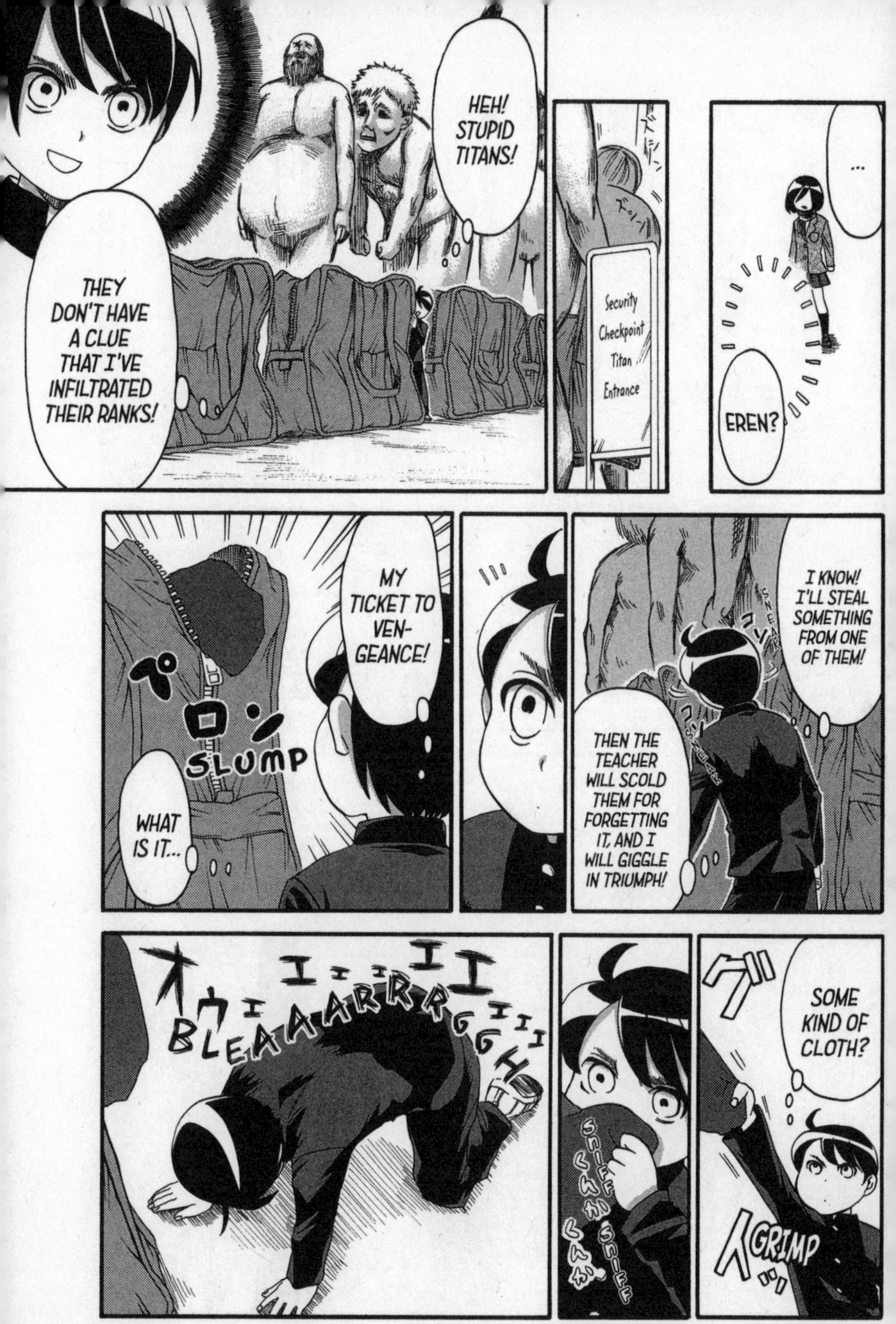
...
EREN?
Security Checkpoint Titan Entrance
HEH! STUPID TITANS!
THEY DON'T HAVE A CLUE THAT I'VE INFILTRATED THEIR RANKS!
I KNOW! I'LL STEAL SOMETHING FROM ONE OF THEM!
SNEAK
SNEAK
THEN THE TEACHER WILL SCOLD THEM FOR FORGETTING IT, AND I WILL GIGGLE IN TRIUMPH!
MY TICKET TO VEN-GEANCE!
SLUMP
WHAT IS IT...
SOME KIND OF CLOTH?
GRIMP
SNIFF
SNIFF
BLEAAARRRGGH

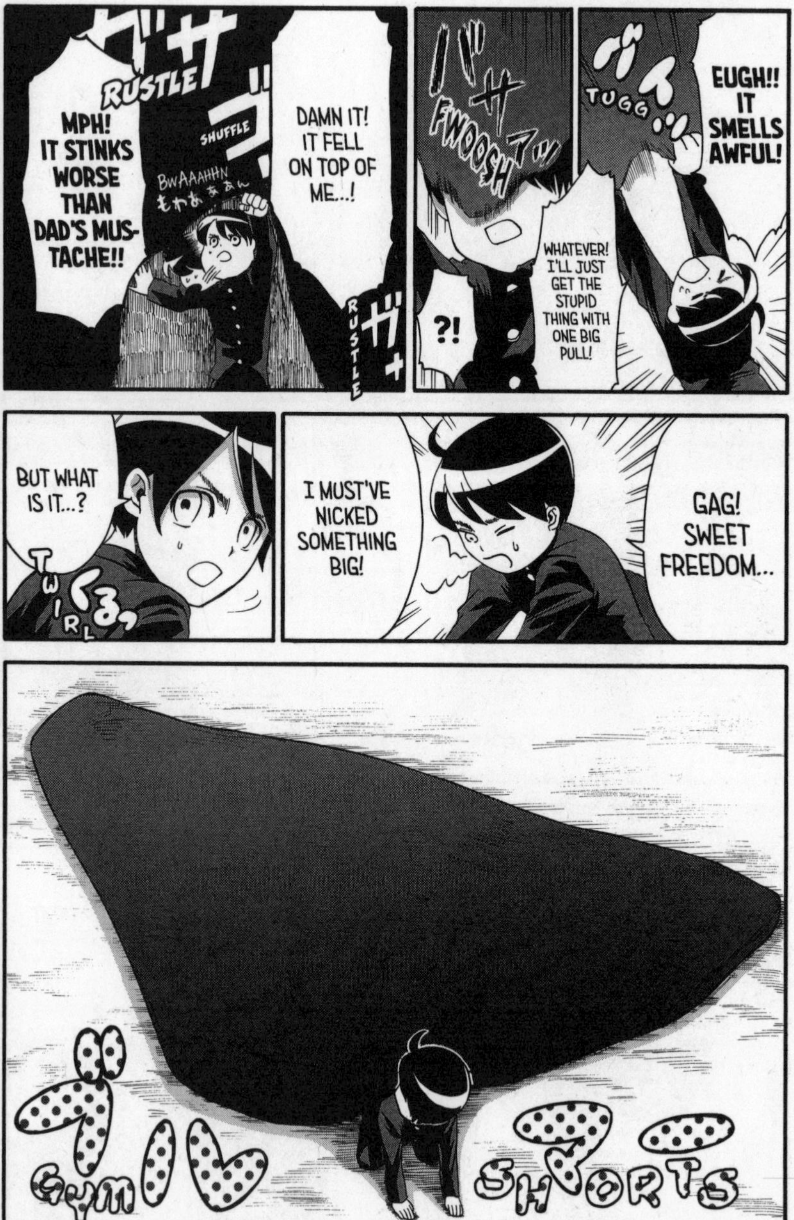

EUGH!! IT SMELLS AWFUL!
ヴィ
TUGG
WHATEVER! I'LL JUST GET THE STUPID THING WITH ONE BIG PULL!
?!
バサァッ
FWOOSH
DAMN IT! IT FELL ON TOP OF ME...!
ガサ
RUSTLE
ゴ
SHUFFLE
MPH! IT STINKS WORSE THAN DAD'S MUS-TACHE!!
BWAAAHHN
もわぁぁん
ガサ
RUSTLE
GAG! SWEET FREEDOM...
I MUST'VE NICKED SOMETHING BIG!
BUT WHAT IS IT...?
くるっ
TWIRL
ブルマ
GYM SHORTS

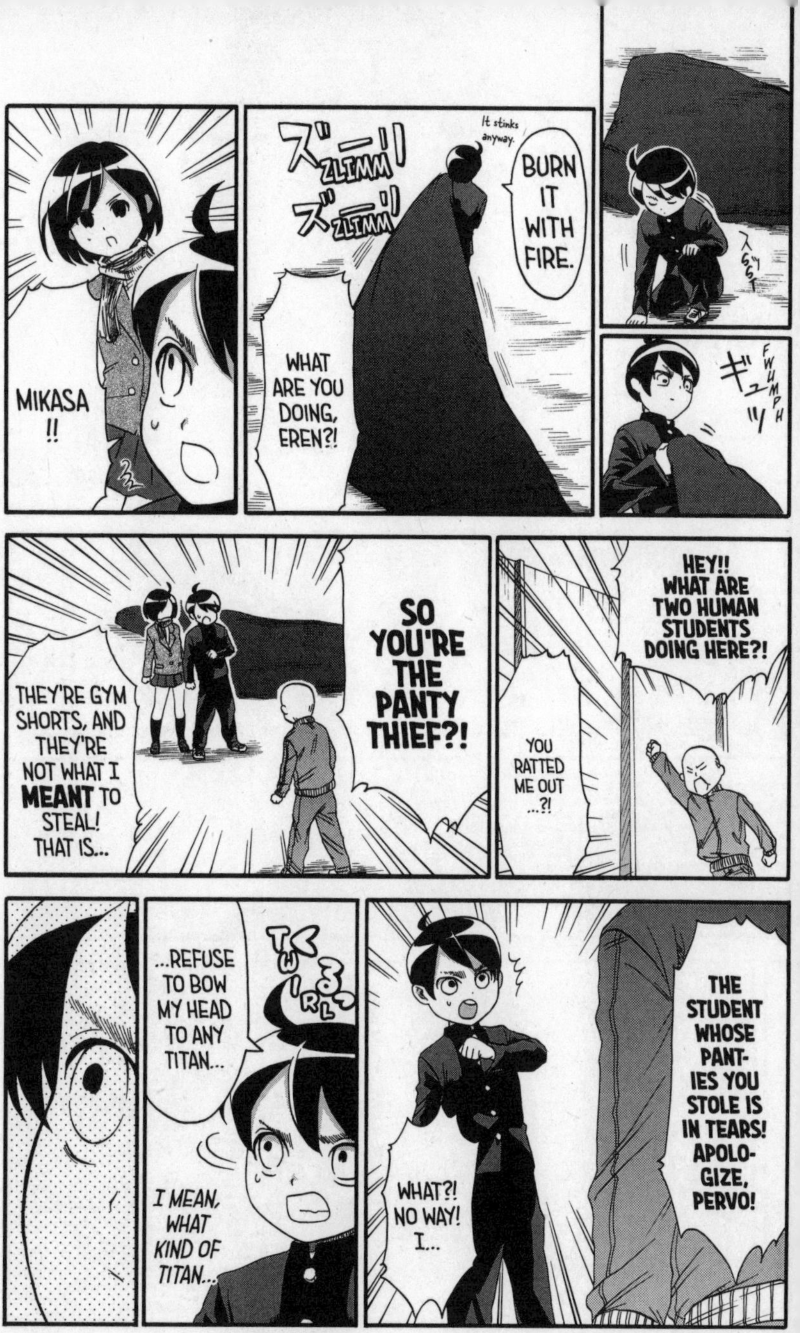
スッ SST
ギュッ FWUMPH
ズーリ ZLIMM
ズーリ ZLIMM
It stinks anyway.
BURN IT WITH FIRE.
WHAT ARE YOU DOING, EREN?!
MIKASA!!
HEY!! WHAT ARE TWO HUMAN STUDENTS DOING HERE?!
YOU RATTED ME OUT...?!
SO YOU'RE THE PANTY THIEF?!
THEY'RE GYM SHORTS, AND THEY'RE NOT WHAT I **MEANT** TO STEAL! THAT IS...
THE STUDENT WHOSE PANTIES YOU STOLE IS IN TEARS! APOLOGIZE, PERVO!
WHAT?! NO WAY! I...
くるっ TWIRL
...REFUSE TO BOW MY HEAD TO ANY TITAN...
I MEAN, WHAT KIND OF TITAN...

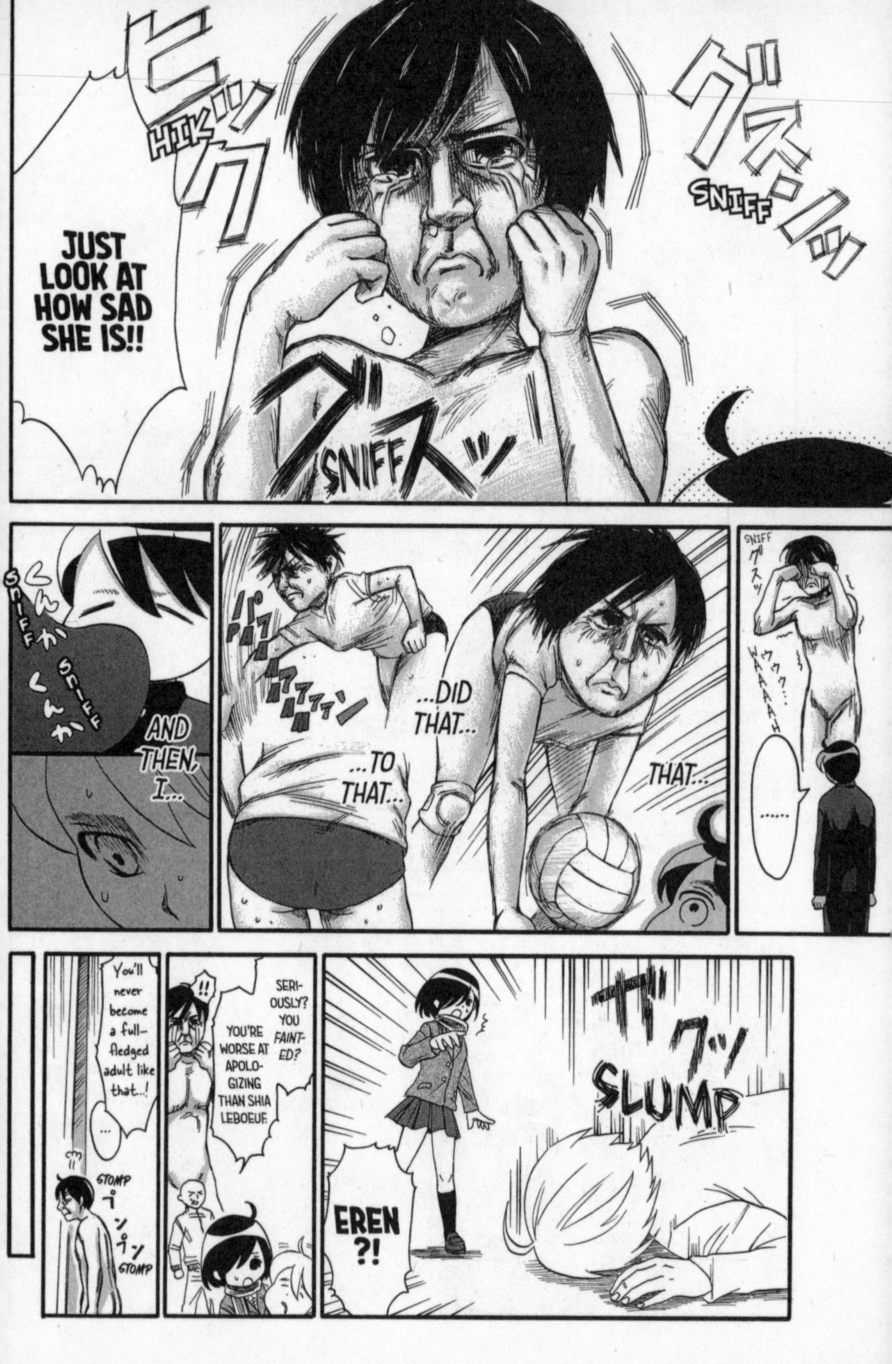
HIK
SNIFF
JUST LOOK AT HOW SAD SHE IS!!
SNIFF
SNIFF
WAAAAH
......
...DID THAT...
...TO THAT...
THAT...
SNIFF
SNIFF
AND THEN, I...
SLUMP
EREN?!
SERI-OUSLY? YOU FAINT-ED?
!!
YOU'RE WORSE AT APOLO-GIZING THAN SHIA LEBOEUF.
You'll never become a full-fledged adult like that...!
...
STOMP
STOMP

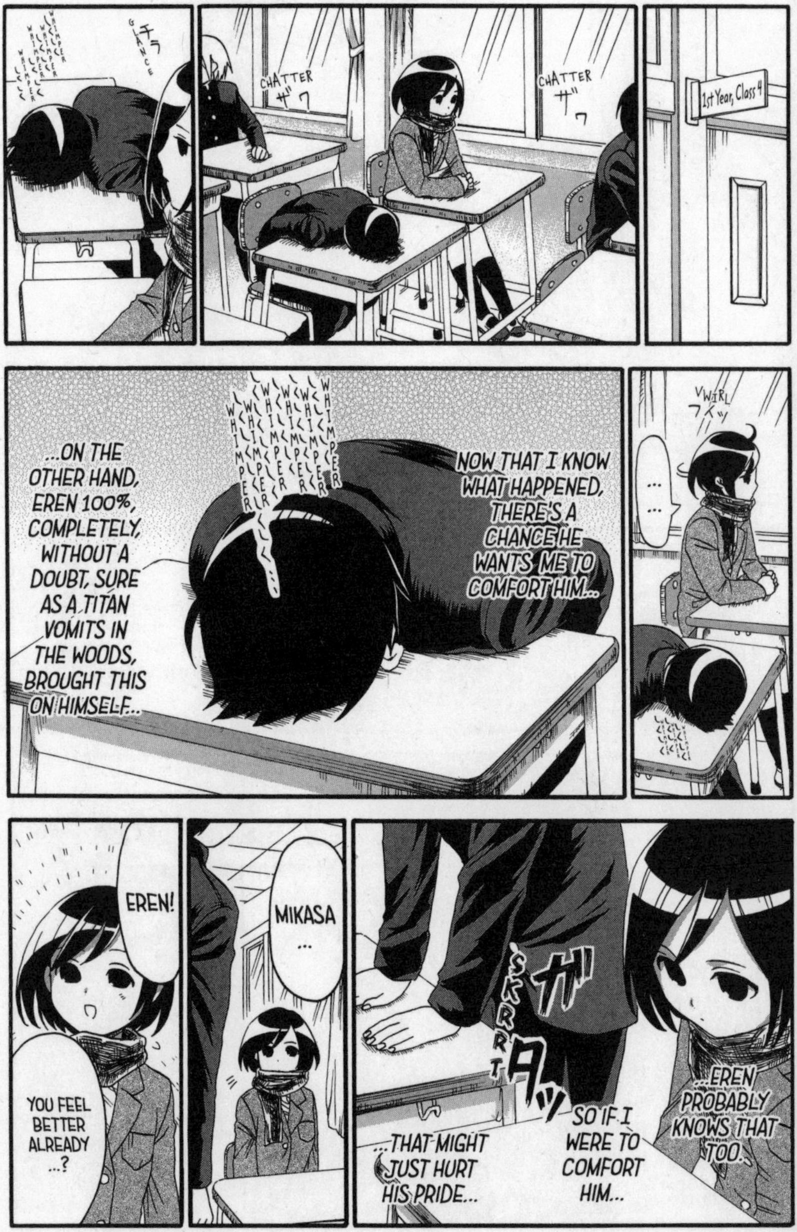
1st Year, Class 4
CHATTER ザワ
CHATTER ザワ
GLANCE チラ
WHIMPER
VWIRL フイッ
... ...
NOW THAT I KNOW WHAT HAPPENED, THERE'S A CHANCE HE WANTS ME TO COMFORT HIM...
...ON THE OTHER HAND, EREN 100%, COMPLETELY, WITHOUT A DOUBT, SURE AS A TITAN VOMITS IN THE WOODS, BROUGHT THIS ON HIMSELF...
WHIMPER
...EREN PROBABLY KNOWS THAT TOO.
SO IF I WERE TO COMFORT HIM...
...THAT MIGHT JUST HURT HIS PRIDE...
SKRRRT ガタッ
MIKASA ...
EREN!
YOU FEEL BETTER ALREADY ...?

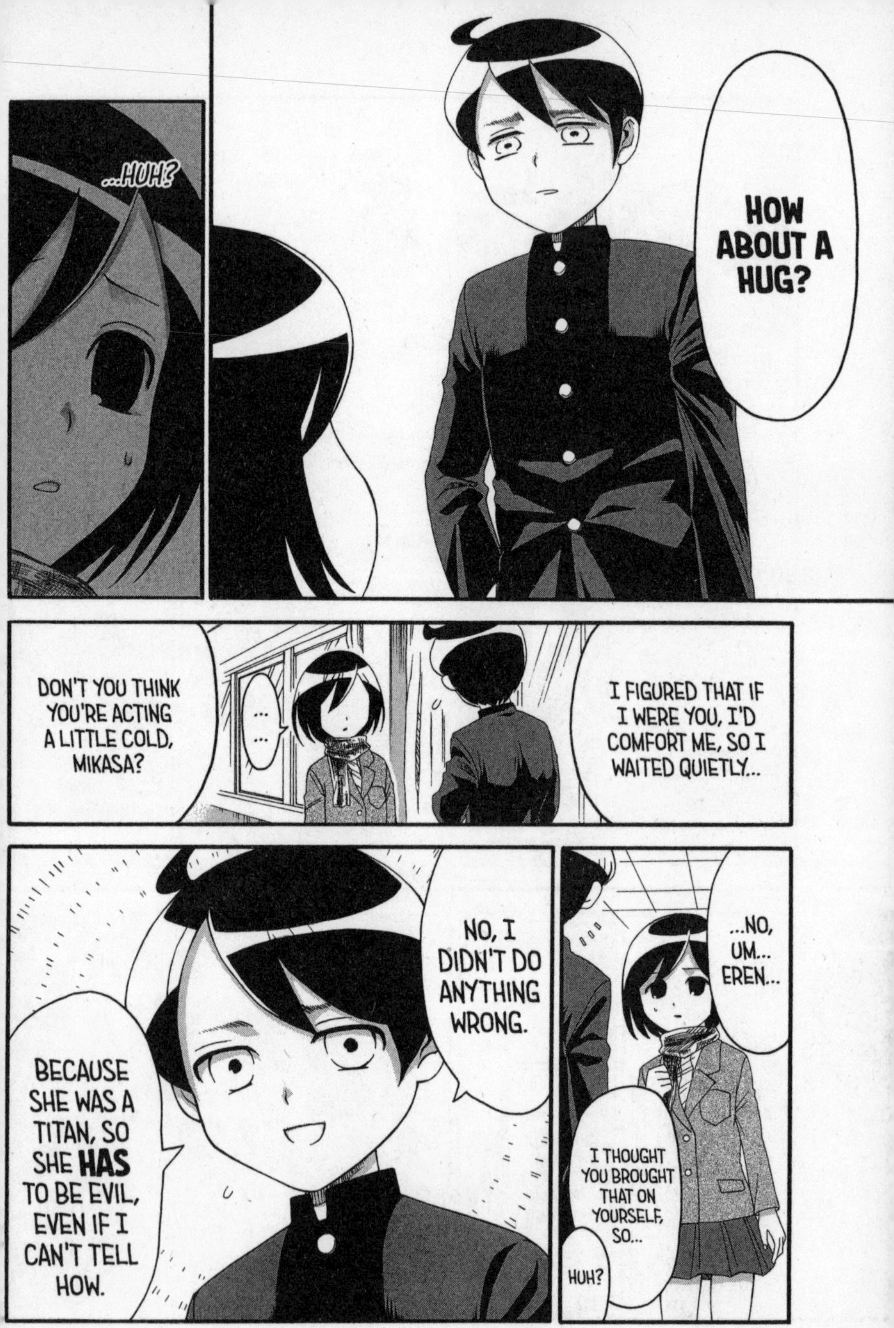
HOW ABOUT A HUG?
...HUH?
I FIGURED THAT IF I WERE YOU, I'D COMFORT ME, SO I WAITED QUIETLY...
... ...
DON'T YOU THINK YOU'RE ACTING A LITTLE COLD, MIKASA?
...NO, UM... EREN...
I THOUGHT YOU BROUGHT THAT ON YOURSELF, SO...
HUH?
NO, I DIDN'T DO ANYTHING WRONG.
BECAUSE SHE WAS A TITAN, SO SHE **HAS** TO BE EVIL, EVEN IF I CAN'T TELL HOW.

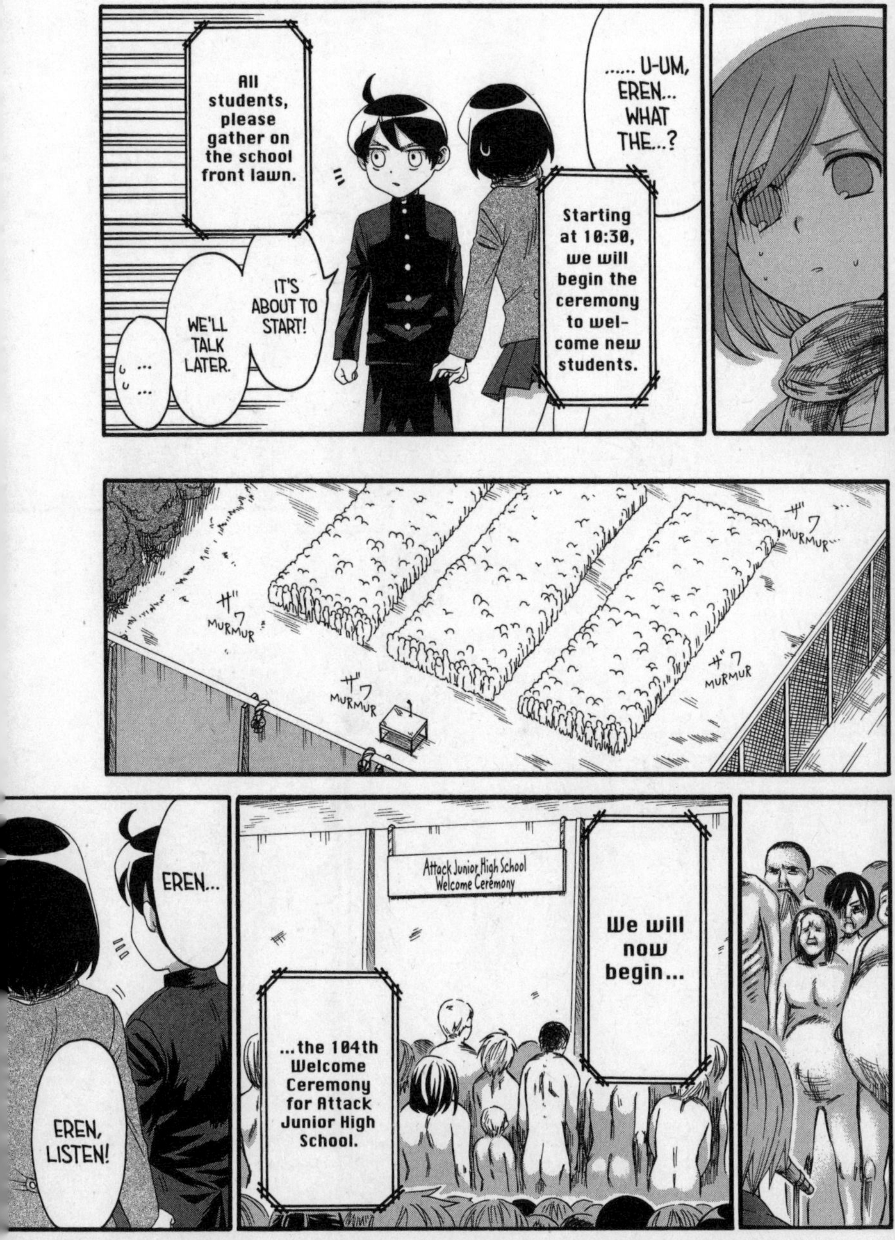

...... U-UM, EREN... WHAT THE...?
All students, please gather on the school front lawn.
Starting at 10:30, we will begin the ceremony to wel-come new students.
IT'S ABOUT TO START!
WE'LL TALK LATER.
...
...
ザワ MURMUR...
ザワ MURMUR
ザワ MURMUR
ザワ MURMUR
Attack Junior High School Welcome Ceremony
We will now begin...
...the 104th Welcome Ceremony for Attack Junior High School.
EREN...
EREN, LISTEN!

Read more in Attack on Titan: Junior High Vol. 1, available now!

SANKAREA
undying love

"I ONLY
LIKE
ZOMBIE
GIRLS."

Chihiro has an unusual connection to zombie movies. He doesn't feel bad for the survivors – he wants to comfort the undead girls they slaughter! When his pet passes away, he brews a resurrection potion. He's discovered by local heiress Sanka Rea, and she serves as his first test subject!

KC
KODANSHA
COMICS

NO.6

A PERFECT LIFE
IN A PERFECT CITY

For Shion, an elite student in the technologically sophisticated city No. 6, life is carefully choreographed. One fateful day, he takes a misstep, sheltering a fugitive his age from a typhoon. Helping this boy throws Shion's life down a path to discovering the appalling secrets behind the "perfection" of No. 6.

KC
KODANSHA
COMICS

Attack on Titan: Before the Fall volume 1 is a work of fiction. Names, characters, places, and incidents are the products of the author's imagination or are used fictitiously. Any resemblance to actual events, locales, or persons, living or dead, is entirely coincidental.

A Kodansha Comics Trade Paperback Original

Published in the United States by Kodansha Comics, an imprint of Kodansha USA Publishing, LLC, New York.

Publication rights for this English edition arranged through Kodansha Ltd, Tokyo.

First published in Japan in 2013 by Kodansha Ltd., Tokyo as *Shingeki no kyojin Before the fall*, volume 1.

ISBN 978-1-61262-910-0

Character designs by Thores Shibamoto
Original cover design by Takashi Shimoyama (Red Rooster)

Printed in the United States of America.

www.kodanshacomics.com

9 8 7 6 5 4 3
Translation: Stephen Paul
Lettering: Steve Wands
Editing: Ben Applegate